£55 Amazon

D1795673

Global Perspectives on Spirituality and Education

In recent decades, and around the world, much attention has been given to the role of spirituality in the education of children and young people. While educationalists share many common goals and values in nurturing the spiritual lives of children and young people, national and regional cultures, religions and politics have impacted on the approaches scholars and practitioners have adopted in their investigations and practices. The different contexts across nations and regions mean that educators face quite distinct conditions in which to frame their approaches to spiritual education and research, and the nature and impact of these differences is not yet understood.

This book brings together thinkers from around the globe and sets them the task of explaining how their research on children's spirituality and education has been shaped by the historical, cultural, religious and political contexts of the geographic region in which they work. The book presents contributions in three sections—Europe and Israel, Australasia, and The Americas—and concludes with a chapter highlighting what is common and what is contextually unique about global approaches to spirituality and education.

Jacqueline Watson is Lecturer in Educational Research at the School of Education and Lifelong Learning, University of East Anglia.

Marian de Souza is Senior Lecturer at the School of Religious Education at Australian Catholic University.

Ann Trousdale is Associate Professor of Children's Literature at Louisiana State University.

Routledge Research in Education

Global Perspectives on Spirituality and Education

Edited by Jacqueline Watson,
Marian de Souza and Ann Trousdale

Routledge
Taylor & Francis Group
NEW YORK   LONDON

First published 2014
by Routledge
711 Third Avenue, New York, NY 10017

and by Routledge
2 Park Square, Milton Park, Abingdon, Oxon OX14 4RN

*Routledge is an imprint of the Taylor & Francis Group,
an informa business*

© 2014 Taylor & Francis

The right of Jacqueline Watson, Marian de Souza and Ann Trousdale to
be identified as the authors of the editorial material, and of the authors for
their individual chapters, has been asserted in accordance with sections 77
and 78 of the Copyright, Designs and Patents Act 1988.

All rights reserved. No part of this book may be reprinted or reproduced or
utilised in any form or by any electronic, mechanical, or other means, now
known or hereafter invented, including photocopying and recording, or in
any information storage or retrieval system, without permission in writing
from the publishers.

Trademark Notice: Product or corporate names may be trademarks or
registered trademarks, and are used only for identification and explanation
without intent to infringe.

Library of Congress Cataloging-in-Publication Data
  Global perspectives on spirituality and education / edited by Jacqueline
Watson, Marian de Souza and Ann Trousdale
      pages cm. — (Routledge research in education)
  Includes bibliographical references and index.
  1. Religious education—Study and teaching.   2. Religious education—
Teaching methods.   I. Watson, Jacqueline, 1932–   II. De Souza,
Marian   III. Trousdale, Ann M.
  BL42.G66 2013
  200.71—dc23
  2013016991

ISBN13: 978-0-415-63619-3 (hbk)
ISBN13: 978-0-203-08557-8 (ebk)

Typeset in Sabon
by IBT Global.

Contents

Preface

Jacqueline Watson, Marian de Souza and Ann Trousdale

In recent decades, much attention has been given to the role of spirituality in education. While this has not happened uniformly across the world, it has occurred in enough countries to warrant a discussion of the perspectives and practices that have emerged to date. While educationalists share many common goals and values in nurturing the spiritual lives of children and young people, national and regional cultures, religions and politics have all impacted on the approaches scholars and practitioners adopt in their investigations and practice. Educationalists, therefore, face distinct conditions in which to frame their approaches to spiritual education and research, and the nature and impact of these differences is not yet well understood. This book aims to make some of these distinctions explicit in order to build a better understanding of the global picture.

With the dawning of a new century, *spirituality* has become a word and concept which has been moved out of theological and religious frameworks to enter public discourse. With a decline in traditional religious influences, there has been a new consciousness emerging at the grass-roots level, a spiritual consciousness, where people are searching for meaning and purpose along both religious and secular avenues. In the first decade of the 21st century, we find ourselves on the threshold of new thinking and understandings about spirituality and its role in social and religious constructs. In particular, this has affected children and young people as we transit from traditional to contemporary structures, thinking and practices. Research from a variety of different disciplines, including neuroscience, psychology, sociology, social work and education, has led to a recognition of spirituality as a vital element in human life and endeavour across the globe.

This book, then, focuses on one of these disciplines: education. The idea for this book was born out of discussions at the Ninth International Conference for Children's Spirituality, held at Canterbury Christ Church University in the United Kingdom in 2009. The multiple voices that came together to share research, ideas and practices in the area of spirituality for children and young people were inspiring. In particular, it was refreshing to hear how different regions and cultures were developing innovative educational approaches to addressing the spirituality of their students. It became clear that, for some, identifying and nurturing spirituality was seen as a significant way forward to meet the challenges and issues that were evident amongst the young people in their respective countries. It is equally apparent that, in a global world which followed a colonized world, the education systems in many countries have been founded on a Western education system where competition, compartmentalization and an unprecedented emphasis on the acquisition of knowledge and skills, and on performativity in literacy, numeracy, science and technology, have gained precedence over other aspects of a holistic education. This has also included an overemphasis on valuing certain character and personality traits over others, so that many children and young people across the world feel less valued and struggle to cope in the high-pressure performance culture in which they find themselves, both academically and socially.

While many of us enjoy a high standard of living, the downsides of this imbalance are seen in the statistics showing increased levels of poor physical and mental health amongst children and young people; and serious problems such as eating disorders, depression, alienation, bullying, violence and self-harm have increasingly become areas for study and research. Some of the strategies that are being developed and applied to address these problems include developing self-esteem, engendering a sense of belonging and connectedness, creating frameworks of meaning, and building resilience. These latter elements may be identified as spiritual characteristics and they confirm that contemporary spirituality has a distinct role in education today.

Another reason to support this argument is the pluralistic nature of society in many countries. The past 50 years have seen large movements of people across different regions so that different cultures and religions have now become next-door neighbours. This has raised questions about ways in which to educate today's children about the diverse beliefs and practices they may encounter or engage with throughout their lives. Developing a spiritual dimension to education is one way forward. This is emphatically different from confessional approaches to religious education (or religious instruction or religious knowledge), but also goes beyond multifaith approaches to religious education (RE). The latter is about a study of religious traditions in historical, sociological and theological contexts and it creates compartments within which each tradition may be placed and drawn out to be examined, compared and comprehended. Spirituality cannot be compartmentalized. Therefore, a spiritual approach to education, and to religious education, offers the potential to transcend boundaries generated by region, culture, religion and social class, perhaps leading to a recognition that Eastern and Western worldviews complement one another and promote an understanding of the total human condition.

A concern for spirituality in education emerges from, but is not yet sufficiently valued by, today's post-secular, pluralistic, globalized societies, where a spiritual rebalancing can contribute to the social cohesion and wellbeing essential in promoting both prosperous and healthy communities. If children and young people are able to find a sense of self and identity, belonging and connectedness, and are able to make meaning from their life experiences through their school programs, they are more likely to develop into proactive, caring and compassionate citizens of the future.

We are aware there is a great deal of research and practice in this field and that it is being carried out in a greater number of countries than are represented in this book. We would refer the reader to the *International Journal of Children's Spirituality* for further insight into global perspectives on spirituality in education, particularly in relation to Eastern Europe and African countries.

The authors who contributed to this book responded to a call for contributions to this project, and patiently worked with the co-editors to fulfil a key aim of the book by contextualizing their research and practice within the historical, cultural, religious and political contexts of the geographic region within which each has worked. The three co-editors took responsibility for gathering and commenting on contributions to three, rather roughly drawn, regions of the world: Europe and Israel, Jacqueline Watson; Australasia, Marian de Souza; and the Americas, Ann Trousdale. We should like to acknowledge and thank the authors for their considerable work and commitment to this project. We are very grateful to them for their dedication and patience, and for their invaluable insights. We should also like to thank Taylor & Francis/Routledge for responding positively to our project and publishing this book, and especially thank Jennifer Morrow and Lauren Verity for their support in bringing the book together.

We offer this collection with the anticipation that it will be valuable to the international community in supporting thinking about the role of spirituality in education. We hope the book will highlight what is common and what is contextually unique about global approaches to spirituality and education and contribute to clarifying our understanding of the global landscape, so that a spiritual approach to education may be further developed and applied in ways that are responsive to both global and local contexts.

Part I

Spirituality and Education in Europe and Israel

Part I
Introduction

Jacqueline Watson

This section includes contributions from Europe and Israel. Because of the religious and political histories and educational policies of the countries represented in this section, whether their state schools are secular or religiously affiliated, religious education is compulsory. Inevitably, therefore, the contributors make a strong correlation between spirituality and the school subject of religious education. The first three chapters also discuss spirituality in terms of the whole curriculum because educational policy in the United Kingdom (UK) and the Republic of Ireland requires this broader approach. Besides grappling with meaningful ways to include spirituality in education within their regional contexts, the authors in this section include innovative new approaches to religious education which are responsive to the spirituality of children and young people.

In Chapter 1, Ron Best presents a study of the place and development of spirituality in education in all of the four countries which make up the United Kingdom (UK): Scotland, Northern Ireland, England, and Wales. In these countries as well as in the Irish Republic (discussed in Chapter 3), the law and educational policy require that spirituality is addressed across the curriculum and not just in religious education (and collective worship); this is true for all schools, including all state-funded schools. This has driven much discussion and debate around the meaning of a notion of spirituality that is not necessarily synonymous with religion. That debate is examined in depth by Ron Best and is also explored in Chapter 2 by Kate Adams. Chapter 2 focuses on one specific country in the UK, England. Adams gives attention to the challenge of addressing spiritual development in the context of secular schools which, in one sense she argues, are advantaged by being legally obliged to give attention to children's spirituality, but where there is an attendant lack of confidence about what spirituality means when schools have no religious affiliation. In Chapter 3, James O'Higgins Norman and Caroline Renehan trace the crucial influence of the Catholic Church on the spiritual education of children and young people in Ireland, as well as the effects of British colonial rule on the country and its education. They describe recent changes to law and education policy in the Republic of Ireland which mean that, as in the

UK, children's spiritual development is seen as broader than religious education. They explore this opportunity for better addressing the spiritual healing and wellbeing of children and young people.

In Chapter 4, Annemie Dillen writes about spirituality in education in Flanders, a region of Belgium. Here, religious education is compulsory and most children study Catholic religious education, although they can also choose from a further five religious alternatives as well as one nonreligious choice. In the context of a strongly Catholic country, Dillen describes and discusses recent changes to religious education inspired by a consideration of children's spirituality, using a hermeneutical-communicative model based on openness toward individuals' beliefs and plurality in society. In Chapter 5, Adrian Gellel describes changes currently being made to Catholic religious education in Malta, where an emphasis on spirituality has led to the development of a curriculum that places less emphasis on doctrine, takes a constructivist and hermeneutical approach to religious knowledge, and has an openness to other faiths and viewpoints.

In Chapter 6, Kirsi Tirri and Martin Ubani discuss spirituality in the context of religious education in Finland, where Lutheran Christianity is the major religion. Here, religious education presents a choice of 13 distinct subjects for different religious groups, including secular ethics. Tirri and Ubani equate spirituality with post-secular religiosity and emphasise the importance of research which studies and measures children's and young people's engagement with aspects of post-secular spirituality. In Chapter 7, Yaacov Katz discusses his research in the Israeli education system and his use of spiritual wellbeing instruments to measure spiritual sensitivity in children and young people. Katz's research measured and compared young people's spiritual sensitivity in Israel's three types of Jewish schools, each having different types of religious education: state secular schools, emphasising humanistic values; ultra-orthodox schools, emphasising faith-based religious education; and state religious schools, which emphasise both. His findings suggest that the latter approach develops more spiritually sensitive young people.

Adams, along with Tirri and Ubani, emphasises the need for more research in the field of spirituality in education and greater dissemination of research findings. Finally, authors in this section, along with several authors in the book as a whole, point to the need for a new approach to teacher education that has greater empathy with children and young people, is willing to listen to their voices, and has an understanding of the complexity of the post-secular, spiritual landscape.

1 Spirituality, Faith and Education
Some Reflections from a UK Perspective

Ron Best

THE CONTEXT

The education system of any nation is inevitably both a reflection of recent and current policies and a vestige of bygone ages. Where a nation consists of more than one country—as is the case in the United Kingdom—regional variations and subcultural proclivities will add a further layer to what is already a complex historical and social artefact.[1] While educational provision in Wales has been closely tied to that of England, and parallels with developments in Northern Ireland and Scotland can be discerned, there are significant differences, especially in regard to Scotland which has long had its own Department of Education. The devolution of political power from the UK Government in Westminster to the Northern Ireland Executive in 1998 (after 27 years of direct rule from Westminster), and to the Scottish and Welsh Governments in the following year, made possible an increase to the regional variation which already existed.[2]

Under the current coalition Government, the situation in England and Wales is in a state of flux, with new categories of school being created and a number of other changes underway, often with little or no public consultation. The system had already seen a great deal of change in the previous 25 years. Following the 1988 Education Reform Act under Prime Minister Thatcher, the introduction of a statutory National Curriculum for England and Wales, direct funding of schools under the heading of 'local management of schools' (LMS), and a radically reduced and reconfigured education brief for Local Education Authorities (LEAs) began a trend of 'reforms' which has gone on unabated ever since. Amongst these were the advent of a new and (some would say) oppressive Office for Standards in Education (Ofsted) to take over the bulk of the work of the old (and more benign) Her Majesty's Inspectorate (HMI) and substantial changes in the structure and control of higher education, including the education and training of teachers. The return of a ('New') Labour government in 1997, led by Prime Minister Blair (who famously listed his top three priorities as 'Education,

Education, Education'), brought with it relatively little that was new; by and large, the changes made in the previous 18 years were retained and, if anything, extended.

In England and Wales there is now a daunting array of different kinds of 'state' school, from the remnants of the post-WW2 tripartite system, consisting of secondary grammar, technical and 'modern' schools, and the neighbourhood comprehensives with which many such schools were replaced, through city technology colleges to quasi-independent 'academies' and 'free schools'. Differences in funding and control are reflected in categories such as 'community-', 'foundation-' and 'trust-schools', and there are further distinctions according to the age ranges of their students, subject specialisms and faith-group affiliation. With regard to the last of these, a very substantial number of schools in the state sector are church schools, voluntarily aided or controlled by the state, and many of the independent schools, which provide for 7% of children, are faith schools.[3] The matter of faith schooling is discussed later in this chapter, but it is pertinent here to note that, in all the countries of the UK, but particularly in Northern Ireland and Scotland, religion is a major and enduring dimension in the organisation of state schooling.

Generalisations about the place of spiritual education within such complex systems should be treated with caution, but one permissible generalisation is that the meaning and place of the *spiritual* in education in the UK is, and has long been, ambiguous.

If one were to equate 'spiritual education' with 'religious education' (an unwise but tacit assumption for many people, and for most schools until at least the 1980s),[4] then spirituality has been a feature of UK schooling since the Middle Ages. With the social and economic pressures of the Industrial Revolution, the Christian churches along with philanthropists guided by Christian principles became the providers and patrons of most elementary and secondary schooling. The Government's first financial intervention, in 1833, involved a grant from the taxpayer of £20,000 towards the establishment and running of schools, to be distributed via the National Society for the Promotion of the Education of the Poor in the Principles of the Established Church (Anglican), and the nonconformist British and Foreign Schools Society (Lawson & Silver, 1973; Holness, 2005, pp. 209–210). Herein lie the beginnings of the English 'dual system' of state and voluntary schools developed through the second half of the 19th century, formalised in the incorporation of (some) Anglican and Roman Catholic schools into the state system in the 1902 (Balfour) Education Act, and untouched by the otherwise sweeping revisions of the 1944 Act (Holness, 2005, p. 211).[5]

In Northern Ireland, schooling was organised along denominational lines from 1921 onwards, with the Protestant Churches accepting absorption into the state system as 'controlled' schools, but the Catholic schools refusing to do so. Today, almost all of the Region's schools are fully state funded, but provision remains most accurately described as a 'dual' system of Catholic and Protestant schools with a small 'integrated sector' (Armstrong, 2012, p. 33). In Scotland, attempts to construct a centralised system can be traced at least as far back as the 1872 Education (Scotland) Act, which followed the 1867–1868 reports of the Argyle Commission set up to investigate what was perceived to be a fragmentary and incomplete system of schooling in crisis (McKinney, 2008a, p. 46). A key moment in this development was the 1918 Education (Scotland) Act, resulting in Catholic schools, which had previously declined to lose their independence after the 1872 Act (McKinney, 2008c, p. 259), eventually being "fully incorporated into the Scottish state educational system and . . . inextricably bound to the post-1918 history of schooling in Scotland" (McKinney, 2008a, p. 47).

Under the 1980 Education (Scotland) Act "the right of children to receive 'religious instruction' and to take part in 'religious observance' is guaranteed by law" (Hartshorn, 2008, p. 375). In England and Wales, the 1944 Act had required that Religious Education (RE) be taught in all state schools, and that there should be a daily act of collective worship, which as Adrian Thatcher (1999b, p. 35) points out, is a "uniquely British phenomenon". The place of both RE and the act of worship was confirmed in the 1988 Education Act, and despite the increasingly multicultural character of British society, the expectation that they will be broadly Christian continues. The 1944 Act also required of LEAs that they "contribute towards the spiritual, moral, mental and physical development of the community" (cited in Keast, 2003, p. 157), a requirement also endorsed by the 1988 Act. In Scotland, the influential Millar Report (Scottish Education Department, 1972), entitled *Moral and Religious Education in Scottish Schools*, reviewed the provision of RE in the so-called 'nondenominational' (i.e. not Catholic) schools and informed subsequent legislation and curriculum development, not least with what became known as Religious and Moral Education (RME).

In the early 1990s it soon became clear that the assumption that RE and the act of collective worship in England and Wales could alone deliver what quickly became known as 'spiritual, moral, social and cultural development' (SMSC), was dubious, with the equivalent provision under RME in Scotland also coming under scrutiny. In Northern Ireland, there seems to have been rather less concern, with Religious Education remaining the main context for spiritual development, but here, too, the stated values underpinning the wider curriculum eventually came to include "each individual's unique capacity for spiritual, moral, emotional, physical and intellectual growth" (Council for the Curriculum, Examinations and Assessment [CCEA], 2007). In England and Wales, this part of the curriculum remains contentious, especially in a postmodern society in which there now exist, alongside the Anglican schools, what Halstead calls the 'old' religious schools of the nonconformist ('free') churches and the Jewish community, and the 'new' which includes those established by evangelical

Christian groups as well as Muslim, Jewish, Sikh, Greek Orthodox, Seventh Day Adventist and secular schools (Halstead, 2002, 2009).

Against this background, planning for SMSC became a pressing concern to those responsible for designing the curriculum of state schools, with the precise meanings of 'spiritual development' and 'spiritual education' being particularly elusive (Keast, 2003; Best, 2005; Bigger, 1999).

FAITH SCHOOLS

Perhaps the most animated debate with relevance to spiritual education in the UK in recent years has been that surrounding faith schools (e.g. Humanist Philosophers' Group, 2001; Gardner, Cairns & Lawton, 2005; Parker-Jenkins, Hartas & Irving, 2005; McKinney, 2008b). One reason for this is that the concept of 'faith schools' is itself complex and unclear. Schools founded by religious groups in the UK go back a long way, and as noted above, many of them have been absorbed to greater or lesser degrees into the state systems of all parts of the UK. As a consequence of ongoing immigration and contemporaneous demographic changes involving industrial growth and decline and associated geographic mobility, the majority of children attending such schools today may not, even nominally, belong to the faith of their founders. For this reason, some commentators prefer to talk about faith-*based* schools rather than faith schools per se (Parker-Jenkins et al., 2005, chap. 3).

Such schools vary greatly in the degree to which they promote and celebrate a particular faith. A school which is nominally Anglican, for example, but serves a zone of inward migration of non-Christian groups, may judge it inappropriate to make much of its religious roots. Even schools serving communities broadly of the faith of their founders vary in the degree to which their curricula, assemblies and observances are transparently religious, and the number of their staff who actively practise the faith. In regard to the desirability or otherwise of faith schools, the distinction between more or less *religious* schools may be more pertinent than that between faith and non-faith schools.

In fact, the debate about the desirability or otherwise of faith schools is not so much one debate but many (Best, 2003, p. 4; Halstead, 2009), including debates about the disputed compatibility between the concepts of education and religious nurture, parental rights in choosing children's education (Marples, 2005), the divisive effect of separate schools for different faiths and state funding for faith schools. Broadly similar issues have been identified as characterising the debate in Scotland (McKinney, 2008a, 2008b, 2008c) and Northern Ireland (Gallagher, 2005), where the populations are less heterogeneous but sectarianism more visible.

A substantial body of literature surrounding the faith schools debate has been written from a primarily philosophical perspective. Most influential is that of the late Terence McLaughlin. In a series of papers (including McLaughlin, 2003, 2008a, 2008b; McLaughlin & Halstead, 2005;

Alexander & McLaughlin, 2003), he pursued, amongst other things, a number of related questions concerning common and separate schools and their justifications in modern societies. McLaughlin's influence has continued since his tragically early death in 2006, not least in the publication of a selection of his papers in 2008 entitled *Liberalism, Education and Schooling* (Carr et al., 2008) and a book of essays in his memory entitled *Faith in Education* (Haydon, 2009). The second of these seems to me to represent very well the current state of debate and the issues around which it revolves.

In terms of the implications for spiritual development, the predominant issue in *Faith in Education* is that of indoctrination (Grace, 2009; Callan, 2009; Alexander, 2009). If faith schools exist to promote initiation into a faith, however broadly conceived, whether one sees them as desirable or repugnant will greatly depend upon whether one sees it as *indoctrination* (the enemy of autonomy) or as necessary if the individual is to flourish as a 'whole person' (i.e. as *education*). That said, in neither the debate about faith in education nor the debate about faith *schools* is much attention given to the concept of the spiritual per se.

SPIRITUALITY AND THE CURRICULUM

In the 1990s, this concept became a thorn in the side of those responsible for the design and assessment of the National Curriculum in England and Wales, and those responsible for inspecting schools to ensure its delivery.

John Keast (2003, p. 157) notes that the promotion of the spiritual development of the community was required explicitly in the preamble to the 1944 Education Act, and that the word 'spiritual' did appear in some official documents in the 1970s and 1980s, but it became a focus of particular attention after the 1988 Act. With the increased emphasis placed on the spiritual, moral, social and cultural development of pupils following the introduction of the National Curriculum in England and Wales in 1989 and its Northern Ireland equivalent a year later (O'Callaghan & Lundy, 2002, pp. 21–23), the precise meaning of the 'spiritual' could no longer be taken for granted. Even then, as Keast (2003, p. 158) records, "no real attention was paid to the promotion of spiritual development until the National Curriculum Council (NCC) published an NCC Discussion paper in 1993".

Discussion papers and other guidance documents were published by the Schools Curriculum and Assessment Authority (SCAA), which had replaced the NCC, and by Ofsted, in which attempts were made to specify how spiritual development might be promoted via the curriculum. None of these seems to have been particularly successful, primarily because an acceptable and coherent definition of the spiritual was so elusive. A review of the content of the 1993 Ofsted *Framework for Inspection* and the SCAA and Ofsted discussion papers of 1994 and 1996, as well as the 1998 *Draft Guidance for Schools* produced by SCAA's successor, the Qualifications and Curriculum Authority (QCA), revealed an astonishing array of nebulous, inconsistent and sometimes seemingly incompatible descriptions of spirituality (Best, 2005), including (amongst many others):

> An inclination to believe in God, the 'other' or 'the ultimate'. . . .
> A powerful force that determines what we are, our self-understanding, our outlook on life, others and the world, and consequently shapes our behaviour. . . .
> [T]hat aspect of inner life through which pupils acquire insights into their personal experiences which are of enduring worth. . . .
> A unique personal characteristic [whose] development for many individuals, depends in part . . . upon human interaction. (quoted in Best, 2005, pp. 71–72)

In light of these attempts at a definition, knowing how to inspect schools' provision for spiritual development was going to be as difficult as teaching it. As Ofsted commented in the 1994 Discussion Paper: "If spiritual development is about a unique inner life, it is not easy to inspect" (quoted in Best, 2005, p. 72).

It was the lacuna of the spiritual in the National Curriculum and the manifest difficulties in agreeing a definition that prompted me, together with colleagues[6] at (what was then) Roehampton Institute in London, to hold a conference on the theme "Education, Spirituality and the Whole Child" in 1994. The success of this venture testified to the felt need amongst teachers and educationalists for the definitional gap to be filled. A selection of the papers was subsequently published under the same title, and the interest aroused by the event resulted in an annual international conference on this theme being held at Roehampton until 2003. Elsewhere, interest in the place of children's spirituality in education was also growing. Notable here was the appearance of the *International Journal of Children's Spirituality* in 1997 and the international conferences associated with it ever since.[7] What these developments had in common was a concern with three fundamental questions:

> What do we mean by the 'spiritual'?
> What is 'spiritual development'?
> What can schools do to 'spiritually develop' their pupils?

In a liberal pluralist society, where respect for differences in values, beliefs and practices and the principles of multiculturalism, democratic rights and individual liberty are enshrined, finding answers to these questions that are acceptable to all, and offensive to none, is pretty well impossible.

In 1996–1997, SCAA attempted to resolve this problem by establishing a *National Forum on Values in Education* in the hope that some set of universal values could be identified as a basis for curriculum planning. The statement which emerged was not entirely unhelpful, in that it identified four aspects of life towards which our values may be oriented—our selves, our relationships, our society and the environment—but precisely *what* values in respect of these ought to be taught remained contentious. In any event, it can be argued that the spiritual is 'lost' amidst the social, moral and cultural within such a range of values.

The work of the Forum was one inspiration for an attempt by the QCA to produce a framework for planning SMSC across the curriculum. The fields of self, relationships, society and environment were cross-related with SMSC and learning outcomes, producing an unwieldy matrix of 64 cells to be filled (16 of which were 'spiritual').[8] Not surprisingly, the scheme was criticised, most powerfully by Paul Yates (1999, 2000), as both a bureaucratic nightmare and as powerfully constraining the content of SMSC while creating the illusion of freedom for schools to determine this for themselves. It is perhaps as well that, despite being piloted in 150 schools, the framework was never implemented (Keast, 2003, p. 160). With regard to the spiritual dimension of the framework, the project was dogged by the enduring difficulty of finding an adequate definition of spiritual development.

To focus on attempts by government and quasi-governmental agencies to define or describe spiritual development as a prerequisite for curriculum planning is, however, to beg the question of whether such involvement is either desirable or has any chance of success. Keast, who was himself the senior officer at the QCA with responsibility for religious education, argues that

> [t]he work of agencies such as the QCA . . . has not so much described spiritual development as such as marked out the 'space' that spiritual development might occupy in school life and the curriculum (Keast, 2003, p. 163)

before conceding that it

> is possible to argue that in all the descriptions, definitions, statements of values, what is missing is that which only particular and real institutions can provide—the actual values, beliefs and their applications of them, where the source, nature, authority and prescription of values is articulated and practised. (Keast, 2003, p. 163)

In other words, perhaps only schools and the communities they serve can answer the question of what should be taught under this heading, although this runs counter to the 'top-down' direction of centralised planning and inspection which seems to have been presumed by those who conceived of a *national* curriculum.

RELIGION AND THE MEANING OF 'SPIRITUALITY'

In the academic debate—no less than the political one—the fundamental question of the meaning of the 'spiritual' has been stubbornly resistant to all attempts at a succinct and coherent definition. The following is not unrepresentative:

> Spirituality is an expression of human longing to approach a supreme entity or power situated beyond human control and grasp. . . . [It] is realised in abstract aspects of human life that constitute part of one's secular or religious being. The definition of spirituality consists of two basic constructs: transcendence and an encounter with a supreme being or deity. . . . An examination of research on spirituality yields three distinct approaches to the relationship between spirituality and religiosity. . . . [of which one] identified nine non-religious components that constitute what they define as humanistic spirituality which are distinct from religious forms of spirituality. . . . [Moreover] Spirituality is not a natural stance. . . . The way individuals conceptualise spirituality is highly correlated with the special circumstances they encounter and experience, which affect how they internalise, manifest and interpret it. (Gross, 2012, pp. 199–200)

Such approaches seem not to get us any nearer the 'Holy Grail' of a clear definition acceptable to all, but they do indicate the key issues in the field, including whether the spiritual is intrinsically linked with religion and belief in God.

Gross's reference to a 'humanistic spirituality' invites the question, Is a concept of spirituality unconnected with religion sensible or viable? This was a question McLaughlin visited on more than one occasion, as he distinguished between what he called 'tethered' and 'un-tethered' spiritualities:

> Religiously 'tethered' spirituality takes its shape from various aspects of the religion with which it is associated and which makes it possible to identify the nature and shape of 'spirituality' within that context, including criteria for spiritual development. (McLaughlin, 2003, p. 191)

In contrast:

> Religiously 'un-tethered' spirituality involves beliefs and practices that are disconnected from, and may even be discomforting to, religions. (McLaughlin, 2003, p. 192)

Given the requirement to provide for religious education and spiritual development in a multifaith society where the majority of the population are probably de facto agnostic and many are atheists, the attraction of a spirituality untethered from any specific religion is great. Thus meditation (Erricker & Erricker, 2001) and other experiences such as 'stilling' and 'silent sitting', as sometimes used in Circle Time, and in curricular schemes such as that of the Human Values Foundation,[9] are considered to facilitate, if not actively promote spirituality without risking offence to any specific religion or the charge of indoctrination.[10]

However, as McLaughlin puts it, in contrast to the 'tethered' variety, such 'spirituality'

> may lack a definite shape and structure and may be unconnected to any wider tradition of belief, practice and value, thereby making it difficult to specify criteria for spiritual development in relation to them. (2003, p. 192)

Thus unconnected, the very concept may lose its meaning, as Adrian Thatcher asserts: "Once wrenched from its religious meaning, it has to be *assigned* a meaning by its advocates, and there is lack of agreement about what it signifies" (1999a, p. 3). And the more the meanings which are assigned to the term, the more human experience it seems to touch (if not include), and the less precise its meaning actually becomes.

A Superfluous Concept?

It is arguable that much of the frustration and confusion about spiritual education could be avoided if we simply stopped using such words altogether. There are two perspectives here. One is that, unlike the cognitive, physical, social and moral development of the child which are *at least in principle* possible to observe and measure, the lack of consensus about what constitutes spiritual development means that it cannot easily be operationalised in this way, not to mention the fact that in some conceptions of the Spirit, it *defies* observation. If we can't 'see' it (if you like), what's the point of talking about it? The second is that we do not *need* a concept of the spiritual, because that which it is used to describe is at least as well (if not better) described in other terms, notably those relating to the emotions.

Of the first of these perspectives, suffice to say that an inability physically to observe or measure something is poor grounds for not referring to it, and even poorer grounds for not providing opportunities for it to be experienced in schools. After all, aesthetic experience is both culturally and personally relative and no more observable than the spiritual, but teaching the appreciation of art does not seem to raise anything like the controversy surrounding the spiritual. It does, however, share with it a strong affective component or accompaniment.

The emotional impact of 'spiritual' experiences leads some commentators to wonder whether there is anything more to it than that. For example, Roger Marples (2006) argues that the idea of spirituality as a search for meaning or 'spiritual quest' is highly problematic, even within a religious context. Such formulations (he asserts) seem to lack a grounding in the kind of clear, shared and rule-governed language necessary for them to be viably meaningful. It is in any case unclear why such a 'quest' would not be quite properly described as 'philosophical' rather than spiritual. Interestingly, such a view seems to underlie a key component of the Scottish Curriculum in Religious and Moral Education (RME) entitled *Personal Search,* which is defined as "a process by which pupils can discover and develop their own beliefs and values. It involves them in making up their minds on religious and moral issues by developing skills associated with critical thinking and evaluation" (quoted in Hartshorn, 2008, p. 376). So much of the language of spirituality (Marples argues) and so many of the 'manifestations of spirituality in life' are either so vague as to be meaningless, or may be understood as experiences of other kinds (e.g. emotional, aesthetic), or as character traits or virtues, or predispositions to act in certain ways. There is nothing he can see which justifies the label 'spiritual' as essential to their adequate description. 'Un-tethering' the concept from religion is no escape from these problems; if anything, the word only becomes even more superfluous.

I have argued elsewhere (Best, 2008), that Marples's thesis is open to a number of serious objections, not least that 'spiritual' fits comfortably within one particular discourse and that Marples's disinclination to accord that discourse parity with those of (say) philosophy and psychology is not enough to rule it out of court. A second objection is that his argument simply ignores the kinds of experience which people are talking about when they use the word 'spiritual' and that no other words (such as 'emotional' or 'aesthetic') *on their own* can do justice to describing them.

Despite the weaknesses (which I think are considerable) in Marples's thesis, the question he poses as to whether the concept of the spiritual is either necessary or viable in regard to education is a serious one. Lambourn (1996) warns against using it merely to fill whatever 'gaps' are left by other concepts, and suggests that there may be no remainder if the 'personal' and 'social' are fully understood.

Examining 'Spiritual' Experience

I see two main ways of approaching the examination of spiritual experience: (a) we may look at *the way we use the word* 'spiritual' in relation to experiences; (b) we may examine *the subjective perceptions and apprehensions of those personal experiences which we describe as 'spiritual'* (a phenomenological approach). While these may appear to be two sides of the same coin, the outcomes suggest otherwise. The first was the path taken (in a philosophically unsophisticated way) by Ofsted, SCAA and others in the 1990s, and we have noted already how this obfuscates rather than illuminates. The second may lead to the identification of experiences for which no other description seems satisfactory, and this is helpful provided we are not 'smuggling in something which should perhaps be examined more explicitly' (Lambourn, 1996, p. 157).

Researchers in the UK and elsewhere have empirically researched children's and adolescents' concepts of spirituality and their descriptions of experiences which might be described as 'spiritual' (e.g. McCreery, 1996; Champagne, 2001; Nesbitt, 2001; Bosacki & Ota, 2000; Adams, 2001; Reimer & Furrow, 2001; Engebretson 2004, 2006). Perhaps best known of these in the UK context is the research undertaken by Hay and Nye (1998) who interviewed 38 children between the ages of 6 and 11, using photographs and other means to get them to talk about spirituality. The authors concluded that children's descriptions of what might be called spiritual experiences were characterised by a single 'compound property' which they called *relational consciousness*—that is, they were moments of exceptional consciousness and perceptiveness in contexts where the child related to something or someone, including God (Hay with Nye, 1998, p. 113).

The descriptions reported in such research are often idiosyncratic and surprising, and our difficulty in grasping what children say in such contexts seems to demonstrate the impossibility of finding the right words to capture their distinctiveness and power. Adult descriptions of similar experiences are often like this, too. I have been struck by a number of examples amongst those for whom spirituality is a major interest, not least Professor John Hull's account of the discovery of an ancient altar in Iona Abbey (Hull, 1997, pp. 195–196)[11] and the theologian Don Cupitt's description of a moment of insight which was

> . . . like the moment when a tightly-coiled spring begins to release its energy, and then a violent explosion of pure happiness which passed so rapidly that I became conscious of it and identified it only as something that was already fast receding and becoming forgotten. I found myself snatching at it as it slipped away, melting though my fingers. (Cupitt, 1998, p. 8)

While it is possible to challenge the use of 'spiritual' to describe such experiences, it is not easy to see what other words can do them justice. The suggestion that these are no more than powerful emotional experiences won't do. They are strong in affect, it is true, but that is not the same thing.

In a recent paper (Best, 2011), I contrasted a moment of heightened relationship as I danced with my 4-year-old granddaughter in my arms with a period of emotional agony when she was born, to demonstrate that the dance episode lacked the dimensions of cognition (recognition or understanding) and desire (motivation or goal-directedness) which philosophers tell us are two other components of emotions (Best, 2011, pp. 364–365). I noted that the experience involved an unspoken but profound level of *trust* and a *letting-go of self* in order to allow the other to fill my world and bring a sense of wholeness. It was also a *total* experience—physical or bodily—as well as awareness and affect, and there was an element of play or *playfulness*. I do not suggest that all spiritual experiences are like this, but this one does, for me, epitomise a kind of experience for which 'spiritual' is the only descriptor which does justice. It also implies something about the conditions under which certain kinds of experience may be facilitated (Best, 2011, pp. 366–367).

CONCLUSION

A comprehensive account of the place, purpose and meaning of children's spiritual development in the education systems of the countries of the United Kingdom would take a whole book. What I have tried to provide in this chapter is but an overview of some of the historical and political factors at work in multiethnic, multicultural and multifaith societies, together with a flavour of the ongoing debates about the meaning of spirituality and how spiritual development might be included in the curriculum of such societies. It should be clear from the discussion that the big questions are by no means resolved to everyone's (*any*one's?) complete satisfaction and that what we live with is inevitably a set of compromises and a continuing struggle for a better understanding.

I am aware that I have said little about the *pedagogy* of spiritual education, but it should be clear that for teachers charged with 'delivering' spiritual education—'tethered' or 'un-tethered' to religion—the challenges are great. Given the difficulties of definition and the historic and problematic relationship between spirituality and religion, the option of simply ignoring spiritual development in curriculum planning is not unattractive. In my view, to do so would be a serious mistake. As for the elusive definition, it matters less what something is called than what we do with it. If there is a sense of the person as a 'whole' in which certain sorts of experience are transcendent and enriching, and if there are genuine connections between such experiences and the moral and religious traditions of a society or a faith, an education which simply ignored these experiences and traditions would not be much of an education at all.

While there is great variety in the kinds of experiences which are labelled 'spiritual' by different groups, there are some (such as those which often happen between adults and children) which seem to me to epitomise what it is to be fully human, fully alive, and wholly at-one with another. It is what it is to love and be loved. To facilitate the development of a capacity for such experiences should surely be a fundamental purpose of education.

NOTES

1. I am grateful for guidance received from Stephen McKinney and James Nelson regarding what I say about faith schools and religious education in Scotland and Northern Ireland, respectively. Any errors which remain are mine alone.
2. Amongst these variations were the curriculum and assessment framework in Scotland, which already had "its own distinctive and flexible qualification

framework that is separate for the National Curriculum based framework used in England, Wales and Northern Ireland", and the inclusion of Welsh as a core subject on the National Curriculum requirements for Wales. Retrieved Jan. 31, 2012, from www.schoolswork.co.uk/media/files/Understanding_the_UK_education_system.pdf.

3. According to the Department for Education website, "around 34 per cent of maintained schools in England are schools with a religious character. That is 6750 maintained faith schools out of a total of 19,783 maintained schools". RetrievedMar.3,2013,fromhttp://www.education.gov.uk/schools/leadership/typesofschools/maintained/b00198369/voluntary-and-faith-schools. For a description of some of the categories of school in respect of faith-based schools, see Parker-Jenkins, Hartas and Irving, 2005, chap. 2.

4. As Adrian Thatcher (1999a, p. 9) comments: "A telling comparison between the lobbying groups which were responsible for the insertion of spiritual development in the 1944 and 1988 Education Acts concludes that each believed in the conflation of doctrinal Christianity, an ambiguous concept of 'spiritual', and the use of education to promote 'national moral virtue'".

5. Which is not to say that the merger was achieved without heated debate between representatives of the established Church, nonconformists and non-believers. On the contrary: See Lawson and Silver, 1973; Holness, 2005, p. 211; Best, 2005, p. 69.

6. David Rose and Elaine McCreery of the Religious Education section of the Faculty of Education.

7. Key movers in these developments were located in higher education institutes at Chichester and Winchester, notably Clive Erricker, Jane Erricker and Cathy Ota.

8. I have to confess to having played a (very minor) role in the discussions which resulted in the matrix; I have regretted it ever since and am relieved that the scheme was eventually dropped.

9. To see their programme *Education in Human Values* (EHV), for 5–12-year-olds, visit www.humanvakluesfoundation.com/ehv (Retrieved May 24, 2012).

10. Not entirely successfully, however. I have heard evangelical Christian students argue that 'emptying the mind' in this way was an invitation to the Devil to move in.

11. John Hull is Emeritus Professor of Religious Education at the University of Birmingham. He is profoundly blind. In his book *On Sight and Insight—A Journey into the World of Blindness*, he recounts how he explores the ancient Abbey at dead of night when he has the place to himself and his blindness is irrelevant. His description, which makes no explicit reference to God or religion, of happening upon the ancient altar, measuring it with his body and examining its blemishes and surfaces with his fingers and his tongue, is an excellent example of what I have in mind as a 'spiritual' experience.

REFERENCES

Adams, K. (2001). God talks to me in my dreams: The occurrence and significance of children's dreams about God. *International Journal of Children's Spirituality*, 6(1), 99–111.

Alexander, H. A. & McLaughlin, T. H. (2003). Education in religion and spirituality. In N. Blake, P. Smeyers, & P. Standish (Eds.), *The Blackwell guide to philosophy of education* (pp. 356–373). Oxford: Blackwell.

Alexander, H. A. (2009). Autonomy, faith and reasons: McLaughlin and Callan on religious initiation. In G. Haydon (Ed.), *Faith in education. A tribute to Terence McLaughlin* (pp. 27–45). London: University of London Institute of Education.

Armstrong, D. (2012). Northern Ireland. In L. P. Barnes (Ed.), *Debates in religious education* (pp. 33–39). London: Routledge.

Best, R. (2003). *Faith schools—A review of the debate.* Paper presented to the Centre for Religious Education and Development, University of Surrey, Roehampton. 6th February.

Best, R. (2005): Spiritual development and affective education: An English perspective. In S. Karppinen, J. Katz, & S. Neill (Eds.), *Theory and practice in affective education. Essays in honour of Arja Puurula* (pp. 65–84). Helsinki: University of Helsinki.

Best, R. (2008). In defence of spiritual education: A reply to Roger Marples. *International Journal of Children's Spirituality, 13*(4), 321–329.

Best, R. (2011). Emotion, spiritual experience and education: A reflection. *International Journal of Children's Spirituality, 16*(4), 361–368.

Bigger, S. (1999). Spiritual, moral, social and cultural education. In S. Bigger and E. Brown (Eds.), *Spiritual, moral, social and cultural education. Exploring values in the curriculum* (pp. 3–15). London: David Fulton.

Bosacki, S. & Ota, C. (2000). Preadolescents' voices: a consideration of British and Canadian children's reflections on religion, spirituality and their sense of self. *International Journal of Children's Spirituality, 5*(2), 203–219.

Callan, E. (2009). Why bring kids into this? McLaughlin and Anscombe on religious understanding and upbringing. In G. Haydon (Ed.), *Faith in education. A tribute to Terence McLaughlin* (pp. 9–26). London: University of London Institute of Education.

Carr, D., Halstead, M. & Pring, R. (Eds). (2008). *Liberalism, Education and Schooling.* Exeter: Imprint Academic.

Champagne, E. (2001). Listening to . . . listening for . . . : A theological reflection on spirituality in early childhood. In J. Erricker, C. Ota, & C. Erricker (Eds.), *Spiritual education. Cultural, religious and social differences* (pp. 76–87). Brighton: Sussex Academic Press.

Council for the Curriculum, Examinations and Assessment (CCEA). (2007). *The statutory curriculum at Key Stage 3.* Belfast: Council for the Curriculum, Examinations and Assessment.

Cupitt, D. (1998). *The revelation of being.* London: SCM Press.

Engebretson, K. (2004). Teenage boys, spirituality and religion. *International Journal of Children's Spirituality, 9*(3), 263–278.

Engebretson, K. (2006). 'God's got your back': Teenage boys talk about God. *International Journal of Children's Spirituality, 11*(3), 329–345.

Erricker, C., & Erricker, J. (2001). *Meditation in schools.* London: Cassell.

Gallagher, T. (2005). Faith schools and Northern Ireland: A review of research. In R. Gardner, J. Cairns, & D. Lawton (Eds.), *Faith schools. Consensus or conflict?* (pp. 156–165). Abingdon: RoutledgeFalmer.

Gardner, R., Cairns, J., & Lawton, D. (Eds.). (2005). *Faith schools. Consensus or conflict?* Abingdon: RoutledgeFalmer.

Grace, G. (2009). Terence McLaughlin: Contributions to the study and practice of faith schooling and Catholic education. In G. Haydon (Ed.), *Faith in ducation. A tribute to Terence McLaughlin* (pp. 1–8). London: University of London Institute of Education.

Gross, Z. (2012). Editorial. The chicken grows as the egg decays: War and spirituality as contradictory and complementary forces. *International Journal of Children's Spirituality, 15*(3), 199–208.

Halstead, J. M. (2002). Faith and diversity in religious school provision. In L. Gearon (Ed.), *Education in the United Kingdom* (pp.146–157). London: David Fulton.

Halstead, J. M. (2009). In defence of faith schools. In G. Haydon (Ed.), *Faith in education. A tribute to Terence McLaughlin* (pp. 46–67). London: University of London Institute of Education.

Hartshorn, B. (2008). Religious and moral education. In T. G. K. Bryce & W. M. Humes (Eds.), *Scottish education: Beyond devolution* (3rd ed., pp. 375–380). Edinburgh: Edinburgh University Press.

Hay, D., with Nye, R. (1998). *The spirit of the child*. London: Fount/Harper Collins.

Haydon, G. (Ed) (2009). *Faith in education. A tribute to Terence McLaughlin*. London: University of London Institute of Education.

Holness, M. (2005). Brief historical survey: The need to recognise old wine in new bottles—The structural roots of voluntarism in the English schooling system. *International Journal of Children's Spirituality, 10*(2), 207–214.

Hull, J. (1997). *On sight and insight—A journey into the world of blindness*. Oxford: One World.

Humanist Philosophers' Group. (2001). *Religious schools: The case against*. London: British Humanist Association.

Keast, J. (2003). Spiritual development and the Qualifications and Curriculum Authority. In D. Carr & J. Haldane (Eds.), *Spirituality, philosophy and education* (pp. 157–169). London: RoutledgeFalmer.

Lambourn, D. (1996). 'Spiritual' minus 'personal-social' = ? A critical note on an 'empty' category. In R. Best (Ed.), *Education, spirituality and the whole child* (pp. 150–158). London: Cassell.

Lawson, J., and Silver, H. (1973). *A social history of education in England*. London: Routledge & Kegan Paul.

Marples, R. (2005). Against faith schools: A philosophical argument for children's rights. *International Journal of Children's Spirituality, 10*(2), 133–147.

Marples, R. (2006). Against (the use of the term) 'spiritual education'. *International Journal of Children's Spirituality, 11*(2), 293–306.

McCreery, E. (1996). Talking to young children about things spiritual. In R. Best (Ed.), *Education, spirituality and the whole child* (pp. 150–158). London: Cassell.

McKinney, S. J. (2008a). Do Catholic schools in Scotland cause or promote sectarianism?. In S. J. McKinney (Ed.), *Faith schools in the twenty-first century* (pp. 41–55). Edinburgh: Dunedin Academic Press.

McKinney, S. J. (2008b). Catholic schools in Scotland and divisiveness. *Journal of Beliefs and Values, 29*(2), 173–184.

McKinney, S. J. (2008c). Catholic education in Scotland. In T. G. K. Bryce & W. M. Humes (Eds.), *Scottish education: Beyond devolution* (3rd ed., pp. 257–265). Edinburgh: Edinburgh University Press.

McLaughlin. T. H. (2003). Education, spirituality and the common school. In D. Carr & J. Haldane (Eds.), *Spirituality, philosophy and education* (pp.185–199). London: RouletdgeFalmer.

McLaughlin, T. H. (2008a). The ethics of separate schools. In D. Carr, M. Halstead, & R. Pring (Eds.), *Liberalism, education and schooling; Essays by T. H. McLaughlin* (pp.175–198). Exeter: Imprint Academic.

McLaughlin, T. H. (2008b): Distinctiveness and the Catholic school: Balanced judgement and the temptations of commonality. In D. Carr, M. Halstead, & R. Pring (Eds.), *Liberalism, education and schooling; Essays by T. H. McLaughlin* (pp.199–217). Exeter: Imprint Academic.

McLaughlin, T. H., & Halstead, M. (2005). Are faith schools divisive? In R. Gardner, J. Cairns, & D. Lawton (Eds.), *Faith schools. Consensus or conflict?* (pp. 61–73). Abingdon: RoutledgeFalmer,.

Nesbitt, E. (2001). Religious nurture and young people's spirituality: Reflections of research at the University of Warwick. In J. Erricker, C. Ota, & C. Erricker (Eds.), *Spiritual education. Cultural, religious and social differences* (pp. 130–142). Brighton: Sussex Academic Press.

Nixon, G. (2008). Religious and Moral Education (RME). In T. G. K. Bryce & W. M. Humes (Eds.), *Scottish education: Beyond devolution* (3rd ed.) (pp. 557–561). Edinburgh: Edinburgh University Press.

O'Callaghan, M., & Lundy, L. (2002). Northern Ireland. In L. Gearon (Ed.), *Education in the United Kingdom* (pp.16–28). London: David Fulton.

Parker-Jenkins, M., Hartas, D., & Irving, B. A. (2005). *In good faith. Schools, religion and public funding.* Aldershot: Ashgate.

Reimer, K. S., & Furrow, J. L. (2001). A qualitative exploration of relational consciousness in Christian children. *International Journal of Children's Spirituality*, 6(1), 7–23.

Scottish Education Department. (1972). *Moral and religious education in Scottish schools.* The Millar Report. Edinburgh: Her Majesty's Stationery Office.

Thatcher, A. (1999a). Theology, spirituality and the curriculum—An overview. In A. Thatcher (Ed.), *Spirituality and the curriculum* (pp. 1–11). London: Cassell.

Thatcher, A. (1999b). Values—Secular or Christian?: A response to Mary Grey. In A. Thatcher (Ed.), *Spirituality and the curriculum* (pp. 33–54). London: Cassell.

Yates, P. (1999): The bureaucratisation of spirituality. *International Journal of Children's Spirituality*, 4(2), 179–193.

Yates, P. (2000). The spirit and the empty matrix: The social construction of spiritual, moral, social and cultural education. In R. Best (Ed.), *Education for spiritual, moral, social and cultural development* (pp. 22–36). London: Continuum.

2 Spiritual Development in Schools with No Faith Affiliation
The Cultural Ambivalence Towards Children's Spirituality in England

Kate Adams

In the summer of 2012, the opening ceremony of the Olympic Games in London conveyed to the world some archetypal images of England which permeate the psyche of the nation. It showcased extracts, both dark and light, from the country's history through the means of drama, art and music. One centrepiece was a grassy setting depicting serene village life, echoing the well-known words of poet William Blake, "in England's green and pleasant land". Such cottages surrounded by lush gardens filled with colourful flowers epitomised a sense of nostalgia and symbol of aspiration for many; indeed, the garden holds an affectionate place in the country's history, immortalised in the lyrics of a traditional folk song, 'English country garden', which celebrates the vibrant display of the native flowers, birds and insects which inhabit them. Serving as a tranquil retreat from the frenzied world of work and other pressures of life, the garden also offers an apt metaphor for spirituality in its broader sense: a place bursting with vitality; of strong majestic trees with solid roots; young shoots emerging from the ground seeking new life as other growth inevitably wilts and dies; a place where connectedness with nature is at its heart.

Perhaps the garden metaphor could also be applied to England's state education system which is, on the face of it, in a privileged position with regards to children's spirituality. Unlike most international education systems, England's enjoys a long-standing legal requirement to promote children's spiritual development—an obligation which is conceivably the envy of advocates of spirituality across the world. However, the picture is not quite as rosy as one might hope.

This chapter focuses on state-maintained schools in England which have no religious affiliation. These schools are in the majority, comprising approximately two-thirds of all state-maintained schools. The remaining third have a religious affiliation, the vast majority of which are Christian (Department for Education, 2012). There is regional variation in policy within the UK and readers interested in the historical development of those variations are directed to Best's chapter in this volume (Chapter 1). The place of spiritual development in England's education policy is considered briefly in this chapter, attending to the religious and cultural forces which have shaped it. As the chronological account nears the 21st century, the discussion focuses on the wider contemporary challenges facing those who seek to nurture spiritual development in schools which have no religious affiliation. The chapter explores the wider cultural ambivalence towards spirituality in general and children's spirituality in particular. It argues that these factors contribute to the feelings of many children encapsulated in the words of 9-year-old Ranjit: "People don't listen, they think you make things up and sometimes they laugh at you". Other children's voices are woven into relevant sections of this chapter to highlight similar issues of lack of voice, as evidenced in research. The chapter concludes by proposing ways forward for supporting children in the experience and exploration of their spiritual worlds which often remain 'unseen' (Adams, 2010).

THE HISTORICAL ROOTS OF SPIRITUAL DEVELOPMENT

The phrase 'spiritual development' first appeared in legislation in the 1944 Education Act, which obliged education authorities to contribute to the spiritual, moral, mental and physical development of the community. Wright (2000) states that the 1944 Act constituted a blueprint for the moral and spiritual rejuvenation of the country following the trauma of World War II. At that time the Church of England had a clearly established and dominant position in a country which had a strong Christian heritage. Indeed, the origins of schools for the masses in England lay with the church. Marples (2005) argues that without the Church of England's early concern for elementary schooling, together with the National Society and the British and Foreign School Society, there would have been little formal education for the vast majority of children before 1870. Postwar, this dominance of Christianity continued to reign and the 1944 Act effectively created a dual system of Church and state-sponsored schools (Wright, 2000). At this time, references to the spiritual were to directly correlate to Christian beliefs. Religious Instruction was a legal requirement in schools, again pertaining only to Christianity and schools were to hold a daily act of collective worship which also served to instil Christian beliefs and values. Consequently, spiritual development was also firmly rooted in Christianity at that time.

As society changed, becoming increasingly multicultural over the ensuing decades, and particularly from the 1940s and 1950s onwards, so new political and cultural influences inevitably emerged in education policy. Wright (2000, p. 65) argues that the rise of a 'moral and liberal humanism' in the 1970s effectively superseded the Christian agenda of the 1944 Act. Now education had become progressive, seeking to promote freedom and tolerance, a change that was occurring alongside a collapse in the Christian consensus. The late 1970s witnessed discussions about the spiritual in education at government level, and the subsequent 1988 Education Reform Act launched a National Curriculum which included the promotion of the spiritual, moral, cultural, mental and physical development of pupils at the school and of society. In fact, this was one of only two aims of this new 'broad and balanced' curriculum, the other being to prepare pupils for the opportunities, responsibilities and experiences of adult life (Her Majesty's Stationery Office, 1988, 1.1.2a).

Alongside the legal requirement came attempts to clarify what was meant by the term 'spiritual development'. Government education bodies promptly published guidance for teachers (e.g. National Curriculum Council, 1993), advocating that spirituality and religion were not synonymous. However to some extent it can be argued that schools were relatively free to disregard the spiritual, particularly given the ambiguity and contestation surrounding its meaning. That situation was to subsequently change with the Education (Schools) Act 1992 which created the government inspection body, the then Office for Standards in Education (Ofsted).[1] The Act stated that the Chief Inspector for England should keep the Secretary of State informed of the spiritual, moral, social and cultural (SMSC) development of pupils at the schools which it inspected. Inspection requirements continued to appear in the School Inspections Act 1996 and most recently were reiterated in the Education Act 2011. The wording had changed slightly from the 1988 Education Reform Act, now losing 'mental and physical' development and inserting 'social', but on paper the spiritual remained not only at the core of the curriculum but even retained its position as the first in the list of these child-centred foci. More importantly perhaps, by placing SMSC on the agenda for inspections, teachers were, and continue to be, urged to pay attention to spiritual development as they would be held to account over its delivery—in theory at least.

SPIRITUALITY IN THE WIDER LANDSCAPE

At least on the political surface, spiritual development appears to have a secure base, shaped and influenced by England's historical traditions, with consecutive governments ensuring its continued inclusion in the curriculum. But below that surface lurk a host of issues which challenge its potential to flourish, most notably in those state schools with no religious affiliation. As Erricker, Ota and Erricker (2001) observe, schools with a faith affiliation are able to ground their approach to spirituality in their own religious traditions. Schools with no such affiliation do not have that grounding, of course, and are advised to heed Ofsted's guidance (Ofsted, 2004) which states that the spiritual should be cross-curricular and not confined to Religious Education, a stance which has proved contentious in itself and one on which educators continue to differ (King, 2008).

In many of these nonaffiliated schools, spiritual development has a very low priority and is often subsumed within its wider brief of SMSC. To examine why this might be the case, and subsequently consider possible ways forward, the wider landscape of spirituality needs consideration. This journey begins with the complexities of the country's changing (though contested) attitudes towards children and religion/spirituality.

Attitudes towards Children

In terms of previous and past government policy, children are understandably afforded a relatively high profile. Various initiatives and legislation to improve children's lives in a range of social arenas have been introduced on a regular basis. For example, recent laws have included the Children Act 2004; the Apprenticeships, Skills, Children and Learning Act 2009; and the Education Act 2011 (National Society for the Prevention of Cruelty to Children, 2012). National policy and legislation also sit within the context of international guidance, most notably the United Nations Convention on the Rights of the Child (UNCRC) which, in 1989, sought to lay foundations to improve children's life experiences on a global scale. It outlined protection, provision and participation rights for children. Of particular relevance to spirituality, the UNCRC included the right for children to have freedom of expression (Article 13) and the right to thought, conscience and religion (Article 14) (Handley, 2005). Of course, not all policies are effective, and none are without their critics, but they evidence the desire of successive governments to improve children's lives.

However, despite practical and well-intentioned systemic support for increasing the quality of children's lives, there are wider cultural issues which affect attitudes towards children particularly in relation to their spirituality. Whilst it may make sense to begin with an exploration of wider cultural attitudes towards spirituality, I make no apologies for starting this section with a discussion about children. If adults are to fully understand children's spirituality, it is essential that children's voices are heard in the debate. Without adults developing empathy with children through hearing how they perceive childhood and their inner experiences, and perhaps reconnecting with their own childhood experiences, a full understanding is not possible (Adams, 2010). Listening to the child's voice is thus an essential focus of research, even if—and perhaps particularly when—children's views do not resonate with contemporary theoretical perspectives.

With regards to children's spirituality, a variety of studies both in the UK and in North America found that children regularly report that they do not share their spiritual experiences for fear of ridicule or dismissal (see Robinson, 1983; Hart, 2003; Hay with Nye, 2006; Adams, Hyde & Woolley, 2008; Adams, 2010). Children's reasons for such fears have not been explored in sufficient depth but similar themes emerge in the aforementioned studies. For example, in my interviews with 94 children about their spiritual dreams, one-third stated that they had not revealed the dream to anyone else. Emily, aged 11, explained,

I would be crazy to tell anyone I had a dream about Jesus 'cos all my friends would say I was mad so I told my teacher not to tell them I was coming to talk to you.

Whilst a small number wished to keep the experience private (as all children have a right to), the majority made references to fears of ridicule or not being believed, as Jack, aged 9, explained:

Once I told my Dad that I had this dream about Gran in heaven, she was in white clouds and looked happy but Dad laughed and said "silly boy, there's no such thing as heaven" which made me cry. I don't know why he laughed at me.

Wider cultural influences impacted on the children's attitudes. In some cases the attitude stemmed from a personal experience such as describing an intriguing dream to a parent who did not have time to respond, which the child deemed as lack of interest. In other cases, children stated that peers would laugh at them so they chose to remain quiet (Adams, Hyde & Woolley, 2008). Similarly, Hay and Nye (2006) observed that few children in their UK study had previously discussed aspects of their spirituality with others prior to their research project. Children discussed fears of being "embarrassed, ridiculed or undermined" if they shared their thoughts and experiences (p. 127). Writing in the US, Hart (2003) made similar observations, going so far as to entitle his book *The Secret Spiritual World of Children*.

Unsurprisingly, studies in the UK and North America with adults have also revealed similar findings (see Hay, 1985; Scott, 2004; Adams, 2010). If many adults avoid telling others about spiritual experiences for fear of ridicule themselves, it is only to be expected that children will not openly discuss theirs either because, in part, they do not hear them being discussed by adults. Thus a notion of a social taboo emerges whereby society deems it somehow inappropriate to talk about such matters. I have argued elsewhere (Adams, 2009a) that whilst much policy and practice in developed countries has increasingly addressed the need to hear the child's voice, particularly since the declaration by the UNCRC, the same attitudes have not been focused on the children's 'spiritual voice(s)' (p. 117). Whilst many practitioners have sought to acknowledge and act upon the thoughts and wishes of children in matters of health, social work and education, the spiritual voice has often remained unrecognised by many adults and has gone unheard for many children. A key factor contributing to such a trend lies in cultural attitudes towards religion and spirituality.

Attitudes towards Religion and Spirituality

There are many complexities surrounding the term 'spirituality', not least the well-rehearsed debates about what it is and if it can be defined at all, and whether or not spirituality has to be linked to religion. In addition, increasing globalisation complicates any claims of a society having either positive or negative cultural attitudes towards spirituality. With populations in countries such as the UK becoming more varied in terms of cultural background, an increasing number of religious and/or spiritual views are inevitably brought into the social arena. So too are claims of increasing secularisation—a complex argument in itself. However, what has occurred in England, as in other countries such as the US and Australia, is a rise of 'popular' spirituality which has become part of a mainstream discourse via publications and courses for the general public. Initially the umbrella term of 'New Age' emerged and more recently the phrase 'Mind, Body, Spirit' has appeared, particularly in bookstores. Some elements of contemporary spiritualities draw on ancient religious traditions, often mixed and reinterpreted, whilst others are more secular in nature, often with a focus on the personal and individual (King, 2008). Tacey (2004) cautions that the New Age is in fact an industry, but one which has captured the minds of many young people in his home country of Australia as well as in Britain.

Such alternative conceptions of spirituality are instantly accessible to children via the media; Hyde (2008) reports how Catholic children in Australia talked of New Age ideas such as horoscopes, as well as drawing on beliefs from religions other than their own such as belief in reincarnation. One boy, Jake, told how his pet dog Scamper had died. Jake explained,

> Now the lady down the street has a dog that has just had pups. They were born right around the time that Scamper died. I think that maybe Scamper's spirit is sort of alive in one of those baby pups . . . one of them even looks a bit like Scamper. (p. 14)

Children in England have very similar exposure to such contemporary spiritualities and, in their quest to find meaning, are able to shape their own ideas drawn from an eclectic mix: a radical departure from the historical backdrop of a society once dominated by Christian belief.

Family attitudes towards spirituality can affect children's willingness to discuss and express it. If children are raised in an environment where talk of spiritual matters is accepted and even encouraged, they are more likely to be articulate in these personal matters of life and more confident in expressing them. Yet whilst it may be safe to assume that children from a spiritually/ religiously open family may feel comfortable discussing such matters, this is not always the case. Children from such homes have also claimed that their spiritual thoughts were not taken seriously (Adams, Hyde & Woolley, 2008). For example, Adam, who was from a Christian family, said "no one in my house talks about God even though we go to church every week". The education system thus potentially plays an important role in supporting those children who do not have confidantes at home, and the legal requirement to promote spiritual development offers a key means of doing so.

THE SPIRITUAL LANDSCAPE OF THE FUTURE

Given the important role that education can play in nurturing children's spirituality, how might the spiritual landscape look in the future? England is currently experiencing a diversification of types of state-maintained schools, many of which are seeing greater freedoms over curriculum, a change which marks uncharted territory for spiritual development. Whilst this trend has the potential to facilitate greater emphasis on spirituality, counterforces such as a focus on test results and league tables combined with a wider cultural lack of interest in children's spirituality conspire to fight the former option. Whilst there is also currently a political drive to create new state-maintained faith schools, whose policies and practices will obviously be shaped by religion, those which are not affiliated to a faith will most likely increasingly differ in their approaches to spiritual development. Factors such as the aims and values of the school, its leaders and staff will be highly influential, so it is essential that teacher training places spiritual development firmly on its agenda to influence those new to the profession.

Over a decade ago, Wright (2000) observed that initial teacher training often paid scarce attention to spirituality, leaving newly qualified teachers with little understanding of what it is. In addition, he suggested that senior managers often lacked confidence in establishing strong guidelines. There is little to suggest that initial teacher training in this area has improved since Wright expressed his views, with practice most likely being variable, in part depending on staff expertise and interest at various institutions engaged in training. More recently, Woolley (2010) surveyed student teachers at eight universities and found that only 28% claimed their training had given detailed input on spiritual development; a worrying 44% said they had received little or no input. In addition, over a fifth of respondents thought they would 'rarely' or 'never' have to deal with spiritual development in their first teaching job.

Initial teacher training institutions in England (predominantly higher education institutions who work in partnerships with schools) have not succeeded as well as they might with regards to providing high quality input on spiritual development. Such input is variable across the sector, indicating that the inclusion of spiritual development in legislation and the inspection of it in schools are not sufficient to guarantee that is understood, valued and nurtured (Adams, 2009b).

Change in teacher training is needed if newly qualified staff are to enter the profession with an understanding of spiritual development. Indeed, in England change in training is on the horizon. The government is altering the mode of initial teacher training, aiming to have one-third of all new teachers (approximately 10,000 per year) trained in schools (Gove, 2012). One of the concerns about these new proposals for those engaged in nurturing children's spirituality lies in the inconsistency of the training that schools are likely to offer. If a school places little emphasis on spiritual development, the trainee will have little or no exposure to high quality provision of the requirement (even if other areas of the school's performance are effective). Trainees will need exposure to mentors who are advocates of spiritual development, particularly in school where they can experience its implementation in practice. However, if such role models are not widely available across the country, trainees' experience of observing spiritual development will continue to be inconsistent and the status quo of variable provision in initial teacher training will remain.

RELIGIOUS EDUCATION AND SPIRITUAL DEVELOPMENT

As noted above, Ofsted has long maintained that spiritual development should be cross-curricular although there is recognition that it has a special relationship with Religious Education (RE), the teaching of which is also a legal requirement (Ofsted, 2004). Many schools, however, blur the spiritual, moral, social and cultural. Whilst there is a general consensus that there are overlaps across the four strands (Eaude, 2006) there is confusion amongst many teachers, particularly in schools without a faith affiliation, who struggle to identify what the spiritual is. Whilst Ofsted's (2004, 2011) guidelines to support teachers have attracted criticism, particularly for offering definitions so inclusive that they say little, the matter is further complicated by confusion over meaning amongst Ofsted inspectors themselves, as Watson (2001) discovered. Furthermore, RE is often perceived to be the natural home for spiritual development even though a cross-curricular approach is required. However, Ofsted (2010) recently published a report into the strengths and weaknesses of RE in primary and secondary schools based on visits to 94 primary and 89 secondary schools in England. A key finding of the report was that RE made little contribution to students' spiritual development—a finding that applied to six out of ten secondary schools. Again, the role of initial teacher training is paramount to prepare students to teach Religious Education effectively but so too is the role of schools' senior leaders to ensure that it is being delivered, and being delivered effectively, as a matter of course.

WAYS FORWARD

With the current state of flux in England's education system, the task of proposing ways forward is more complex given that changes to the curriculum and to initial teacher training are inevitable but not yet fully formulated. However the following more generic principles are proposed with regards to state schools with no faith affiliation.

One of the difficulties facing those engaged in researching and/or promoting children's spirituality is that we inevitably 'preach to the converted'. The readers of this volume and other texts like it, for example, are unlikely to be those who have no interest in spirituality. So how best can we promote children's spirituality to those engaged in education but have no interest in it? Certainly, a drive to increase evidence-based policy making is a key motivator. Increasing numbers of rigorous and systematic studies on spirituality can contribute to a larger evidence base. Examples of possible studies include collecting more data on the views of teachers in schools not affiliated to a faith, which could facilitate greater understanding of their perceptions and practices; and more data on children's views could facilitate greater understanding of their needs in various school contexts.

Certainly, there is a strong call for more research which includes children's voices, which has much potential to at least impact on practice in the classroom. Children often make very poignant comments to researchers not only about their spiritual experiences and reflections but also about how they felt impeded in expressing them. Robinson cited a woman's recollection of an early childhood spiritual experience:

> This inner knowledge was exciting and absorbingly interesting, but it remained unsaid because, even if I could have expressed it, no one would have understood. Once, when I tried, I was told I was morbid. (1983, p. 12)

Similarly, Sinats et al. (2010, p. 23), drawing on a study of spirituality as it appeared in women's diaries and poetry written in their youth, offer an extract from a girl who wrote, at the age of 13, "I also believe in levitation. Once when I was three I levitated, but no one else believes me". Perhaps children's words can impact positively on teachers and can motivate and inspire them to not only understand children's spirituality more fully but also to engage in various pedagogies (for example, listening, talk, art, drama and writing) to facilitate expression.

Undertaking research projects, especially large-scale studies, brings difficulties. A first difficulty is in obtaining funding for educational research which is progressively more competitive in the UK, as in some other countries. Bidders face significant barriers in many disciplines, with an increasing trend for research councils to only fund projects which meet their predetermined topics. A second difficulty is engaging policy makers with research findings. The impact of educational research on government policy has long been debated, with concerns raised over governments' selective approach to which research they choose to inform policy. However, opportunities to disseminate research findings via workshops, symposia, conferences, books and professional and academic journals are essential means of reaching current and intending practitioners. Whilst impact via these means may only reach a small percentage of teachers and academics, it is an essential method of making spirituality more visible in educational arenas until policy can be influenced more effectively.

Another key barrier facing teachers lies in mounting workload pressures, including a trend towards a performance management system based on measurable outcomes. Publicly available Ofsted reports and student grades have added to teachers' workload and stress, contributing to an unprecedented rise in the number of teachers leaving the profession (Vasagar, 2012). Such pressure on teachers and pupils could, and perhaps should, facilitate a greater emphasis on matters of the spiritual to counter the performance discourse; of course in reality many teachers who work in schools which do not pay attention to the spiritual are unlikely to explore ideas which are new to the school when their workload is already high. However, an increasing diversity of schools is leading to greater autonomy over curricula in many cases, and may open the door for increasing provision of spiritual development. Whilst the publication of league tables and government inspections and associated pressures show no sign of disappearing, less prescription over what is taught may enable staff to develop and ensure the promotion of children's spiritual development. In order to do so, of course, spirituality needs to be valued by staff who are willing to lead in pursuing it. With wider dissemination of research findings and good practice, and more widespread teaching about spirituality in colleges and universities in general, and in teacher training in particular, there will be some potential to influence current and intending teachers. Those interested parties cannot change a nation's attitude towards the importance of spirituality but they can still make a difference to many children's lives.

CLOSING THOUGHTS

As for the spiritual garden of England's education system, the cultural and political threats loom large. Whilst the system is privileged to have spiritual development and Religious Education in its legislation, that has not been sufficient to secure high quality training and implementation in these areas across the board. This situation means that change is needed to nurture and grow the seeds, shoots and flowers of spirituality in all schools, particularly those with no faith affiliation. Whether the wider proposed changes to initial teacher training will be a cultivator or a destroyer of spirituality remains to be seen, though most likely provision will be patchy. In the meantime, each and every one of us, as contributors to wider society's values, should not shy away from nurturing spirituality in the children around us. Not all schools provide a safe haven for children to express themselves, so it is incumbent upon us all to give children the opportunity to develop resilience against those who seek to ridicule or dismiss what is at the very heart of being human—so that they may flourish themselves.

NOTES

1. Now the Office for Standards in Education, Children's Services and Skills.

REFERENCES

Adams, K. (2009a). The rise of the child's voice; the silencing of the spiritual voice. *Journal of Beliefs and Values, 30*(2), 113–122.

Adams, K. (2009b). Seeking and sharing the spiritual in the classroom. In M. de Souza, L. J. Francis, J. O'Higgins Norman, & D. Scott (Eds.), *The international handbook of education for spirituality, care and wellbeing* (pp. 809–820). Dordrecht: Springer.

Adams, K. (2010). *Unseen worlds: Looking through the lens of childhood.* London: Jessica Kingsley.

Adams, K., Hyde, B., & Woolley, R. (2008). *The spiritual dimension of childhood.* London: Jessica Kingsley.

Department for Education (DfE). (2012). *Faith schools.* Retrieved November 11, 2012, from http://www.education.gov.uk/schools/leadership/typesofschools/b0066996/faith-schools.

Eaude, T. (2006). *Children's spiritual, moral, social and cultural development—Primary and early years.* Exeter: Learning Matters.

Erricker J., Ota, C., & Erricker, C. (2001). *Spiritual education: Cultural, religious and social differences.* Brighton: Sussex Academic Press.

Gove, M. (2012). *Michael Gove at the National College annual conference.* Retrieved June 21, 2012, from http://www.education.gov.uk/inthenews/speeches/a00210308/michael-gove-at-the-national-college-annual-conference.

Handley, G. (2005). Children's rights to participation. In T. Waller (Ed.), *An introduction to early childhood: A multidisciplinary approach* (pp. 1–12). London: Paul Chapman.

Hart, T. (2003). *The secret spiritual world of children.* Maui: Inner Ocean.

Hay, D. (1985). Suspicion of the spiritual: Teaching religion in a world of secular experience. *British Journal of Religious Education, 7,* 40–147.

Hay, D., with Nye, R. (2006). *The spirit of the child* (2nd ed.). London: Jessica Kingsley.

Her Majesty's Stationery Office. (1988). *Education Reform Act 1988.* London: Author.

Hyde, B. (2008). *Children and spirituality: Searching for meaning and connectedness.* London: Jessica Kingsley.

King, U. (2008). *The search for spirituality: Our global quest for a spiritual life.* New York: BlueBridge.

Marples, R. (2005). Against faith schools: A philosophical argument for children's rights. *International Journal of Children's Spirituality, 10*(2), 133–147.

National Curriculum Council. (1993). *Spiritual and moral development: A discussion paper.* York: National Curriculum Council.

National Society for the Prevention of Cruelty to Children (NSPCC). (2012). *NSPCC factsheet: An introduction to child protection legislation in the UK.*

Retrieved June 11, 2012, from http://www.nspcc.org.uk/Inform/research/questions/child_protection_legislation_in_the_uk_pdf_wdf48953.pdf.

Ofsted. (2004). *Promoting and evaluating pupils' spiritual, moral, social and cultural development.* London: Author.

Ofsted. (2010). *Transforming religious education: Religious education in schools 2006–09.* London: Author.

Ofsted. (2011). *The framework for school inspection from January 2012.* London: Author.

Robinson, E. (1983). *The original vision.* New York: The Seabury Press.

Scott, D. (2004). Retrospective spiritual narratives: Exploring recalled childhood and adolescent spiritual experiences. *International Journal of Children's Spirituality, 9*(1), 67–79.

Sinats, P., Scott, D. G., McFerran, S., Hittos, M., Cragg, C., Leblanc, T., & Brooks, D. (2010). Writing ourselves into being: Writing as spiritual self-care for adolescent girls. Part One. *International Journal of Children's Spirituality, 10*(1), 17–29.

Tacey, D. (2004). *The spirituality revolution. The emergence of contemporary spirituality.* Hove: Routledge.

Vasagar, J. (2012). Stress drives teachers out of school. *The Guardian.* Retrieved June 21, 2012, from http://www.guardian.co.uk/education/2011/apr/25/stress-drives-teachers-out-of-schools.

Watson, J. (2001). OFSTED's Spiritual Dimension: An analytical audit of inspection reports. *Cambridge Journal of Education, 31*(2), 205–219.

Woolley, R. (2010). *Tackling controversial issues in the primary school: Facing life's challenges with your pupils.* Abingdon: Routledge.

Wright, A. (2000). *Spirituality and education.* London: RoutledgeFalmer.

3 The Custody of Spiritual Education in Ireland

James O'Higgins Norman and Caroline Renehan

INTRODUCTION

This chapter will explore the historical and sociological context of spiritual education in the Republic of Ireland. It will show how spirituality in education in Ireland has mostly been characterised by *Jansenistic* themes such as original sin, human depravity and the necessity of divine grace. Consequently, spirituality in education in Ireland has mostly been associated with Religious Education with an emphasis, although not exclusively, on cognitive learning. This understanding of spirituality, particularly with the development of non-faith-based schools, is only beginning to be replaced by a more holistic view of the person in which the spirit does not have to be identified with religious knowledge. In this chapter we understand spirituality as a fundamental concept that defines humanity as distinct from all other living things. It has to do with our relationship with self, with all other people, with the environment and with the transcendent. A person who has achieved some level of integration between all of these relationships in his or her life then can be said to be spiritual. Human spirituality is transformational in that it takes one out of one's self to connect with and be concerned for everything else outside of self. We can recognise people's spirituality in their capacity for love, compassion, patience, tolerance, forgiveness, happiness, generosity, responsibility and harmony. Spirituality is nourished by connecting with the transcendent but not in any abstract or theoretical way. For some this connection will be maintained through prayer while for others it is achieved through quality relationships that raise us up and out of ourselves. In this sense, to recognise the spiritual in oneself is to challenge oneself and the quality of the relationships that contribute to who we are and how we live.

HISTORICAL CONTEXT OF SPIRITUAL EDUCATION IN IRELAND

The close association between spirituality and academic learning in Ireland is well expressed in the characterisation of Ireland as the 'Land of Saints and Scholars'. It seems that early monastic schools which were founded in the 6th century saw no conflict between their love of God and love of learning. It was through the influence of the monastic schools in the 8th and 9th centuries that schools and colleges spread rapidly all over the country (Raftery, 2009). In these schools, secular as well as religious (ecclesiastical) learning was catered for. Their subjects included divinity, the scriptures, the classics, literature and science. In those great seminaries, religion in education appeared to sit seamlessly alongside education in secular subjects. As time progressed, religion and education became intertwined between love of God and love of learning. In the words of Raftery, "the history of the labyrinthine connections between the churches, the State and schooling in Ireland . . . dates back at least to the sixth century" (2009, p. 9). Nor were all of their students destined to enter the Church, for a large proportion of them were the sons of chiefs and kings preparing to take their place in civil or military life (Hyland & Milne, 1987).

A sense of the seamlessness between life and education, education in religion and other disciplines in the monasteries was a feature of early education in Ireland in monasteries such as that founded by Colmcille (or Columba), the son of a Donegal Chief at Iona who facilitated the spreading of Christianity to the Orkney and Shetland Islands in Scotland and also in northern England. Another, Columbanus born in Co Meath, emerged from the austerity of Celtic Christianity and became one of the most outstanding sources of cultural, educational and spiritual renewal in Europe. Travelling from Ireland to Italy, he and his followers established numerous monasteries in France, Switzerland, Germany, Austria and Italy, which became strongholds of safety, education, employment and culture amidst the turmoil of the so-called 'Dark Ages'. These monasteries continued for centuries to serve both religious and social life in Ireland at one and the same time. The typical monastery was like a little village of huts and small houses surrounding the central church. The Irish Church at this stage was largely independent of the structure and influence of Rome and hence developed spirituality along its own cultural lines.

This association between religion and learning continued and became a function of the colonisation of Ireland. Dunn argues that from "the early days of the Tudor conquest, schooling in Ireland became intimately bound up with the process of colonisation and with the consequent ascendancy of the English language" (1988, p. 95). In the same way, education in religion became part of Tudor policy in respect of the Church of England's Reform tradition. According to Glendenning (2007), the Tudors were the first to legalise the promotion of the religious principles of the Reformation. Following the Battle of the Boyne (1690), the Protestant ascendancy in Ireland came increasingly to the fore dominating education in religion through the Reform tradition. Tudor policies were instrumental in spreading the influences of the Reformation for approximately the next century and a half. Throughout the 17th and 18th centuries, Glendenning recounts that "England relied upon a comprehensive series of repressive legislative measures, (the Penal Laws), to implement its policies in Ireland thereby affecting four crucial areas of Catholic life: property; religion; personal disabilities and education" (2007, p. 13). Education in religion delivered from the perspective of Catholic Christianity was particularly adversely affected by these laws as Catholic teachers were forbidden either from teaching or running a school. Any teacher or member of the clergy found not adhering to these laws received punitive treatment mostly in the form of heavy fines (Glendenning, 2007). Of particular importance was the Education Act (1695).[1] This forbade Catholics from sending their children to Catholic education centres in countries such as Spain and France (Rafferty, 2009, p. 11). Hyland and Milne explain that the Act specifically wanted to protect children from being educated anywhere by "any Jesuit, seminary priest, friar, monk, or other popish person" (1987, p. 47). The effect of the Penal Laws in Ireland was to embed deep in the psyche of the Roman Catholic majority population a continued identification of learning and religion as one. It is important to note that throughout the Penal Law period in Ireland, Church leaders continued to emphasise that spiritual development was achieved through religious knowledge. As early as 1730, the Catholic diocesan statutes of Dublin required every "parish priest to have a schoolmaster in his parish to teach Catholic doctrine" (McCracken, 1986, p. 95). These men kept a careful watch on education in religion. Corish observes that the hedge schoolmaster "was expected to teach Catechism. . . . If he did not he was carpeted; if he could not he was instructed" (Corish, 1981, p. 102).

This concern for the teaching of Catholic doctrine within schools continued and was well established by the final lifting of the Penal Laws with the Relief Act (1829) and the introduction of *national schools* from 1831 onwards. These new primary schools were developed on the recommendations of the then Chief Secretary for Ireland Edward Stanley and addressed to the Duke of Leinster. In the so-called 'Stanley Letter' he recommends that these new schools could

> afford combined literary and moral, and separate religious instruction, to children of all persuasions, as far as possible, in the same school, upon the fundamental principle that no attempt shall be made to interfere with the peculiar religious tenets of any description of Christian pupil. (Stanley Letter, 1831)

However, it can be argued that the effect of Stanley's recommendations was an overconcern for the place of religious knowledge within schooling to the detriment of spiritual development. This concern continued even beyond the foundation of Irish Free State in 1921. This can be seen in the provisions of The Constitution (1922), The Constitution (1937) and the subsequent *Rules for National Schools* (1965) where it is stated:

Of all parts of a school curriculum Religious Instruction is by far the most important, as its subject matter, God's honour and service, includes the proper use of all man's faculties, and affords the most powerful inducements to their proper use. Religious Instruction is, therefore, a fundamental part of the school course, and a religious spirit should inform and vivify the whole work of the school. (Rule 68)

The centrality of Religious Education thus was taken as a given emanating from (i) The Constitution (1922), (ii) The Constitution (1937) and the *Rules for National Schools* (1965), and it was not until the Education Act (1998) that we find the first signs of divergence between spirituality and religious education or religion. The Act states that the purpose of the school is to

promote the moral, spiritual, social and personal development of students and provide health education for them, in consultation with their parents, having regard to the characteristic spirit of the school. (Section 9.d)

This failure of the education system in Ireland until recently to acknowledge that spiritual development and Religious Education are not synonymous means that we are only now beginning to consider what the implications of this reality are for children, families and wider society.

CURRENT ANALYSIS OF SPIRITUALITY IN EDUCATION

Historically modern Irish society has emerged out of a postcolonial context in which for centuries the Crown and the churches had strongly influenced, if not controlled, most aspects of people's lives. In fact, the relationship between these authorities and the individual permeated all aspects of life, even aspects that we might consider to be private such as family life, sexuality and spirituality. An example of this can be seen from the late 19th century onwards in the growth of institutions established to reform or rehabilitate women. These so-called 'Magdalene' asylums and laundries increasingly took on the character and punitive ethos of prisons where inmates were expected to do hard labour and work long hours unpaid (McAleese, 2013). In the eyes of the churches and society the women who were sent to these institutions were removed from family, community and society because they had sinned sexually or to ensure that they would be protected from impurity. They were often viewed as second-class people who had failed and this extended to the children they bore. Those who managed these institutions understood their role as agents of church and society ensuring that neither the women nor the children in their care would be further associated with their families or communities through any scandal. To a considerable extent, it could be said that these institutions operated through an ethos that was paternalistic and punitive towards those who were viewed as sinners and the offspring of sinners resulting in a spirituality characterised by correction and external rituals of piety.

With the emergence of the Irish Free State in 1922 the newly formed government was mostly composed of middle class Catholics who had come from landed and professional families, and as such were more inclined to value and maintain the status quo where religious and spiritual education were concerned. In that context, the spiritual education of those who lived in Magdalene institutions and those who attended mainstream schools remained unchanged. It could be argued that the Jansenistic ethos that permeated Irish educational institutions was strengthened through its validation by the newly formed organs of the state. Recently exposed scandals and crimes of a physical and sexual nature carried out against children in the care of the state and the churches have revealed that a particular view of childhood had dominated educational provision in Ireland from the 18th century up to the end of the 20th century when the last so called 'Magdalene laundry' closed in 1996. There is little evidence to suggest that prior to the late 20th century the collective consciousness of Irish society considered spiritual education among children to be anything other than serving the purpose of overcoming original sin and depravity. The publication of the Ryan Report in 2009 and the Murphy Report, also in 2009, for example, reveal that children in general were not believed to have the same rights as adults and those who had been born outside of wedlock or who came from poverty were viewed as a burden to the state and an outrageous challenge to the societal norms and mores that were officially and informally sanctioned at the time.

The symbiotic relationship established between churches and the state in education continues to the present day and while it may have been acceptable to argue in the past that the status quo in Irish schooling reflected the values of the majority of the population, the need for greater diversity in the provision of Irish schooling has become apparent to both institutions. Recent deliberations between churches and state in the past decade or so now show that considerable progress is being made in understanding the relationship between a religious and nonreligious school-based ethos, particularly at primary school level (Drumm, 1997; Coolahan, Hussey & Kilfeather, 2012). In this context, it is therefore timely for those interested in the spiritual education of the young to revisit the essential dynamic at play between spiritual and religious education and to give equal and specific attention to these essential aspects of human life.

DEFINING SPIRITUALITY IN EDUCATION

For at least a century educators have argued that a gap exists between what is taught in schools and what a person needs to function fully and to be successful in society (Dewey, 1916/1966; Lindeman, 1926; Coyle, 1947; Pring, 2007). The same can be said in relation to spirituality as, quite often, schools equate spiritual development solely with religious education and adherence to officially sanctioned forms of spirituality to the detriment of diversity (Watson, 2000). Too often, schools have focused largely on scholastic development to the extent that the interpersonal skills required for a full spiritual development are often neglected. Almost one hundred years ago John Dewey (1916/1966) argued that there is an intimate connection between education and the quality of societies. He claimed that democratic societies could only continue to exist if schools promoted exploration and growth rather then repressing expression and creativity. Progressive educationalists have identified the qualities that are needed to manage life intelligently and to participate in society, namely, critical thinking, problem solving, communicating and collaboration (Dewey, 1916/1966; Lindeman, 1926; Coyle, 1947; Williams, 2007), all of which can be promoted through spiritual development.

Educational settings have been found not always to be the most suitable environments for this type of transformational process to be experienced. Apart from a strong focus on scholastic achievement, modern schools often reflect what Bauman (1991) refers to as society's 'solid' form and attempt to remove all unknowns and uncertainties in the educational process. A modern concern with instrumental and organisational goals in schooling has resulted in other aspects of education, such as spiritual development, receiving less attention in many schools in Ireland. These somewhat intangible aspects of a school's remit include cultural activities, the formation of character, the cultivation of attitudes, the transmission of values and freedom of thought, all of which are important for spiritual development. While these expressive goals are important as a source of cohesion and unity within a school as well as providing the foundations of democracy and collaboration in wider society, they are also important for an individual child's spiritual development. In fact, a lack of these qualities can contribute to a society where citizens are competitive, individualistic and overly concerned with material wealth resulting in a lack of concern for others.

In response to this historical problem of goal displacement where spiritual development is concerned, the new Primary School Curriculum (1999) in Ireland was developed to integrate spirituality across all aspects of children's learning. The inclusion of spiritual development is explicitly related to learning that includes religious education but is not limited to that syllabus:

> The importance that the curriculum attributes to the child's spiritual development is expressed through the breadth of learning experiences the curriculum offers, through the inclusion of religious education as one of the areas of the curriculum, and through the child's engagement with the aesthetic and affective domains of learning. (Primary School Curriculum, 1999, p. 27)

Arising from this particular vision of schooling, it is intended that children will understand and learn how to live life with concern for others, to solve issues related to global perspectives, to contribute to society and experience a sense of belonging to that society. While there is no shortage of evidence for the spiritual element in approaches to faith formation and development at both primary and post-primary levels in Religious Education classes, particularly in faith-run schools, the spirituality element is also evident in non-class situations such as prayer services, sacramental preparation (at primary), class Masses, beginning and end of year school Masses and Advent, Lent, Easter liturgies, reconciliation services, special services for the bereaved, carol services, prayers at the beginning of class and ecumenical and interreligious services, all of which can be spiritually uplifting. These are found not only in faith-run schools but also in multidenominational schools, The relationship between Religious Education and spirituality is accepted without question and they are by and large recognised as synonymous with one another. In these circumstances the Religious Education teacher is given not only an academic remit but also a spiritual one, albeit faith based. In many schools in the Republic of Ireland, in respect of developing the spiritual education of the child, the Chaplain and the Religious Education teacher share the responsibility between them. Nonetheless, there is still a great deal more work to be done given the heritage of unilateral restraint imposed on schools by churches, state and society in the country's past.

CHALLENGES FOR SPIRITUAL EDUCATION IN SCHOOLS

For too many young people in Ireland in the past, teaching and learning relationships at school were characterised by violence and tension which was experienced and accepted as the norm by school authorities, parents and wider society. Punitive approaches to classroom management and to pupil learning undermined the possibility of a young person developing the balance or integration that is the hallmark of spirituality. Martin explains that "children living in an atmosphere of fear and tension are unlikely to be psychologically available to engage in life in school" (2006, section 3, paragraph 8) and as such spiritual development was difficult.

Recent research in Ireland found that 84% of admissions to psychiatric hospitals were children aged 15–17 years (Hanfin et al., 2008) while a previous study revealed that 15.6% of pupils aged 12–15 years had a current psychiatric disorder (Lynch , Mills, Daly, and Fitzpatrick, 2006). Research in other countries such as Norway, France and Finland found that about 12–15% of children and young persons aged from 10 to 19 years self-reported mental health problems (Van Roy, Grøholt B., Heyerdahl, S., and Clench-Aas J., 2006; Fombonne, 1998; Puura et al., 1998) with a higher prevalence of 19% of young people in this age group in Germany suffering from anxiety disorders and 18% from depression (Essau, Karpinski, Peter-mann, and Conradt., 1998). The importance of social cohesion and relationships, as well as the ability to be involved in decision-making and a sense of belonging and safety in different situations, has been highlighted as crucial in promoting wellbeing among young people (Morrow, 2000; World Health Organisation Regional Office for Europe, 2007) and cannot be ignored by schools in relation to spiritual development.

In order to respond to this problem, schools will have to consider to a greater extent the employment of empathetic strategies that might be useful to help children and young persons to achieve an integration of self. Furthermore, schools will need to continue to find ways that help young people, despite their personal struggles, to transcend their own psychological, spiritual and material wounds and to connect with the needs of their brothers and sisters in the global family. Schools are now increasingly looking for praxis-orientated approaches that will offer greater opportunity for young people to engage courageously with their own desires for healing and wholeness. A *praxis* approach synthesises our thoughts, our intentions, our judgements and our actions. At a practical level, it helps us to serve others, to rediscover the goodness of life and commits us to acts of kindness and love. Specifically, *praxis* calls upon us to remove any such barriers that keep our fellow human beings marginalised. Without it, any ethical, moral or spiritual system has a lesser chance of understanding the vulnerability or the fragility of the human condition. Educators are seeking to respond to these deeper issues of the human heart and to be able to help young people to question issues relating to belonging and loneliness, good and evil, peace and division, healing and suffering, meaning and meaninglessness, hope and despair, love and apathy, justice and injustice, freedom and repression and, ultimately, life and death questions. Ultimately, it is through the development of an integrated life, achieved through positive relationships, that a young person will achieve wellbeing, which includes spiritual wholeness. This should challenge young people to grow in nonviolence, work for human rights, be merciful and seek liberation of all, and most of all deepen their relationship with God, others, the environment and self (O'Higgins Norman and Hall, 2011) . These questions are rooted in an essential pastoral perspective when teachers, chaplains, guidance counsellors and school leaders pass over from clinical definitions of emotional disturbance and engage young people to envision realistic alternatives. Such alternatives include the healing narratives of the relationships between the material and the spiritual realms of existence, between spirituality and education, between spirituality and religious education. In this environment, young people can move from the narratives of the battered and the broken to inclusiveness and wholeness, from the abyss of emptiness to the hope of fullness and fulfilment.

Sometimes, simple mechanisms can be used by teachers to promote spiritual development among their students, but it is also essential that those who 'teach' spiritual development have experienced spiritual growth themselves. For example, Miller and Athan (2007) provide an example of how working with graduate student teachers enabled them in turn to become conduits for spiritual development among their pupils. This was achieved by engaging student teachers in a programme in which they were encouraged to bring "private, raw, neglected and often discredited stories" from their own personal experience to be explored in a supportive encounter with their teacher educators (2007, p. 21). Miller and Athan outline a four-stage approach that can be adapted into most classroom contexts and used as a basis for spiritual development. The process is built on the work of Freire (1993) and the premise that educators redefine the traditional teacher/learner relationship by 'authorising' the student as a partner in a democratic process of education based less on the belief that the teacher and institution are the source of knowledge and more on the belief that the learner is empowered to learn and grow as a human person. The ultimate aim of the process outlined by Miller and Athan is to reveal the spiritual dimension of life as significant and evocative, equipping students to cope with the high points and challenges of their life journeys (2007, p. 31).

The role of empathy in promoting spiritual development is also extremely important and has been highlighted in research (Zembylas, 2012; Cooper, 2010; de Souza and McLean, 2012). However, the work of teachers is continually expanding and becoming more pressurised as schools and curricula are increasingly identified as the means by which society expects to select young people for the labour market and by which competent citizens will be developed. Research in Ireland by Boldt (2000) and more recently in the UK by Cooper (2010) on this issue found that while teachers deeply desire to play a more empathetic and caring role in the lives of their pupils a number of factors mitigate against them being able to achieve their pastoral goals. A lack of time, a fragmented and rigid curriculum, bureaucracy of modern education and the large number of pupils all work to undermine teachers' ability to be empathetic and caring in schools. This has serious consequences for spiritual education, and in Ireland the presence of a terminal examination in post-primary schools, the results of which are used to select students for places in higher education, also puts additional pressure on teachers thus reducing the time and space available to develop and model personal and empathetic relationships with their pupils.

CONCLUSION

It is clear that the people of Ireland have since ancient times placed a high value on learning. For much of the history of Ireland learning and spirituality have been understood as synonymous activities, albeit that the spiritual aspect of learning has been overidentified with the acquisition of religious knowledge, thence Religious Education continues to be a core activity of modern primary and post-primary schooling in Ireland.

It is only since the introduction of the Education Act (1998) that there has been official recognition by the state that spiritual development and Religious Education are separate concepts and activities in schooling. Schools in Ireland are still struggling to deconstruct centuries of practice whereby responsibility for children and young people's spiritual development is assigned to teachers and priests who have tended to rely on overly cognitive methods to the detriment of experiential approaches to spiritual development. However, the ongoing evolution of non-faith-based schools and greater awareness among teachers in the faith-based school of new pedagogies that can be used to promote spirituality among young people will hopefully contribute to a greater emphasis on spirituality education as a distinct activity within schools in Ireland.

NOTES

1. Its long title is "An Act to restrain Foreign Education".

REFERENCES

Bauman, Z. (1991). *Modernity and ambivalence*. Ithaca, NY: Cornell University Press.

Boldt, S. (2000). A vantage point of values—Findings from school culture and ethos questionnaires. In C. Furlong & L. Monahan (Eds.), *School Culture and Ethos*. Dublin: Marino.

Coolahan, J., Hussey, C., & Kilfeather, F. (2012). *The Forum on Patronage and Pluralism in the Primary Sector*. Dublin: Department of Education and Skills.

Cooper, B. (2010). Empathy, interaction and caring: Teachers' roles in a constrained environment. *Journal of Pastoral Care in Education, 22*(3), 12–21.

Coyle, G. L. (1947). *Group experience and democratic values*. New York: Women's Press.

Corish, P. J., *The Catholic community in the seventeenth and eighteenth centuries*, (Dublin: Catholic Historical Society of Ireland, 1981).

Department of Education, (1965). Rule for Primary Schools. Dublin: Stationery Office.

de Souza, M., & McLean, K. (2012). Bullying and violence: Changing an act of disconnectedness into an act of kindness. *Pastoral Care in Education: An International Journal of Personal, Social and Emotional Development, Special Edition, 30*(2), 165–180.

Dewey, J. (1916/1966). *Democracy and education*. New York: The Free Press.

Drumm, M. (1997). Symposium The future of religion in Irish education. In P. Hogan & K. Williams (Eds.), *The future of religion in Irish education* (pp.108–127). Dublin: Veritas.

Dunn, Seamus., 'Education, religion and cultural change in the Republic of Ireland', in *Christianity and Educational Provision in International Perspective*, ed. by W. Tulasiewicz and C. Brock (London: Routledge, 1988), pp. 87–99.

Essau, C.A., Karpinski, N.A., Petermann, F. & Conradt, J. (1998). Häufigkeit und Komorbidität psychischer Störungen bei Jugendlichen: Ergebnisse der Bremer Jugendstudie. Zeitschrift für Klinische Psychologie, Psychiatrie und Psychotherapie, 46, 105–124.

Fombonne, E. (1998). Increased rates of psychosocial disorders in youth. *European Archives of Psychiatry and Clinical Neuroscience, 248*, 14–21.

Freire, P. (1993). *Pedagogy of the oppressed*. New York: Continuum.

Glendenning, Dympna, (2007). *Education and the Law*. West Sussex: Tottel.

Government of Ireland, (1998). Education Act. Dublin: Government Publications.

Government of Ireland, (1999). Primary School Curriculum. Dublin: Government Publications.

Hanafin,S., Brooks, A., Macken, A., Brady, G., McKeever, R., Judge, C., Ryan, B., . . . Gavin, A. (2008). *State of the nation's children*. Dublin: Department of Health and Children, Office for the Minister for Children and Youth Affairs.

Hyland, Aine and Milne, Kenneth., (eds) *Irish Educational Documents*, Vol. 1, (Dublin: Church of Ireland, College of Education, 1987).

Lindeman, E. C. (1926). *The meaning of adult education*. New York: New Republic. Republished in a new edition in 1989 by The Oklahoma Research Center for Continuing Professional and Higher Education.

Lynch, F. , Mills, C, Daly, I., and Fitzpatrick, C. (2006). Challenging times: Prevalence of psychiatric disorders and suicidal behaviours in Irish young persons. *Journal of Adolescence, 29*(4), 555–573.

Martin, M. (2006). *School matters: Indiscipline in second level schools*. Report of the National Task Force. Dublin. Government Publications.

McAleese, M. (2013). *Report of the Inter-Departmental Committee to establish the facts of State involvement with the Magdalen Laundries*. Dublin: Department of Justice and Equality.

McCracken, J. L., 'The ecclesiastical structure, 1714–1760' in *A New History of Ireland. Eighteenth-Century Ireland 1691–1800*, ed. by T. W. Moody and W. E. Vaughan (Oxford: 1986).

Miller, L., & Athan, A. (2007). Spiritual awareness pedagogy: The classroom as spiritual reality. *International Journal of Children's Spirituality, 12*(1), 17–35.

Morrow V. (2000). *Networks and neighbourhoods: Children's and young people's perspectives*. London: Health Development Agency.

O'Higgins Norman, J., & Hall, E. (2010). Violence and conflict in schools, negotiating pathways to well-being. In M. de Souza, L. Francis, J. O'Higgins Norman, & D. Scott (Eds.), *International handbook of education for spirituality, care and wellbeing* (pp. 1101–1114). Netherlands: Springer.

Pring, R. (2007). The common school. *Journal of Philosophy of Education, 41*(4), 503–522.

Puura, K., Almqvist, F., Tamminen, T., Piha, J., Räsänen, E., Kumpulainen, K., . . . Koivisto A.-M. (1998). Psychiatric disturbances among prepubertal children in Southern Finland. *Social Psychiatry and Psychiatric Epidemiology, 33*(7), 310–318.

Raftery, D. (2009). The legacy of legislation and the pragmatics of policy: Historical perspectives on schooling for Irish children. In S. Drudy (Ed.), *Education in Ireland: Challenge and change* (pp. 9–23). Dublin: Gill & Macmillan.

Van Roy, B., Grøholt B., Heyerdahl, S., and Clench-Aas J. (2006). Self-reported strengths and difficulties in a large Norwegian population 10–19 years. Age and gender specific results of the extended SDQ-questionnaire. *European Child & Young Person Psychiatry, 15*(4), 1435–1465.

Watson, J. (2000). Whose model of spirituality should be used in the spiritual development of school children? *International Journal of Children's Spirituality, 5*(1), 91–101.

Williams, K. (2007). *Education and the voice of Michael Oakeshott*. Exeter: Imprint Academic.

World Health Organisation Regional Office for Europe. (2007). *Social cohesion for mental wellbeing among young persons*. WHO/HBSC Forum Report. Copenhagen: World Health Organisation.

Zembylas, M. (2012). Pedagogies of strategic empathy: Navigating through the emotional complexities of anti-racism in higher education. *Teaching in Higher Education, 17*(2), 113–125.

4 The Complex Flavour of Children's Spirituality in Flanders

Fostering an Open Catholic Spirituality

Annemie Dillen

RELIGIOUS LIFE IN FLANDERS

Although Belgium has been an autonomous country since 1830 it is almost impossible to speak about the general Belgian context, since Belgium consists of two major regions—Flanders and Wallonia.[1] The two regions have different languages and little intercultural exchange, they have separate educational systems, and most aspects of Church life are organized separately and independently. Most Belgians live in Flanders, however, and this chapter will focus on Flanders, which is also the context in which I myself work and live.

Flanders has traditionally been a strongly Catholic region, with, in 1981, about 75% of the population identifying themselves as Catholic. Nowadays, only 50% of the population say they are members of the Catholic Church and 43% identify themselves as not belonging to any church (Dobbelaere, Billier & Voye, 2009, pp. 13–14). A minority consider themselves to be Protestant, Muslim or Jewish. Nonetheless, 75% of children and adolescents attend Catholic schools, and 82% opt for Catholic religious education in either public schools or Catholic schools (Onderwijs Vlaanderen, 2011, p. 430). Many institutions and groups in Flanders still have the label 'Catholic' in their names; this includes not only schools, but also universities, youth movements, women's and men's movements, labor movements and health care institutions.

More recently, however, many of these institutions and groups, including schools, have begun to reconsider what the word 'Catholic' means. For some this has led to a renewed attention to what a 'Catholic' can be; for others it has led to the dropping of the word 'Catholic' in favour of what is often called 'active pluralism'. Those organizations that stay 'Catholic' and 'recontextualize' its meaning (Pollefeyt & Bouwens, 2010; Boeve, 2006) generally seek to ensure that their Catholicism is considered open to plurality, but they also claim that this openness to the identity of others must be accompanied by a positive acknowledgement of their own identity. At the same time there has been a tendency by a minority of groups to reconfessionalize their institutions.

SCHOOLS, CATHOLIC IDENTITY AND DEBATES
ABOUT RELIGIOUS EDUCATION

The tendency toward reconfessionalization can be seen particularly in a few Catholic schools, where a small minority of parents and Catholic leaders desire a stronger Catholic identity for schools, refocusing on specific Catholic practices such as prayer and the Eucharist. Recent research at my Faculty of Theology and Religious Studies in Leuven, carried out with parents of children attending primary and secondary Catholic schools (Centrum Academische Lerarenopleiding Faculteit Theologie en Religiewetenschappen KU Leuven,2011) showed, however, that most parents are content with the Catholic identity of their children's school: they do not want to drop the Catholic identity, but neither do they desire a reconfessionalization. These parents would prefer a form of 'recontextualization', a renewed thinking about what Catholicism can mean when it is accompanied by an openness toward individuals' beliefs and toward plurality in society in general. Additionally, many Muslims attend Catholic schools and participate in Catholic religious education classes together with the other students, and these children often feel welcomed and respected. The religious education is legitimized by both the schools and the Catholic Church, with curricula that offer education 'from' the Catholic religion with an openness toward other religions. There are only a few private Muslim and Jewish schools.

In public schools, children and adolescents can choose to follow religious education or nonconfessional philosophical moral education for two hours every week in one of six religious affiliations or denominations (Anglican, Muslim, Jewish, Catholic, Orthodox, Protestant religion) or a nonconfessional course (Edulex, 2012). The content of these classes does not fall under the authority of the schools or the government, but is controlled by the various religious or nonconfessional philosophical affiliations. This system works quite well but nonreligious policy makers or intellectuals sometimes refer to a small number of mostly evangelical Protestant or Muslim teachers who express ideas that could be considered as radical, maybe fundamentalist. In 2011, a major debate took place between atheistic humanists and Catholics concerning religious education (Jagers, 2001), with some humanists challenging religious education because the content is determined by the religions or worldviews themselves. This led to two new proposals. The first was to introduce a general, *neutral*, course in the final two years of secondary education (ages 17 and 18) instead of religious education (Loobuyck, Abicht, Beeckman, Chikha, Blancke, Boudry & Bracke et al., 2011). The second proposal suggested that, in addition to one hour of religious education, a second hour should be given to comparative religion (*De Morgen*, 2011). These proposals, coming in general from atheistic humanists, were not welcomed by most Catholics. For example, my colleague Didier Pollefeyt argued that the present curricula already offer all the advantages of these proposals, including a fundamental openness to the beliefs of others, a recognition of the personal views of the teacher, and a challenge to the student to reflect on his or her personal ideas and beliefs (Pollefeyt, 2011). Pollefeyt argued that *neutral* teachers, or *neutral* religious/moral education, do not exist.

In May 2012, however, the Flemish parliament decided that the present forms of religious education did not have to change, but that the representatives of the various religious groups should as a rule take it upon themselves to ensure that interreligious competences should always be part of the curricula (Ysebaert, 2012). They also decided that diversity and dialogue should receive more attention, although these elements were already important. The curricula of Catholic religious education, introduced in 2000, were already inspired by what is called the 'hermeneutical-communicative model', and focused on an open dialogue with other religions. Recently it was once again made clear that the state will not intervene in matters of religious education, with the exception of urgent matters, related to, for instance, extremism or fundamentalism.

CHILDREN'S SPIRITUALITY AND FAMILY LIFE

In addition to schools, families are a significant environment where the spirituality of children is lived and nurtured. Here we see that children with a Muslim or another minority religious background often experience a stronger religious education in their families than Catholics (Pollefeyt et al., 2004). In Catholic families, many children are still baptized but numbers are decreasing. In 2008, 67.1% of newborn children in Flanders were baptized, which is higher than the figures for Belgium in general (57.3%) (Botterman & Hooghe, 2009). For a lot of families, baptism is above all a 'rite of passage' that gives expression to the thankfulness and happiness at the birth of a child, or that allows children to fully participate in Catholic cultural life, with First Communion taking place around the age of 7 or 8.

In general, religious initiation of children in families in Flanders is democratically structured in the sense that the focus is less on control and compulsion, and more on freedom and communication (Pollefeyt et al., 2004). Many parents are strongly in favor of allowing their children complete freedom of choice, and thus even refuse to offer their children any form of initiation into a religion, on the basis of the idea that a 'neutral' education is possible. Other parents wish to do 'something with religion', but feel incompetent or insecure and prefer to leave the religious education of their children to the school or the parish. Although a great deal of adequate didactical material exists for children within families, such as children's Bibles, religious storybooks, questions and answers, music, religious symbols and prayer books, these materials are only used by a small number of families (Pollefeyt et al., 2004). Bible reading within the family is limited, which may partly be explained by Catholic culture where the reading of the Bible takes place in the context of liturgical celebration such as the Eucharist, especially at Christmas and Easter, and the focus is much more on participation in the sacraments and rituals.

PARISHES AND CHILDREN'S SPIRITUALITY

In parishes—local Catholic church communities—initiatives in relation to children's spirituality are mainly focused on the catechetical preparation of the initiation sacraments, especially First Communion and Confirmation. Depending on the diocese and/or parish, First Communion takes place at the age of 7 or 8 and Confirmation at the age of 12, sometimes at 13, or more exceptionally 17. For First Communion, there is at present a tendency to prepare children within the parish, and sometimes in relation to the family. Until recently, in most places the preparation for First Communion was exclusively the responsibility of the school and the task of the teacher of religious education (within Catholic primary schools, this person is usually the class teacher). Confirmation catechesis is generally organized by volunteers from the parish. Although recently more attention has been given to children's own spirituality and to theologizing with them, in some places there is still a form of (an all too) simple 'correlation' catechesis taking place. Concretely, this means that life experiences are discussed and that elements of Christian belief are presented as an answer to these human experiences without much critical thinking and sometimes also in a forced way. In some cases, the Christian tradition will remain absent as too much focus is laid on the general experiences of children, without coming to theological reflections (Dillen & Pollefeyt, 2011). Although the search for a 'mutual critical correlation' between experience and Christian tradition—in line of the theological developments of, among others, Schillebeeckx (1974) and Tracy (1975), and further developed internationally in many catechetical methods—is very relevant, caution must be given to an all too easy form of correlation and possible blind spots. In line with many critical reflections on correlation theology and didactics, researchers within the KU Leuven have developed a more complex approach, which they call multicorrelational and hermeneutical (Pollefeyt, 2008). Insights of this 'hermeneutical approach' are applied both on catechetical contexts and on religious education in schools.

Since 2006, a stronger focus on adult catechesis has developed, since this was considered by the bishops to be lacking (Bisschoppenconferentie van België, 2006). The aim was to make clear that catechesis is not only something for children and to offer adults a clearer view of what the Christian tradition is, with a much stronger focus on tradition and the Bible than in most forms of children's catechesis. This tendency has reduced the attention of Church policy on children's spirituality. More recently, a greater emphasis is being given to intergenerational catechesis and to the role of the community in all catechetical processes (Interdiocesane commissie voor catechese, 2010). In certain (main) parishes, various parishioners come together on a Sunday morning for a catechetical moment for adults and for children (sometimes separately, sometimes together), before going together to participate in the Eucharist and to share lunch. Those who are preparing for a sacrament, especially children preparing for First Communion or Confirmation or adults preparing for marriage, are particularly welcome at this catechesis. Another intergenerational project involves family vacations, organised by diocesan groups, mostly in an abbey in Belgium. Families stay for about four days together in an abbey, where they participate in the liturgical life, discuss their own spirituality and have fun together, with a special program organized for children.

In 2012, various people in Belgium became familiar with a creative method for religious communication called 'Godly play' (Berryman, 1991). As Chair of the Interdiocesan Council for Family Ministry, I am now, together with many others, searching for ways to encourage the method and vision of 'Godly play' within the Flemish Catholic landscape, both in schools and in parishes (see www.godlyplay.be). This method—with a profound theology of children's spirituality behind it—may be used even with very young children (aged 3 and up) as well as with adults.

PASTORAL CARE AND CHAPLAINCY WITH CHILDREN

Another place where children's spirituality is especially important is in forms of pastoral care and chaplaincy. In most Belgian hospitals, chaplains from various denominations and worldviews (especially Catholic, Protestant and humanist-atheist) are employed and paid by the hospital itself, which is partly financed by the government, but as the large majority of hospitals are Catholic, in most situations chaplains have a Catholic profile. Hospital chaplains have the opportunity to stimulate children's spirituality—at least in theory—but, in practice, there are various obstacles (Vandenhoeck, 2011). In Belgium, few chaplains are specialized in hospital chaplaincy in a pediatric context. Most intensive spiritual caregiving for children is done in university hospitals, where more children tend to be present. However, it is not easy for hospital chaplains to become integrated in a pediatric context, as many hospital employees tend to associate them with death, or because many nurses, educators and other caregivers surrounding the children have little insight into the relevance of their specialized spiritual caregiving. In other cases, the caregivers may be afraid that Christian chaplains will impose their Christian view on children or may have many reservations about nurturing spirituality themselves, partly because of the difficulty of putting the suffering of the children within a religious context. In other hospital units, chaplains may also meet children who are chiefly family members of patients. Even in this case, however, many would question what the chaplains have to offer children. Therefore, there is a long way to go to stimulate more pastoral care with children in hospitals and to make sure that caring for children's spirituality is an important part of good general caregiving in hospital.

KEY CHALLENGES

Having already mentioned various challenges to the nurturing of children's spirituality, I will now bring some of these together and argue—in line with my previous work and the arguments developed by my colleague Didier Pollefeyt—that the nurture of children's spirituality requires a general 'hermeneutical-communicative' position, which I will subsequently explain and which will be applied within the various contexts of education in schools and families, as well as pastoral work with children in parishes and hospitals.

A first key issue for discussion concerns the analysis of the situation and the anthropological view that influences decisions concerning children's spirituality. For this, I will distinguish three approaches. The first two are quite common and widely used by policy makers within church and society. The third is a position that is proposed here as the most preferable (see also Knieps & Dillen, 2013). A second general theme for discussion concerns the *aim* of nurturing children's spirituality and related questions concerning an adequate method for nurture.

A Discussion of the Contemporary Religious Situation and Desirable Practices for Nurturing Children's Spirituality

On the basis of a classical form of (often implicit) secularization theory, various people would suggest that there is a decline in knowledge of and interest in the Christian (i.e. Catholic) tradition. The gap between culture and Catholic or Christian tradition is increasing rapidly and is difficult to bridge (Kaufmann, 1989; Hervieu-Léger, 1993, 2000; Davie, 1994; Dobbelaere, 2002). Others will say religiosity is not fading but has become individualized, experienced in various, more subjective ways, outside the traditional institutions (Boeve, 2005; Heelas & Woodhead, 2005; Gräb & Charbonnier, 2008).

Both the secularization theory and the individualization theory begin with a negative view of what is possible in nurturing the spirituality of children from a Christian perspective. On the basis of the secularization theory, or similar theories focusing on the gap between culture and Christianity, many will say that what children need is first of all a clear initiation into what the Christian tradition is and the experience of a Christian community. The focus may be put more strongly on the 'handing down' of the tradition in a rather 'deductive' way (top-down, starting from general ideas and then applying them to concrete reality). The risk is that the children's own agency, their own spiritual awareness, remains unseen or unheard. The anthropological presumptions accompanying this approach are rather negative: children need to be socialized within the Christian tradition and their own spiritual capacities remain unexplored. Whereas in earlier times, religious education was strongly focused on finding links (correlation) between children's experiences and the tradition, this approach is viewed more critically today. In Catholic reflection concerning nurturing children's spirituality in Flanders, this position, with a focus on the gap between culture and Christianity and an accompanying emphasis on handing down the Christian tradition, is the most dominant.

On the basis of the individualization theory, or similar theories focusing on new spiritual developments outside Christianity, nurturing children's spirituality may be chiefly focused on a more general concept of spirituality, without reference to the Christian tradition. In practice, one can find such approaches in schools where religious education is reduced to 'learning values' and where the starting point is that children are now completely unfamiliar with the Christian tradition and that neither children nor parents are really interested in it. This approach might be accompanied by an optimistic anthropology that believes in the general spiritual competences of children. There might be a strong focus on children's own 'spirituality', but the danger is present that children may not be further challenged or may not be offered insights into traditional religious expressions and ideas.

In addition to these two positions, a third position—which I consider to be the most adequate—is also possible and needs further development. This third position starts from the idea that Catholic religiosity has not totally disappeared in Flanders and that many people continue to feel more affiliated to Catholicism than is often assumed—they might be called 'secular Catholics' (Beaudoin, 2011). However, this relation to the Catholic religion has also changed: people feel free to pick and choose at their own discretion from the Catholic tradition, and Catholic religiosity subsequently becomes subjective in its experience. This becomes clear on consideration of the large group of people who desire initiation rituals, such as baptism, First Communion, Confirmation or marriage, or on consideration of the ongoing demand for Catholic funerals or rituals in the face of terminal illness and death. For many people it is not so much a question of receiving a 'real' sacrament, offered by a priest, but more of undergoing a sort of ritual that is related to a certain tradition. These sorts of rituals, for instance for sick or dying people, are also offered by Catholic lay chaplains and express a personal form of religiosity that is not totally independent of Catholic religion but does not adhere to classical forms and tradition. The same is true for the way in which many people prefer a subjectivized form of marriage or baptism. At the same time, this subjectivization is relative, as many people are content with texts that are offered by a pastor, but would like to personalize the ceremony, mainly by choosing songs and music. This third position might support an approach to nurturing children's spirituality which takes into account children's own thinking and feeling and also offers elements from the Christian tradition. This does not need to be done in a classical correlational way (with a focus on a rather harmonious link between general human experience and the Christian tradition as an answer to existential problems), where there is a danger that neither children's experiences nor the Christian tradition are really taken seriously.

A hermeneutical-communicative and abductive approach—as I explain below—fits well with this third position in the analysis of the contemporary situation concerning spirituality and religion. The anthropological view behind this approach is based on a strong belief in the possibilities children possess, without overestimating them or considering them as 'little saints'. Children are both active agents and vulnerable persons in terms of spirituality (Dillen, 2007b, 2011).

A Discussion of the Aims and Methods of Nurturing Children's Spirituality

The general view behind the Catholic religious education curriculum in primary education is based on what is called the 'hermeneutical-communicative' model. This model has strong links with general hermeneutical approaches internationally (Lombaerts & Pollefeyt, 2004), but has also been developed in a specific way at the Faculty of Theology and Religious Studies, KU Leuven, originally under the influence of Herman Lombaerts. Didier Pollefeyt, who was appointed professor in religious education in 2000, was one of the inspirational voices in the process of writing the curriculm for Catholic religious education (Erkende Instantie, 2000a, 2000b). In the period after 2000, the hermeneutical-communicative model was further developed at the KU Leuven (Dillen & Pollefeyt, 2011; Maex, 2003) and in the religious landscape in Flanders, especially in secondary education. Most teachers in (secondary) religious education in Flanders support this model as it is included in the obligatory curricula (Van Lierde, 2008). It forms the basis of the widely used Thomas website for religious education (www.godsdienstonderwijs.be) and is applied in various handbooks for religious education. I will briefly sketch some core elements of this model and discuss possible criticisms.

The term 'hermeneutical-communicative' refers to two elements that belong together: hermeneutical and communicative. Whereas 'hermeneutical' refers more to theological, content-related positions, 'communicative' refers to didactical processes, but neither can be separated from the other.

'Hermeneutical' means focused on various interpretative positions, stimulating interpretations and inquiry. It refers to a theological position where truth is not fixed and absolute, but rather open and related to an eschatological perspective: we will continue searching for aspects of truth. The most common criticism of the hermeneutical-communicative model, often expressed in oral discussions, is that it is focused on intellectual competences concerning interpretational conflicts. Critical voices argue that it is limited in possibilities as many people, especially children, do not have large intellectual capacities and as religion is much more than an intellectual activity. This criticism is based on a limited interpretation of what 'hermeneutical' can mean and a limited view of people's capacities.

In line with much research about children's spirituality, one can state that children are often much more competent than we believe (Dillen, 2007a). The success of programs involving philosophizing with children, even with preschool toddlers, shows that we do not have to underestimate their capacities. Of course, the way in which the 'reflection' is organized and conceptualized varies, and one does not expect the same level of abstract reflection from young children and adolescents. Children are often very sensitive to symbols and stories, and are often able to see links with their own life experiences. The example of Godly play, also offered to very young children, shows that a form of 'reflection' is possible with children. The other aspect of the critique as formulated above, that 'hermeneutical' only refers to intellectual activities, is a narrow interpretation of the concept 'hermeneutical'. 'Hermeneutical' refers to interpretation, but this interpretation is also always related to experiences, to concrete materials (e.g. media, texts, discussions, arts), to bodily actions, to symbols or rituals.

The vision behind the hermeneutical-communicative model is that it is important to offer children (or adolescents) various experiences—reading a text, but also participating in a ritual, or watching a short movie, or looking at a painting—and then working with this experience, showing that various interpretations are possible and searching for a possible meaning that is appropriate for a particular child. Often, the concept of 'mystagogical catechesis' is used where the focus is put on the experience, and 'hermeneutical' is then considered as less experience oriented and more intellectually/verbally focused. However, the concept 'hermeneutical' as I present it here, and as it is used in the curricula for Catholic religious education, refers to a broad understanding, including experiences. The concept 'mystagogical' might also be misleading, as it is nowadays often used as a form of introducing children (adults) into a form of (broad) religious experience, which could be deepened and could lead to an understanding of the Christian tradition. In early Christianity however, mystagogy referred to a strong and explicit Christian initiation after baptism. The difficulty with the contemporary use of the concept 'mystagogy' however is that the relation between general spiritual or religious experiences and the Christian tradition is not always evident and may not be forced. The concept 'hermeneutical' tries to avoid easy or forced relations between experience and tradition, and refers clearly to various possible interpretations.

The idea of 'abductive learning' is closely related to hermeneutical-communicative learning and with the third analysis of the contemporary situation as expressed above (Lombaerts & Pollefeyt, 2004). 'Abductive learning' can be considered as part of the hermeneutical-communicative model. Abduction is a third way in addition to induction and deduction, and refers to the idea that one cannot easily surmount the gulf between experience and tradition by just believing in the power of either experience (induction) or tradition (deduction). Experience and tradition can be related and can be brought into dialogue with each other in learning processes because they are already interwoven: children are often aware of some aspects of the Christian tradition and the tradition is related to concrete experiences as well. An abductive learning process starts with the aspects that are already related to each other; for example, children lighting candles or looking at a nativity stall might be elements that stimulate further exploration of both experiences and religious traditions.

The term 'communicative' refers to a dialogical approach, where it is not the teacher/catechist who knows everything, but where the interpretation of children and exchanges in the group are stimulated. Starting from a theological concept where religious tradition and truth are not fixed, but an open process of searching which can be stimulated by learning from each other, this communicative approach is very important. Within the Flemish context, however, theoretical discussions concern the degree of 'guiding' by the teacher in open learning contexts. Are there things that cannot be said if they are contrary to orthodoxy? Does the teacher have to stimulate a specific interpretation in the communicative process, one that is 'better' than the others? In the context of experimenting with 'Godly play' as a new and open, communicative form of nurturing spirituality with children, these are questions some adults (teachers and catechists) raise, but they apply to various forms of religious education. The background to these questions is the search for a form of 'control', to have some 'power over' what happens in groups of children, and about a certain 'right' interpretation of the Christian tradition. A possible answer might be that if one trusts the group process and the competences of children themselves, stimulated by a competent teacher/catechist, the children will discover together that not every interpretation is helpful or valuable. They will challenge each other and might be challenged by the teacher as well (Dillen, 2011). The teacher, however, does not have to block the searching process, as this would not stimulate children's own reflection and would presuppose the theological idea of a 'closed tradition', with only one possible interpretation. Nevertheless, it is important that some input is offered: if children are fully free, they will not be confronted with elements from the tradition, with valuable rituals, symbols or texts. So the focus on open communication does not mean that 'identity' or 'theological input' have to disappear. On the contrary, the communication can only be stimulated when it is centred on something—which may however be interpreted in various ways.

CONCLUSION

This overview of various ways in which children's spirituality is nurtured within a Catholic context in Flanders indicates the relevance of trusting children's own possibilities and recognizing their agency. If this trust in children and the communicative process among them, guided by competent adults, is stimulated and accompanied by a hermeneutical and thus open perspective on religion, there is no reason for anxiety. Both from an atheistic humanistic perspective and from a more classical Catholic perspective, nurturing children's spirituality is sometimes approached with caution. These perspectives consider contemporary ways of nurturing children's spirituality often as either too narrow (monoreligious) or too open (multireligious). However, when one looks at the contemporary pluralistic context in which children in a Flemish Catholic context grow up, there is a need for a dialogical theological view, an open hermeneutical learning, where children are offered basic insights in a specific (their own) religion, in dialogue with other religions. This demands further development of adults (teachers, catechists, pastors) able to guide these processes on various levels, in schools, parishes and hospitals, and further communication to answer many prejudices coming both from within and from without the Catholic tradition/religion.

NOTES

1. For Brussels, religious education and church-related questions are mostly organized around the language: people in Brussels will either fall under the Dutch-spoken or under the French-spoken groups. There is also a small group of people in Wallonia who speak German.

REFERENCES

Beaudoin, T. (2011). Secular Catholicism and practical theology. *International Journal of Practical Theology, 15*(1), 22–37.

Berryman, Jerome W. (1991). *Godly play. An imaginative approach to religious education.* Augsburg: Fortress.

Bisschoppenconferentie van België. (2006). *Volwassen worden in het geloof. Catechese in het leven van de kerk.* Brussel: Licap.

Boeve, L. (2005). Religion after detraditionalization: Christian faith in a post-secular Europe. *Irish Theological Quarterly, 70,* 99–122.

Boeve, L. (2006). The identity of a Catholic university in post-Christian European societies: Four models. *Louvain Studies, 31,* 238–258.

Botterman, S., & Hooghe, M. (2009). *Religieuze praktijk in België 2007. Een statistische analyse.* Leuven: KU Leuven Centrum voor Politicologie.

Centrum Academische Lerarenopleiding Faculteit Theologie en Religiewetenschappen KU Leuven. (2011). *Hoe kijken ouders naar de katholieke identiteit van de school? Presentatie van onderzoek uit 21 primaire en secundaire katholieke scholen verspreid over Vlaanderen in de periode 2008–2011 uitgevoerd door het Centrum Academische Lerarenopleiding Faculteit Theologie en Religiewetenschappen van de Katholieke Universiteit Leuven.* Retrieved October 8, 2012, from http://www.kuleuven.be/thomas/page/identiteit-ouders/#66057.

Davie, G. (1994). *Religion in Britain since 1945: Believing without belonging.* Oxford: Blackwell.

De Morgen. (2011, Dec. 1). *Vlaams parlement trekt discussie over godsdien-stonderwijs op gang.* Retrieved October 8, 2012, from http://www.demorgen.be/dm/nl/1344/Onderwijs/article/detail/1356474/2011/12/01/Vlaams-Parlement-trekt-debat-over-godsdienstonderwijs-op-gang.dhtml.

Dillen, A. (2007a). Religious participation of children as active subjects: Toward a hermeneutical-communicative model of religious education in families with young children. *International Journal of Children's Spirituality, 12*(1), 37–49.

Dillen, A. (2007b). Between heroism and deficit: Challenges to research on children's spirituality from a Christian theological standpoint. *Concilium: International Review of Theologie—English Edition, 5,* 57–68.

Dillen, A. (2011). Empowering children in religious education: Rethinking power dynamics. *Journal of Religious Education, 59*(3), 4–12.

Dillen, A., & Pollefeyt, D. (2011). Catechesis inside out. A hermeneutical model for catechesis in parishes. *The Person and the Challenges, 1*(1), 151–177.

Dobbelaere, K. (2002). *Secularization. An analysis at three levels.* Brussels: Lang.

Dobbelaere, K., Billier, J., & Voye, L. (2001). Religie en kerkbetrokkenheid in een ver veranderende samenleving. In K. Abts (Ed.), *Ethiek, religie en institution-eel vertrouwen in EVS* (pp.11–22). Leuven: Centrum voor Sociologisch Onder-zoek. Retrieved October 8, 2012, from http://www.kuleuven.be/emeritiforum/update/Forumgesprekken/2011–2012/25%20november%202011/Presentatie_Emeritiforum_Koen_Abts.pdf.

Edulex. (2012). *Onderwijsinspectie over de erkende godsdiensten en de niet-con-fessionele zedenleer.* Retrieved October 8, 2012, from http://www.ond.vlaan-deren.be/edulex/database/document/document.asp?docid=13255.

Erkende Instantie. (2000a). *Leerplan rooms-katholieke godsdienst voor het secun-dair onderwijs in Vlaanderen.* Brussel: Licap.

Erkende Instantie. (2000b). *Leerplan rooms-katholieke godsdienst voor het lager onderwijs in Vlaanderen.* Brussel: Licap.

Gräb, W., & Charbonnier, L. (Eds.). (2008). *Individualisierung–Spiritualität–Religion.* Berlin: LIT.

Heelas, P., & Woodhead, L. (2005). *The spiritual revolution. Why religion is giv-ing way to spirituality.* Oxford: Blackwell.

Hervieu-Léger, D. (1993). *La religion pour mémoire.* Paris: Cerf.

Hervieu-Léger, D. (2000). *La religion en mouvement. Le pèlerin et le converti.* Paris: Flammarion.

Interdiocesane commissie voor catechese (2010). *Pastoraal bij het vormsel. Cat-echese en gemeenschap.* Brussel: Licap.

Jagers, J. (2011, Nov. 30). Eenheidsvak over levensbeschouwing invoeren? *Knack.* Retrieved October 8, 2012, from http://www.kuleuven.be/thomas/images/algemeen/actualiteit/visie/toekomst-godsdienstonderwijs/KnackPollefeyt.pdf.

Kaufmann, F.-X. (1989). *Religion und Modernität. Sozialwissenschaftliche Pers-pektiven.* Tübingen: Mohr.

Knieps, T., & Dillen, A. (2013). *(N)Iets voor dummies!? Op zoek naar de spiritu-ele expertise van de leek in de kerk.* Antwerpen: Halewijn.

Lombaerts, H., & Pollefeyt, D. (Eds.). (2004). *Hermeneutics and religious educa-tion.* Leuven: Peeters.

Loobuyck, P., Abicht, L., Beeckman, T., Chikha, C.B., Blancke, S., Boudry, M. & P. Bracke et al. (2011, Nov. 30). LEF voor de burgers van morgen. Academici en schrijvers bepleiten schoolvak levensbeschouwing, ethiek, burgerschap en filosofie. *De Morgen.* Retrieved October 8, 2012, from http://www.kuleuven.be/thomas/images/algemeen/actualiteit/visie/toekomst-godsdienstonderwijs/DeMorgen20111130–1.jpg.

Maex J. (2003). *Een hermeneutisch-communicatief concept vakdidactiek gods-dienst. Een fundamenteel-theoretisch en empirisch onderzoek.* (Doctoral dissertation). Katholieke Universiteit, Leuven.
Onderwijs Vlaanderen. (2011). *Statistisch Jaarboek Vlaams Onderwijs. Onderwijs niet-confessionele zedenleer en godsdienst. Basis- en secundair onderwijs 2010–2011.* Retrieved October 8, 2012, from http://www.ond.vlaanderen.be/onderwijsstatistieken/2010–2011/statistisch_jaarboek_pdfs/18_425_434.pdf.
Pollefeyt, D. (2008). Difference matters. A hermeneutic-communicative concept of didactics of religion in a European multi-religious context. *Journal of Religion Education, 56*(1), 9–17.
Pollefeyt, D. (2011, Dec. 1). *Levensbeschouwelijke diversiteit en de vakken gods-dienst en niet-confessionele zedenleer Voorstel tot mogelijke wijziging art. 55 van het decreet van 31 juli 1990 betreffende onderwijs II, vakken godsdienst en niet-confessionele zedenleer.* Speech presented at Commissie voor Onderwijs en Gelijke Kansen Vlaams Parlement, Antwerp. Retrieved October 8, 2012, from http://www.kuleuven.be/thomas/page/discussie-levensbeschouwelijke-vakken.
Pollefeyt, D., & Bouwens, J. (2010). Framing the identity of Catholic schools. Empirical methodology for quantitative research on the Catholic identity of an education institute. *International Studies in Catholic Education, 2*(2), 193–210.
Pollefeyt, D., Hutsebaut, D., De Vlieger, M., Lombaerts, H., Dillen, A., Maex, J., & Smit, W. (2004). *Godsdienstonderwijs uitgedaagd: jongeren en (inter)levens-beschouwelijke vorming in gezin en onderwijs. Opzet, methode en resultaten van empirisch onderzoek bij leerkrachten rooms-katholieke godsdienst en leer-lingen van de derde graad secundair onderwijs in Vlaanderen. With a summary in English.* Leuven: Bibliotheek van de Faculteit Godgeleerdheid—Peeters.
Schillebeeckx, E. (1974). *Jezus, het verhaal van een levende.* Baarn: Nelissen.
Tracy, D. (1975). *Blessed rage for order: The new pluralism in theology.* New York: The Seabury Press.
Vandenhoeck, A. (2011). Over de grenzen. Pastoraat en pediatrie. Great Ormond Street Hospital for Children in Londen. *Pastorale Perspectieven, 150,* 75–78.
Van Lierde, E. (2008). Onderzoek ontkracht clichés over godsdienstles. Dossier 10 jaar leerplan godsdienst. *Tertio, 9*(447), 1, 7–9.
Ysebaert, T. (2012, May 2). Doorbraak in het godsdienstonderwijs. *De Standaard.* Retrieved October 8, 2012, from http://www.standaard.be/artikel/detail. aspx?artikelid=693PCON8.

5 An Emerging Approach to Spiritual Development through Religious Education in Maltese Schools

Adrian-Mario Gellel

INTRODUCTION

Spirituality is an underlying force of human existence, both at the communal level and at the individual level. Due to its pervasive nature, there are many diverse ways in which spirituality is experienced and expressed. So while religion may be considered by many as the preferred way to access and to express this fundamental dimension, it is undeniable that spirituality is also expressed through a variety of human activities, including the arts, philosophy and even scientific enquiry. Consequently, it is not surprising that spirituality is considered to be an essential component of a holistic education. In this regard, UNESCO's Delors report (1996) established that the education of the 20th century should be based on four main pillars: to know, to do, to live with others and to be. On the latter point, the commission explicated that "education should contribute to every person's complete development—mind and body, intelligence, sensitivity, aesthetic appreciation and spirituality" (1996, p. 95). Similarly, in providing a general comment on the Convention on the Rights of the Child, the United Nations Committee for the Rights of the Child specified that

> article 29 (1) insists upon a holistic approach to education which ensures that the educational opportunities made available reflect an appropriate balance between promoting the physical, mental, spiritual and emotional aspects of education, the intellectual, social and practical dimensions, and the childhood and lifelong aspects. The overall objective of education is to maximize the child's ability and opportunity to participate fully and responsibly in a free society. (United Nations, 2001, note 12)

Indeed, spirituality has found its place in various curricula, including in the then-atheist Soviet Union where it was understood as instilling inspiration and promoting moral capacity, courage, wisdom and social responsibility (Halstead, 1994). Social, political, historical and cultural circumstances shape the way, and determine to what extent, schools deal with the spiritual education of their students.

The Maltese way of dealing with the spiritual education of students is in this sense peculiar. The pervasiveness of Catholicism in Maltese life, together with local politics, and, more recently, secularisation and globalisation, are the main factors that have been shaping the spiritual education of Maltese students.

THE MALTESE CONTEXT

Malta is the smallest member state in the European Union. Its eurocentric identity was constructed over the centuries by the dominating influences of the major Mediterranean and European powers. Due to various historical circumstances, Catholicism has been an essential contributor to the construction of Maltese identity, with the institutional Church playing an important role in the political, communitarian and cultural life of the islands.

Catholic symbols are readily available in both spatial and temporal dimensions, both in public and private spaces. Churches, niches, statues and houses named after saints are only a few examples of the symbolic repertoire that is immediately evident to any local or foreign visitor. Social and family life still follow the religious calendar and are thus full of religious events marked by Church, community and/or family traditions. The public year is organised around three main moments: Lent and Easter, the village *festa*, and Advent and Christmas, while the individual temporal dimension is marked by celebrations of the sacraments as well as major rites of passage. Many parishes still organise some seven public processions a year, usually accompanied by anywhere between 30 and 1000 participants. Even on a national level, 8 of the 14 public holidays commemorate religious festivities.

Indeed, contrary to most European countries, one cannot argue that Malta is a secular society, even though a sizable part of the population relate and operate through a secular mentality, and the majority of the population experience reality in both secular and nonsecular terms (Gellel & Sultana, 2008). The European Union's Social Values Survey demonstrated that, when compared to their European counterparts, Maltese have the highest belief in God (95%), the lowest nonbelieving group (2%) and the lowest group of believers in a life force or spirit (3%) (European Commission, 2005). The European Values Survey has given similar results over the past 30 years. From the latest report it transpired that 96.1% of the Maltese population claim to be Catholic and 90.3% feel that religion is important in their lives. The Maltese data contrasts with data from the other EU countries. For instance, the importance Maltese attribute to God (72.6%) is significantly higher than the EU average of 21.6%.

Similarly, in contrast to the EU average, Maltese are interested in spirituality (76.5% against 52.5%) and claim to be religious (72.9% against 64.4%) (European Values Survey Foundation/Tilburg University, 2010). This European 'anomaly' can only be explained through an understanding that religion and spirituality are largely shaped by context. This explanation is in agreement with the observations of a number of geographers, social scientists and theologians who point to the reality of contextual difference within the same regions and/or worldviews (see for instance Ivakhiv, 2006; Dangor, 2004).

Yet one should not be misled into thinking that the Maltese have been completely immune to the secularisation process. The European Values Survey (2010) reveals a noticeable decline in the religious practice of the Maltese population, with those participating in religious celebrations at least once a week decreasing from 92.3% in 1981 to 80.2% in 2008. It also transpires that the Maltese have become less and less satisfied with the answers the Church gives to issues related to moral problems, family and even spiritual needs.

RELIGIOUS AND SPIRITUAL UPBRINGING OF CHILDREN

In a culture and society imbued with a Catholic worldview, it is not unreasonable to find that spiritual nurture is normally understood to be part of religious upbringing. Following a traditional Catholic understanding, religious upbringing in Malta is generally considered to be the responsibility of the family, the parish community and the school. It is very normal for the nuclear family to have frequent contacts with the extended family, especially with grandparents who normally help in the child's upbringing. Research conducted among 11–13-year-olds revealed that a high proportion of pre-teens (77.4%) spend some time during the week alone with their grandparents (Barbara, 2010). It is thus plausible to assume that some form of intergenerational learning occurs, including on a religious and spiritual level. The family is also sustained by the wider community through its practices and activities directed towards children and the family in general. Popular religiosity and, in particular, feasts, religious drama and processions during the village festa, Christmas, Lent and Easter expose children to rich religious symbolism and narrative, while catechesis and Catholic associations aim at the religious and social formation of the child. Most children attend catechesis classes twice a week in the evening, at least for a year, before they receive the sacraments of Eucharist and Confirmation at the ages of 7 and 11, respectively. Furthermore, it is also common practice for children and adolescents to be involved in Catholic associations, such as Catholic Action or local youth groups. Two separate research projects conducted among 11–13- and 13–16-year-olds found that 37.8% and 48.3%, respectively, are members of a Catholic association (Barbara, 2010; Xuereb, 2008).

By the end of 2008, the state provided for the compulsory education of 60.5% of school-aged children, while church schools and independent schools provided for the education of 29.4% and 10.1% of school-aged children, respectively (National Statistics Office, 2011). All schools have to follow the National Minimum Curriculum and the syllabus published by the state authorities (Ministry of Education and Employment, 2012). In all of these schools, children receive formal Religious Education (RE) and, in most circumstances, schools also provide non-time-tabled spiritual/religious pastoral care as well as religious/spiritual activities. Although the current National Minimum Curriculum makes reference to the development of spiritual values, these are implicitly understood to be part of the Religious Education component. The National Curriculum Framework (Ministry of Education and Employment, 2012) also speaks of the need to help students develop their potential as lifelong learners in the areas of moral and spiritual development. However, spiritual development is only mentioned under the Religious Education and Ethics learning area. The new curriculum also proposes the introduction of an Ethics Education component as an alternative for those who withdraw from the Catholic Religious Education Programme, although the National Curriculum Framework remains silent on what this proposed programme will consist of (Ministry of Education and Employment, 2012).

With the exception of just three independent schools which provide Muslim or Protestant Religious Education, there are practically no differences between state, church and independent schools in the adoption of the Catholic Religious Education (CRE) syllabus or in the way these lessons are inserted in the curriculum. Although parents have the constitutional right to withdraw their children from these classes, less than 2% choose to do so (Malta, House of Representatives, 2009). In terms of the 1989 agreement between the Republic of Malta and the Holy See,[1] CRE lessons in state schools are given at least two and a half hours a week during the six years of primary and at least one and a half hours a week during the five years of secondary education (Republic of Malta & Holy See, 1989).

Besides the formal CRE lessons, students are nurtured in Catholic spirituality through religious extracurricular activities organised during the scholastic year. The number of such activities varies between primary and secondary education and between church and state schools. Furthermore, all state and church schools are required to provide the service of an ordained Religious Counsellor who takes care of the religious and moral guidance of students (Republic of Malta & Holy See, 1989).

THE SPIRITUAL DIMENSION IN CHILDREN'S EDUCATION

While it may appear that spirituality is being adequately catered for in children's upbringing and education, in reality the spiritual nurture of children has been very much weakened over the years by the profound changes that are occurring in Maltese society. In particular, the increasing signs of an individualistic mentality, which started in the mid-90s (Abela, 1994; Tabone, 1995; Tonna, 1997), has weakened a sense of community that used to be so much stronger in Maltese society.

In analysing the European Values Survey data of these past two decades, Abela (2006) concluded that the Maltese seem to be experiencing a communitarian-individualistic divide. On the one hand, there is an inherited national identity which is related to people's attachment to Church and religion and, on the other, a growing identity which is driven by the values of individualism and secularism. In the Maltese context, individualism (and not just individuality) and secularism have been spurred on by economic growth and the consequent change in the standard of living and lifestyle (Gellel & Sultana, 2008). While secularity can, and should, promote spiritual nurture, individualism weakens collective memory, relationships, and the ability to access and use the symbolic repertoire available.

Given this scenario, it seems imperative to find an acceptable working definition of 'spirituality' and thereafter what is meant by spiritual education. The developments that have been occurring in Western society have made it possible to conceptualise a spirituality that is separate from religion. For instance, in a study among religious ministers of the three monotheistic religions, Hyman and Handal (2006) demonstrated that conceptually, religion may be identified with what is objective and external, while spirituality may be understood to be subjective, internal and involving a relationship with, or experience of, God. Zinnbauer et al. (1997) also confirm that the major difference between spirituality and religion lies in the former being perceived as more personal and the latter more objective. Yet these researchers also found significant high correlation between self-rated spirituality and religiosity, with 74% of respondents defining themselves as both religious and spiritual. In another study, Hill et al. (2000) concluded that the two realities are intertwined and that it is counterproductive to have either narrow or broad definitions, or to provide polarised terms, as this would oversimplify the constructs.

For the purpose of this chapter, it is acknowledged that spirituality may be experienced and expressed in and through diverse ways and that there are a number of characteristics which indicate its presence and nature. It is also understood that spiritual development, which is not always a linear reality, is composed of three major cores: connectedness and belonging, awareness and the development of a way of life. These core components are embedded and interact with other dimensions of human life, and use worldview, cultural and family beliefs, meta-narratives and traditions as interpretative frameworks (Roehlkepartain, Benson, Scales, Kimball & Ebstyne King, 2008).

As Van der Hoogen (2011) argues, lived spirituality is better understood within a contextual framework. It is through narratives, rituals, beliefs and symbol systems that the inexpressible is given form and can thus be accessed and experienced. This necessity of contextual frameworks leads to rich interactions and diverse ways of experiencing and understanding similar realities. This view implies that the spiritual dimension is considered to be a human fundamental shared by believers and nonbelievers alike. The way spirituality is being understood here is in line with social constructivist theory: meaning is not something given but is continuously reconstructed and reinterpreted by a community. Thus, spirituality, and the manner in which it is sensed and experienced, is interpreted before, during and after the same experiences through a given worldview and cultural context (Hense, 2011).

THE SITUATION IN SCHOOLS

When browsing through Maltese school textbooks published over the past two centuries, one is impressed by the extent to which spiritual, moral and religious education were intertwined, and how these dimensions passed through various scholastic subjects. Thus, for instance, an early 19th century Maltese reading book includes an impressive array of biblical proverbs, ancient Greek fables, Christian moral stories and exhortations aimed at a holistic education of students as witnessed by the words stated by the teacher in the textbook, *Ejjeu ∩andi ulŷdi; jŷn n∩allymkom yl byza∩ t'Alla* (Come to me, my children, and I will teach you the fear of God) (*Ktyb-yl-qari, ∩at-Tfal,* 1831). As one might expect, with the advance of secularisation, the prominence of religious language in textbooks, other than religious ones, has diminished considerably. Nonetheless, the Maltese primary school reading textbooks published during the 1970s, and then re-edited during the 1980s, still included a number of texts that saw children's spiritual, moral and religious education as a primary objective, even if this was to a much lesser degree than the 19th century textbooks. Thus, 8-year-olds in the first few days of their fourth year in primary school were exhorted to love God, the environment and all people since

> *Kull m'hawn ahwa ġod-dinja,* (All that exist in this world are
>   brothers/sisters)
> *Ilkoll tfal tal-Bambin* (All children of God/Baby Jesus)
> (Mejlaq, 1981)

Maltese society is changing and so is the way people construct and interact with reality. The fragmentation of knowledge and a labour market–oriented education have led to utilitarian curricula that leave little or no space for spiritual education. On the other hand, the Religious Education curricula have practically remained the same for three decades: the current RE textbooks for primary schools were published between

1982 and 1987, while those for secondary schools were published between 1997 and 1999. When reviewing the textbooks for primary level, it is evident that they were written in a particular sociocultural milieu when the Catholic meta-narrative was well known and religious socialisation occurred in the family and the wider community.

Furthermore, preference is given to religious knowledge, with affective and spiritual education occurring only sporadically or, by inference, through moral stories, para-liturgical celebrations and/or religious information. At secondary level, RE becomes more cognitively based and aims at helping students evaluate the Christian message and Maltese culture in an objective and critical manner, while constructing an answer to the existential dimension of life (Kummissjoni Kateketika Nazzjonali, n.d.). In both RE cycles much depends on the teacher's methods, approach and ability to help students transform arid cognitive content into personally meaningful resources.

SPIRITUAL EDUCATION AS A MAIN COMPONENT OF RELIGIOUS EDUCATION

A concrete attempt to promote spiritual education in the curriculum was recently made by the Catholic Church. As already mentioned, the state recognises that the Church is responsible for the development of the CRE curricula, syllabi and textbooks (Republic of Malta & Holy See, 1989). In 2006, the Secretariat for Catechesis, the Church entity responsible for the curriculum development of CRE, asked me, in my capacity of area specialist at the university, to chair and coordinate a committee with the intent of analysing the current situation of RE in Malta and to propose necessary reforms in the religious education of students attending compulsory education. A draft policy document open for public consultation was published in 2008 (Gellel et al., 2008). The policy document sets a definition of CRE that tries to meet the current requirements of society, students and their families. Given that, to date, there is no formal distinction between school-based RE and parish-based catechesis, one of the major proposals was to clearly distinguish between the two. The document argued that while

> Catechesis aims at educating the faith of the person within a *faith community*, Religious Education aims at helping the student to clarify the basic human religious and spiritual questions and needs, and at equipping the student to live the transcendental dimension in the context of the *learning community*. Whilst in the former, the individual is invited to build a deeper relationship with God, in the latter the student acquires critical understanding and the ability to use and develop religious and spiritual language. (Gellel et al., 2008, p. 28)

The document insists on the principle that the target population, as well as the setting where education takes place, determine the aims and the nuances of the content presented. RE is not understood as religious learning but as a contribution towards meaning-making. According to these recommendations, CRE should offer an intellectual approach to the content and the various expressions of the Christian faith, as well as provide students with the language and skills necessary to access, comprehend, express and evaluate their religious, moral and spiritual dimensions. The policy document recommends that CRE is understood as a service

> towards the understanding and development of those tools that have sustained and contributed to the development of different generations of Maltese individuals and communities. Similarly, the Maltese Catholic Community is duty bound to help individual students access, understand and take advantage of the wisdom that different generations of believers have put together in the quest to live the good life and develop a healthy relationship with Self, Others, Creation and God. (Gellel et al., 2008, p. 29)

This way of conceptualising CRE has paved the way for a less doctrinally based approach to RE and to acknowledge and value spiritual education as an area that merits specific attention whilst still being an integral part of RE. While arguing that spirituality and religion are inextricably tied to each other, the document understands spirituality to be broader than the social and cultural dynamics of religion and to be about sustaining one's life journey.

Unfortunately, at the time of writing this chapter, while having the approval of the Maltese Catholic Bishops Conference, the draft policy paper has not yet been formally endorsed. Nonetheless, the principles of the draft policy have influenced the new National Curriculum Framework (NCF) (Ministry of Education and Employment, 2012). In defining Religious Education and Ethics as one of the eight main Learning Areas of the curriculum, the framework makes explicit the need that

> learning in this area [Religious Education & Ethics] nurtures and enhances a sense of spiritual self. . . . The spiritual dimension of the self should be supported by promoting values that include justice, personal responsibility, respect, reflection and active engagement in moral issues. (Ministry of Education and Employment, 2012, p. 35)

Following the impetus of the draft policy paper on CRE, the National Curriculum Framework (NCF) establishes that the new CRE curriculum should be developed over four learning strands, namely

   i. Religious Language
  ii. Spiritual Dimension
 iii. Beliefs (which in the document are referred to as the Word of God) and
  iv. the formation of a Personal Catholic Worldview.

It is thus positive to note that the NCF formally recognises the importance of including specific attention to the education of students' spirituality. While the NCF does not go into further detail about the learning outcomes and the content within the four identified strands, the Diocesan Office of Religious Education has already refined the scope and objectives of these strands. The documents prepared by the Diocesan Office of RE, although still not published, posit that the four strands should not be understood as being independent of each other. Indeed, each contributes to the construction of the others. They are conceptualised in such a way as to provide a balance between the cognitive, affective and spiritual dimensions of knowledge, thus empowering students and facilitating transformative knowledge.

In a more recent unpublished document the 'Spiritual Dimension' strand is understood to comprise three main areas, namely,

   i. educating the sense of beauty and wonder, of emotions and of attitudes,
  ii. enabling students to formulate, express, and possibly answer, fundamental existential questions, and
 iii. educating connectedness with oneself, others, all creation and God (Office of Religious Education, 2010).

Moreover, the Office of Religious Education understands that the 'Spiritual Dimension' strand is further sustained through the narratives, beliefs, rituals and attitudes developed in the 'Beliefs' and the 'Personal Catholic Worldviews' strands.

The 'Beliefs' strand should provide a concrete language for accessing and expressing the spiritual by presenting the beliefs of the Catholic community through the life experiences of individuals and communities of the Old and the New Testament period, and of various Christians in different cultures throughout the ages.

At the same time, the 'Personal Catholic Worldview' strand should foster the development of virtues and values, as well as higher order thinking skills that enable students to evaluate and synthesise what they would have learnt and to critically apply this to their own lives.

The Religious Language strand should provide the necessary background to help students read and interpret symbols and religious language, as well as help them acquire information and encourage them to be challenged by other religions.

FROM THEORY TO ACTION

Although the CRE policy document presented for discussion in 2008 has still not been formally endorsed, the Bishops formally approved the Syllabus for Form 1 students (Office of Religious Education, 2010). The document, which follows the guidelines and principles of the CRE policy document, was then used to design and prepare the current RE textbook for Form 1 students (Polidano, Gerada, Gellel, Micallef & Gatt, 2011).

The preparatory syllabus document reiterated that, through RE, students should be able to "**connect** to, **respond** to, and **express** their **spiritual dimension** by expressing awe, value and be committed to beauty, formulate and express fundamental questions and connect/relate through Jesus Christ, with oneself, others, creation and God" (Office of Religious Education, 2010, p. 15). The document also claimed that at least a quarter of the learning outcomes in the Form 1 syllabus aim at facilitating students' spiritual education. It is also positive to note that the whole theme of the Form 1 syllabus centres on spiritual imagery. During their first year in secondary education, students are invited to consider their lives as adventurous journeys. Through this journey they are encouraged to relate their own personal experiences with the experiences/adventures of biblical persons and communities as well as individuals who have experienced joys and faced challenges throughout the past two millennia. Focusing on the personal life of the student, the syllabus encourages students, along with other goals, to

   i. reflect on, acknowledge and celebrate their uniqueness;
  ii. be open to change;
 iii. foster a sense of connectedness with others and to be socially responsible;
  iv. become aware of God's active presence in their lives and develop a personal relationship;
   v. deal with existential issues (in particular, beauty, suffering and death) and draw from the experiences of others and face life challenges; and
  vi. become able to make life choices upon evaluating consequences.

The fact that these objectives are made concrete through a Catholic worldview is not a contradiction or a limitation for the spiritual education of students, especially given that the content and methods of the syllabus are shaped by an invitation to approach the Catholic faith with an open mind. Indeed, the content and method of the textbook insist that there is no one way of being Catholic, and that one may be authentic to oneself and to the message in a variety of cultures and life situations. The invitation to reflect on one's life issues, and to correlate them with the same issues that other believers have faced in a variety of contexts, encourages students to develop their own language and way of life.

CONCLUDING REFLECTIONS

In the current changing Maltese context, characterised by tension between an inherited Catholic tradition and global secularisation, the need to equip students with tools that help them access and express what makes them intrinsically human is urgent. There have been some notable developments in these past few years and the very fact that the spiritual dimension has been identified as an area that merits educational attention is positive. Yet the pace of reforms in the area is slow, and the direction still not clear. Much has already been achieved, but considerable work is still needed to ensure that students' entitlement to a truly holistic education, which includes their spiritual growth, is met. Although currently the only subject that gives attention to this dimension is RE, it is hoped that in the near future the whole of the curriculum will promote student spiritual education through the different subjects.

NOTES

1. In 1989, the Holy See and the Republic of Malta recognised the contribution and place of Catholic faith in the life of the Maltese community. Both parties also acknowledged the value of RE in the holistic formation of the individual. On these basis of these observations the two states signed an international agreement to regulate Catholic Religious Education in Maltese state schools.

REFERENCES

Abela, A. M. (1994). *Shifting family values in Malta: A Western European perspective*. Floriana: DISCERN.

Abela, A. M. (2006). Shaping a national identity. *International Journal of Sociology, 35*(4), 10–27.

Barbara, D. (2010). *The religious culture of pre-teens*. (Doctoral dissertation). University of Malta, Malta.

Dangor, S. (2004). The many voices of Islam. *Religion and Theology, 11*(3/4), 331–342.

Delors, J. (1996). *Learning: The treasure within—Report to UNESCO of the International Commission on Education for the Twenty-First Century*. Paris: UNESCO Publishing.

European Commission. (2005). *Social values, science and technology*. Eurobarometer 225/Wave 63.1. Brussels: European Commission. Retrieved May 15, 2012, from http://ec.europa.eu/public_opinion/archives/ebs/ebs_225_ report_en.pdf.

European Values Survey Foundation/Tilburg University. (2010). *European Values Study 2008, 4th wave, Integrated Dataset.* Cologne: GESIS.

Gellel, A., Chircop, L., Debono Curmi, M., Deguara, G., Gatt, S., Magro, E., . . . Sultana C. M. (2008). *Religious education in Malta: Reflections by the Catholic community.* Malta: Archdiocese of Malta, Secretariat for Catechesis.

Gellel, A., & Sultana, M. (2008). Leaping from non-secular to post-secular. A study of the Maltese scenario. In H. G. Ziebertz & U. Riegle (Eds.), *Europe as a postsecular society: Reflections on religion and societal cohesion* (pp. 111–126). Berlin: Lit Verlag.

Halstead, J. M. (1994). Moral and spiritual education in Russia. *Cambridge Journal of Education, 24*(3), 423–439.

Hense, E. (2011). The quest for interdisciplinary theories on spirituality. In E. Hense & F. Mass (Eds.), *Towards a theory of spirituality* (pp. 5–14). Leuven: Peters.

Hill, P. C., Pargament, K., Hood, R. W., McCullough, M. E., Swyers, J. P., Larson, D. B., & Zinnbauer B. J. (2000). Conceptualizing religion and spirituality: Points of commonality, points of departure. *Journal for the Theory of Social Behaviour, 30*(1), 51–77.

Hyman C., & Handal P. J. (2006). Definitions and evaluation of religion and spirituality items by religious professionals: A pilot study. *Journal of Religion and Health, 45*(2), 264–282.

Ivakhiv, A. (2006). Towards a geography of "Religion": Mapping the distribution of an unstable signifier. *Annals of the Association of American Geographers, 96*(1), 169–175.

Ktyb-yl-Qari, ∩*at-Tfal.* (1831). Malta.

Kummissjoni Kateketika Nazzjonali. (n.d.). *Sillabu tar-Reliġjon għall-Klassijiet I, II, III—Prinċpji gwida.* Malta: Author.

Malta, House of Representatives. (2009). *Tfal eżentati mit-tagħlim tar-reliġjon: Parliamentary Question 11995.* Retrieved November 10, 2011, from http://www.pq.gov.mt/PQweb.nsf/10491c99ee75af51c12568730034d5ee/c1256e7b0 03e1c2dc1257669004e4bea?OpenDocument.

Mejlaq, M. (1981). Inħobbu 'l Alla. In V. Fenech, L. Scerri, J. L. Camilleri, & P. Mifsud (Eds.), *Id-Denfil, Ir-Raba' Ktieb* (2nd ed., p. 6). Malta: Dipartiment tal-Edukazzjoni.

Ministry of Education and Employment. (2012). *A curriculum framework for all.* Malta: Author.

National Statistics Office. (2011). *Education Statistics 2006/2007, 2007/2008.* Malta: Author.

Office of Religious Education. (2010). *Sillabu tal-Ewwel Sena (Sekondarja): L-Avventura ta' Ħajti.* (Unpublished document). Malta: Office of Religious Education, Secretariat for Catechesis.

Polidano, D., Gerada, V., Gellel, A. M., Micallef, S., & Gatt, K. (2011). *L-Avventura ta' Ħajti. Ktieb tar-Reliġjon għall-ewwel sena tal-iskola sekondarja.* Malta: Segretarjat għall-Katekeżi.

Republic of Malta & Holy See. (1989). Accordo tra la Repubblica di Malta e la Santa Sede per meglio ordinare l'istruzione e l'educazione Religiosa Cattolica nelle Scuole statali. *Acta Apostolicae Sedis, 90*(1), 30–41.

Roehlkepartain, E. C., Benson, P. L., Scales, P. C., Kimball, L., & Ebstyne King, P. (2008). *With their own voices: A global exploration of how today's young people experience and think about spiritual development.* Minneapolis: Search Institute. Retrieved March 22, 2010, from http://www.search-institute.org/system/files/with_their_own_voices_report.pdf.

Tabone, C. (1995). *Maltese families in transition.* Malta: Ministry for Social Development.

Tonna, B. (1997). *The sign of the here and now criterion*. Malta: DISCERN.

United Nations. (2001). *Convention on the rights of the child. Appendix General Comment 1 (2001): The Aims of Education*. Retrieved May 10, 2012, from http://www.unhchr.ch/tbs/doc.nsf/(symbol)/CRC.GC.2001.1.En?OpenDocument.

Van der Hoogen, T. (2011). Elements of theory about 'lived spirituality'. In E. Hense & F. Mass (Eds.), *Towards a theory of spirituality* (pp. 15–27). Leuven: Peters.

Xuereb, D. (2008). *Emerging trends amongst Maltese adolescents: A qualitative study into Taylor's culture of authenticity*. (Master dissertation). University of Malta.

Zinnbauer, B. J., Pargament, K. I, Cole, B. C., Rye, M. S., Butter, E. M., Belavich, T. G., . . . Kadar, J. L. (1997). Religion and spirituality: Unfuzzying the fuzzy. *Journal for the Scientific Study of Religion*, 36(4), 549–564.

6 Spirituality and Education in Finland

Meeting the Socio-Demographic Changes with Empirical Research

Kirsi Tirri and Martin Ubani

INTRODUCTION

This chapter focuses on Finnish research and practice into spirituality and education. In this chapter we give an overview of the recent research into spirituality conducted in the last ten years in the educational context. The last decades have been significant in academic and socio-demographic terms with regards to spirituality in Finland. The changes in Finnish academia are discussed in more detail in Section 3. The shift from religiosity to spirituality in Finnish academic research coincides with changes in Finnish population and educational policy toward pluralism in the 21st century.

Currently about 80% of the Finnish population belong to the Lutheran Church. The next largest religious groups are the Greek Orthodox with 60,000 and Muslims with 40,000 members. Especially in the urban areas, there has been a rapid decrease in Church membership. In Helsinki, in 2010, about 67% of the population belonged to the Lutheran Church. Instead of becoming members of another religious tradition, more and more people choose to stay unaffiliated. Allegedly, spirituality in Finland is becoming like that of Western culture in general in that it is deinstitutionalised, individualised and privatised (Hay, 1998, p. 18; Pargament, 1999, p. 7; Davie, 2000). On the other hand almost the whole population of Finnish youth (approximately 90%) attends Evangelical Lutheran confirmation school at the age of 15 (Helve, 2006) and it is a very important part of Finnish youth culture among boys and girls (Helander, 2005). Confirmation school has several religious, spiritual and social learning goals (The Evangelical Lutheran Church of Finland, 2001). In this chapter we review the latest research conducted by Finnish researchers related to spirituality in different contexts in educational domains including church, school, homes and work life.

SPIRITUALITY IN THE FINNISH EDUCATIONAL CONTEXT

In Finland, we have a state school system. Religious Education is a compulsory school subject for all students. The subject is taught both in basic education (7–15-year-olds) and upper secondary school (16–18-year-olds). Currently, in Finnish schools there is a choice of 13 different RE subjects, such as Lutheran, Greek Orthodox and Roman Catholic Christianity, Islam and Judaism, and Secular Ethics for the children who do not belong to any religious denomination. Wicca is the most prominent religious tradition without state religious education. It is not considered a full religion in the sense that it lacks the level of organisation and membership required by the Board of Education/School legislation.

Finnish state school religious education is under increasing pressure to change into a common nondenominational RE. The current RE solution in Finland has been considered 'weak confessional' as the students are given RE according to their own religious traditions, with content based on the respective tradition, but the instruction does not include the elements of religious devotion or commitment (Kallioniemi & Ubani, 2012).

In the Finnish National Curriculum for Basic Education (Finnish National Board of Education, 2004) there is no direct reference to spirituality. The concept 'spirituality' is only used in the official English translation of the National Core Curriculum as a substitute for 'religious' in the Finnish document. In the English document it is stated that the aim is to get to know Finnish spiritual heritage. The only exception that explicitly cites the spiritual aspect to be part of the whole curriculum is that concerning early childhood education (National Research and Development Centre for Welfare and Health, 2003).

The cultural and linguistic context may explain the lack of the concept 'spirituality' in the Finnish curriculum. For instance, Finnish curriculum goals mention themes related to worldview, identity, ethics and purpose at each grade level (Finnish National Board of Education, 2003, 2004). In the Nordic context, 'worldview' or 'view of life' can be used broadly to refer to spirituality (Stifoss-Hanssen, 1999). Furthermore, in contemporary Finnish there are two words that derive from the Finnish equivalent of 'spirit'. The first one could be roughly translated as 'religious spirituality' or 'spirituality connected with religion'. This would often refer to Christian individual or communal devotional life. The second word refers to 'nonreligious spirituality' and increasingly to 'non-Christian spirituality'. In this category belong diverse traditions and actions such as theosophy, new religious movements and sometimes even some aspects of psychology. In addition to these, there is a third word or concept which is the exact Finnish equivalent of 'religiosity'. Of the previous concepts, it is most clearly connected with religious faith and religious practices. Finnish theology has also been increasingly applying a fourth concept derived from the German 'Spiritualität' or the Swedish 'spiritualitet' to refer to Christian devotional life. However, religious education and educational research also have been applying the very same concept, but with a broader meaning that covers the meanings of all previous concepts (e.g. Tirri, 2004).

RESEARCH INTO SPIRITUALITY IN FINLAND

The Background to Finnish Research into Spirituality

In the early 21st century spirituality emerged as a new research focus in religious education in Finland. Until the early 21st century research into religiousness and (religious) spirituality in Finland was dominated for decades by the preceding cognitive religious psychological research tradition on religious development (Tamminen, 1991; Räsänen, 2002). There was little new activity, either in this branch of research or in general, which related to religious or spiritual education. However, in the early 2000s spirituality became central to the research activities of Finnish researchers in religious education. With funding from the Academy of Finland, Professor Kirsi Tirri started a research project with several doctoral students interested in spirituality as a human quality that could be taught in homes, church, schools and work life (Ryhänen, 2006; Ubani, 2007a; Valtonen, 2009; Hanhimäki, 2011; Holm, 2012). At the same time the largest European association on learning and instruction (EARLI) established a special interest group (SIG) for researchers interested in religious and spiritual education. For several years Tirri acted as the SIG chair for this group and, later, a book series on religious and spiritual education was established by Waxmann with van der Zee, Tirri and Riegel as editors. Many Finnish doctoral students published their dissertations in this book series (Kuusisto, 2011; Hanhimäki, 2011; Holm, 2012). With these developments empirical research into spirituality became a leading focus for religious education in Finland. This research differentiated itself from the systematic theological discussion on devotional spirituality (Kotila, 2005).

In this chapter we present the main discussion and research into spirituality and education in Finland from four viewpoints: 1. Spiritual intelligence (SQ); 2. Spiritual sensitivity; 3. Spirituality as expression of post-secular religiosity; and 4. Spirituality as a contributor to positive youth development. These viewpoints are to be seen as overlapping themes because some of the individual studies have relevance to two or even three areas of research. In general Finnish research into spirituality has emphasised empirical approaches. The theoretical basis has been international rather than domestic. For this reason the following sections include a brief description of the main theories and conceptualisations used in the Finnish research within the presented viewpoints.

Spiritual Intelligence

In line with the international research on spiritual intelligence, the Finnish research on the topic stems from Howard Gardner's multiple intelligences theory (Gardner, 1983). The most recently suggested intelligence types include emotional and spiritual intelligence (Goleman, 1995; Zohar &

Marshall, 2000). Howard Gardner (1999, pp. 54–58) has identified three domains of spiritual intelligence. First, he attributes the "concern with cosmic or existential issues" to the sphere of spiritual intelligence. In fact, Gardner (1999, p. 60) has considered whether it would be more appropriate to consider spiritual intelligence as a form of existential intelligence. Second, he emphasises the "spiritual as achievement of a state of being" which represents the psychological states and phenomenal experiences that are called spiritual. The third domain is "spiritual as it affects others", a social aspect, which also coincides with the term 'charisma' and is an important ingredient in bringing other people towards fulfillment of the first two domains in their lives. Spiritual intelligence and its measurability has been a widely debated topic (Emmons, 2000; Gardner, 2000; Mayer, 2000) and the discussion continues.

Tirri, Nokelainen and Ubani (2007) have discussed the possibility that the concepts of spiritual intelligence and spiritual sensitivity could be synonymous. In their study they found that academically gifted students rated their spiritual sensitivity higher than average ability students. With this observation they asked whether gifted students have higher spiritual intelligence. Furthermore, in another study by Tirri and Ubani (2007), preadolescent girls rated their spiritual intelligence higher than boys of the same age.

The study by Ryhänen, Nokelainen and Tirri (2006) examined the spiritual intelligence profile of Finnish peacekeepers, and Ryhänen (2006) continued the discussion in his dissertation on Finnish peacekeepers' spirituality. In a recent book by Tirri and Nokelainen (2011), the concepts of intelligence and sensitivity are further explored with a collection of instruments for measuring multiple intelligences and moral sensitivities in education.

Spiritual Sensitivity

David Hay's (1998) research has been the conceptual basis for Finnish research into spiritual sensitivity. In short, Hay has identified three categories of spiritual sensitivity. *Awareness sensing* refers to an experience of a deeper level of consciousness when we choose to be aware by 'paying attention' to what is happening. The second category of spiritual sensitivity is *mystery sensing* which is connected to our capacity to transcend everyday experience and to use our imagination. The third category of spiritual sensitivity is *value sensing*. This category emphasises the importance of feelings as a measure of what we value. Among such values are issues that touch our existential questions and meaning seeking (Hay, 1998, pp. 70–74). In the study of spiritual sensitivity of gifted students by Kirsi Tirri, Petri Nokelainen and Martin Ubani (2006, 2007), a social dimension was added to Hay's three categories of spiritual sensitivity. The fourth subscale of spiritual sensitivity is called *community sensing* and is based on the work of Bradford (1995).

Based on the foregoing, Tirri has studied the spiritual sensitivity of the academically gifted and identified their strength in the mystery-sensing dimension of spirituality (Tirri, 2005). Ubani has studied the spiritual sensitivity of gifted preadolescents (N = 95) (Ubani, 2007a) and also explored the gender differences among them (Ubani, 2007b, 2013). Spirituality is very much concerned with the meaning of life, and girls and boys express differences also in that domain. In the qualitative studies the girls (N = 15) seemed to emphasise relationship in their search more than the boys (N = 12). In contrast the boys' search seemed to be characterised by deduction, relating to principles and theories as well as taking a position of observing different phenomena in life from a distance (Tirri & Ubani, 2005; Ubani, 2010, 2013). Furthermore, Ubani's (2010) study of gifted sixth-grade boys echoed Tirri's results concerning the prevalence of mystery in the spiritual lives of the pupils. Additionally, the sense of mystery was connected to their knowledge of and interest in science.

In a cross-cultural study of preadolescents' (N = 975) moral, religious and spiritual questions with data from Finland, Hong Kong, Bahrain and the US (Tirri et al., 2005) cultural differences were found in the spiritual and religious questions asked by preadolescents. In all the data sets, girls asked more questions of a spiritual and religious nature than boys. The Christian influence could be seen in the data for Finland and the United States. The Bahrain data clearly reflected a Muslim influence in the nature of religious questions (Tirri et al., 2005). Another study with Finnish youth (N = 316) explored how concepts about the future develop from preadolescence to adolescence. This study showed how the number and nature of different types of questions develop as students get older. The number of spiritual questions about the future increased while the number of moral questions decreased from preadolescence to adolescence. Both preadolescent and adolescent girls asked more religious questions than did boys of the same age. The increase in spiritual questions with age can be explained by psychological developments in adolescence. The struggle for a sense of significance and purpose in life is greatest during adolescence (Tirri & Nokelainen, 2006).

Spiritual sensitivity is also present in the lives of schoolteachers (Hanhimäki, 2011) and in church youth workers' professional identity (Valtonen 2009). In these two recent Finnish studies, which used narrative methods, spirituality was found to be an important aspect in the identity formation and professional morality of teachers and youth workers.

Spirituality as an Expression of Post-Secular Religiosity

The Finnish research has also been affected by the sociology of religion's definition of spirituality as post-secular religiosity (Tirri, 2008, 2009). According to the German researchers Hans-Georg Ziebertz and Ulrich Riegel (2008), post-secularity represents a discursive mode of religiosity. They build their definition on Habermas's (2001) philosophy in which post-secular religion meets three criteria: acceptance of plurality, communicating by reasoning and acknowledgement of fundamental rights. In the light of these criteria spirituality can be seen as one form of post-secular religiosity (Tirri, 2008, 2009).

According to recent British and Finnish empirical studies, an increasing number of people call themselves spiritual rather than religious (Heelas & Woodhead, 2005; Mikkola, Niemelä & Petterson, 2007). The British researchers Paul Heelas and Linda Woodhead argue that people do so because they are reluctant to commit themselves to hierarchies and would rather grow and develop as their own unique selves instead of going to churches and submitting to their teaching (Heelas & Woodhead, 2005, pp. 1–11). In a recent Finnish qualitative study, preadolescents also perceived spirituality to be more connected to these qualities than the concept of religion (Ubani & Tirri, 2006). Today, religion cannot be poured over the people from outside in the form of habits or rituals. It is something to be experienced within a person. Traditional religion is seen to be bound to tradition and institutions, whereas spirituality is associated with contemplation of self and inner existentialism and concentration on experiences. Compared to previous generations, the new generations in Finland are trying more actively to search for meaning and make sense of life themselves without ready answers given by the church. Spirituality now refers to what was earlier referred to as religion in the broadest and nontraditional sense (Mikkola et al., 2007, p. 111).

Spirituality as a Contributor to Positive Youth Development

The Finnish research on spirituality and youth development draws its influence and theoretical basis from different sources and evidence. Spiritual and moral development have been studied widely in the context of developmental psychology of religiosity (e.g. Reich, Oser & Scarlett, 1999; Oser, Scarlett & Bucher, 2006). In Finland and abroad we also have empirical research concerning the relations between religious and moral thinking (Duriez & Soenens, 2006; Tirri, Nokelainen & Mahkonen, 2009), motivation and spirituality (Hirsto & Tirri, 2009), and religion, spirituality and identity (Tirri, 2006).

The American researchers Mariano and Damon's (2008) models of the possible relationships between spirituality, religious faith and purpose contribute to the discussion on the roles of religion and spirituality in supporting purpose in life. These models provided the framework for case studies on purposeful youth in Finland and in the US (Tirri & Quinn, 2010). Mariano and Damon proposed five working models to describe these relationships in young people. Model 1 suggests that spirituality helps young people learn that they want to contribute, which eventually leads to contribution. Model 2 suggests that spirituality infuses the extant personal goals of young people with meaning and value, opening pathways for these goals to become purposeful. Model 3 imagines spirituality as a support for the desire young people have to develop moral character, which then leads to the actual development of such character. Religious community enters the framework with Model 4, which suggests that the community of religious faith provides a framework in which purpose is shared, which, in turn, supports the purpose of the young person. Finally, Model 5 represents the integration of all of these aspects; spirituality, religious faith and the goals of the young person are inextricably linked to a coherent purpose for the young person.

In their discussion of the positive contributions of spirituality and religion to youth development, Tirri and Quinn (2010) adhere to King's (2008) concepts that help explain why spirituality might be what she calls "fertile ground" for positive youth development: *plasticity* and *context*. Plasticity refers to the ability of people to change over the course of development and context emphasises the importance of the relationship between the young person and his or her environment. As King argues, given that positive youth development suggests that young people optimistically change over time, spirituality offers a rich context for this change. This context is provided in three ways: ideological, social and transcendent. This means that the young person who engages the spiritual self has an ideological framework in which to test new discoveries, social support and models for those who do reach greater levels of contribution, and a language and model of connecting to something greater than the self.

FINNISH CONTRIBUTIONS TO RESEARCH AND EDUCATION ON SPIRITUALITY

In this chapter spirituality was examined within the educational framework in Finland. We identified four main approaches to research into education for spirituality. First, spirituality was explored in a psychological framework as a new possible intelligence type. The scientific debate about the existence of spiritual intelligence is still going strong. However, in the educational context, a majority of researchers and educators agree on the importance of developing the spiritual sensitivity of our youth. The Finnish research has developed instruments to measure this kind of sensitivity with empirical results from children, youth and adults.

Second, the sociological approach sees spirituality as an expression of post-secular religiosity. Recent European writings on the faith and values of young adults were presented as examples of this approach and new empirical research findings from Finnish studies were reported and discussed. According to both theoretical and empirical reflections on the values and religiosity of the new generation, the concept of spirituality has proved to be an appropriate expression of post-secular religiosity.

The third approach where spirituality is studied as an expression of post-secular religiosity opens up new ways of studying religiosity (Tirri, 2009).

The empirical approaches and instruments in studies of religiosity have very much operationalised religiosity as dogmatic beliefs (such as a belief in a Christian God) or religious rituals (praying, attending services). We need new research instruments that are relevant for the new generation and which acknowledge the current ways of expressing religiosity. These new ways include taking quiet moments in the midst of everyday life, mystical and aesthetic experiences to complement rational thinking and the search for meaning and values in life. This new generation also wants to act in ways that promote peace and human rights. Understanding spirituality as an expression of post-secular religiosity gives more room for young adults to participate in communicative actions concerning religion. This promotes discursive religiosity in the spirit of Habermas, in which a plurality of religious beliefs and practices are acknowledged and a dialogical and interreligious approach advocated.

Fourth, spirituality as a contributor to positive youth development emphasises the positive aspects of spirituality. It can be seen as the whole-person approach in spiritual education (Tirri, 2012). Recent handbooks and special issues (Engebretson et al., 2010; de Souza et al., 2010; Van der Zee & Tirri, 2009) in the field include several contributions that address the whole-person approach to religious and spiritual education. This approach seems to be growing in our field, which is understandable because it can combine many of the strengths from the other approaches presented earlier and can be implemented by an autonomous teacher with strong pedagogical content knowledge and competence in the art and science of teaching.

REFERENCES

Benson, P. (2008). Foreword. In R. Lerner, R. Rosser, & E. Phelps (Eds.), *Positive youth development and spirituality: From theory to research* (pp. vii–x). West Conshohocken, PA: Templeton Foundation Press.

Benson, P. L., Roehlkepartain, E. C., & Rude, S. P. (2003). Spiritual development in childhood and adolescence: Toward a field of inquiry. *Applied Developmental Science, 7*(3), 205–213.

Bradford, J. (1995). *Caring for the whole child: A holistic approach to spirituality.* London: The Children's Society.

Davie, G. (2000). *Religion in modern Europe. A memory mutates.* Oxford: Oxford University Press.

de Souza, M., Francis, L., O'Higgins Norman, J., & Scott, D. (Eds.). (2010). *International handbook of education for spirituality, care and wellbeing.* Dordrecht: Springer.

Duriez, B., & Soenens, B. (2006). Religiosity, moral attitudes and moral competence: A critical investigation of the religiosity-morality relation. *International Journal of Behavioral Development, 30*(1), 76–83.

Emmons, R. (1999). *The psychology of ultimate concerns. Motivation and spirituality in personality.* New York: Guilford.

Emmons, R. (2000). Is spirituality an intelligence? Motivation, cognition, and the psychology of ultimate concern. *International Journal for the Psychology of Religion, 10*(3), 26.

Engebretson, K., de Souza, M., Durka, G., & Gearon, L. (Eds.). (2010). *International handbook of inter-religious education*. New York: Springer.
The Evangelical Lutheran Church of Finland. 2002. *Life-Faith-Prayer. Confirmation training plan 2001*. Helsinki: Church Council Education and Youth Work.
Gardner, H. (1983). *Frames of mind*. New York: Basic Books.
Gardner, H. (1999). *Intelligence reframed: Multiple intelligences for the 21st Century*. New York: Basic Books.
Gardner, H. (2000). A case against spiritual intelligence. *International Journal for the Psychology of Religion, 10*(3), 27–34.
Goleman, D. (1995). *Emotional intelligence*. New York: Bantam Books.
Habermas, J. (2001). Glaube und Wissen. Rede zur verleihung des "Friedenspreises des deutschen Buchhandels", Paulkirche Frankfurt. *Frankfurter Allgemeine Zeitung, 15*(10), 9.
Hanhimäki, E. (2011). *Moral professionalism in interaction. Educators' relational moral voices in urban schools*. Münster: Waxmann.
Hay, D., with Nye, R. (2006). *The spirit of the child* (2nd ed.). London: Jessica Kingsley.
Heelas, P., & Woodhead, L. (2005). *The spiritual revolution: Why religion is giving way to spirituality*. Oxford: Blackwell.
Helander, E. (2005). Finland: Optimistic realism and individualistic solidarity. In H. G. Ziebertz & W. Kay (Eds.), *Youth in Europe I: An international empirical study about life perspectives. International practical theology* (pp. 137–150). Münster: LIT.
Hirsto, L., & Tirri, K. (2009). Motivational approaches to studying theology in relation to spirituality. *Journal of Empirical Theology, 22*(1), 88–102.
Holm, K. (2012). *Ethical, intercultural and interreligious sensitivities: A case study of Finnish urban secondary school students*. Münster: Waxmann.
Kallioniemi, A., & Ubani, M. (2012). Religious education. In H. Niemi, A. Kallioniemi, & A. Toom (Eds.), *The miracle of PISA* (pp. 177–187). Rotterdam: Sense.
King, P. E. (2008). Spirituality as fertile ground for positive youth development. In R. Lerner, R. Rosser, & E. Phelps (Eds.), *Positive youth development and spirituality: From theory to research* (pp. 55–73). West Conshohocken, PA: Templeton Foundation Press.
Kotila, H. (2005). Contemporary worship as an expression of post-modern spirituality. In K. Tirri (Ed.), *Religion, spirituality and identity* (pp. 65–84). Bern: Peter Lang.
Kuusisto, A. (2011). *Growing up in affiliation with a religious community: A case study of Seventh-Day Adventist youth in Finland*. Münster: Waxmann.
Lerner, R. M., Roeser, R. W., & Phelps, E. (2008). Positive youth development, spirituality, and generosity in youth: An introduction to the issues. In R. M. Lerner, R. W. Roeser, & E. Phelps (Eds.), *Positive youth development and spirituality: From theory to research* (pp. 3–22). West Conshohocken, PA: Templeton Foundation Press.
Mariano, J. M., & W. Damon. (2008). The role of spirituality and religious faith. In R. M. Lerner, R. W. Roeser, & E. Phelps (Eds.), *Positive youth development and spirituality: From theory to research* (pp. 210–230). West Conshohocken, PA: Templeton Foundation Press.
Mayer, J. (2000). Spiritual intelligence or spiritual consciousness? *International Journal for the Psychology of Religion, 10*(3), 46–47.
Mikkola, T., Niemelä, K., & Petterson, J. (2007). *The questioning mind. Faith and values of the new generation*. Tampere: Church Research Institute, Finland.
National core curriculum for basic education. 2004. Helsinki: Finnish National Board of Education.

National core curriculum for upper secondary schools. 2003. Helsinki: Finnish National Board of Education.

National curriculum guidelines on early childhood education and care in Finland. 2003. Helsinki: National Research and Development Centre for Welfare and Health.

Nokelainen, P., Ryhänen, T., & Tirri, K. (2006). The intelligence profile of Finnish peacekeepers. *Gifted and Talented International, 20*(2), 19–30.

Oser, F., Scarlett, G., & Bucher, A. (2006). Religious and spiritual development throughout the life span. In W. Damon & R. M. Lerner (Eds.), *Handbook of child psychology. Volume 1: Theoretical models of human development* (6th ed.). Hoboken, NJ: Wiley & Sons.

Pargament, K. (1999). The psychology of religion and spirituality? Yes and no. *The International Journal for the Psychology of Religion, 9*(1), 3–16.

Reich, K. (1996). A logic-based typology of science and theology. *Journal of Interdisciplinary Studies, 8*(1–2), 149–167.

Reich, K. (1998). Psychology of religion: What one needs to know. *Zygon: Journal of Religion and Science, 33*(1), 113–120.

Reich, K. H. (2000). What characterizes spirituality? A comment on Pargament, Emmons and Crumpler, and Stifoss-Hansen. *The International Journal for the Psychology of Religion, 10*(2), 125–128.

Reich, K. H., Oser, F. K., & Scarlett, W. G. (Eds.). (1999). *Psychological studies on spiritual and religious development. Being human: The case of religion* (Vol. 2). Legerich: Pabst Science.

Ryhänen, T. (2006). *Spirituality of Finnish peacekeepers* (Doctoral dissertation). University of Helsinki, Department of Practical Theology, Helsinki.

Ryhänen, T., Nokelainen, P., & Tirri, K. (2006). The spiritual intelligence profile of Finnish peacekeepers. In K. Tirri (Ed.), *Nordic perspectives on religion, spirituality and identity* (pp. 146–164). Helsinki: University of Helsinki.

Räsänen, A. (2002). *Aikuisen uskonnollisuus. Tutkimus Fritz Oserin uskonnollisen arvioinnin kehityksen teoriasta ja sen pätevyydestä aikuisilla suomalaisilla koehenkilöillä.* [Religiousness of the adult. A research on Fritz Oser's theory of religious judgment and validity among Finnish adult participants]. (Doctoral dissertation). University of Helsinki, Helsinki.

Stifoss-Hanssen, H. (1999). Religion and spirituality: What a European ear hears. *The International Journal for the Psychology of Religion, 9*(1), 25–33.

Tamminen, K. (1991). *Religious development in childhood and youth*. Annales academiae scientarium Fenniae ser. B/259. Helsinki: Federation of Finnish Scientific Societies.

Tirri, K. (2004). Spirituality in religious education. In R. Larsson & C. Gustavsson (Eds.), *Towards a European perspective on religious education* (pp. 344–352). Bibliotheca theologiae practicae 74. Skellefteå: Artos & Norma bokförlag.

Tirri, K. (2005). Spiritual sensitivity of the academically gifted. *Proceedings*. Paper presented at the 4th International Conference: Developmental Distinctiveness and Potential Realization of Gifted Children, 11–13. November, 2004, Bratislava, Slovenia.

Tirri, K. (Ed.). (2006). *Religion, spirituality and identity*: Bern: Peter Lang.

Tirri, K. (2007). *Spirituelle Empfindsamkeit junger Erwachsener*. In A. A. Bucher (Ed.), *Moral, Religion, Politik: Psychologisch-pädagogische Zugänge* (pp. 269–277). Münster: LIT.

Tirri, K. (2008). Spirituality as an expression of post secular religiosity. In H. G. Ziebertz & U. Riegel, *Europe as a post secular society (EPOS). Reflections on religion and societal cohesion. Empirical studies and theoretical reflections* (pp. 155–166). Muenster: LIT.

Tirri, K. (2009). Spirituality in education. In T. Ahlbäck (Ed.), *Scripta Instituti Donneriani Aboensis,* Vol. 21: *Postmodern spirituality* (pp. 245–258). Åbo, Finland: Donner institute for Research in Religious and Cultural History.

Tirri, K. (2012). Religious and spiritual education as contributors to the development of the whole person. In T. van der Zee & T. Lovat (Eds.), *New Perspectives on Religious and Spiritual Education.* Research on Religious and Spiritual Education: Band 4 (pp. 269–280). Münster: Waxmann.

Tirri, K., & Nokelainen, P. (2006). Gifted students and the future. *KEDI Journal of Educational Policy, 3*(2), 55–66.

Tirri, K., & Nokelainen, P. (2011). *Measuring multiple intelligences and moral sensitivities in education.* Rotterdam: Sense.

Tirri, K., Nokelainen, P., & Mahkonen, M. (2009). How morality and religiosity relate to intelligence. A case study of mathematically talented adolescence. *Journal of Empirical Theology, 22*(1), 70–87.

Tirri, K., Nokelainen, P., & Ubani, M. (2006). Conceptual definition and empirical validation of a spiritual sensitivity scale. *Journal of Empirical Theology, 19*(1), 37–62.

Tirri, K., Nokelainen, P., & Ubani, M. (2007). Do gifted students have spiritual intelligence? In K. Tirri (Ed.), *Values and foundations in gifted education* (pp. 187–202). Bern: Peter Lang.

Tirri, K., & Quinn, B. (2010). Exploring the role of religion and spirituality in the development of purpose: Case studies of purposeful youth. *British Journal of Religious Education, 32*(3), 189–200.

Tirri, K., Tallent-Runnells, M., & Nokelainen, P. (2005). A cross-cultural study of preadolescents' moral, religious, and spiritual questions. *British Journal of Religious Education, 27*(3), 207–214.

Tirri, K., & Ubani, M. (2005). How do gifted girls perceive the meaning of life? *Gifted Education International, 19*(3), 266–274.

Tirri, K., & Ubani, M. (2007). The differences in the intelligence profiles of Finnish 12–13 -year old academically gifted girls and boys. In K. Tirri & M. Ubani (Eds.), *Holistic education and giftedness.* Series 111 (pp. 31–44). Helsinki: Department of Practical Theology, University of Helsinki.

Ubani, M. (2006). What makes life spiritual? In K. Tirri (Ed.), *Religion, spirituality and identity* (pp. 119–134). Bern: Peter Lang.

Ubani, M. (2007a). *Young, gifted and spiritual—The case of Finnish sixth-grade pupils.* (Doctoral dissertation). Research report 278. Department of Applied Sciences of Education. University of Helsinki, Helsinki.

Ubani, M. (2007b). Gender, giftedness and spirituality. In K. Tirri & M. Ubani (Eds.), *Holistic education and giftedness.* Series 111 (pp. 73–90). Helsinki: Department of Practical Theology, University of Helsinki.

Ubani, M. (2010). Malehood, giftedness and spirituality. An empirical study of Finnish gifted boys. *Religious Education Journal of Australia, 25*(1), 7–13.

Ubani, M. (2013). Existentially sensitive education. In T. Lovat & J. Arthur (Eds.), *International handbook of education, religion and values* (pp. 42–54). London: Routledge.

Ubani, M., & Tirri, K. (2006). How do Finnish preadolescents perceive religion and spirituality? *International Journal of Children's Spirituality, 11*(3), 357–370.

Valtonen, M. (2009). *Stories of students' development into church professions. Church youth work leader students' spirituality and professional identity.* Helsinki: Publications of DIAK 23.

Van der Zee, T., & K. Tirri (Eds.). (2009). Research on religious and spiritual education. *Journal of Empirical Theology, 22*(1), 1–6.

Ziebertz, H. G., & Riegel, U. (2008). Postsecular Europe: A concept questioned. In H. G. Ziebertz & U. Riegel (Eds.), *Europe as a post secular society (EPOS). Reflections on religion and societal cohesion. Empirical studies and theoretical reflection* (pp. 9–41). Muenster: LIT.

Zohar, D., & Marshall, I. (2000). *SQ—Spiritual intelligence the ultimate intelligence*. London: Bloomsbury.

7 Spirituality in Israeli State Jewish Education

Possible Guidelines for National Education Systems

Yaacov J. Katz

INTRODUCTION

Israel's multiethnic and multinational population of about 8 million is approximately 75% (6 million) Jewish, about 20% (1.5 million) Arab, around 2% (160,000) Druze and Circassians and the remaining 3% (240,000) migrants and foreign workers. The Jewish population of Israel may be described as one of immigrants with almost 90% of the population stemming from families that immigrated to Israel since the founding of the modern Zionist movement in the 1880s. Thus the Israeli Jewish population is particularly heterogeneous and comprises individuals who have different cultural and religious backgrounds. Approximately half of the Jewish population are of oriental origin and cherish a richly developed culture significantly influenced by Middle Eastern and North African attributes, while the remaining half of the Jewish population are of mainly European origin, maintaining a culture influenced by Eastern European traditions. In addition, about 20% of the Jewish population may be described as religiously observant, with about one-third of those following an ultra-orthodox lifestyle and two-thirds adhering to a modern orthodox way of life; 60% of the Jewish population can be described as traditional Jews, who believe in the Jewish religion without strictly observing religious rituals; and the remaining 20% perceive themselves as totally secular without any affinity to Jewish religious traditions.

The Israeli parliament took these sociological and anthropological population issues into account when debating the National Education Bill (Ministry of Education, 1994), according to which state education would be divided into three parallel and separate Jewish educational sectors, namely state secular education, state religious education and ultra-orthodox education, as well as providing one sector each for the Arab and Druze-Circassian minorities. All sectors are subject to the rules and regulations of the national Ministry of Education and a common national curriculum was prescribed, but autonomy was granted to all sectors in implementation of the curriculum, especially regarding the inclusion of content matter dealing with religious, secular, cultural and historical viewpoints to be addressed by the school system.

This chapter will address the relationship between religious values and spirituality as well as the relationship between humanistic values and spirituality in the Israeli Jewish educational system. The chapter, in describing Israeli society, will address the complexity of the Israeli Jewish educational system, which includes state secular, state religious and ultra-orthodox schools, and will define the different religious and values education curricula in the three educational sectors. The chapter will specifically focus on two major perceptions of spirituality, the first related to and deriving from religiosity and the second related to and deriving from humanistic perceptions. Theory and research pertaining to the relationship between religious values and spirituality on the one hand, as well as to the relationship between humanistic values and spirituality on the other, will be addressed. Consideration will be given to the results of two research studies that compared aspects of spirituality of elementary and high school students studying in Israeli Jewish state secular, state religious and ultra-orthodox schools. How the studies addressed the issue of when and where the two types of spirituality, namely spirituality related to religiosity and spirituality linked to humanistic values, come to the fore in the Israeli educational system will be described.

JEWISH EDUCATION IN ISRAEL

Israel is characterized as being both a traditional and modern society at one and the same time (Eisenstadt, 1996). Katz (2004) indicated that when the State of Israel gained independence in 1948, the first Israeli prime minister, David Ben-Gurion, immediately engineered the adoption of a national policy whereby the state education system served as a social agent for the enhancement of integration of the different religious, cultural and Jewish ethnic groupings in Israeli society. Over the years this policy, designed to bring about cultural integration in the Israreli population failed, and as a result led to the understanding that all sectors in Israeli society should be legitimately encouraged to foster their sectorial needs, including specific sectorial needs in the domain of religious education (Katz, 2007).

Katz (2004) described how the Jewish education system in Israel is divided into three major sectors: state secular, state religious and ultra-orthodox. The Ministry of Education is responsible for the curriculum and closely coordinates the educational processes and curricula that characterize the secular and state religious state sectors, with the ultra-orthodox sector given significantly more autonomy and flexibility in choice of educational processes and curriculum. The three sectors exist side by side, with Ministry of Education inspectors responsible for supervising the educational process in their particular sector. In addition to the usual range of mandatory core subjects such as Hebrew (mother tongue), English (foreign language), mathematics, science and history, the national curriculum stipulates that religious education be studied as a mandatory subject in all three educational sectors, with the particular and specific religious needs of each sector emphasized in the sectorial religious education curriculum. In addition, religious education is perceived by the educational authorities as the core subject within which the issue of spirituality, which includes a feeling of well-being, coherence and self-worth, is to be addressed (Katz, 2006; Ministry of Education, 1994).

Education in the Israeli State Secular Sector

In the Israeli state secular sector core curricular subjects are taught from a humanistic values point of view that does not aim to promote any particular ideology apart from the humanistic and democratic values that characterize Western society more generally (Katz, 2010). Religious education (described as heritage education in the state secular curriculum) is a mandatory subject characterized by its knowledge-based roots. Students are taught about religion, the history of religion, religion as a part of culture, and religious tradition and folklore from the humanistic point of view. Students are encouraged to understand how religion in general and the Jewish religion in particular developed, the place of religion in the moulding of national identity and the connection of religion to the humanistic values consensually accepted within Western society. In knowledge-based religious education, the Jewish religion is perceived as centre-stage but other religions may also be studied from a pluralistic point of view. Parents choose this sector for their children mainly because they have a secular lifestyle with no particular religious commitment and wish their children to experience an all round secular education that emphasizes knowledge of Jewish heritage as well as humanistic values, citizenship and academic knowledge and achievement. Parents do not perceive the goal of religious education as taught in the state secular sector as one of enhancing religiosity or religious observance but solely as one of promoting historical, cultural and traditional knowledge.

Education in the Israeli State Religious Sector

In the state religious sector the emphasis is placed on achievement in the different core subjects offered to the students as well as on specialization in a range of religious subjects that are taught from a Jewish orthodox point of view, with a major emphasis placed on values that are congruent with orthodox Judaism (Katz, 2010). Mention should be made that state religious education is totally orthodox in demanding all students to be observant Jews according to the strict letter of traditional Jewish law (Bar-Lev & Katz, 1991). State religious education does not have any pretensions of being pluralistic and does not offer education to the conservative stream of Judaism, which attempts to adapt Jewish tradition and observance to the needs of modern-day society (Gordis, 1990), or to the reform or liberal streams of Judaism, which emphasize the feeling of spiritual identity rather than demanding observance of traditional rituals, precepts and commandments (Jacobs, 1995). Thus teachers in this sector are intent on inculcating an orthodox way of life in their students and view Western civilization and citizenship through the Jewish orthodox prism. Religious education in the state religious sector is both faith and knowledge based and students are not only provided with religious knowledge regarding the history of religion and religion as part of humanistic culture, but are also encouraged to carry out religious precepts and commandments. At one and the same time students are exposed to the academic study of religion as well as to other core curriculum subjects. In state religious educational ideology the Jewish religion is taught with emphasis being placed on tolerance and open-mindedness towards those with different levels of religious commitment, such as modern-orthodox, traditional-orthodox and strictly-orthodox, with observance of Sabbath and dietary laws perceived as the lowest common denominator of observance for all in this sector. Parents choose this sector mainly because of their traditional religious persuasion and their belief that religious education should be faith as well as knowledge based and should contribute to the religiosity and religious observance of students without compromising their secular knowledge and achievement, as well as their sensitivity to the needs and beliefs of other Jewish sectors in the population.

Education in the Israeli Ultra-Orthodox Sector

As noted by Katz (2004), the ultra-orthodox sector of the education system specifically caters to the needs of the ultra-orthodox Jewish population. Parents belonging to this sector of Israeli society send their children to schools in this educational sector because they perceive the school to be a direct extension of the ultra-orthodox family, where strict observance of religious precepts, commandments and traditions is of paramount importance. Thus the schools in this sector perceive religious instruction to be totally faith based and to include both the imparting of religious knowledge to the students and the ensuring of strict religious observance of the ultra-orthodox way of life by the students. Intensive religious studies are the main goal of the school curriculum in the ultra-orthodox educational sector. Teachers in ultra-orthodox schools are committed to the inculcation of religious knowledge and observance in their students and are obliged to ensure that their students maintain high standards of ultra-orthodox religious observance throughout their school careers. Although these schools are formally expected to implement the national curriculum, achievement in general subjects is perceived as a secondary goal of the school system with the major thrust directed to religious instruction and observance.

DEFINITIONS OF SPIRITUALITY

There are many different definitions of spirituality and some of these are general and rather loose in their nature. For example, Wright (2000) defined spirituality as the concern for the ultimate meaning and purpose of life; Starratt (2004) postulated that spirituality is a way of being sensitive to the most profound realities of one's world; and Kumar (2000) proposed that spirituality may be defined as a deep feeling of compassion and unity, relatedness and connection with existence.

Davis, Hook & Worthington (2008) attempted to conceptualize what they perceive to be the major themes underpinning spirituality. They identified four types of spirituality as follows: religious spirituality, humanistic spirituality, nature spirituality and cosmos spirituality. As the aim of this chapter is to focus on clearly defined aspects of spirituality addressed in the Israeli state educational system (following Katz, 2012, 2013; Ministry of Education, 1994), only two of the four types identified by Davis, Hook and Worthington, namely religious spirituality and humanistic spirituality, will be reviewed.

Worthington and Aten (2009) stated that religious spirituality involves a sense of closeness and connection to the sacred as described by a specific religion (e.g. Christianity, Islam, Judaism) and that humanistic spirituality involves a sense of closeness and connection to humankind. According to Worthington and Aten both types of spirituality are commonly found in modern society, with religious spirituality characterizing individuals who are more religious in their beliefs and humanistic spirituality typifying those who are more secular in their worldview.

According to Zinnbauer and Pargament (2005) there are individuals who are both religious and spiritual and there are individuals who are only one or the other. Prior research (e.g. Cohen, 2002; Johnstone, Yoon, Franklin, Schopp & Hinkebein, 2009; Larson & Larson, 2003; Wills, 2009) has generally indicated that spirituality is an adaptive aspect of human functioning and a major variable related to psychological well-being and adaptivity. For example, Piechowski (2003) suggested a list of common themes that recur in spirituality. These themes include (among others) ecstasy, timelessness, oneness with nature, pulsating energy and life force, pro-social behavior and techniques of achieving heightened states of consciousness. Thus spirituality relates to psychological well-being and positive social adaptivity.

Religious Values and Spirituality

Gollnick (2005) defined religion as belief in God which includes profound experience of the holy or the sacred. Spirituality can be defined as an awareness and concern for the human spirit and a feeling of oneness or wholeness. Waaijman (2007) stated that spirituality is a complex whole, constructed out of elements which are complementarily interrelated. Spirituality is a relational process in which God and man are reciprocally related. Humans in various ways strive via the enhancement of spirituality to prepare themselves for union with God in order to grow in the direction of perfection as found in God.

Zinnbauer and Pargament (2005) proposed that religion and spirituality are interrelated. Religion concerns involvement in practices and commitment to beliefs or ideologies, whereas spirituality is more about the individual's complementary quest for meaning and well-being. According to Jackson and Bergeman (2011) religion and spirituality are strongly linked, with religion having more organizational and behavioral connotations than spirituality, which is oriented towards personal experiences. Indices of religion and spirituality are robustly associated and interrelated with positive outcomes concerning happiness and well-being (van Dierendonck, 2012; Wills, 2009). Patrick and Kinney (2003) and Ellison and Fan (2008) intimated that individuals who are more committed to their religious faith and spiritual convictions are happier and healthier, with more coping resources at their disposal than those for whom religion and spirituality are less important. Religious and spiritual persons tend to have better mental and physical health (Rosmarin, Pirutinsky, Pargament & Krumrei, 2009; Lawler-Row, 2010), enjoy greater life satisfaction (Steger & Frazier, 2005) and engage in more pro-social behaviors (Gibson, 2008; Hardy & Carlo, 2005). Thus there is much empirical evidence that religion and spirituality lead to a sense of well-being, to feelings of wholeness and congruence, as well as to a feeling of commitment to community and to society (Dillon, Wink & Fay, 2003).

The evidence presented above indicates a clear relationship between religious values and spirituality. In addition the evidence suggests that a religious orientation is conducive to the development of spirituality as well as to the positive psychological characteristics that are related to enhanced spirituality.

Secular Values and Spirituality

There are a number of sources testifying to the existence of enhanced spirituality among individuals who have secular and humanistic inclinations, without their having to ascribe to religiosity in any way. Breitbart (2007) pointed out that the tradition of existential philosophy contains both theistic and secular worldviews. Character strengths or habits, such as integrity, forgiveness, kindness and gratitude were originally identified with reference to the virtues espoused by the great faith traditions of the world (Peterson, 2006). However, positive psychology (following Seligman & Csikszentmihalyi, 2000), which promotes the nurturing of human talent as well as making normal life more fulfilling, talks of these faith traditions with respect, but essentially understands them as receptacles that have housed and nurtured these very same character strengths and may now be ready to give them up to the secular world. Positive psychology thus has a definite 'spiritual but-not religious' orientation. Schermer (2003) observed what he called 'spiritual awakening' in psychiatric patients. This awakening, which had nothing to do with religiosity, included renewed family life, a sense of hope and faith, improved self-esteem, restored careers, access to a greater range of feelings and an increased ability to establish intimacy. Schermer added that similarities can be found among spiritual teachings to living systems and modern relativity concepts or to quantum and chaos/complexity theories, none of which are related to religiosity.

Tacey (2004) described spirituality as the refuge for many of those who have rejected the false gods of wealth and status and instead chosen the substitutes of a life lived in spiritual wholeness. In addition, those espousing spirituality rather than material wealth have striven to regain the universal spiritual wisdom that once guided humankind. For those who are spiritually awakened, social responsibility becomes a sacred imperative, and through it they are impelled to go outside themselves and serve others and the world. Schneiders (2003) added that while religion is losing its popularity, spirituality is ascending and there is increasing justification among those who have traded the religion of their past for the spirituality of their present.

Emmons (2000) stated that spirituality includes universal morals and values such as the capacity to engage in virtuous behavior, to show forgiveness, to express gratitude, to be humble and to display compassion. Claxton (2002) argued that spirituality includes a heightened sense of vitality, a sense of being at ease in the world and peace of mind. He rejected any supernatural element to spirituality. His emphasis was on the psychological and in contrast with those who describe spirituality as being inextricably related to religiosity.

Comparison of Spirituality in the Three Israeli Educational Sectors

In order to more fully understand how spirituality fits into the curricula of schools in the Israeli school system, two studies (Katz, 2012, 2013) were undertaken to examine spirituality as observed in the system and to present an evidence-based understanding of how spirituality is actively promoted in schools affiliated to the three different Jewish educational sectors in Israel. The studies were necessary because enhancement of spirituality in the Israeli educational system is in its infancy and the discourse linked to spirituality is predominantly philosophical without being related to evidence-based educational activity (Tadmor, 2012). Thus, the two studies initiated by Katz (2012, 2013), examined if and how the prescribed parallel forms of religious and values education (Katz, 2006; Ministry of Education, 1994), namely knowledge-based religious education offered in state secular schools, faith- and knowledge-based religious education characteristic of state religious schools and faith-based religious education provided in ultra-orthodox schools, enhance spirituality in each of the respective educational sectors.

The first study investigated the spirituality of 230 tenth-grade students (aged 16) and the second study examined the spirituality of 363 eighth-grade elementary school students (aged 14). Both samples consisted of male and female students and, although the samples were randomly chosen, they typically represented students studying at state secular, state religious and ultra-orthodox schools. The state secular schools were coeducational with male and female students studying in the same classes, but the state religious and ultra-orthodox schools were single-sex schools catering separately for male and female students. All students were assigned to regular classes and were not diagnosed as having special needs.

Spirituality was assessed using valid and reliable questionnaires. The questionnaire administered to the eighth-grade students was based on the Spiritual Well-Being Questionnaire (Fisher, 2009), and the questionnaire completed by tenth-grade students was based on the Daily Spiritual Experiences Scale (Underwood & Teresi, 2002). Both questionnaires addressed the factors considered by many researchers to be closely associated with both religious spirituality and humanistic spirituality (Breitbart, 2007; Davis, Hook & Worthington, 2008; Ellison & Fan, 2008; Jackson & Bergeman, 2011; Lawler-Row, 2010; Peterson, 2006; Worthington & Aten, 2009). These factors included the following: self-identity, self-awareness, joy in life, inner peace, meaning in life, relationship with God, worship of the creator, love of God, closeness to God, prayer in daily life, love of others, acceptance of others, respect for others, kindness towards others and trust between individuals.

Results of the statistical analyses conducted on the data collected in both studies indicated that students studying in state religious schools were significantly characterized by factors associated with religious spirituality and to a lesser extent by factors linked to humanistic spirituality, whereas students attending state secular schools were significantly typified by factors related to humanistic spirituality and moderately characterized by factors related to religious spirituality. The results of the statistical analyses also indicated that students studying in ultra-orthodox schools had less intensive feelings of both religious spirituality and humanistic spirituality than their counterparts attending state religious or state secular schools.

DISCUSSION OF RESULTS OF EMPIRICAL RESEARCH ON SPIRITUALITY IN THE ISRAELI SCHOOL SYSTEM

The research findings from these two research studies indicated that students attending state religious schools are characterized most especially by religious spirituality but also by humanistic spirituality. This may be understood in the light of what Katz (2004) confirmed as the most important factor influencing state religious education, namely, that students at state religious schools come from religious homes that emphasize faith- and knowledge-based religious education, a demand that is fully met by the schools. This complex integrated faith- and knowledge-based religious education includes subject matter that, on the one hand, emphasizes faith-based observance of religious precepts and commandments by students and, on the other, integrates knowledge-based humanistic values about religion that seem to balance a one-sided narrow approach. It appears that the integration of both faith- and knowledge-based religious education leads to the enhancement of both religious and humanistic spirituality from a mixed religious-humanistic point of view. Thus the integration of faith- and knowledge-based religious education provides a broader platform for the enhancement of spirituality not available in either exclusively knowledge-based or faith- based religious education that respectively provide rather narrower perspectives of religious education.

Students at state secular schools, who received knowledge-based religious education congruent with the wishes of their parents, were significantly characterized by humanistic spirituality and to a lesser extent religious spirituality. It appears that the humanistic aspect of knowledge-based religious education is perceived as a major educational focus and thus intensively contributes to the enhancement of humanistic spirituality but also moderately contributes to the enhancement of religious spirituality.

Students at ultra-orthodox schools receive strictly faith-based religious education focusing almost exclusively on Jewish religious knowledge and on the enhancement of observance of religious precepts and commandments. The affective aspects of either faith- or knowledge-based religious education are apparently neglected in ultra-orthodox schools, resulting in the almost total sidelining of those aspects of education that emphasize either religious or humanistic spirituality.

The above explanations regarding the types of spirituality that characterize students in the three sectors in the Israeli educational system seem to confirm the observation of Waaijman (2007), who stated that spirituality is a complex whole, constructed out of elements which are complementarily interrelated. In addition it appears that the integration of faith- and knowledge-based religious education which includes reference to both religion and humanism serves as a platform that enhances a sense of well-being, feelings of wholeness and congruence with God, as well as a feeling of commitment to humanity, to the community and to society (following Dillon, Wink & Fay, 2003).

With reference to the findings concerning humanistic spirituality, students in state secular schools were more significantly characterized by this type of spirituality than students in state religious high schools who, in turn, were more significantly characterized by humanistic spirituality than students attending ultra-orthodox schools. It appears that knowledge-based religious education which is overwhelmingly humanistic in its character, and which is provided in state secular schools, enhances the sensitivity of students to the importance of closeness to others and feeling for others (Lasher, 2012). Thus knowledge-based religious education as taught in state secular schools addresses the relationship between individuals significantly more than the integrated faith- and knowledge-based religious education taught in state religious schools or the totally faith-based religious education offered in ultra-orthodox schools. It appears that faith-based education focuses almost exclusively on the relationship between individuals and God as well as on the observance of religious precepts, principles and other religious behaviors (Katz, 2004), and seems to relegate the religious and spiritual aspects of the relationship between individuals to a place of lesser importance in state religious schools and to a situation of total indifference in ultra-orthodox schools (following Joss-Kent, 2012).

The fact that students in state religious and state secular schools were more significantly characterized by religious spirituality than students in ultra-orthodox schools is rather surprising. It appears that both faith- and knowledge-based religious education where humanistic elements of behavior are emphasized, together with either religious observance in the case of the state religious students or a deeper cultural understanding of religion in the case of the state secular students, enhance religious spirituality rather more significantly than the narrow ritualistic and observance-oriented faith-based religious education offered in ultra-orthodox schools. Faith-based religious education may be perceived by students as indoctrination (Dawkins, 2006; Martínez-Torrón, 2005), and thus arouse feelings of resistance by students towards anything related to this type of education, including religious spirituality. Thus it appears that students in ultra-orthodox schools, despite their commitment to ultra-orthodox religious observance, may well resist the development of religious spirituality within totally faith-based religious education because of the negative connotation of possible indoctrination embedded in this educational ideology (following Huttunen, 2003). In addition it appears that the emphasis on observance of precepts and commandments may be developed in ultra-orthodox religious education at the expense of the enhancement of positive feelings towards members of the wider community (following Edgell, Gerteis & Hartmann, 2006; Hammer, 2009; Spiegel, 2011).

CONCLUSION

This chapter highlights the complex relationship between different worldviews underlying religious education and spirituality in the Israeli state Jewish educational system. It appears that totally faith-based religious education offered to students in ultra-orthodox schools is designed almost exclusively to deepen religious observance and behaviour, and is limited in its ability to enhance either religious or humanistic spirituality. Parents of students who attend ultra-orthodox schools insist that these schools complement the home religious outlook which focuses on religious obser-vance at the expense of almost all else including affective education in gen-eral and most especially the promotion of spirituality (following Spiegel, 2011). Knowledge-based religious education, dependent almost entirely on humanistic education, as presented to students in the state secular stream, significantly enhances humanistic spirituality. An integration of faith-based and knowledge-based religious education provided to students in state reli-gious schools significantly enhances religious spirituality and, to a lesser extent, humanistic spirituality.

It appears that the results of the above two studies conducted in the Israeli educational system can offer insights for the policy makers respon-sible for the Israeli educational system as well as for policy makers of other national educational systems that have the goal of enhancing spiri-tuality among their students. The findings indicate that education for the enhancement of spirituality among students seems to be better served by an integrative approach to religious education that promotes a combi-nation of faith-based (religious values) and knowledge-based (humanis-tic values) religious education. This is congruent with the official policy for religious education laid down by the Israeli educational authorities (Ministry of Education, 1994) that emphasizes an integrative and toler-ant approach that could well lead to closer understanding between differ-ent religious sectors within the Israeli Jewish population. It appears that almost totally faith-based or almost exclusively knowledge-based reli-gious education is rather one-sided and narrow, having less of an effect on students' religiosity-related spirituality. A growing number of researchers now argue that enhancement of spirituality contributes to well-being and better mental and physical health (Rosmarin et al., 2009; Lawler-Row, 2010), greater life satisfaction (Steger & Frazier, 2005) and more pro-social behaviors (Gibson, 2008; Hardy & Carlo, 2005), national educa-tional authorities are invited to address the results of this study in order to consider a reform in religious education so as to accommodate the need for enhancement of students' spirituality.

REFERENCES

Bar-Lev, M., & Katz, Y. J. (1991). State religious education in Israel: A unique ideo-logical system. *Panorama—International Journal for Comparative Religious Education, 3*(2), 94–105.

Breitbart, W. (2007). Who needs the concept of spirituality? Human beings seem to! *Palliative and Supportive Care, 5,* 105–106.

Claxton, G. (2002). *Mind expanding: Scientific and spiritual foundations for the schools we need.* Paper presented at the Graduate School of Education Public Lectures (21 October 2002), University of Bristol, UK.

Cohen, A. B. (2002). The importance of spirituality in well-being for Jews and Christians. *Journal of Happiness Studies, 3*(3), 287–310.

Davis, D. E., Hook, J. N., & Worthington, Jr., E. L. (2008). Relational spirituality and forgiveness: The roles of attachment to God, religious coping, and viewing the transgression as a desecration. *Journal of Psychology and Christianity, 27,* 293–301.

Dawkins, R. (2006). *The God delusion.* New York: Bantam Books.

Dillon, M., Wink, P., & Fay, K. (2003). Is spirituality detrimental to generativity? *Journal for the Scientific Study of Religion, 42,* 427–442.

Edgell, P., Gerteis, J., & Hartmann, D. (2006). Atheists as 'other': Moral boundaries and cultural membership in American society. *American Sociological Review, 71*(2), 211–234.

Eisenstadt, S. N. (1996). Comments on the post-modern society. In M. Lissack & B. Knei-Paz (Eds.), *Israel towards the Year 2000* (pp. 19–27). Jerusalem: Magnes Press. (Hebrew)

Ellison, C. G., & Fan, D. (2008). Daily spiritual experiences and psychological well-being among U.S. adults. *Social Indicators Research, 88,* 247–271.

Emmons, R. A. (2000). Is spirituality an intelligence? Motivation, cognition and the psychology of ultimate concern. *The International Journal for the Psychology of Religion, 10*(1), 3–26.

Fisher, J. W. (2009). *Reaching the heart: Assessing and nurturing spiritual well-being via education.* (Unpublished doctoral dissertation). University of Ballarat, Australia.

Gibson, T. (2008). Religion and civic engagement among America's youth. *The Social Science Journal, 45*(3), 504–514.

Gollnick, J. (2005). *Religion and spirituality in the life cycle.* New York: Peter Lang Publishing.

Gordis, R. (1990). Introduction: The commission, the statement, the movement. In Jewish Theological Seminary of America (Eds.), *Emet ve-emunah: Statement of principles of Conservative Judaism* (pp. 9–16). New York: Jewish Theological Seminary of America.

Hammer, J. (2009). *The nature and sequelae of religious discrimination as experienced by atheists.* Paper presented at the 116th Annual Convention of the American Psychological Association 7 August 2009), Toronto, Canada.

Hardy, S. A., & Carlo, G. (2005). Religiosity and pro-social behaviors in adolescence: The mediating role of pro-social values. *Journal of Moral Education, 34,* 231–249.

Huttunen, R. (2003). Habermas and the problem of indoctrination. In M. Peters, P. Ghiraldelli, B. Zarnic, & A. Gibbons (Eds.), *Encyclopedia of philosophy of education.* Retrieved September 11, 2012, from http://www.ffst.hr/ENCYCLO-PAEDIA/doku.php?id=habermas_and_the_problem_of_indoctrination.

Jackson, B. R., & Bergeman, C. S. (2011). How does religiosity enhance well-being? The role of perceived control. *Psychology of Religion and Spirituality, 3*(2), 149–161.

Jacobs, L. (1995). Introduction. In L. Jacobs (Ed.), *The Jewish religion: A companion* (pp. 1–6). New York: Oxford University Press.

Johnstone, B., Yoon, D. P., Franklin, K. L., Schopp, L., & Hinkebein, J. (2009). Re-conceptualizing the factor structure of the brief multidimensional measure of religiousness/spirituality. *Journal of Religion and Health,48*(2), 146–163.

Joss-Kent, P. (2012). *Mother nature versus religion.* Booksie.com Publishers. Retrieved September 20, 2012, from http://www.booksie.com/non-fiction/article/petra_joss_kent/mother-nature-versus-religion/nohead/pdf/ver/8.

Katz, Y. J. (2004). State religious education in Israel: Developmental trends in the Zionist era. In Z. Gross & Y. Dror (Eds.), *Education as a social challenge* (pp. 73–83). Tel-Aviv: Ramot Publishing House, Tel-Aviv University. (Hebrew)

Katz, Y. J. (2006). The core curriculum in Israel: An educational common denominator for all population sectors. In D. Inbar (Ed.), *Towards an educational revolution* (pp. 186–194). Jerusalem: Van Leer Institute and Hakibbutz Hameuchad Publishing House. (Hebrew)

Katz, Y. J. (2007). Values education in the Israeli educational system. In N. Kryger & B. Ravn (Eds.), *Learning beyond cognition* (pp. 291–302). Copenhagen: Danish University of Education Press.

Katz, Y. J. (2010). The state approach to Jewish and non-Jewish education in Israel. *Comparative Education, 46*(3), 325–338.

Katz, Y. J. (2012). Religious education and spirituality: Complementary or contradictory educational concepts? In V. Gersak, H. Korosec, E. Majaron, & N. Turnsec (Eds.), *Promoting the social emotional aspects of education: A multifaceted priority* (pp. 88–93). Ljubljana: University of Ljubljana Press.

Katz, Y. J. (2013). *Spirituality in the Israeli state Jewish educational system.* (Unpublished manuscript).

Kumar, S. (2000). Soul man. *New Scientist, 2243*, 46–49.

Larson, D. B., & Larson, S. S. (2003). Spirituality's potential relevance to physical and emotional health: A brief review of quantitative research. *Journal of Psychology and Theology,31*(1), 37–51.

Lasher, C. (2012). The flowering of ordinary possibilities: Humanistic education and sustainability today. *SGI Quarterly, 68*, 6–7.

Lawler-Row, K. A. (2010). Forgiveness as a mediator of the religiosity-health relationship. *Psychology of Religion and Spirituality, 2*, 1–6.

Martínez-Torrón, J. (2005). School and religion in Spain. *Journal of Church and State, 47*(1), 133–150.

Ministry of Education. (1994). *Shenhar report.* Jerusalem: Pedagogic Secretariat. (Hebrew) Ministry of Education. (2009). *State education bill.* Jerusalem: Division of Society and Youth. Retrieved January 7, 2013, from http://cms. education.gov.il/EducationCMS/Units/Zchuyot/ChukimVeamanot/Chukim/ ChokChinuchMamlachti1953.htm. (Hebrew)

Patrick, J. H., & Kinney, J. M. (2003). Why believe? The effects of religious beliefs on emotional well being. In S. H. McFadden, M. Brennan, & J. H. Patrick (Eds.), *New directions in the study of late life religiousness and spirituality* (pp. 153–170). Binghamton, NY: Haworth Press.

Peterson, C. (2006). The values in action classification of character strengths. In M. Csikszentmihalyi & I. Selga Csikzentmihalyi (Eds.), *A life worth living: Contributions to positive psychology* (pp. 29–48). New York: Oxford University Press.

Piechowski, M. M. (2003). Emotional and spiritual giftedness. In N. Colangelo & G. A. Davis (Eds.), *Handbook of gifted education* (3rd ed., pp. 403–416). Boston: Pearson Education.

Rosmarin, D. H., Pirutinsky, S., Pargament, K. I., & Krumrei, E. J. (2009). Are religious beliefs relevant to mental health among Jews? *Psychology of Religion and Spirituality, 1*, 180–190.

Schermer, V. (2003). *Spirit and psyche: A new paradigm for psychology, psychoanalysis and psychotherapy.* New York: Jessica Kingsley.

Schneiders, S. M. (2003). Religion vs. spirituality: A contemporary conundrum. *Spiritus: A Journal of Christian Spirituality, 3*(20), 163–185.

Seligman, M. E. P., & Csikszentmihalyi, M. (2000). Positive psychology: An introduction. *American Psychologist, 55*(1), 5–14.

Spiegel, E. (2011). *And the study of the Torah is more important than all other precepts.* Jerusalem: The Jerusalem Institute for Israel Studies. (Hebrew)

Starratt, R. J. (2004) The spirituality of presence for educational leaders. In C. Shields, M. Edwards, & A. Sayani (Eds.), *Inspiring practice: Spirituality and educational leadership* (pp. 67–84). Lancaster, PA: Pro-Active Publishers.

Steger, M. F., & Frazier, P. (2005). Meaning in life: One link in the chain from religiousness to wellbeing. *Journal of Counseling Psychology, 52*, 574–582.

Tacey, D. (2004). *The spirituality revolution: The emergence of contemporary spirituality*. Hove: Brunner-Routledge.

Tadmor, Y. (2012). Sustainability, spirituality and essentiality in education. In Y. Tadmor & A. Freiman (Eds.), *Education: Essence and spirit* (pp. 282–288). Tel-Aviv: Mofet Institute. (Hebrew)

Underwood, L., & Teresi, J. (2002). The daily spiritual experience scale: Development, theoretical description, reliability, exploratory factor analysis, and preliminary construct validity using health related data. *Annals of Behavioral Medicine, 24*, 22–33.

van Dierendonck, D. (2012). Spirituality as an essential determinant for the good life, its importance relative to self-determinant psychological needs. *Journal of Happiness Studies,13*(4), 685–700.

Waaijman, K. (2007). What is spirituality? *Acta Theologica, 27*(2), 1–18.

Wills, E. (2009). Spirituality and subjective well-being: Evidences for a new domain in the Personal Well-Being Index. *Journal of Happiness Studies,10*(1), 49–69.

Worthington, Jr., E. L., & Aten, J. D. (2009). Psychotherapy with religious and spiritual clients: An introduction. *Journal of Clinical Psychology: In Session, 65*, 123–130.

Wright, A. (2000). *Spirituality and education*. London: Routledge-Falmer.

Zinnbauer, B. J., & Pargament, K. I. (2005). Religiousness and spirituality. In R. F. Paloutzian & C. L. Park (Eds.), *Handbook of the psychology of religion and spirituality* (pp. 21–42). New York: The Guilford Press.

Part II

Spirituality and Education in the Australasian Region

Part II
Introduction

Marian de Souza

This section of the book brings together multiple voices from Australasia and Asia which offer a variety of regional perspectives on spirituality and education. The countries included are Aotearoa New Zealand, Australia, Bhutan, China, Japan, Singapore and Thailand, some of which share a colonial history so it is not surprising to find both common and diverse elements in their respective histories and practices. The writers have carefully examined the political and historical influences on their educational structures and curricula, and offered specific descriptions of the concept of spirituality as they use it in their individual chapters. Some recognize that in indigenous and Eastern cultures a more holistic understanding of religion and spirituality is evident which develops wisdom and compassion amongst the people. Others acknowledge that spirituality has not always been part of the educational agenda in their countries and, instead, programs have been offered, cultivating spiritual traits of connectedness and belonging and having a sense of responsibility, which are also viewed as desirable characteristics of good citizenship. Nonetheless, all voices argue that spirituality has a distinct role in education to provide nurturing of and wellbeing for their students.

Deborah Fraser and Jane Bone discuss the education system in Aotearoa New Zealand. Aotearoa is a Maori name for New Zealand and both names are used in conjunction with each other, thereby recognizing the influence of Maori culture in the social, educational and political organizations in the country. The research findings offered by both Fraser and Bone, respectively, present different understandings and applications of spirituality and illustrate the fact that spirituality has been part of the New Zealand curriculum for many years. Between the two authors, we gain insights into the broad spectrum of education from early childhood settings to secondary schools, and it is of interest to note the differences between these settings where recent school education policy documents have excluded the word 'spirituality' but it still has a distinct place in the early childhood curriculum. Bone also shows how the New Zealand early childhood curriculum has been very influential in the development of the curriculum in Australia.

The two Australian authors present widely different views. Brendan Hyde identifies the more frequent use of the word 'spirituality' in curriculum and policy documents in the past several years and proceeds to describe a particular approach to learning which may be used to nurture spirituality in children from primary school and early childhood settings. On the other hand, Graham Rossiter examines the secondary education situation to argue that while spirituality may have entered the educational discourse, for the most part it has not really become part of classroom practice. He describes various programs and approaches that could be categorized as Spirituality and Education—such as Religious and Values Education and Personal Development—but makes the point that there is little consistency in the application of spirituality to learning programs across schools.

Two countries that share some features pertaining to history and religion are Bhutan and Thailand. Noa Jones from Bhutan (Chapter 12) and Michael Jones from Thailand (Chapter 16) present detailed pictures of their respective countries as independent kingdoms that were not colonized but have, in the past 70 years or so, opened their doors to outside influences. As a result, they have both introduced a Western-based education system that has tended to erode the influence of Buddhist spirituality amongst their young people. This also reflects the situation in Japan where Shintoism and Buddhism were, once, influential factors in developing spirituality as part of educating young Japanese. However, Yoshiharu Nakagawa (Chapter 14) contends that people have generally become less influenced by their religious traditions and attending to spiritual needs is not a focus. Despite the development of an alternative to religious education in the school system with values-based education, Nakagawa maintains that more needs to be done to recognize a spiritual dimension in education.

Another writer, Ngar-sze Elsa Lau, has provided a detailed examination (Chapter 13) that focuses on four interrelated regions—Mainland China, Hong Kong, Macao and Taiwan. Here we are able to view the conflicts as well as the cooperation between the four regions in striving for an education that will respond to the social and health problems that have become evident amongst their young people. Ngar-sze Lau describes a particular educational program that was introduced in one of the regions—Life Education—and which is now being implemented in various ways in the other regions. Ngar-sze Lau argues that Life Education is one attempt to incorporate spirituality in education.

In the remaining offering (Chapter 15), two authors, Charlene Tan and Kaili Zhang, compare education in Singapore and Hong Kong. Both Tan and Zhang highlight the fact that both these countries share a colonial heritage so that their education systems have been imported from the West. As a result, religious education in one form or another has been offered—for instance, a confessional approach in faith-based schools in Hong Kong or a phenomenological approach in state-based education in Singapore. The role of spirituality in education has not been clearly recognized in these regions and both authors assert that this is something that needs to be addressed.

In general, we hear a range of voices from an array of cultural and religious traditions in this section. Nonetheless, all of the authors identify similar reasons why spirituality should have a role in education. Their ideas and issues are clearly articulated and their concern as educators is apparent as they discuss the problems faced by many of their students. Each of these authors agree that addressing spirituality in education is one way forward to combat these problems and to nurture their children and young people into wholeness and wellness.

8 Taha Wairua
The Spiritual in State Education in Aotearoa New Zealand

Deborah Fraser

INTRODUCTION

Recent years have witnessed a global shift in awareness of indigenous values and practices. This includes the international rights of indigenous peoples to have their narratives and values regarded as valid epistemology and not romanticised as exotic or dismissed as mythical. The decline of modernism in the West has further contributed to the resurgence of ethnic rights including a greater awareness of indigenous worldviews. 'Taha wairua', for instance, is Maori for the spiritual side of humanity. In the New Zealand school curriculum fostering this spiritual side is considered part of the development of well-being for all students. Just what that means, however, is seldom made explicit.

This chapter briefly outlines aspects of Maori spirituality and the impact of colonisation. It notes the incidences of spirituality in the New Zealand school curriculum and discusses the unique and ongoing influence of Maori culture on this curriculum. It concludes with findings from a New Zealand classroom project that focussed on spirituality in state schools. The conclusion has implications for the rights of Maori to an education that is culturally responsive alongside the value of spirituality for all.

INDIGENOUS SPIRITUALITY, COLONISATION
AND EARLY CHRISTIANITY

Maori are the indigenous people of New Zealand and up until the 1860s were the majority of the country's population. Today they comprise approximately 15% of the population, making them the second-largest ethnic group. People of European descent are the majority at 67.6% at the last census. The Maori population is currently increasing with comparatively large numbers of young people (Statistics New Zealand, 2006). Maori language along with English and New Zealand Sign is an official language of New Zealand. For instance, the New Zealand national anthem is sung in both Maori and English at many public occasions such as rugby games, and Maori language is taught in schools but is not compulsory. Despite recent language renewal initiatives, a history of Maori language suppression has resulted in only 4% of New Zealanders speaking Maori (Ka'ai, 2011). New Zealand like many Western countries is also increasingly multicultural (with larger numbers of ethnic groups from Asia and the Pacific, in particular) but remains predominantly monolingual.

The colonisation of New Zealand is a relatively recent event in world history marked by the signing of the Treaty of Waitangi, the founding document of the nation. Signed in 1840 between representatives of the British Crown and 512 Maori leaders, it was "purported to establish a new nation: one where Maori people were promised full participation in the benefits that the new society was to offer" (Bishop, 2005, p. 56). The promise of power sharing was not fulfilled as wars erupted between British settlers and Maori over land ownership and democratic rights. State institutions including the land courts consolidated the subjugation of Maori. Legislation was introduced to make land ownership an individual acquisition which ran counter to the concept of group guardianship of land traditionally practiced by Maori. For Maori, individual land ownership as an economic asset was meaningless and profane. Land was part of Papatuanuku (the earth mother) and was clothed by the children of Tane Mahuta (God of the forest). Maori also identified, then and now, with their local mountain and river as part of their tribal and family whakapapa or genealogy. Their spiritual beliefs made it clear that they were inextricably linked to the land with responsibility for the guardianship of Papatuanuku. Today, Maori are still referred to as tangata whenua, which literally means people of the land, and this spiritual connection is considered part and parcel of their identity. However, through the 20th century, Maori children often found that "their cultural knowledge was unacceptable or belittled, their intentions and motivations misinterpreted, and their language and names mispronounced. This amounted to a systematic assault on their identity and well-being as Maori people" (Bishop, 2005, p. 65). Not surprisingly, Maori failure and poor achievement at school increased despite the fact that they had been a thriving indigenous group with relatively high levels of literacy (a point that is discussed below).

The long- and short-term effects of colonisation are invariably complex but there is compelling global evidence to show that in general terms indigenous people suffer in colonised countries (Bishop, 2012; Illich, 1997; Said, 1993; Shields, Bishop & Mazawi, 2005). The ramifications of colonisation for indigenous people include language loss, poor health, lowered standard of living, high rates of incarceration, low levels of education, and shortened life expectancies. Given these dire trends, the incorporation of indigenous ways of knowing in education is a moral imperative. If education is to benefit all people and not perpetuate injustice then it needs to take seriously the knowledge and beliefs of indigenous people.

Despite the detrimental effects of colonisation, Maori have in many ways preserved their spirituality and adapted what the new religion brought. Prior to the arrival of early European settlers, New Zealand Maori already had strong spiritual beliefs that permeated their everyday lives. "They recognised atua or spiritual powers in nature: in Tane Mahuta's offerings of food and shelter from the forests, in Tangaroa's gifts of fish and shellfish from the sea, even in the cleansing storms and winds of Tawhirimatea" (King, 2003, p. 139). Maori believed in a range of animist Gods, emanating from the lineage of the primordial parent Gods, Papatuanuku (the earth mother) and Ranginui (the sky father). Many Maori were also involved in lucrative trade both within and beyond New Zealand. The arrival of the Christian missionaries around 1814 into this thriving culture initially made little impact.

A stumbling block was the missionary attitude towards Maori spiritual beliefs as naïve or even dangerous. In 1816 the first mission school was opened with the explicit intent of teaching the Bible and assimilating Maori into British culture (New Zealand History Online, n.d.). There was little interest by Maori however until some missionaries began to learn the Maori language and took an interest in Maori spiritual beliefs (Biggs, 1966). Maori translations of the Bible, the prayer book and numerous hymns also helped to raise the profile of Christianity within Maoridom. It is interesting to note that in the 1830s and 40s there were more literate Maori than Pakeha (white New Zealanders), many of whom accessed the written word through the printing and dissemination of both their own narratives and the Christian Bible (Elsmore, 1999).

Moreover, the blending of Maori and Christian ideas produced some unique interpretations with Maori adapting or adopting Christian practices where and how they saw fit (Owens, 1992). This blending and selection of ideas, beliefs and rituals is evident today in events such as the powhiri (formal welcoming ceremony). Maori did not completely abandon their traditional spiritual beliefs. Instead, some adapted their beliefs to include a supreme God alongside the Gods of nature. King concluded that "Maori did not so much convert *to* Christianity as convert Christianity, like so much else that Pakeha brought, to their own purposes" (2003, p. 163).

A census undertaken towards the end of the 1800s found that most of the British settlers declared a religious, mainly Christian, affiliation. Anglicans came to outnumber the others but the Church of England did not become the established authority. Christian groups had an influence on education and welfare, especially during the gold-rush years in the 19th century with church-sponsored schools and welfare support for destitute women and neglected children (Graham, 1992). Mormons from the US became more noticeable after 1870 and are a thriving group in New Zealand. Their national temple in Hamilton, New Zealand, was the first in the southern hemisphere.

Despite a general tolerance of different Christian groups, the 1877 Education Act signalled the formal separation of church and state due to disagreement over which version of Christianity and which version of the Bible would be used. State schools as a result of this Act were obliged to provide a free, compulsory and secular education, although legally this only pertained to primary schools.

Today there are more than 400 'special character' (mostly Roman Catholic) schools which teach religion as a central part of the curriculum and receive full state funding, but most state schools remain secular. While the secular is distinct from religion it does not preclude spirituality and in New Zealand, spirituality is part of the state school curriculum. Its survival, however, is precarious which has ramifications for Maori and for all students.

SPIRITUALITY IN THE STATE SCHOOL CURRICULUM

The New Zealand school curriculum includes a number of references, past and present, to spirituality. In 1937, the state school syllabus promoted the following liberal policy:

> There still survives in the schools a great deal of the old-fashioned formalism that regarded education more as a mechanical process than as a means of securing for every child the fullest possible spiritual, mental and physical development. It is hoped that the present Syllabus will give encouragement to those teachers—and fortunately there are many of them—who regard the child not as inanimate clay in the hands of the potter, or as an empty vessel sent them for filling, but as a soul, a personality, capable of being developed and trained for the wider service of humanity. (Department of Education, 1937, p. 65)

This statement reflects a very contemporary view and could have been written in this decade. While the spiritual and the soul are not defined in this syllabus, at least they are not ignored. Little has been mentioned in official curriculum documents since this progressive statement on the subject but the word 'spiritual' has reappeared. A curriculum statement in the early 1990s acknowledged spirituality within the realm of health, referring to the "spiritual dimensions of a person's growth" (Ministry of Education, 1993, p. 16). As with the 1937 syllabus, care was taken to avoid mention of religion or religious beliefs in keeping with the separation of church and state. Spirituality, with its rather vague connotations, is considered less controversial and more palatable for state education policy.

Passing mention is also made of spirituality in the now defunct art education syllabus which stated, "Art education helps students to respond to their experience in ways that enrich their sensory, emotional, spiritual and intellectual awareness" (Department of Education, 1989, p. 6), and "because art is closely linked to social, cultural and spiritual action and belief, its contribution is particularly important" (p. 20). It is interesting to note that in the current arts curriculum (which combines music, art, drama and dance) there is less reference to a spiritual dimension. Only two very general statements are made: the assertion in the preamble that the arts "enrich our emotional and spiritual lives" (Ministry of Education, 2000, p. 9) and the rather vague claim that "visual arts link social, cultural, and spiritual action and belief" (p. 70).

The Health and Physical Education curriculum statement (Ministry of Education, 1999) attempted a definition of spirituality. It is here that the relationship between spirituality and religion is mentioned. It defines spiritual well-being (in Maori, taha wairua) as "the values and beliefs that determine the way people live, the search for meaning and purpose in life, and personal identity and self-awareness. (For some individuals and communities, spiritual well-being is linked to a particular religion; for others, it is not.)" (p. 31). This statement signals an inclusive approach that accommodates religious beliefs but is not limited to religion nor does it mean the teaching of religion. The health and physical education curriculum definition is so broad, however, that it risks trying to be all things to all people and therefore, nothing much to anyone at all, a criticism that is common in reviews of spirituality (e.g., Thatcher, 1999). Nonetheless, it does attempt to be inclusive rather than exclusive and the challenge of any inclusive policy is ensuring that heterogeneity is acknowledged within an all-encompassing paradigm. In this case it does not mean an unquestioned homogeneity but rather the embracing of multiple views and expressions. There is room within the definition for the religious and the nonreligious to be acknowledged, underlining the broader meaning of the word 'spirituality'. In many respects this makes 'spirituality' a less divisive word than 'religion' and a word that acknowledges the plurality of contemporary society. As noted earlier, spirituality also allows room for traditional Maori spiritual beliefs to coexist with religious ones.

New Zealand's state school curriculum, through these documents, makes evident the belief that spirituality is not antithetical to secularity nor does it exclude those who have a religious faith. Nevertheless, the latest curriculum policy document (Ministry of Education, 2007) makes the briefest allusion yet to spirituality. It is couched in Maori (as taha wairua), with no English translation, and only in relation to health and well-being. This raises questions as to the longevity of spirituality in the state curriculum and has implications for both teachers and students. It also implies that spirituality is largely superfluous and can easily be minimised or made redundant.

In a number of ways Maori culture has influenced and continues to influence how spirituality is defined and regarded in New Zealand state education. It seems that without this influence the mention of spirituality today in the curriculum may be erased and for many reasons, Maori students, in particular, may be disenfranchised if spirituality disappears from the curriculum. Some of these influences and reasons, respectively, are outlined next.

CURRENT AND FUTURE ISSUES

While the curriculum provides a secular view of spirituality it also takes cognisance of a Maori perspective with reference to Durie[1] (1994) and his whare tapawha model (literally, the four walls of the house, a metaphor for the dimensions of each person). In this model, well-being or hauora comprises four components: the physical, the mental and emotional (taken as one), the social, and the spiritual. Durie argued that all four dimensions are necessary for strength and overall health and that there are reciprocal influences between each one.[2] It is no surprise that well-being includes a spiritual dimension in his model as the spiritual is regarded as a natural part of te ao Maori (the Maori world) and also one of the paths to learning (Pere, 1995). In addition, there is an expectation in Maoridom that spiritual abilities are used in the service of others (Bevan-Brown, 2011a). This obligation to use one's talents to enable others is strongly embedded in the cultural fabric. Bevan-Brown (2011b) argued that this "stems back to traditional times when it was believed that gifts were handed down from the gods, not for personal aggrandisement but to help one's whanau, hapu and iwi (tribe)" (p. 12).

A strong sense of ancestral connection permeates Maori philosophy with the belief that Maori as individuals, families and tribes are inextricably linked to the living, the land and those extended family members who have died. As one Maori teacher commented:

> When I talk with a child, about what he is doing, I do not just see that child in front of me. I see all the people connected to that child, going back generations in a great cluster. So I feel that whatever I'm saying is not just to that child but to all his relations, all those who are living and dead. I also realise that what the child does is not just his efforts but reflects a whole line of influences.

Hence, approaches in schools that are based upon individual analysis of a student's observable behaviour are severely limited if cognisance is not taken of this strong sense of intergenerational, past-present connectedness. A focus on the individual, visible, autonomous self has little relevance or credibility from this Maori perspective. One of the main challenges for teacher education has been to understand Maori perspectives, such as their strong group and family orientation, and consider implications for practice (Bishop, 2012). Most teachers in New Zealand are Pakeha (white New Zealanders) and many of the students they teach are increasingly *not* Pakeha given the country's growing multiculturalism. The Maori population is the second-largest group with numbers increasing with one out of three under 15 years of age (Statistics New Zealand, 2006), yet Maori students out-number other cultural groups in this country when it comes to referrals for learning and behavioural support. Understanding Maori perspectives on a range of issues is imperative, therefore, if teachers are to build bridges of respect, communication and support with the country's indigenous culture (Bevan-Brown, 2011b; Whitinui, 2011). This inevitably includes taha wairua, the spiritual side of well-being, which is an inextricable dimension of Maoridom and humanity.

It is not unusual for state schools with high proportions of Maori students to greet visitors through the kawa or protocol of the local iwi (tribe) or hapu (subtribe). Young people, Maori and non-Maori alike, learn the ways of knowing that are central to the powhiri and it is a distinct example of where Maori epistemology and ontology determine how things are done. The influence of Maori views of spirituality and beliefs about existence on education constitute a vast area that this chapter can only introduce. Generally, there is no division between spirituality and the rest of human experience in te ao Maori (the Maori world) as captured in Durie's model. So the powhiri is as much a spiritual experience as an emotional, physical, intellectual and social one. For instance, Koro Apirana, the grandfather in the book *The Whale Rider*, explains that such a relationship is integral to Maori culture:

'You have all seen the whale,' he said. 'You have all seen the sacred sign tattooed on its head. Is the moko there by accident or by design? Why did a whale of its appearance strand itself here and not at Wainui? Does it belong in the real world or the unreal world?'

'The real,' someone called.

'Is it natural or supernatural?'

'It is supernatural,' a second voice said.

Koro Apirana put up his hands to stop the debate. 'No,' he said, 'it is both. It is a reminder of the oneness which the world once had. It is the pito joining past and present, reality and fantasy. It is both. It is both,' he thundered, 'and if we have forgotten the communion then we have ceased to be Maori.' (Ihimaera, 1987, p. 115)

This worldview emphasises that the rational and empirical is not in opposition to the spiritual and intangible but rather, part of the wholeness of what it means to be human. Such wholeness is evident in the powhiri (formal welcoming ceremony), karakia (prayer), whaikorero (speech making), kapahaka (action dance) and waiata (song) which are explicit expressions of both Maori culture and spirituality. These expressions are evident in state schools where there is strong Maori leadership in the school and where Maori culture is honoured. Education for indigenous people such as Maori should not come at the expense of their cultural values, but "rather should enhance further the relationship between culture and education" (Whitinui, 2004, p. 89). The importance of the spiritual dimension to Maori and their unified perspective on the integration of the spiritual with the temporal and secular cannot be separated from the learning-teaching context if schools are to be culturally responsive.

IMPLICATIONS FOR TEACHERS

Maori views on spirituality have implications for teachers in state schools. The following examples are drawn from a New Zealand study on spirituality in state education (Fraser & Grootenboer, 2004). The study involved nine teachers from two multicultural primary schools. Six of the participants identified as Christian and three as agnostic. Four were Maori and two of them taught largely in the Maori language, incorporating a Maori worldview in their pedagogy. Data collection consisted of a brief survey and three focus group interviews; two at each school site and one combined interview. The data analysis reveals that the most common theme or core category (Charmaz, 2005) to which the other themes related was connection. The teachers shared a number of experiences they believed fostered this sense of connection. Some of these had nothing to do explicitly with the teachers' lessons but indicate instead a climate that these teachers fostered. This is illustrated by an account from Helena's classroom about a group of Maori boys:

> One of my boys had a problem with his parents splitting up and he came in and all my kids knew something was wrong and all the boys said, "Are you all right?" He didn't answer but they sensed something and all shuffled over and gave him a hug and I'm sitting there going, "Wow, how did that happen?" I could see my girls wanted to hug him as well, but they knew that was for boys. [Normally] you never would see these big boys go up and give a hug and sit there and rub his back. He was feeling really good [comforted]. And that's not something you teach them, that's sort of, they sort of know and that just happens. I was sitting there feeling really good.

Helena identified this as a moment where the children's spirituality came to the fore in her classroom and she was particularly moved by the boys' lack of self-consciousness as they supported their classmate. Amongst these 11- and 12-year-old boys it was not considered normal or 'cool' to hug and comfort one another, and yet there was a sense that they knew this was the appropriate thing to do and no one seemed concerned about what the others might think about them. Moreover, Helena appreciated the significance of this event for all the boys and had the sensitivity to not interfere or comment.

Another example that was student initiated occurred in Marama's classroom. In this instance the sense of connection reported by Marama was beyond the visible and temporal:

Marama: A few years ago I had a girl come into the unit and she was really, really, really shy and she could hardly speak and you couldn't hear her when she spoke. She had really low self-esteem. After a while . . . because she was a girl, the expectation is that the girls in that class would train up in karanga (the formal calling on of visitors in welcome at the powhiri) and the boys in the class would train up in whaikorero (speech making). So we were preparing her for this and I was really dreading the day when it was going to be her turn because I knew she would get all teary and nervous, and you just know when kids are not ready. One day she surprised me and I can't remember who was coming into the class or school but she said she wanted to do it. So she puts on the skirt and she goes out there and I remember standing in the room really nervous thinking, "Oh my God she's going to crack", and then when she opened her mouth I could hear her tupuna (ancestor) come out of her body and that was just sooo awesome. After it was all over I just held her. I felt like crying because suddenly she had found this voice. It was wicked.

Deborah: So the tone, the sound, the resonance, everything was . . . ?

Marama: Everything was not her voice; it was an old lady from her line. 'Cause we're not related to her so I didn't know who she was . . .

Deborah: Do you think she was conscious at any stage of that? Was she . . . ?

Marama: She was going with the flow. I was watching her and she was just away and then afterwards when she came back she said, "Was that all right?"

I said, "You sounded so awesome you know I could hear your tupuna in you" and she understood what I meant by that and she didn't get frightened; she was just all smiles and beams.

Deborah: How did the other children respond to her after that?

Marama: After that, it was like okay who's going to karanga and everybody was pushing her out the door, you know . . .

Deborah: So it changed how they related to her as . . .

Marama: Oh yes she became [more confident] . . .

Deborah: And how she was viewed and valued?

Marama: Oh Yeah. Newfound respect. And her parents were so overwhelmed, like her mum cried and you know her dad was just standing with his head down and you could just see the pride.

This experience appeared transformational for the girl and moving for her parents. She had risen to the occasion in a way that belied her timorous demeanour. Moreover, her transformation appeared to be more than just fleeting as this experience changed the way in which the other children related to her. They recognised, for the first time, her leadership qualities and her skill in the karanga. The teacher's explanation reflected Maori tikanga (or cultural beliefs)—gifts, talents, strengths and courage are passed down by ancestors, genetically and spiritually. It is also common in te ao Maori to consider a close and ongoing relationship between the living and the dead, the natural and the supernatural as discussed earlier.

Given that teachers are often socioculturally distanced from many of the children they teach (Hargreaves, 2001), they often struggle to connect with children who belong to cultures different from their own (Delpit, 1995). How, then, does a majority culture (in this case, Pakeha) make sense of and space for the beliefs of a minority culture when the subject matter is sensitive as is the case with spirituality? The following extract provides a response to this difficult question:

> One of the most touching things that happened was a little boy in my room last year and this year and they're brothers and they both wanted to make their brother a birthday card and their brother died before they were born. And on Mother's Day they make their mum a card and that says you know, we love you and this card is from . . . and they always add their dead brother's name to theirs and to me that's really cool. When we go round and do statistics and graphing and how many children in your family, you know Te Manu will talk about Anaru, even though he's dead he's still my brother and really open so that's cool, so you put two brothers and a sister. He gets in our graph because the child is kept as important in the family structure. It's important for him to feel that he's included in his world and I could shut that down so easily. I could say, "No! he's not alive, he doesn't count". It's easier to shut it down than it is to nurture it. You know just because people aren't in our world any more, they're still part of us. I get quite teary about that story. It's funny, it's always been sitting in the back of my mind, that's the child coming to you and saying this is important and we've got to value that moment and nurture it.

It seems that the teacher, who is not Maori, found a way to honour the relationship between life and death in a naturally inclusive way. Her willingness to listen to the child and include his acknowledgement of his dead brother showed a sensitivity to what was deeply important to that child. The seamless relationship between life and death is a central belief amongst many Maori and is acknowledged in countless ways from the structure of the wharenui (meeting house) to the karanga at the powhiri. This example from a primary classroom illustrates how this spiritual value can be acknowledged within a secular context in a natural and inclusive fashion.

How we respond to children coping with the death of a loved one is important; the extract shows how teachers can create a climate where "children can safely bring what they know and who they are into the learning relationship" (Bishop, 2012, p. 44).

CONCLUSION

The extracts above provide illustrations of how spirituality can be expressed in state schools in ways that honour spiritual beliefs. The wider purpose of education is not to reinforce injustice and the oppressive effects of colonisation. Yet there is much evidence internationally to show that indigenous people fare badly in colonised countries (Bishop, 2012; Illich, 1997; Said, 1993; Shields, Bishop & Mazawi, 2005). Addressing this is complex and requires multiple initiatives across the domains of economics, health, politics and education. An appreciation and encouragement of the spiritual dimension goes some small but significant way towards creating schools that embrace rather than disenfranchise Maori. Schools that honour spirituality and find ways for nurturing spiritual expression avoid deficit or exotic views of Maori culture and instead, build respectful ways of relating to what it means to be Maori.

A current issue is the scant mention of spirituality in the latest curriculum document. It is mentioned only once and in terms of 'taha wairua' (the spiritual side) within health education. It raises the risk of leaving children spiritually bereft (Hyde, Ota & Yust, 2012) within state schools. It could be argued that without the influence of Maori culture today, the spiritual dimension may not feature in education policy despite the fact that it was first mentioned in the 1937 syllabus. This runs the risk of demarcating spirituality as a mainly Maori concern and of little relevance to others. While this chapter has deliberately focussed upon the important influence of Maori culture the question remains about the place of spirituality in the education of all children. The current curriculum is ardent in its desire that young people are enterprising, confident and curious, becoming "active seekers, users and creators of knowledge" (Ministry of Education, 2007, p. 8). But it is silent on the nurturing of spirituality for and with children. This silence is one that requires urgent discussion and debate if education is to remain relevant to Maori and speak deeply to all children.

NOTES

1. Mason Durie is a retired professor of psychiatry. For 40 years he was a leader in health and in 2010 was knighted for services to Maori health and public health services.
2. Salter (2000) explained that an earlier model with five sides existed (known as the niho taniwha or dragon's teeth) with the fifth dimension referring to whenua or land, reinforcing the close association Maori have with land. It may have been omitted due to the political ramifications of land claims, many of which are ongoing.

REFERENCES

Bevan-Brown, J. (2011a). Gifted and talented Maori learners. In R. Moltzen (Ed.), *Gifted and talented: New Zealand perspectives* (3rd ed., pp. 82–110). Auckland: Pearson.

Bevan-Brown, J. (2011b). Indigenous conceptions of giftedness. In W. Vialle (Ed.), *Giftedness from an Indigenous perspective* (pp. 10–23). Wollongong, NSW: AAEGT/DEEWR.

Biggs, B. G. (1966). Maori myths and traditions. In A. H. McLintock (Ed.), *Encyclopaedia of New Zealand* (pp. 447–454).Wellington: Government Printer.

Bishop, R. (2005). Pathologizing the lived experiences of the Indigenous Maori people of Aotearoa/New Zealand. In C. Shields, R. Bishop, & A. Mazawi, *Pathologizing practices: The impact of deficit thinking on education* (pp. 55–84). New York: Peter Lang.

Bishop, R. (2012). Pretty difficult: Implementing kaupapa Maori theory in English-medium secondary schools. *New Zealand Journal of Educational Studies: Te Hautaki Matai Matauranga o Aotearoa, 47*(2), 38–50.

Charmaz, K. (2005). Grounded theory in the 21st century: Applications for advancing social justice studies. In N. K. Denzin & Y. S. Lincoln (Eds.), *The Sage handbook of qualitative research* (3rd ed., pp. 507–536). Thousand Oaks, CA: Sage.

Delpit, L. (1995). *Other people's children: Cultural conflict in the classroom.* New York: New Press.

Department of Education. (1937). *Syllabus of instruction for public schools.* Wellington: Government Printer.

Department of Education. (1989). *Art education: Junior classes to form 7—Syllabus for schools.* Wellington: Learning Media.

Durie, M. (1994). *Whaiora: Maori health development.* Auckland: Oxford University Press.

Elsmore, B. (1999). *Mana from heaven: A century of Maori prophets in New Zealand* (2nd ed.). Auckland: Reed Publishing Ltd.

Fraser, D., & Grootenboer, P. (2004). Nurturing spirituality in secular classrooms. *International Journal of Children's Spirituality, 9*(3), 307–320.

Graham, J. (1992). Settler society. In G. W. Rice (Ed.), *The Oxford history of New Zealand* (2nd ed., pp. 112–140). Auckland: Oxford University Press.

Hargreaves, A. (2001). Emotional geographies of teaching. *Teachers College Record, 103*(6), 1056–1080.

Hyde, B., Ota, C., & Yust, K. (2012). Are we leaving our children spiritually bereft? *International Journal of Children's Spirituality, 17*(3), 201–202.

Ihimaera, W. (1987). *The whale rider.* Auckland: Reed Publishing.

Illich, I. (1997). Development as planned poverty. In M. Rahnema & V. Bawtree (Eds.), *The post-development reader* (pp. 94–101). London: Zed Books.

Ka'ai, T. (2011). Imagining Maori success in education in the 21st century. In P. Whitinui (Ed.), *Kia tangi te titi: Permission to speak* (pp. 215–226). Wellington: NZCER Press.

King, M. (2003). *The Penguin history of New Zealand.* Auckland: Penguin Books.

Ministry of Education. (1993). *The New Zealand curriculum framework.* Wellington: Learning Media.

Ministry of Education. (1999). *Health and physical education in the New Zealand curriculum.* Wellington: Learning Media.

Ministry of Education. (2000). *The arts in the New Zealand curriculum.* Wellington: Learning Media.

Ministry of Education. (2007). *The New Zealand curriculum*. Wellington: Learning Media.

New Zealand History Online (n.d.). *The Christian missionaries*. Retrieved March 30, 2013, from http://www.nzhistory.net.nz/culture/the-missionaries.

Owens, J. M. R. (1992). New Zealand before annexation. In G. W. Rice (Ed.), *The Oxford history of New Zealand* (2nd ed., pp. 28–53). Auckland: Oxford University Press.

Pere, R. (1995). *Te wheke: A celebration of infinite wisdom*. Wairoa: Ao Ako Global Learning.

Said, E. (1993). *Culture and imperialism*. New York: Knopf.

Salter, G. (2000). Marginalising indigenous knowledge in teaching physical education: The sanitising of hauora (well-being) in the new HPE curriculum. *Journal of Physical Education, 33*(1), 5–16.

Shields, C., Bishop, R., & Mazawi, A. (2005). *Pathologizing practices: The impact of deficit thinking on education*. New York: Peter Lang.

Statistics New Zealand. 2006 Census Data. Retrieved from http://www.stats.govt.nz/Census/2006CensusHomePage.aspx

Thatcher, A. (1999). *Spirituality and the curriculum*. London: Cassell.

Whitinui, P. (2004). The Indigenous factor: The role of kapa haka as a culturally responsive learning intervention. *Waikato Journal of Education, 10*, 85–98.

Whitinui, P. (Ed.). (2011). *Kia tangi te tītī/Permission to speak: Successful schooling for Māori students in the 21st century—Issues, challenges and alternatives*. Wellington: New Zealand Council of Educational Research Press.

9 Spirituality and Early Childhood Education in New Zealand and Australia

Past, Present and Future

Jane Bone

INTRODUCTION

The role of spirituality in early childhood education has been acknowledged in both Australia and New Zealand. In New Zealand the spiritual has been embedded in the early childhood curriculum, *Te Whariki*, since 1996 (Ministry of Education, 1996). In Australia spirituality has been included in The Early Years Learning Framework for Australia (EYLF) produced by the Australian Government Department of Education, Employment and Workplace Relations (DEEWR, 2009). This chapter is primarily written from a New Zealand perspective and highlights the importance of spirituality in that context. Research is presented from New Zealand and Australia and the historical and cultural connections between these countries are acknowledged. Also noted, are the reciprocal agreements and respect, despite disparities in size, population and wealth, that bind the two countries together as allies in the Pacific region. Narratives and discourses that construct understandings of spirituality in both places are described. These connections are emphasised in terms of early childhood education and spirituality, and a wider, more political view of children and childhood in these places is presented.

A research study carried out in three early childhood settings in New Zealand is discussed where a major finding about the spiritual experience of young children in New Zealand was that an "everyday spirituality" (Bone, 2007, 2010a) is possible in early childhood settings. This qualitative case study research took place in a Montessori preschool, a Rudolph Steiner kindergarten and in a small private kindergarten. Teachers, parents and children participated. More recent research with a group of teachers in Australia (City of Casey Early Childhood Research Collective. (2012).) highlights the voices of educators as they make links to the Australian framework (DEEWR, 2009). An aspect of this research included a spiritual perspective in their interpretation of curriculum learning outcomes. The Australian framework uses the definition of 'curriculum' from the New Zealand document, *Te Whariki* (Ministry of Education, 1996) and this shared meaning emphasises the strong association between the two countries and gives credibility to the connections made in this chapter.

CONTEXT AND HISTORY

New Zealand, an island in the Pacific, had already been settled for centuries when it was given this name by Dutch explorers in the 1640s. The name achieved this final form from the time of Cook's explorations in the 1770s (Salmond, 2003). It is also known as Aotearoa, or 'land of the long white cloud'. This name is based, as many indigenous place names are, on close observation of the landscape; the sky in New Zealand is often streaked with clouds that follow the line of the horizon. The indigenous people of New Zealand are collectively known as Māori and the people who came from elsewhere identify as Pākehā—non-Māori or, more specifically, as European, Asian or Pasifika peoples (Tongan, Samoan or from Fiji, Nuie or the Cook Islands). New Zealand society is changing like everywhere else in the world as a result of human mobility and globalisation. Despite this, the notion of partnership and the emphasis on biculturalism persists, primarily because of the political act that brought Māori and Pākehā into partnership through the Treaty of Waitangi/Te Tiriti o Waitangi signed in 1840. Not all Māori Chiefs signed this document that created a partnership with the English Crown but enough did so to make the Treaty a lasting and influential document. This Treaty still underpins political decision-making, and the notion of partnership, while contested, was key to the construction of a bicultural early childhood curriculum document, *Te Whāriki*, in 1996 (Ministry of Education, 1996).

Historically New Zealand is a place where the stranger, as explorer and adventurer, was met with some enthusiasm because of trading possibilities and because there were shared interests between peoples (Salmond, 2003). Important relationships forged bonds between indigenous Māori and new settlers and also meant that conflict was inevitable. In documentation about these conflicts spirituality is always present and some of the leaders in times of war were also important spiritual influences. In an account about *Parihaka*, a small community that produced a great leader, Te Whiti o Rongomai, there is a description of him as being influential and having "spiritual authority, incorruptible integrity and innovatory leadership" (Savage, 2005, p. 14). In New Zealand, like any place with an indigenous population, spirituality is all about deep relationships with the land, acknowledged in the *United Nations Declaration on the Rights of Indigenous People* (2008, p. 2). This document affirms the right of indigenous people to their "cultures, spiritual traditions, histories and philosophies, especially their rights to their lands, territories and resources". In terms of relationships in society Dei (2011, p. 4) points out that "indigenous knowledge speaks of the inseparability and inter-dependence of selves and the

collective". This orientation to life "heralds the mind, body, and spirit connections and connectedness of society, culture and nature in the ways we
come to know ourselves and our worlds" (Dei, 2011, p. 4).

Historical accounts from New Zealand include well-documented stories of battles and struggles, including Binney's *Redemption Songs* (1997),
a study of prophets and heroes. These stories have spiritual significance
as they have seeped into the national psyche and remain attached to the
sense of place. The importance of a sense of place is reflected in the New
Zealand curriculum through the prominence given to 'belonging' as an
aspect of learning that is essential for children. Belonging as a strand in the
early childhood curriculum for New Zealand is also featured in The Early
Years Learning Framework for Australia: *Being, Belonging and Becoming*
(DEEWR, 2009). In New Zealand it is part of the curriculum that children
are required to learn about their place in the land and to know their local
mountains, rivers and other significant landmarks. In this way children and
their families have a 'place to stand' or *turangawaewae* and this enables
them to have a strong sense of community and spiritual ties to the land
which are affirmed through the development of a strong sense of identity,

THE IMAGE OF THE CHILD

The traditional image of the child in New Zealand is of a 'free spirit'. This is
a romantic image of the child as understood by Rousseau, an 18th century
French philosopher who proposed that children should be unfettered and
free, allowed to "grow up in accordance with nature" (Cunningham, 2005,
p. 63). The free spirit is at once a child of nature defined by innocence and
purity, an image that has links to the colonising notion of 'the noble savage' (Vercoe, 2004, p. 36). This image is linked to the idealisation of New
Zealand as an isolated island perceived to be an unspoiled Paradise, the
"geography of our imagination" (Julian, 2004, p. 112). Reedy (2003, p. 72)
described a traditional Māori image of the child as embodying "the spark
of godliness in each human being" and acknowledged the importance of
the sacred in relation to young children. These images of the child as inno-
cent or redemptive (Dahlberg & Moss, 2005) in an untouched landscape
have been challenged by events in recent years. Like many places in the
world, New Zealand is prey to global changes and has suffered from man-
made and natural disasters, for example, oil spills, mining disasters and
the Christchurch earthquake. Some sectors of the population work hard to
retain a 'clean and green' ecologically friendly environmental image. However, the arcadian dream (Vercoe, 2004) that underpins ideas of a spiritual
childhood in New Zealand exists as a feature of postcolonial society with
all the challenges this entails.

In educational encounters, teachers need to see beyond the notion of
spirituality as an extension of the free spirit, somehow disconnected from

the rest of life. Thus, the finding that in early educational contexts an "everyday spirituality" (Bone, 2007) is possible had these implications: spirituality is in the day to day renewal of relationships (Bone, 2008), in the rituals and celebrations that mark the days, weeks and seasons of the year (Bone, 2010b) and the spiritual life of the child may be affirmed daily in play and the imagination (Bone, 2010a). This research advocated for a spirituality that permeates daily life and at the same time goes beyond it; this is the paradox of *everyday spirituality.*

CURRICULUM AND CONTEXT

New Zealand is the context for the early childhood curriculum *Te Whāriki* (the woven mat). (Ministry of Education, 1996) and is thought of in spiritual terms as it is increasingly regarded in New Zealand as a *taonga*, a treasured artefact. It is a unique document in that it reflects both the Māori and Pākehā language and culture and attempts to reconcile different worldviews. It has defined the field of early childhood education in New Zealand, while being recognised as internationally significant (Carr & May, 2000) and influencing the national curriculum framework for Australia (DEEWR, 2009). The Australian curriculum describes spirituality as "a sense of awe and wonder" (DEEWR, 2009, p. 46), a descriptor often used for spirituality that affirms the capacity of children for curiosity and the ability to have an appreciation of the marvellous in everyday life (Bone, 2010a).

Definitions

Rresearch about spirituality was underpinned by the curriculum document *Te Whariki* (Ministry of Education, 1996) and used the following working definition for spirituality:

> [It] connects people to each other, to all living things, to nature and the universe. Spirituality is a way of appreciating the wonder and mystery of everyday life. It alerts me to the possibility for love, happiness, goodness, peace and compassion in the world. (Bone, 2007, p. 9)

In the curriculum document, spirituality was about being connected to land, belonging and having a sense of wellbeing. The opening aspirational statement articulated a wish that children grow up to be

> competent and confident learners and communicators, healthy in mind, body and spirit, secure in their sense of belonging and in the knowledge that they make a valued contribution to society. (Ministry of Education, 1996, p. 9)

In Australia, the spiritual has been defined in the EYLF as "a range of human experiences including a sense of awe and wonder, and an exploration of being and knowing" (DEEWR, 2009, p. 46). The inclusion of spirituality in both documents is an acknowledgement of the importance of holistic approaches to education and a growing emphasis on what Martin (2005, p. 29) calls "relatedness", a sense of connection that encompasses all dimensions, the physical, emotional, cognitive and spiritual.

In Aotearoa indigenous knowledge has contributed to understandings about spirituality, or 'spiritualities' (Bone, 2010a); the pluralisation of the word indicates that spirituality can be understood in multiple ways (Bergin & Smith, 2004). Darragh (2004, p. 2) notes, "as one of the last places on the surface of the planet to play host to human beings, Aotearoa New Zealand has been the receptacle of many spiritualities developed in places across the Pacific Ocean". This privileging of the multiple is endorsed by Martin (2005, p. 28) who in commenting about the danger of generic understandings of her own Aboriginal culture suggests that "one size does not fit all because the one-size-fits-all model is not respectful".

Myths and Sense of Place

The history of Aotearoa New Zealand includes narratives that filter through a network of fact and myth. Young children hear that Maui, the trickster god, dragged the North Island of New Zealand up from the sea when out fishing with his brothers (New Zealand in History, 2012). The North Island is shaped like a fishhook and from this introduction to mythic stories children learn that place is important and unique as they are introduced to special stories about the formation of the land. An understanding of place and in particular an emphasis on 'the land' is important when the connection to the land is a source of spirituality as it is in New Zealand. Some Māori people may describe themselves as 'tangata whenua' or people of the land. In translation from *te reo* Māori (the Māori language) *tangata* means people and *whenua* means both the placenta, or afterbirth, and land (Pere, 1991). In New Zealand it is a spiritual practice to return the placenta to the land and this ritual connected to birth is something that many people appreciate as new life is celebrated and marked by this symbolic connection to the earth. If families and communities choose to recognise the spiritual there are opportunities for doing so and it is possible to recognise the importance of children as spiritual beings through practices such as this.

The Right to Spiritual Beliefs

In New Zealand, at the time of the signing of the Treaty of Waitangi, there was a commitment to tolerance of other religions that continues to the present (Human Rights Commission, 2012). Called "the most secular country in the world" (Geering, 2005, p. 20), people in Aotearoa New Zealand can worship whoever or wherever they like. New Zealanders engage with spirituality and do so from a position that affirms pluralism. Pluralism is the recognition and tolerance of the beliefs of others, an acceptance of the many rather than one, and an acknowledgement of minority, and occasionally unusual beliefs. Likewise in Australia efforts are made to acknowledge diversity, and tolerance of multiple approaches to the spiritual can be seen as a feature of a post-secular society. Recently, Fischer, Hotam and Wexler (2012) stated that "religion, which was the first to go in the long shadow of modernity's triumph, was more easily vanquished in the names of science, rationality, and Enlightenment. It survived mostly in compartmentalization, as the separate sphere of 'the sacred'" (p. 261). It appears that including the sacred in society answers a fairly universal imperative.

Both curriculum documents, in New Zealand and Australia, put emphasis on the partnership with parents and families (DEEWR, 2009; Ministry of Education, 1996). It is seen as part of the ethos of quality early childhood settings. Many ideas can be conceptualised as spiritual in secular societies. Teachers in the original study (Bone, 2007) talked about living an ethical life, being green and environmentally conscious, tolerant of difference and familiar with their own cultural and family values. To recognise the spiritual for these educators was to be tolerant and accepting of difference.

IMPLICATIONS FOR AUSTRALIA

In New Zealand the influence of indigenous spiritualty, linked to well-being, contributed to a bicultural framework and made a consideration of spirituality essential. This is not the same in Australia despite the cultural knowledge of indigenous Australians including aspects of the spiritual (Martin, 2005). The Eary Years Learning Framework is also called *Belonging, Being and Becoming* (DEEWR, 2009). Ontological perspectives of identity and place as well as a potential for transformation through living and learning are particular features and the spiritual can be perceived to be part of these constructs. The curriculum writers point out that the document was written to balance flexibility with political risk. Accordingly, Sumsion et al. (2009, p. 8) say "we endeavoured to deliberately weave in words that can cross borders and divides, resonate with diverse audiences, and be taken up differently within different discourses and narratives". The framework seeks to stay 'open' and the learning outcomes of this curriculum (like the principles of *Te Whariki*) can be connected to a spiritual perspective.

AUSTRALIAN CREATION STORIES

The creation narratives of Indigenous Australians concern the Dreamtime and sacred spaces. The stories are about a deep connection to place and feature animals and birds as aspects of the spirit, underlining the connection with the land. In the Dreamtime stories and in most creation stories people have to learn about their place in the scheme of things (Mayo & Brierley, 1995). These stories about the creation of the world sit alongside colonial tales of adventurers like Ned Kelly; they create culture and construct a sense of identity. Children get to know these stories and this begins to influence who they are, where they live and their understanding of the world. The EYLF mentions the right of children to be connected with and to contribute to their world and this becomes evident as they "explore the diversity of culture, heritage, background and tradition" that makes up this world. Understanding is extended by including spirituality and the definition in the EYLF refers to "an exploration of *being* and knowing" (DEEWR, 2009, p. 46).

In a recent project about workforce best practice and innovation, research with teachers made it possible to see how educators in Australia work with the EYLF (City of Casey Early Childhood Research Collective, 2012). It was possible to make links with the spiritual aspect of the framework. This project supported interpretations of the learning outcomes promoted in the Australian curriculum through a spiritual lens.

CURRICULUM FRAMEWORKS THROUGH A SPIRITUAL LENS

In the research project educators were asked to discuss each learning outcome at a workshop and follow up this reflective process by reporting back about how they had worked with the learning outcome in the following week. This project involved conversations with university lecturers and educators from a range of early childhood settings. Conversations were recorded and transcribed and the material eventually became a booklet for thinking about the EYLF (City of Casey Early Childhood Research Collective, 2012). Here the teachers' perspectives on early childhood practice can be analysed from two different contexts.

LEARNING OUTCOMES AND TEACHER VOICES

The EYLF features five major learning outcomes (DEEWR, 2009). Learning Outcome One requires that children will develop a strong sense of identity. The subsequent discussion with teachers showed that in their practice this outcome encouraged them to focus on relationships. In the discussion they suggested that being in the world does not happen in an isolated or individualistic way; it is impossible to 'be' a separate entity. In the New Zealand–based research it was suggested that an everyday spirituality could be conceptualised as a series of relational spaces (Bone, 2007). One of these, being 'spiritually with'(Bone, 2007, p. 147), was conceptualised as a major spiritual category, as follows:

The act of being spiritually with another person is a form of loving attention that emphasizes the spiritual aspect of relationships. In each context this was achieved differently but the intention is the same: to be alongside children and their parents, to help children fulfil their potential, to encourage children to become who they are and will be in the fullest possible sense. (Bone, 2007, p. 173)

It is clear that identity is not automatically seen in either place as fixed or individualised; it is more about being together and interrelating when interpreted through the spiritual lens.

Learning Outcome Two mentions that children must be connected with and contribute to their world. Again, this is a major spiritual conceptualisation—the idea of connectedness. One of the educators in the Australian group who talked about connecting recognised that it was possible to have a shared cultural experience in early childhood settings and she tried to develop connections through her work with families and the community. In her teaching practice she used the Sanskrit word "kushala" which means 'happiness' and this was the name of her kindergarten group; a place to come together and be happy. When talking about connectedness different notions of time and space, of being and becoming, as well as ideas about the importance of the environment, art and cooking, were included in a conversation that ranged from the esoteric to the mundane. The stories told formed the 'little narratives' that make up everyday life in the preschool (Dahlberg & Moss, 2005, p. 164).

Wellbeing is Learning Outcome Three of the EYLF and is also a major aspect of the New Zealand curriculum framework. This holistic notion is sometimes difficult to grapple with and everyone seems to have their own idea of what constitutes wellbeing. One of the teachers participating in the Australian research project[1] stated that "spirituality is key to understanding wellbeing for so many people. For many people, life is lived with a spiritual worldview and wellbeing is part of that" (City of Casey Early Childhood Research Collective, 2012, p. 17). The idea that spirituality is always an aspect of wellbeing was slightly controversial in the Australian group whereas teachers in New Zealand saw it as completely linked and understood holistic ideals as inextricably connected to the spiritual. In New Zealand the Māori word for wellbeing is *mana atua*. A/*atua* means a higher being. In some sense a search for oneness and the sacred aspects of existence are tied to wellbeing. One of the Australian teachers wrote that her version of wellbeing was expressed spiritually through the practice of "being in the moment, accept, know, and believe" (City of Casey Early Childhood Research Collective, 2012, p.18).

The fourth outcome from the EYLF is that children become confident and involved learners. Participants in the project critiqued an emphasis on individuality and competitive interpretations of learning. The Australian educators stressed the high levels of engagement and commitment that support this learning outcome. A spiritual interpretation of this might be that in their planning and assessment, and through what the EYLF calls "intentional teaching", a space is created for an educator to show caring and awareness of each child as they take part in different learning experiences. The notion of a space as being *spiritually in-between* (Bone, 2010b) encompasses this aspect in terms of a spiritual component in early childhood education. In this space the educator and child may be in a space of not knowing, of finding out together; a space for mutual discovery. This is exciting and has the potential for shared intellectual endeavours. This liminal space, the *in-between*, may support a spiritual sense of (un)certainty in the moment; the moment just before knowing happens. This is also a space for routines and rituals that create an environment that can build confidence and support children to be involved in their own learning.

The final learning outcome states that children must become effective communicators and mentions the importance of interacting with others and 'attunement' (Siegel, 1999, as cited in DEEWR, 2009, p. 39). As effective communicators they can express themselves, making meaning and sharing thoughts. Educators in the Australian project see communication as essential to the social world of children and discuss language and literacy linked to information technologies (Bone & Edwards, 2012). Their concern is for how children connect with their friends and families in a world of highly sophisticated symbols and images. This desire for constant communication can be seen as symptomatic of a spiritual need to interrelate and be together. This can also be recognised in the longing for stories and the perpetuation of myths and narratives in early childhood settings. The repetition of certain stories was seen by an teacher in the New Zealand context as speaking to something in the soul, a means of opening the gateway to the imagination, or as Bone (2010a) noted, this is the space of the *spiritual elsewhere*, a place of transformation and creativity.

THE DOMINATED SPIRIT AND THE SUBDUED LAND

The curriculum frameworks for Australia and New Zealand are aspirational documents, reflecting what Sumsion et al. (2009) describe as "narratives of hope" (p. 10). In early childhood education spiritual perspectives may be an aspect of hope or of the Utopian thinking described by Dahlberg and Moss as a way of thinking about "radical and transformative change" (2005, p. 178). Such thinking reveals a desire to ameliorate the situation of many children. In Australia and New Zealand the land is always under threat from developers and multinational corporations, mining companies and deep sea oil speculators. Money and the economy appear to be more important than the environment, including sacred spaces. There seems to be very little respect for spirituality when economics are at stake. At the same time economic strength does not seem to change the situation of people who have lost their land and their spiritual traditions.

CONCLUSIONS

This chapter has provided an overview of the role of spirituality in early childhood education in two countries, close but connected, similar but different. In early childhood education the curriculum documents provide a framework for best practice and, working closely with these documents, can support excellence in early childhood educational settings. The historical and cultural backgrounds of both places support a spiritual dimension in education. Research from both countries shows that the spiritual aspects of education can be practised in the day to day life of busy early childhood settings. Learning outcomes that are common to both curriculum documents are interpreted in this chapter through a spiritual lens.

Spirituality is an important aspect of a holistic approach to education, something upheld by the curriculum frameworks of both countries. According to Miller in conversation with Four Arrows, holistic education has three basic principles: "holding a sense of the sacred, valuing the web of life, and educating the whole human being" (Four Arrows & Miller, 2012, p. 9). Despite policy changes it seems that spirituality, as part of a holistic education system, is still a marginalised area. Acknowledging that this is so leads me to close with a question: how can spiritual perspectives, especially in education, support the creation of a better world for ALL children? This was the hope of Tilly Reedy as she addressed an audience of early childhood teachers in New Zealand when plans for the curriculum were launched in the mid-1990s (Reedy, 2003). What does the future hold for children in places like Australia and New Zealand, places that represent hope for so many people and yet places that grapple with significant global issues: climate change, movement of people, economic downturns and shifts of power on the international stage. In New Zealand and Australia some people are guardians of the spiritual; in these places, where generations have struggled to make new lives for themselves, it is important to promote aspects of spirituality with our youngest children, including wellbeing, compassion, creativity and environmental awareness.

NOTES

1. The Australian project was funded by the Department of Education, Employment and Workforce Relations 'Workforce Innovation' Scheme (2010–2011).

REFERENCES

Bergin, H., & Smith, S. (2004). *He whenua, he wahi. Land and place: Spiritualities from Aotearoa New Zealand*. Auckland: Accent.

Binney, J. (1997). *Redemption songs*. Auckland,: Auckland University Press & Bridget Williams.

Bone, J. (2007). *Everyday spirituality: Supporting the spiritual experience of young children in three early childhood educational settings.* (Doctoral dissertation). Massey University, Palmerston North, New Zealand.

Bone, J. (2008). Creating relational spaces: Everyday spirituality in early childhood settings. *European Early Childhood Education Research Journal, 16*(3), 355–368.

Bone, J. (2010a). Play and metamorphosis: Spirituality in early childhood settings. *Contemporary Issues in Early Childhood, 12*(4), 402–414.

Bone, J. (2010b). Spirituality and early childhood education: 'Belonging, being and becoming' at a Midwinter festival. *Journal of Religious Education, 58*(3), 26–35 (Special Edition: Children's Spirituality and Religious Education).

Bone, J., & Edwards, S. (2012). Thinking together—EYLF learning outcomes—identity. *Every Child, 18*(4), 3–4.

Carr, M., & May, H. (2000). Te Whariki: Curriculum voices. In. H. Penn (Ed.), *Early childhood services: Theory, policy and practice* (pp. 53–74). Buckingham: Open University Press.

City of Casey Early Childhood Research Collective. (2012). *In practice and in theory: A booklet for thinking about the five learning outcomes and the early years learning framework.* Melbourne: Australian Catholic University.

Cunningham, H. (2005). *Children and childhood in Western society since 1500.* Harlow: Pearson.

Dahlberg, G., & Moss, P. (2005). *Ethics and politics in early childhood education.* Abingdon, Oxon: Routledge.

Darragh, N. (2004). Foreword. In H. Bergin & S. Smith (Eds), *He whenua, he wahi. Land and place: Spiritualities from Aotearoa New Zealand* (pp. 1–5). Auckland: Accent.

Dei, G. J. S. (2011). Introduction. In G. J. S. Dei (Ed.), *Indigenous philosophies and critical education: A reader* (pp. 1–13). New York: Peter Lang.

Department of Education, Employment and Workplace Relations [DEEWR]. (2009). *Belonging, being and becoming: The early years learning framework for Australia.* Barton, ACT: Commonwealth of Australia.

Fischer, S., Hotam, Y., & Wexler, P. (2012). Democracy and education in postsecular society. In K. M. Borman, A. B.Danzig, & D. R. Garcia (Eds.), *Education, democracy, and the public good. Review of research in education* (Vol. 36), (pp. 261–181). Washington, DC: American Educational Research Association.

Four Arrows, & Miller, J. (2012). To name the world: A dialogue about holistic and indigenous education. *ENCOUNTER: Education for meaning and social issues, 25*(3), 1–11.

Geering, L. (2005). *God in 20th century New Zealand: A personal perspective.* Hocken Lecture, July 12, 2005, University of Otago, Dunedin.

Human Rights Commission. (2012). *Religious diversity in New Zealand, 2004–2010.* Retrieved March 30, 2013, from http://www.hrc.co.nz.

Julian, E. (2004). Landscape as spiritual classic: A reading from Paekakariki. In H. Bergin and S. Smith (Eds), *He whenua, he wahi. Land and place: Spiritualities from Aotearoa New Zealand* (pp.97–115). Auckland: Accent.

Mayo, M., & Brierley, L. (1995). *The Orchard book of creation stories.* London: Orchard.

Martin, K. (2005). Childhood, lifehood and relatedness: Aboriginal ways of being, knowing and doing. In J. Phillips & J. Lampert (Eds.), *Introductory indigenous studies in education: The importance of knowing* (pp. 27–40). Frenchs Forest, NSW: Pearson.

Ministry of Education. (1996). *Te Whāriki: He whāriki mātauranga mo ngā mokopuna o Aotearoa. Early childhood curriculum.* Wellington: Learning Media.

New Zealand in History. (2012). *Maori myths and legends*. Retrieved March 30, 2013, from http://history-nz.org/maori9.html.

Pere, R. T. (1991). *Te wheke: A celebration of infinite wisdom*. Gisborne: Ao Ako Global Learning.

Reedy, T. (2003). Toku rangatiratanga na te mana-Mātauranga: "Knowledge and power set me free . . .". In J. Nuttall (Ed.), *Weaving Te Whāriki* (pp. 51–79). Wellington: NZCER.

Salmond, A. (2003). *The trail of the cannibal dog: Captain Cook in the south seas*. London: Penguin.

Savage, P. (2005). Parihaka: The weighty legacy of unfinished business. In T. M. Hohaia, G. O'Brien, & L. Strongman (Eds.), *Parihaka: The art of passive resistance* (pp. 12–16). Wellington: Victoria University Press.

Sumsion, J., Barnes, S., Cheeseman, S., Harrison, L., Kennedy, A., & Stonehouse, A. (2009). Insider perspectives on developing Belonging, Being and Becoming: The Early Years Learning Framework for Australia. *Australian Journal of Early Childhood, 34*(4), 4–13.

United Nations. *United Nations Declaration on the Rights of Indigenous People*. (2008). Retrieved March 30, 2013, from http://www.un.org/esa/socdev/unpfii/documents/DRIPS_en.pdf.

Vercoe, C. (2004). The many faces of paradise. In *Paradise now? Contemporary art from the Pacific* (pp. 34–48). New York: Asia Society & David Bateman.

10 Nurturing Spirituality through a Dispositional Framework in Early Years' Contexts

Brendan Hyde

THE CONTEXT

There are a number of distinct features that comprise Australia's historical, cultural, political and religious landscape which have impacted upon my research in the field of children's spirituality in education. For many in Australia, spirituality is still perceived as a by-product of, or an appendage to religion, and for this reason, there exists particular wariness amongst policy makers and educators in articulating a spiritual dimension in learning. The Education Act of 1872 made clear that state education was to be free, compulsory and secular. Lovat (2010) argues that documents which followed the Education Act in the 1880s and 1890s in some of the then colonies of Australia made reference to religion (and by implication spirituality because of its then close association with religion) and permitted volunteers from church denominations to provide, with their parents' permission, religious instruction to students. However, most state school children did not receive much in the way of religious or spiritual education. The free, compulsory and secular tenets of education in Australian state schools have remained virtually intact to the present day, with little provision in legislation for the inclusion of religion or spirituality within the formal curriculum.[1] Education has tended to remain compartmentalised and content driven, with assessment focused on the achievement of demonstrable standards and the attainment of particular benchmarks.

However, the political climate in which the Australian education system now finds itself has resulted in the publication of three recent documents, all of which, for the first time, make explicit reference to the spiritual dimension. The first of these documents, titled *National Goals for Schooling in the 21st Century* (Ministerial Council on Education Employment Training and Youth Affairs [MCEETYA], 1999) also known as the Adelaide Declaration, stated that schooling provides a foundation for young Australians' intellectual, physical, social, moral, spiritual and aesthetic development.

The second of these documents, superseding the Adelaide Declaration, is the *Melbourne Declaration on Educational Goals for Young Australians* (MCEETYA, 2008). This document states, "Schools play a vital role in promoting the intellectual, physical, social, emotional, moral, spiritual and aesthetic development and wellbeing of young Australians" (p. 4) and that students should "have a sense of self-worth, self-awareness and personal identity that enables them to manage their emotional, mental, spiritual and physical wellbeing" (p. 9).

The third and most recent of these documents is Australia's first and landmark national statement on the education of young children between birth and 5 years of age, *Belonging, Being, Becoming: The Early Years Learning Framework for Australia* (Australian Government Department of Employment Education and Workplace Relations [DEEWR], 2009). This document explicitly makes several references to the spiritual aspects of children's lives and considers the role of the spiritual in children's learning and wellbeing. For example, it acknowledges that children's learning is "dynamic, complex and holistic. . . . Physical, social, emotional, spiritual, creative, cognitive and linguistic aspects of learning are all intricately interwoven and interrelated" (p. 9). This marks a significant shift in the perception and nature of the human person from the Australian government's normally secular perspective. For the first time, Australian Early Years' educators are being called upon to consider children's spirituality in learning and wellbeing.

While each of these documents has made explicit the importance of children's spirituality in education, a number of critical elements have been left unaddressed. For instance, *how*, practically speaking, might educators address the spiritual dimension of children's lives. Also, and particularly in relation to the Early Years Learning Framework, there is an assumption that Early Years teachers are clearly aware of their own beliefs and values in relation to addressing the spiritual dimension in their professional practice. The documents remain silent on such issues, and, as Grajczonek (2011) notes, such silence, potentially, creates ambiguity which can result in the omission of the spiritual from teaching pedagogy.

Given that the documents described above explicitly identify the importance of the spiritual dimension, the challenges which now arise centre on how to address spirituality in learning given that the contemporary education system in Australia continues to maintain a focus on the achievement of demonstrable standards. One possible way forward involves the use of a learning dispositional framework. Such frameworks have been advocated for use in education by Claxton (2007, 2008) and in early childhood education by Carr (2001) and Claxton and Carr (2004). In building upon this work, Hyde (2010a, 2012) refined a dispositional framework which, although originally intended for use in religious education in Catholic schools, also has the potential to nurture children's spirituality more broadly in early contexts and beyond. This chapter will focus on the development and application of this framework.

LEARNING DISPOSITIONS

The concept of a disposition in developmental psychology stems from Dewey's (1966) work. It is seen as generally describing the qualities or attributes possessed by a person, often used to signal temperament. These have been variously termed 'dispositions' (Katz, 1988; Perkins, Jay & Tishman, 1993); 'orientations' (Dweck, 1999) and habits of mind (Costa, 2000); for example "she has a cheerful disposition". However, Carr (2001) notes that, when motivation is considered in the description, learning dispositions comprise a set of participation repertoires from which the learner recognises, selects, edits, responds to, resists, searches for and constructs learning opportunities. Alternatively, learning dispositions indicate that a learner is "ready, willing and able to participate in various ways: a combination of inclination, sensitivity to occasion, and the relevant skill and knowledge" (p. 21). In drawing on the work of Pierre Bourdieu, Comber (2000) argues that young children bring to school their "economic, cultural, social, symbolic and linguistic capital and their *habitus*, sets of dispositions acquired in daily life, that incline people to act in particular ways" (p. 46, my italics). Given that children bring these sets of dispositions with them, Claxton (2008) argues that education can and should influence the development of these particular inclinations, alongside influencing the development of knowledge and skills associated with different subject areas. Further, Claxton and Carr (2004) argue that when learning dispositions form the basis of an educational approach, attention is given to the long-term trajectories, rather than to the accumulation of particular bodies of knowledge and skills. Additionally, Claxton (2007) contends that when educators think only in terms of teaching skills or problem-solving competencies and neglect the need to cultivate dispositions, they often find that any apparent gains in acquiring such skills and competencies are relatively short-lived—they fail to "last, spread or deepen" (p. 6).

A dispositional framework does not negate the teaching of particular content, knowledge and skills. Although necessary and important, they are viewed as one part of a larger picture. A dispositional framework is concerned not so much with the short-term aim of having students acquire particular content knowledge but rather with the long-term trajectory which includes the habits and orientations towards learning in general. These are strengthened (or perhaps, weakened) in the learning process. It is concerned with *how* students learn—the *process*—rather than with what they learn, since these processes can be applied across disciplines. A dispositional framework then shifts attention towards the process of learning and the ways in which students' learning dispositions grow and change (Claxton, 2007). In the Australian educational context, this represents a significant movement away from the traditional content-focused curriculum aiming for demonstrable competencies and benchmarks.

In her work in early childhood contexts in New Zealand, and linked to the strands of the national early childhood curriculum *Te Whariki* (Ministry of Education, 1996), Carr (2001) identified five domains of dispositions: taking an interest, being involved, persisting with difficulty or uncertainty, communicating with others and taking responsibility. These are intended to contribute towards the development of orientations, or habits of mind, across a range of discipline areas comprising the early childhood curriculum. Drawing upon Carr's work and other references to the literature in education and in religious education, more specifically, Hyde (2010a) refined these domains of learning dispositions for religious education in the Early Years in Australian Catholic schools. Accordingly, he identified five domains: curiosity, being dialogical, persisting and living with uncertainty, meaning-making and taking responsibility. Although refined initially with Early Years religious education in mind, these particular domains of learning dispositions are discussed, next in the context of how each might nurture the spirituality of children.

Curiosity

Curiosity is the first domain of learning dispositions. Being curious entails not only capturing interest, but also concerns having a sense of wonder and awe. Hay and Nye (2006) strongly describe curiosity in terms of mystery-sensing, which pertains to the sense of wonder and awe, and to the fascination and questioning that is characteristic of children as they interact with their world. They note that for young children in particular, any distinction between the commonplace and the profound may not yet have meaning. Therefore, children's sense of wonder can be awakened by that which may appear to an adult to be ordinary and mundane, such as striking a match or turning on a tap.

The notion of curiosity—and wonder—may offer a way of talking with children about the Transcendent (God). Children (as well as adults) encounter mystery through wonder and through imagination. For instance, Godly Play (Berryman, 2002, 2009) explicitly utilizes the notion of wonder (and develops children's predisposition towards it) as a way of enabling children to use and play with religious language to discern meaning in life. A sense of curiosity and wonder enables children to use their imagination and to open up the creative process in relation to religious language. The story teller, through her or his "dependable presence" (Melchert & Proffitt, 1998) and through her or his own disposition towards curiosity, allows children the freedom to be curious, and to wonder:

> When the teacher is truly wondering, the children sense wonder in the air. It manifests itself in the playfulness present in the room. Permission and reinforcement are present to encourage it. When the teacher enters religious language with wonder, he or she shows the children by example how to open the creative process. (Berryman, 1991, p. 62)

A key responsibility for teachers here is to acknowledge children's predisposition towards wonder and to nurture it using their own sense of wonder as an impetus,

> not only in their way of being with students, but also in shaping the learning process to include and honour learners' wonder. They must

be aware of, and willing to let into the classroom the contingency of life, at the same time creating a sense of dependability for the learners. (Melchert & Proffit, 1998, p. 31)

In being curious and in possessing a sense of wonder, children are then able to recognise the familiar, while also being empowered to enjoy the unfamiliar and to wonder about it. Spirituality may be nurtured through this disposition since the wonder, curiosity and awe experienced by children often incorporates a sense of mystery and, at times, sacredness in what they see (Adams, Hyde & Woolley, 2008). For many children, the predisposition towards curiosity provides a gateway for speaking about the transcendent, and may offer an impetus for introducing appropriate religious and spiritual language for children's exploration and use.

Being Dialogical

Being dialogical refers to more than being willing to speak and to enter into conversation with others. Being dialogical refers to the disposition of being a willing participant in the type of dialogue that leads to genuine understanding. It involves the willingness to enter into discourse with another without having a predetermined agenda—to be open to the possibilities of new insights that may be developed between the dialogue partners.

The philosophical thought of Gadamer (1989) sheds light upon this particular disposition. Gadamer put forward the metaphor of *conversation* as an ideal for that which ought to occur during the hermeneutical process. Conversation exemplifies the qualities of responsiveness, creativity and freedom that are central to genuine understanding. Of importance is the notion that genuine dialogue cannot be controlled by the conversation partners:

> We say that we 'conduct' a conversation, but the more genuine a conversation is, the less its conduct lies within the will of either partner. Thus a genuine conversation is never the one we want to conduct. Rather, it is generally more correct to say that we fall into conversation, or even that we become involved in it. The way one word follows another, with the conversation taking its own twists and reaching its own conclusion, may well be conducted in some way, but the partners conversing are far less leaders of it than the led. No one knows in advance what will be the 'outcome' of a conversation. Understanding or its failure is like an event that happens to us. Thus we can say that something was a good conversation or that it was ill fated. (p. 383)

Dialogue works most effectively when the subject matter of the conversation assumes control, while those in dialogue allow themselves to be led by it. A conversation is foiled when one dialogue partner seeks to dominate by imposing her or his own point of view. The prerequisite for genuine dialogue is that the conversation partners give in to the "ebb and flow of the conversation as the subject matter unfolds" (Sharkey, 2001, p. 23). The object of the dialogue then is that which both partners seek to understand. It is this joint object, rather than the partners, that conducts the dialogue (Weinsheimer, 1985).

That those involved in the dialogue are partners is important. In Gadamer's philosophical thought, the concept of a partner implies equality (Weinsheimer, 1985). Therefore, both conversation partners—student and student, or student and teacher—are equal and contribute to the ebb and flow of the dialogue in valuable, albeit different ways. Being dialogical then entails that both dialogue partners exhibit respect for the opinion of the other.

In this particular disposition, being dialogical entails deep listening and trust on the part of the dialogue partners. It entails the partners being "seriously playful" (Berryman, 2009) in their exchange of ideas, and playfulness is one of the indicators which may signal spirituality (Adams, Hyde & Woolley, 2008; Berryman, 2001). Spirituality may be nurtured through this disposition when students enter into dialogue with others as genuine dialogue partners. The other with whom the students dialogue may involve another student, the teacher, or indeed the texts and artefacts of a particular religious tradition. Each brings its own horizon of meaning (Gadamer, 1989) to the dialogue. These horizons are fused together by the dialogue partners, thereby creating meaning and understanding.

Persisting and Living with Uncertainty

Persisting and living with uncertainty reflects the predisposition of being able to hold in tension different ways of being in the world and of confronting life's existential concerns and issues. Horell (2003) notes the ambiguity which exists as a result of the shift towards cultural postmodernity and both the challenges and opportunities this presents for educators. While such a shift generally involves movement away from a strict adherence to the traditional religious worldviews, it also involves a greater emphasis on spiritual experiences, and of being able to connect spiritually with Self, Other, the world and with God (p. 102). In exploring the importance of spirituality and connecting beyond the Self, Hyde (2008) notes how children draw upon many frameworks of meaning to weave together their respective worldviews and, in many cases, envision more authentic and life-giving ways of being in the world. Often, these frameworks reflect the uncertainty, the ambiguity and multiplicity of cultural postmodernity. This particular disposition then describes the inclination towards being able to sit with ambiguity, and to engage in deep questioning and genuine wondering about existential issues and questions.

Drawing from psychotherapy and, in particular, from the works of Reinhardt (1950/1960), Yalom (1980) and Cooper (2003), Berryman (1991,

2009) maintains that existential issues mark the boundaries of human experience. They include the experience of what happens at death, the sense of aloneness, the need to create meaning and an appreciation of the experience of freedom. According to Berryman, these limits are as fundamental to the lives of children as they are to adults. While children may experience them, speak of them and approach them in ways different from adults, they are, nonetheless, real for them.

For children to be disposed to persist and to live with uncertainty, therefore, requires them to be able to problem-solve, think laterally, and to wonder deeply and imaginatively in confronting existential issues. That this is the case finds support in a growing body of research. For instance, the work of Berryman (1991, 2009) and, more recently, Hyde (2010b, 2010c) indicates that young children, when given agency and freedom to choose their own work and materials, will return continually to stories and presentations that contain for them meaningful images and motifs in which to persist and make meaning. Persisting and living with uncertainty is then a pertinent learning disposition which, potentially, nurtures spirituality in children, by aiding in its development.

Meaning-Making

Meaning-making is the predisposition of being able to make sense of signs, symbols and events. For young children, play is one of the key means through which they discover and make meaning (see for instance Copple, Cocking & Matthews, 1984; Sawyers & Carrick, 2008), and through which they may also express their spirituality (Berryman, 2009). Exploring this notion further, there are two particular theories about the way in which children make meaning through play—script theory and emotive theory. Shank and Abelson (1977) maintain that script theory involves the type of play in which children imitate events they have experienced. They follow a type of 'script' in imitating and making meaning from the event. Emotive play refers to the way in which children may enact events which enable them to express emotions as a key to their meaning-making (Fein, 1991).

Sociodramatic play (pretend play) is also a key feature of young children's play which enables them to make meaning. Bretherton (cited in Hymans, 1996) describes pretend play as consisting of two levels. The first level—make-believe play—pertains to the 'as if' dimension in which children are involved in familiar situations, such as shopping or having a party. In this type of play, children shop or play party games as if they were actually involved in the real event itself. The second level comprises the 'what if' dimension. Here, children transform the real world into a fictional, or fantasy world, in which a spoon or block of wood becomes the telephone, and in which children pretend to be doctors, nurses, teachers or parents.

Through immersion in these types of deep play, children are able to use both verbal and nonverbal communication as a means to discover and unpack the meaning of an event or story in their lives. In using nonverbal communication in play, their response may be intuitive and beyond words. Through these types of play children may be moved to express or make visible their meaning-making in some way—through artwork, drawing, writing and the like. In creating meaning through play, children learn "the meaning of many of our cultural artefacts, to construct their own meaning in and through those artefacts, and to manipulate meanings according to context" (MacNaughton, 2004, p. 43). When children construct their own meaning in this way, they are, as discussed, potentially expressing something of their spirituality.

Taking Responsibility

As Carr (2001) describes it, taking responsibility includes contributing to shared activities and episodes of joint attention. Several studies indicate the learning potential present in contexts involving reciprocal and responsive relationships with others (e.g. Moore & Durham, 1992; Smith, 1999). However, taking responsibility as it is viewed here extends such understandings. It is concerned with taking action that matters—that is, an inclination to own the learning and to 'think' the learning through into action with positive consequences for the wellbeing of one's self and others. In this way, children are empowered to engage in "reciprocal and responsive relationships with people that weave together the affective, the cognitive and the social into rich fabrics of learning" (Carr, 2001, p. 77).

Taking responsibility empowers children and encourages a commitment to social justice. It inclines children towards being able to recognise situations in which injustice of one kind or another prevails, and to act accordingly. It involves the inclination to make a difference for the good. Several authors (for example Buchanan & Hyde, 2008; de Souza, 2006; Moffett, 1994) argue that learning experiences which have the power to be transformative ought to lead the learner to act upon what has been learnt in ways that benefit self and others. Such action and relationship towards the other accords with the literature's understanding and description of spirituality (see, for example, de Souza, 2006; Hay with Nye, 2006; Hyde, 2008). The disposition of taking responsibility reflects this notion.

CONCLUSION

Each of the five domains of learning dispositions represents the orientations, or habits of mind, that many young children bring with them to early childhood centres and early years' classrooms in schools. They are also avenues through which the spirituality of children may be nurtured and given expression. Therefore, the dispositional framework represents one practical means by which educators in the Australian context might address and nurture the spiritual dimension of children's lives through the curriculum.

However, and while emanating from the Australian context, it is important to note that this work has broader application to educators and classroom practitioners elsewhere. Since the dispositional framework outlined in this chapter draws upon an extensive body of research, its applicability for nurturing the spirituality of *all* children is noted because it represents a shared approach to and understanding of both spirituality and the notion of learning dispositions. For instance, the dispositional framework, with its focus on the processes of how children learn, may provide an alternative perspective to the outcomes-based philosophy that drives contemporary education in many countries. Since the framework is based on contemporary research, it may also provide education policy makers with a valid stance from which to challenge the outcomes-based approach. Classroom practitioners using this framework are well positioned to discover the processes through which their students learn and the ways in which they are predisposed to learn. With such pedagogical learner knowledge at their disposal, they may, consciously and deliberately, plan learning experiences which take account of the ways in which their students are predisposed to learn and include opportunities for the nurturing of their spirituality.

The task now is to devise ways in which such opportunities for the nurturing and expression of these domains of learning dispositions might be incorporated in the curriculum of early years' classrooms. Preliminary work has already begun in this area (see Hyde, 2012; Hyde & Leening, 2012) with a view to devising and articulating possible learning and teaching strategies for nurturing and expressing these learning dispositions, as well as the development of practical tracking tools that can be utilized by educators for recording purposes. In this way, it is hoped that the use of a dispositional framework in early years' education might have the potential to enable Australian educators to consider children's spirituality in learning and wellbeing. In doing this, early years' educators will be well positioned to be attentive to the "[the] Physical, social, emotional, *spiritual*, creative, cognitive and linguistic aspects of learning [which] are all intricately interwoven and interrelated" (DEEWR, 2009, p. 9, my italics).

NOTES

1. This is in contrast to, for instance, England, where the Education Act of 1944 explicitly contains the term 'spiritual', albeit that it is tied closely with religion, and specifically, with Christianity. Subsequent acts, for example, in 1988 have drawn upon and further developed the notion of spirituality in education so that it is now understood as being quite distinct from religion.

REFERENCES

Adams, K., Hyde, B., & Woolley, R. (2008). *The spiritual dimension of childhood*. London: Jessica Kingsley.

Australian Government Department of Employment Education and Workplace Relations (DEEWR). (2009). *Belonging, being and becoming: An early years' learning framework for Australia*. Retrieved March 30, 2013, from http://foi.deewr.gov.au/system/files/doc/other/belonging_being_and_becoming_the_early_years_learning_framework_for_australia.pdf.

Berryman, J. W. (1991). *Godly play: A way of religious education*. San Francisco: Harper.

Berryman, J. W. (2001). The nonverbal nature of spirituality and religious education. In J. Erricker, C. Ota, & C. Erricker (Eds.), *Spiritual education: Cultural, religious and social differences. New perspectives for the 21st century* (pp. 9–21). Brighton, UK: Sussex Academic Press.

Berryman, J. W. (2002). *The complete guide to Godly play* (Vol. 1). Denver, CO: Living the Good News.

Berryman, J. W. (2009). *Teaching Godly play: How to mentor the spiritual development of children*. Denver, CO: Morehouse Education Resources.

Buchanan, M. T., & Hyde, B. (2008). Learning beyond the surface: Engaging the cognitive, affective and spiritual dimensions within the curriculum. *International Journal of Children's Spirituality, 13*(4), 309–320.

Carr, M. (2001). *Assessment in early childhood settings: Learning stories*. London: Sage.

Claxton, G. (2007). Expanding young people's capacity to learn. *British Journal of Educational Studies, 55*(2), 1–20.

Claxton, G. (2008). Cultivating positive learning dispositions. In H. Daniels, H. Lauder, & J. Porter (Eds), *Routledge companion to education*. London: Routledge.

Claxton, G., & Carr, M. (2004). A framework for teaching learning: The dynamics of disposition. *Early Years, 24*(1), 87–97.

Comber, B. (2000). What really counts in early literacy lessons. *Language Arts, 78*(1), 39–49.

Cooper, M. (2003). *Existential therapies*. London: Sage.

Copple, C., Cocking, R., & Matthews, W. (1984). Objects, symbols and substitutions: The nature of cognitive activity during symbolic play. In T. D. Yawkey & A. D. Pelligrini (Eds.), *Child's play: Developmental and applied* (pp. 105–124). Hillsdale. NJ: Erlbaum.

Costa, A. L. (2000). Describing the habits of mind. In A. L. Costa & B. Kallick (Eds.), *Habits of mind: Discovering and exploring* (pp. 21–40). Alexandria, VA: Association for Supervision and Curriculum Development.

de Souza, M. (2006). Rediscovering the spiritual dimension in education: Promoting a sense of self and place, meaning and purpose in learning. In M. de Souza, K. Engebretson, G. Durka, R. Jackson, & A. McGrady (Eds.), *International handbook of the religious, moral and spiritual dimensions in education* (pp. 1127–1139). Dordrecht, The Netherlands: Springer.

Dewey, J. (1966). *Democracy and education: An introduction to the philosophy of education*. New York: Free Press. (Original work published 1916).

Dweck, C. S. (1999). *Self theories: Their role in motivation, personality and development*. Philadelphia: Psychology Press.

Fein, G. (1991). Bloodsuckers, blisters, cooked babies, and other curiosities: Affective themes in pretence. In F. S. Kessel, M. H. Bornstein, & A. J. Sameroff (Eds.), *Contemporary constructions of the child* (pp. 143–158). Hillsdale, NJ: Erlbaum.

Gadamer, H. G. (1989). *Truth and method* (2nd rev. Eng. ed.). (J. Weinsheimer & D. Marshall, Trans.). London: Sheed & Ward. (Original work published 1960).

Grajczonek, J. (2011). Belonging, being and becoming: The early years learning framework for Australia—Opportunities and challenges for early years religious education. *Journal of Religious Education, 59*(3), 23–35.

Hay, D., with Nye, R. (2006). *The spirit of the child* (rev. ed.). London: Jessica Kingsley.

Horell, H. (2003). Cultural postmodernity and Christian faith formation. In T. Groome & H. Horell (Eds.), *Horizons and hopes: The future of religious education* (pp. 81–107). New York: Paulist Press.

Hyde, B. (2008). *Children and spirituality: Searching for meaning and connectedness*. London: Jessica Kingsley.

Hyde, B. (2010a). A dispositional framework in religious education: Learning dispositions and early years' religious education in Catholic schools. *Journal of Beliefs and Values, 31*(3), 261–269.

Hyde, B. (2010b). Agency and non-verbal communication in religious education: A case study from a Godly play classroom. *Journal of Religious Education, 58*(1), 4–11.

Hyde, B. (2010c). Godly play nourishing children's spirituality: A case study. *Religious Education, 105*(5), 504–518.

Hyde, B. (2012). Learning stories and dispositional frameworks in early years' religious education. *Journal of Religious Education, 60*(1), 4–14.

Hyde, B., & Leening, L. (2012). Teachers' perceptions and experiences in using a dispositional framework in Catholic school early years' religious education to track students' learning. *Journal of Catholic School Studies, 84*(1), 56–67.

Hymans, D. (1996). Let's play: The contribution of the pretend play of children to religious education in a pluralist context. *Religious Education, 91*(3), 368–381.

Katz, L. G. (1988). What should young children be doing? *American Educator* (Summer), 29–45.

Lovat, T. (2010). Spirituality and the public school. In M. de Souza & J. Rimes (Eds.), *Meaning and connectedness: Australian perspectives on education and spirituality* (pp. 19–30). Canberra, ACT: Australian College of Educators.

MacNaughton, G. (2004). Exploring critical constructivist perspectives on children's learning. In A. Anning, J. Cullen, & M. Fleer (Eds.), *Early childhood education: Society and culture* (pp. 43–54). London: Sage.

Melchert, C., & Proffitt, A. (1998). Playing in the presence of God: Wonder, wisdom and education. *International Journal of Children's Spirituality, 3*(1), 21–34.

Ministerial Council on Education Employment Training and Youth Affairs (MCEETYA). (1999). *National Goals for Schooling in the 21st Century*. Retrieved March 30, 2013, from http://www.mceetya.edu.au/mceetya/nationalgoals/index.htm.

Ministerial Council on Education Employment Training and Youth Affairs (MCEETYA). (2008). *Melbourne declaration on educational goals for young Australians*. Retrieved March 30, 2013, from http://www.mceecdya.edu.au/verve/_resources/National_Declaration_on_the_Educational_Goals_for_Young_Australians.pdf.

Ministry of Education. (1996). *Te Whariki: He whariki matauranga mo nga mokopuna o Aotearoa, Early Childhood Curriculum*. Wellington, NZ: Learning Media.

Moffett. J. (1994). *The universal schoolhouse: Spiritual awakening through education*. San Francisco: Jossey-Bass.

Moore, C., & Durham, P. J. (Eds.). (1992). *Joint attention: Its origin and role in development*. Hillsdale, NJ: Erlbaum.

Perkins, D. N., Jay, E., & Tishman, S. (1993). Beyond abilities: A dispositional theory of thinking. *Merrill-Palmer Quarterly, 39*, 1–21.

Reinhardt, K. F. (1950/1960). *The existentialist revolt: The main themes and phases of existentialism*. New York: Frederick Unger.

Sawyers, J., & Carrick, N. (2008). Symbolic play through the eyes and words of children. In E. Woods (Ed.), *The Routledge reader in early childhood education* (pp. 136–159). London: Routledge.

Shank, R., & Abelson, R. (1977). *Scripts, plans, goals and understanding.* Hillsdale, NJ: Erlbaum.

Sharkey, P. (2001). Hermeneutic phenomenology. In R. Barnacle (Ed.), *Phenomenology: Qualitative research methods* (pp. 16–37). Melbourne: RMIT Press.

Smith, A. B. (1999). Quality childcare and joint attention. *International Journal of Early Years' Education, 7*(1), 85–98.

Weinsheimer, J. (1985). *Gardamer's hermeneutics: A reading of "Truth and method".* New Haven, CT: Yale University Press.

Yalom, I. D. (1980). *Existential psychotherapy.* New York: Basic Books.

11 A Perspective on Spiritual Education in Australian Schools
The Emergence of Nonreligious Personal Development Approaches

Graham Rossiter

INTRODUCTION

Ever since the origins of the first school systems in Australia in the 19th century, the main area in which they gave specific curriculum attention to a spiritual and moral dimension has been in religious education. This remains the case today, even though there are changes on the horizon—that is, educational initiatives that are based on a notion of spirituality that is not necessarily religious. This chapter, which follows on from a previous chapter describing the religious component to spiritual education in Australian schools,[1] is concerned with some of these new initiatives.

This chapter explores the movement into spiritual, but not necessarily religious, education. This movement is evident in the literature both in Australia and internationally (e.g. de Souza, 2011; Ota & Erricker, 2005), but, as may be the case in other countries, there still remains a significant gap between theory and actual classroom practice. Firstly, attention is given to the emergence of a range of personal development constructs that have become reference points for spiritual education. Here, the discourse is about how schools might promote pupils' spiritual and moral development, where the key terms in the discourse are not religious. Then the Australian school practice of spiritual education under these personal development categories will be documented briefly. Finally, some proposals are made for furthering and enhancing the practice of spiritual education by adopting a view of spirituality that lends itself to a critical, student-centred pedagogy—an approach that can have across-the-curriculum implications. A contemporary spiritual education in schools (even where this is under the auspices of religious education) needs to identify and evaluate the spiritual dimension in personal life and culture—which means interrogating the cultural meanings that can have a shaping influence on people's thinking, valuing and behaviour.

THE NEED FOR A PERSONAL DEVELOPMENT BASIS TO THE DISCOURSE ON SPIRITUAL EDUCATION AND THE PIVOTAL PLACE OF THE CONSTRUCT 'SPIRITUALITY' IN THIS DISCOURSE

There has been a significant change in the landscape of contemporary spirituality which for many Australians no longer has much linkage, if any, with organised religion (Mason, Singleton & Webber, 2007). Hence the discourse about the role of schools in promoting young people's spiritual and moral development cannot remain a relatively exclusive prerogative of religious education; it needs to be based more on *personal development constructs*.

Rossiter (2012) proposed that 'spirituality' was a pivotal personal development construct in discussions of both *religious education* and nonreligious *spiritual education*. The construct 'spirituality' has significant roots in both the *religious sphere* and the *ordinary secular human sphere*. The word originated within Christianity, and until relatively recent times, the words 'religious' and 'spiritual' tended to be synonymous—spirituality was the equivalent of religiosity. Spirituality has also been used as a secular construct for interpreting aspects of personal, spiritual and moral development in a nonreligious way. It is thus strategically placed like a bridge connecting traditional religious ways of seeing people in God's universe with contemporary secular, psychological ways of interpreting personal development. Another valuable quality of spirituality is its growing connection with education (both religious and secular). As illustrated in Figure 11.1, spirituality can be used as a mediating, central construct for interpreting how spiritual education works in both religious and nonreligious spheres.

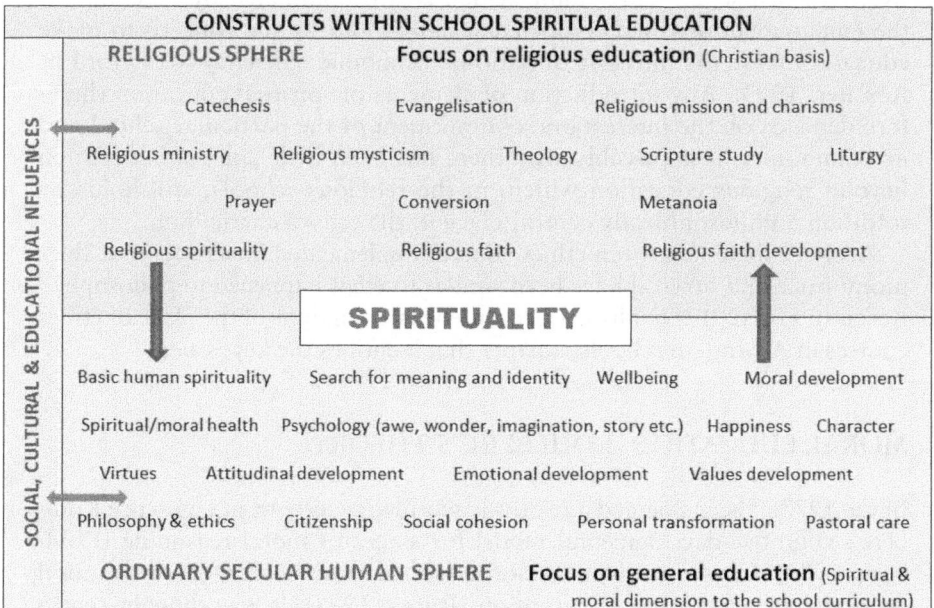

Figure 11.1   Brief sketch of examples of spiritual education in Australian schools referenced to particular personal development constructs.

PHILOSOPHY AND ETHICS

Philosophy and ethics courses have been developed, trialled and introduced to various schools in Australia at both primary and secondary levels. However, as with general religion studies, these practices have been minimal. Nevertheless, an indication of the interest in this form of spiritual education is evident in the operation of an Australasian federation of groups that promote the study of philosophy in schools. It argues a case for including philosophy in the new Australian national school curriculum.

> Philosophy will make a pre-eminent contribution to students' general capabilities. Philosophy education promotes critical thinking, insightful questioning, reasoned argument, metacognitive reflection and problem-solving skills, as well as improving students' social competence and self-management. (Federation of Australasian Philosophy in Schools Associations, 2012)

It is not that the community is opposed to such courses. Spiritual and moral aims for education are now recognised in national statements about the purpose of schools (e.g. Ministerial Council for Education, Early Childhood Development and Youth Affairs [MYCEETYA], 2008). But no matter how noble the spiritual and moral aims proposed for education generally, and for particular forms of spiritual education in particular, at the level of practice, there is usually no room for their introduction in a competitive, crowded school curriculum which is still dominated by outcomes in the employment-oriented competencies area, and by the concern to make education serve the interests of national economic efficiency (Crawford & Rossiter, 1993). Any introduction of elements of spiritual education therefore depends on the interest and commitment of the particular school and its community. It is possibly why there has been little spiritual education beyond religious education which, in the religious schools, still holds by tradition a philosophically central place in the school curriculum.

At times there have been ethics courses implemented in schools. But their prominence and survival have been similar to what happened to philosophy.[2] Recently, Hill (2012) published a comprehensive analysis of the place of ethics courses in Australian schools, a paper that identifies the key issues

MORAL EDUCATION: KOHLBERG'S THEORY

In the 1970s, there emerged a relatively worldwide interest in Lawrence Kohlberg's cognitive-developmental model for stages of moral reasoning (Kohlberg, 1984). Consequently, attention was given to its contribution to moral development and to moral education (Peters, 1978). It was thought that a pedagogy of moral dilemmas would be useful in promoting the moral development of young people in the classroom through their analysis and rehearsal of the motivations in various options within the dilemmas, and through the exposure to motivations from 'higher' levels of moral reasoning.

The extent to which this thinking affected Australian spiritual education in schools is difficult to estimate—a situation that is probably common elsewhere (Lockwood, 1978), but it did influence the thinking and practice of educators, particularly in religious education in church-related schools. For example, seminars on Kohlberg's theory were conducted for church school educators by visiting US scholar P. Travis in 1978. Since that time there has been anecdotal evidence of reference to Kohlberg's work as well as moral dilemma pedagogy in various church school religious education programs. As well, Kohlberg's theory and its links to moral dilemma pedagogy are still considered in some postgraduate education programs in Australia—so it is likely that they have retained some pedagogical interest for spiritual educators in Australia.

Two early pieces by Brian Crittenden, a prominent Australian philosopher of education, gave perspective to the initial interest in Kohlberg's cognitive-developmental model and its potential contribution to moral education—*Bearings in Moral Education* (1978) and 'Moral Education: Some Aspects of Its Relationship to General Values Education and the Study of Religion' (1981). Crittenden's writing was iconic in showing the level of academic thinking about moral education in the country at that time. The other prominent Australian author in this area is Brian Hill. I consider the work of these two scholars to be the best examples of Australian contributions to the theory of moral education in the 20th century. Of special note is Hill's (1981) contribution on a code of teaching ethics. His ethical position of 'committed impartiality' proposed that it was ethically appropriate for teachers to refer to their own beliefs/values in the classroom if and when they judged that this could make an appropriate educational contribution as content along with the other content being examined. This eschewed partiality and indoctrination, and also a stance of neutrality. It meant that the teacher's personal contribution (like students' personal contributions) was in the domain of content to be critically evaluated; it was not 'privileged'. It protected the privacy of both teachers and students. And it gave teachers an ethical stance that was justifiable and accountable.

Moral education has tended to exist more as an academic pursuit than a working area of curriculum in Australian schools. It is not that the theory was irrelevant to school practice, but, as noted in the section on philosophy and ethics, other factors limited any systematic implementation, especially in government schools. Religious educators in church schools always maintained that their work included a significant component of moral education from a religious perspective.

VALUES EDUCATION

Crittenden (1981) provided a useful clarification of links between the broader construct of moral education and values education. The latter tended to revolve around an understanding of values as

[t]he priorities which individuals and societies attach to certain beliefs, objects and experiences when deciding how they shall live and what they shall treasure. (Hill, 1991, p. 5)

Moral education, while subsuming values education, also was concerned with moral development, ethics and issues such as indoctrination.

The operating definition of values education in Australian schools was eventually crystallised into the following national government statement in 2005:

Any explicit and/or implicit school-based activity which promotes student understanding and knowledge of values, and which develops the skills and dispositions of students so they can enact particular values as individuals and as members of the wider community. (Australian Government Department of Education, Science and Training [DEST], 2005)

Nonetheless, in the later decades of the 20th century there was little in the way of formal values education in public school curricula. This was evident in Hill's claim that values education was

a *poor cousin* of other core areas in the curriculum. The openness of value debates, in which clinching proof of a position is often hard to pin down, easily leads to the view that such studies are 'soft' and 'vague'. (Hill, 1991, p. 4)

He went on to explain how values education included not only classroom teaching on values-related issues, but also the subtle influence of implicit values in school organisation, curriculum and social life.

VALUES CLARIFICATION PEDAGOGY

The Australian educational discourse about values and values education in the 1970s gave special attention to the emergence of the *values clarification* movement (Raths, Harmin & Simon, 1978; Kirchenbaum, 1973). In addition to its application to business and community services, there was also an educational focus (Simon, Howe & Kirschenbaum, 1978). The pedagogy was process oriented, concerned with individuals naming, listing and prioritising their values; it was not concerned with values content and it did not engage in the evaluation of values; it was primarily subjective and it was intended to help individuals reflect on their own personal values. These pedagogical emphases were evident in typical values clarification worksheets—they were often made up of blank spaces in which individuals were to record subjective estimates of their values. The extent to which there might or should be personal exchanges about values amongst participants was always a problem. Another potential difficulty with the approach was the judgment by some that it was too relativist about moral values.

Some values clarification activities entered in church school religious education (Marshall, 1981) as well as into church curricula used for teaching denominational religious education in state schools—as evident in the curriculum materials *Religion in Life* developed for Victorian state schools but used in other states as well (Joint Board of Christian Education, 1988). There still remain in recent practice various strategies and curriculum materials that have roots in the values clarification movement. They tend to be used to promote self-reflection and review of lifestyle.

Simulation Games

Related to the use of values clarification materials in religious education in Australian schools was an interest in learning through simulation games (Benson, 1971). Curriculum materials and writings, such as that of Baker and Marshall (1974) and Marshall (1981), were typical of what has been used since the 1970s.

Conflict Resolution

Also related to values clarification strategies was conflict resolution. While this movement had much to do with community and business mediation, it also had educational applications. Typically, conflict resolution worksheets tended to have more content information (on topics like emotions, anger, frustration, conflict, family and so on) and were not so dependent on generating subjective responses as were the values clarification exercises (Lions International, 1989; Conflict Resolution Network, 1989 & 2012).

Values Dimension to Citizenship Education

Further interest in values education was generated by the introduction of a national citizenship education program in 1994. It included a number of values-related issues (Civics Expert Group, 1994). This development related to discussions of citizenship education in the UK. However, its overall impact on values education in Australia seemed to be minimal.

THE AUSTRALIAN NATIONAL VALUES EDUCATION STUDY

The most significant development in the history of values education in Australian schools was the introduction of a federal government initiative, the National Values Education Study in 2003 (Curriculum Corporation, 2003; Department of Education, Employment and Workplace Relations [DEEWR], 2012). While well funded for a number of years, it appears that the program is now being wound down. The final report (Curriculum

Corporation, 2003) and the review of case studies funded in the program (Curriculum Corporation, 2004) give an indication of its scope. In my view, Hill (1991, 2004, 2006) has long been the most prominent academic spokesman and principal consultant for values education in Australia. He was prominent in the work of the National Study. In the light of his writings on values education and of his work in philosophy of education, Christian education, religious education, school chaplaincy and voluntary religious groups, I suggest that Hill has been the most significant and prolific Australian academic in these areas of spiritual education.

In 2005 the Federal Government published the final version of its statement about the national framework for values-based education (DEST, 2005). This included the final set of nine core values that it considered ought to underpin Australian schooling, as well as the values that it hoped that schools might engender in pupils. There were many positives to the National Values program, and while its intentional contribution towards spiritual education is not in question, two key issues for spiritual education generally emerged from it.

Confusion between Organisational and Curriculum Dimensions

Following Halstead and Taylor (1996), the term 'values education' was used to refer to two different but related domains: firstly, *values in education*—the presence of values within the community/organisational dimension of the school, and secondly, *education in values*—pedagogy and content for educating about values in the classroom. It is not that this differentiation is inappropriate but there are problems where talk about the values in a school's life generally came across as counting for, and therefore substituting for, actual classroom teaching related to values.

The Perennial Problem of How Classroom Teaching/ Learning Might Promote Personal Change in Pupils

The second issue is where discourse about 'teaching' values seems to imply that this activity will automatically bring about personal change in the values and beliefs of pupils. It fails to acknowledge that readily identifiable causal links between teaching interventions and knowledge/cognitive skills are not adequate for explaining the much more complicated and uncertain links between teaching about values and the actual adoption of values/ beliefs. This issue is particularly relevant to the whole range of nonreligious spiritual education initiatives that have appeared in Australian schools.

SPIRITUAL HEALTH, WELLBEING AND HAPPINESS

Spiritual Health and Wellbeing

The emerging thinking about a spiritual dimension to health and wellbeing has had some implications for schooling and for spiritual education in

Australia. The term 'spiritual wellbeing', as well as other references to the spiritual, have been used in the Federal Government's framework document for early childhood education (DEEWR, 2009), as well as in national statements about the purposes of schooling (MYCEETYA, 2008). I get the impression that this thinking about spiritual development is more related to pastoral care and student wellbeing than to the school curriculum. Fisher (2000, 2001) has given research attention to the notion of spiritual health and wellbeing in schools, as perceived by students and teachers. As well, a significant social research contribution on young people's personal/spiritual wellbeing has been made by Eckersley who, I would suggest, is one of the most prominent researchers in Australian youth studies (Eckersley, 2005a, 2005b; Eckersley, Wierenga & Wyn, 2005).

Happiness Education

Based on Seligman's work on positive psychology (Seligman, 2003), one private school in Victoria has commenced a joint project on Positive Education. The overview states that

> Seligman defines Positive Education as traditional education plus approaches that nurture wellbeing and promote mental health. Therefore, a focus on wellbeing within schools entails a holistic approach whereby student accomplishment and wellbeing are both valued objectives that contribute to flourishing. . . . [It] highlights the significant value that best practice teaching brings to the knowledge-transfer process and application of the science in real life settings. (Geelong Grammar School, 2012)[3]

CONCEPTUAL SCHEME FOR SPIRITUALITY THAT MAY HELP ADVANCE PEDAGOGY FOR SPIRITUAL EDUCATION IN SCHOOLS

This author has given considerable attention to a view of spirituality, a related critical pedagogy and a conceptual scheme for a spiritual/moral dimension to the school curriculum, with the purpose of advancing the theory and practice of school spiritual education in both secular and religious spheres (Crawford & Rossiter, 2006; Rossiter, 2010a, 2010b, 2011, 2012). In conclusion, some of the key points in this work will be signposted.

The term 'basic human spirituality' is used to cover the way in which a spiritual/moral dimension is implied in an individual's thinking, valuing and lifestyle. It is a natural genetic human capacity; this understanding is consistent with views of contemporary spirituality in the literature as well as with the various interpretations throughout this book. But this basic human spirituality is usually embedded and implied in behaviour and is not always overt; it needs to be teased out to be identified and evaluated (Rossiter, 2010a). It is not as self-evident as religious spirituality which, often, is referenced to religious texts, artefacts and rituals. Religious spirituality can be interpreted as a basic human spirituality with a *cultural religious overlay*.

Basic human spirituality (as well as religious spirituality) is informed and influenced by cultural meanings, often in subtle ways. While there are many cultural meanings in a society, it is possible to identify the sets of meanings with which individuals or groups identify. They are like the background ideas about life (thinking and assumptions) that people draw on to explain or justify their behaviour. They condition the way people think about their lives. A pedagogy for identifying and appraising the cultural meanings that have a shaping influence on people's lives, therefore, becomes a valuable educational tool for studying any sort of spirituality—religious or not.

This approach lends itself to a critical, inquiring, research-oriented, student-centred pedagogy in which the students themselves investigate contemporary spiritual and moral issues. While not the only pedagogy for spiritual education, it is a particularly useful one. It is applicable both within the religious sphere where religious spirituality is investigated as well as within the secular sphere (Rossiter, 2010b). This sort of pedagogy is being used in across-the-curriculum studies, but its scope and extent have not been identified. In some postgraduate programs, the author's students have tried to model this critical research pedagogy for their own classes.[4] Their own investigation of social issues helped convince them of the value of this type of pedagogy in the classroom.

The other key emphasis in the author's work has been in trying to interpret and conceptualise the broader spiritual and moral dimension to the school curriculum in a way that will help break down the hiatus between theory and practice. The discourse about spiritual education implies some sort of *personal* and *spiritual* learning on the part of pupils—and this applies to the areas noted in the lower secular sphere part of Figure 11.1. The following headings summarise the way in which this question has been addressed.

- Despite the increasing prominence of *spiritual and moral development aims* for all Australian schools, there remains a persistent hiatus between these aims and practice. Little has been done to promote any practice of spiritual education outside the domain of religious education. This remains a critical agenda item for the future of Australian education. (Crawford & Rossiter, 2006, pp. 241–254)
- The *expectations* of parents, teachers and students, and of the wider community, as well as from some educational discourses, for a *spiritual and moral role to the school curriculum*. (Crawford & Rossiter, 2006, pp. 255–276)
- Interpretation of linkages between the classroom *content/pedagogy* and *personal/spiritual change* and *development* in pupils. What is involved in personal/spiritual learning? How is personal learning

linked with personal change? Is there a distinctive personal/spiritual pedagogy? (Crawford & Rossiter, 2006, pp. 277–298)

- An interpretation of the changing *landscape of contemporary spirituality* that suggests the need for a pedagogy of *critical interpretation and evaluation of cultural meanings*, together with a student-centred, research-oriented pedagogy on contemporary personal/social issues. (Crawford & Rossiter, 2006, pp. 404–407; Rossiter, 2010a, 2010b)
- A conceptual scheme for interpreting and implementing a *spiritual and moral dimension to the whole school curriculum.* (Crawford & Rossiter, 2006, pp. 299–321)
- Acknowledgment that one of the perennial problems facing spiritual education in schools is that the very subjects and topics that are intended to promote personal/moral learning tend to have their *personal value subverted by the psychology of the learning environment.* Many students and parents see spiritual education as 'low status' compared with the subjects that are important for advancement like English, Maths and Science. (Crawford & Rossiter, 2006, pp. 307–310)

CONCLUSION: POTENTIAL CONVERGENCE BETWEEN RELIGIOUS AND NONRELIGIOUS APPROACHES TO SPIRITUAL EDUCATION

The approach above proposes that a key element for spiritual education in schools is student research on contemporary spiritual/moral issues. This critical pedagogy involves searching out the spirituality and morality in what is happening and making evaluations of the influence of cultural meanings. This is not the only pedagogy needed but it is an essential one for schools in today's Westernised societies.

The approach can be implemented under the various categories listed in the secular educational sphere (lower half of Figure 11.1). It is proposed that the approach is also important for religious education. In secularised societies, many people who are nominally religious construct meaning, purpose and value in life with little reference to religious traditions. Hence, if religious education (in religious and secular settings) is to enhance the spirituality of young people, then it is inadequate if the content is restricted to a study of religious traditions. It is not that this is no longer needed; all children, no matter what their level of religious practice, have a birthright to access their religious tradition even if this is nominal—it is part of their cultural heritage; but this itself is not enough. An investigation of basic human spirituality and of the culture that has a shaping influence on it is a much needed part of contemporary education in schools.

Elsewhere, it is suggested that this formula for spiritual education is needed to enhance the personal relevance of church school religious education (Crawford & Rossiter, 2006, pp. 391–408). More use of non-religious personal development constructs for interpreting spiritual/moral development is needed to make religious education understandable, accessible and meaningful for students and for the community. While this view is shared by many religious educators, not all would agree, as some would not accept the argument that in the secularised situation which tends to be dominated by individualistic, consumerist cultural meanings, a focus on basic human spirituality is fundamentally important for both religion and religious education today (Rossiter, 2010a). Where the argument is accepted, educators can see that there is a convergence between religious education and various nonreligious approaches to spiritual education; the construct 'spirituality' is pivotal in this movement.

NOTES

1. The earlier chapter, *Perspective on Spiritual Education in Australian Schools: Part 1. The Dominant Contribution from Religious Education*, is available for download at the following website: http://203.10.46.30/spiritual/index.html.
2. The political debate about ethics courses in NSW state schools was referred to in the previous chapter—see note 1 for website details.
3. Seligman (2003) and Ben-Shahar (2007) have been principally involved in the ongoing project.
4. The results of their group projects can be viewed at http://203.10.46.30/mre/636/research.html.

REFERENCES

Australian Government Department of Education, Science and Training (DEST). (2005). *National framework for values education in Australian schools*. Canberra: Author.
Baker, P., & Marshall, M. R. (1974). *Using simulation games*. Melbourne: Joint Board of Christian Education.
Ben-Shahar, T. (2007). *Happier: Learn the secrets to daily joy and lasting fulfilment*. New York: McGraw Hill Professional.
Benson, D. (1971). *The fine art of creating simulation/learning games for religious education*. Nashville, TN: Abingdon Press.
Civics Expert Group. (1994). *Whereas the people. Civics and citizenship education: Report of the Civics Expert Group*. Canberra: Australian Government Publishing Service.
Conflict Resolution Network. (1989 & 2012). *Conflict resolution worksheets*. Retrieved March 30, 2013, from http://www.crnhq.org.
Crawford, M., & Rossiter, G. (1993). The future of holistic education: The recession we had to have. *Curriculum Perspectives, 13*(1), 37–46.
Crawford, M., & Rossiter, G. (2006). *Reasons for living: Education and young people's search for meaning, spirituality and identity. A handbook*. Melbourne: Australian Council For Educational Research.

Crittenden, B. (1978). *Bearings in moral education. A critical review of recent work.* Melbourne: Australian Council for Educational Research.

Crittenden, B. (1981). Moral education: Some aspects of its relationship to general values education and the study of religion. In G. Rossiter (Ed.), *Religious education in Australian schools* (pp. 186–201). Canberra: Curriculum Development Centre.

Curriculum Corporation. (2003). *Values education study: Final report.* Melbourne: Author.

Curriculum Corporation. (2004). *Values education in action: Case studies from 12 values education schools.* Melbourne: Author.

Department of Education, Employment and Workplace Relations (DEEWR). (2009). *Belonging, being & becoming: The early years learning framework for Australia.* Canberra: Author.

Department of Education, Employment and Workplace Relations (DEEWR). (2012). *National Values Education Project.* Retrieved March 30, 2013, from http://www.valueseducation.edu.au/values.

de Souza, M. (2011). Promoting inter-spiritual education in the classroom: Exploring a concept at the heart of the perennial philosophy as a useful strategy to encourage freedom of religious practice and belief. *Journal of Religious Education, 59*(1), 40–50.

Eckersley, R. (2005a). *Well and good: Morality, meaning and happiness* (2nd ed.). Melbourne: Text Publishing.

Eckersley, R. (2005b). *What is wellbeing, and what promotes it? Background to a Manifesto for Wellbeing.* Canberra: Australia Institute.

Eckersley, R., Wierenga A., & Wyn, J. (2005). Life in a time of uncertainty: Optimising the health and wellbeing of young Australians. *Medical Journal of Australia, 183*(8), 402–404.

Federation of Australasian Philosophy in Schools Associations (FAPSA). (2012). FAPSA—the Australasian Home of Philosophy in Schools Retrieved March 30, 2013, from http://fapsa.org.au.

Fisher, J. (2000). Understanding spiritual health and well-being: Becoming human, becoming whole. *Journal of Christian Education, 43*(3), 37–52.

Fisher, J. (2001). The nature of spiritual well-being and the curriculum: Some educators' views. *Journal of Christian Education, 44*(1), 47–58.

Geelong Grammar School. (2012). *Promotion of 'authentic happiness' through Positive Education. Overview.* Retrieved March 30, 2013, from http://ggs.vic.edu.au/PosEd/Overview.aspx.

Halstead, J. M., & Taylor, M. (Eds.). (1996). *Values in education and education in values.* London: Falmer Press.

Hill, B. V. (1981). Teacher commitment and the ethics of teaching for commitment. In G. Rossiter (Ed.), *Religious education in Australian schools* (pp. 179–185). Canberra: Curriculum Development Centre.

Hill, B. V. (1991). *Values education in Australian schools.* Melbourne: ACER.

Hill, B. V. (2004, Apr.). *Values education in schools: Issues and challenges.* Keynote Address at the National Values Education Forum, Curriculum Corporation and the Commonwealth Department of Education, Science and Training, Melbourne.

Hill, B. V. (2006). Values in free fall? Religious education and values in public schools. *Journal of Religious Education.* 54 (2): 51–58.

Hill, B. V. (2012). The schooling of ethics. Address to the 40th conference of the Philosophy of Education Society of Australasia. *Educational philosophy and theory.* Retrieved March, 13, 2013, from http://www.tandfonline.com/doi/abs/10.1080/00131857.2012.753376?journalCode=rept20#preview.

Joint Board of Christian Education. (1988). *Religion in life: An introduction to the program.* Melbourne: Author.

Kirchenbaum, H. (1973). *Readings in values clarification*. Minneapolis, MN: Winston Press.

Kohlberg, J. (1975). The cognitive developmental approach to moral education. *Phi Delta Kappan, 56*(10), 670–677.

Kohlberg, L. (1984). *Essays on moral development: The psychology of moral development*. San Francisco: Harper & Row.

Lions International. (1989). *Lions Quest skills for adolescence program*. Oak Brook, IL: Author.

Lockwood, A. (1978). The effects of values clarification and moral development curricula on school-age subjects: A critical review of recent research. *Review of educational research, 48*(3), 325–364.

Marshall, M-R. (1981). The use of values clarification and simulation games in religious education. In G. Rossiter (Ed.), *Religious education in Australian schools* (pp. 202–209). Canberra: Curriculum Development Centre.

Mason, M., Singleton, A., & Webber, R. (2007). *The spirit of Generation Y: Young people's spirituality in a changing Australia*. Melbourne: John Garratt.

Ministerial Council for Education, Early Childhood Development and Youth Affairs (MYCEETYA). (2008). *Melbourne declaration on education goals for young Australians*. Canberra: Author.

Ota, C., & Erricker, C. (Eds.). (2005). *Spiritual education: Literary, empirical and pedagogical approaches*. (Vol. 3 of the *Spirituality in Religious Education* series). Eastbourne: Sussex Academic Press.

Peters, R. S. (1978). The place of Kohlberg's theory in moral education. *Journal of Moral Education, 7*(3), 150–156.

Raths, L., Harmin, M., & Simon, S. (1978). *Values and teaching* (2nd ed.). Columbus, OH: Charles E. Merrill.

Rossiter, G. (2010a). Religious education and the changing landscape of spirituality: Through the lens of change in cultural meanings. *Journal of Religious Education, 58*(2), 25–36.

Rossiter, G. (2010b). A 'big picture' review of K-12 Australian Catholic school religious education in the light of contemporary spirituality. *Journal of Religious Education, 58*(3), 5–18.

Rossiter, G. (2011). Some perspectives on contemporary Youth Spirituality: A 'need to know' for church school Religious Education. *Religious Education Journal of Australia, 27*(1), 9–15

Rossiter, G. (2012). Perspective on children's spirituality and Catholic primary school religious education: A key starting point for reviewing issues in content and pedagogy. *Journal of Religious Education, 60*(1), 31–40.

Seligman, M. (2003). *Authentic happiness: Using the new Positive Psychology to realise your potential for lasting fulfillment*. Boston: Nicholas Brearley Publishing.

Simon, S. B., Howe, L. W., & Kirschenbaum, H. (1978). *Values clarification: A handbook of practical strategies for teachers and students* (rev. ed.). New York: Hart Publishing.

12 Buddhism in Bhutanese Education

Noa Jones

A REFLECTION

> A dry field of cracked mud may appear barren but hidden under-
> ground fertile seeds could be waiting to sprout with the right amount
> of water. If left fallow too long, however, the potential will dry up.
> Similarly, in Bhutan, there is a drying up of spirituality. But with
> just a bit of nurturing, some well-directed teachings by great masters,
> translations of accessible texts into local languages, a true under-
> standing of the wisdom teachings, and a heart connection to the Bud-
> dhist view could easily blossom in the next generation.
>
> —N. Jones

I arrived in the Kingdom of Bhutan in 2002 to write a book about the making
of the first full-length feature film to be shot in the country. I returned several
times since then before moving to the country full time in 2009 to oversee
an education initiative as part of the Lhomon Society, a registered civil society organization dedicated to promoting sustainable development through
grassroots holistic education and training initiatives. My mandate was to
form a team that would design and implement alternatives to the Bhutanese
curriculum in which, currently, 40% of Bhutanese students fail to advance to
higher degrees. Lhomon's founder, Dzongsar Jamyang Khyentse, felt that, at
the expense of meeting Indian standardized testing requirements, Bhutanese
were losing their connection to their own practicality and wisdom.

I spent the first year meeting local educators, organizing education
'zomdus,'[1] and exploring many of the existing progressive education initiatives being carried out in Bhutan in order to ensure that the organization's
work was not replicating projects already established. I also sought Bhutanese partners to ensure that our outcomes would be truly Bhutanese in
character. Through this research and relationship building, I learned much
about Bhutanese pedagogy and was able to construct a plan for implementing change at a grassroots level. Lhomon Society's efforts are focussed on
two primary sectors: 1) Developing holistic, project-based, integrated curriculum units using local wisdom, references, and traditions; and 2) helping

teachers connect more deeply with their spirituality. The belief is that when a teacher truly understands the essence of Buddhism—not just the ritual—wisdom and compassion have a much better chance of becoming imbedded in the everyday classroom environment.

The material presented in this chapter is drawn from personal experience, individuals' narratives, informal interviews, and anecdotal evidence.

EDUCATION IN BHUTAN—HISTORICAL PERSPECTIVE

Bhutan is often regarded as the last remaining Vajrayana,[2] or tantric, Buddhist kingdom, where 14 centuries of Tibetan Buddhist tradition have been transferred through a careful system of monastic education and guru/disciple instruction. Until about one hundred years ago, this tradition, which was limited to males, was the only formal education available in Bhutan. In 2012, the country celebrated its centenary of formal education, dating from 1913, when two Hindi-medium schools[3] were established in central and western Bhutan under the first king, His Majesty Ugyen Wangchuck. The second king, His Majesty Jigme Wangchuck, continued by setting up about 20 coeducational Hindi-medium primary schools throughout the country.

But the current system only dates back to the early 60s. During the reign (1952–1972) of the third king, His Majesty Jigme Dorji Wangchuck, who began to open Bhutan up to the outside world, Hindi schools were converted to English-medium schools based on the West Bengal Board of Secondary Education model. This was a Euro-Indian system with teacher-centred learning that relied heavily on testing for assessment. There is indeed much to celebrate about these developments. With limited resources within a short time span, Bhutan established an education system that produced literate students who passed international exams, pursued college degrees, and assumed leadership posts in the government. But unlike the monastic graduates of a century ago, the average Thimphu graduate today is likely to have little contact with spiritual guides and has only a limited understanding of his or her grandparents' belief systems and the wisdom traditions upon which they were built.

Like the people of other developing nations, the Bhutanese face enormous challenges as they seek to contend with globalization. The effects of the relatively recent introduction of international media (1999), combined with the imported education system from colonized India, a strong tide of rural-urban migration, diminishing family size, and rapid economic development, have contributed significantly to a strong popular trend toward consumerism and a decrease in traditional Buddhist values.[4]

It was common practice just 50 years ago for every Bhutanese family to send their cleverest son to a monastery to train so that nearly everyone had a cousin or an uncle or a brother who would come home to the village from time to time to offer teachings and guidance. This home-schooling provided ample spiritual education for the generation that is now approaching retirement age. A resident in Wamrong offered this recollection:

> I had an uncle who was a monk and he would come tell stories in our local language and we would listen with so much interest. He would tell us the life story of Gesar of Ling and we would immediately memorize it word for word. There were no other distractions.

She also referred to the crucial role her family played in her spiritual development.

> We tended to do what our parents did. We learnt how to fill water bowls and pray. But nowadays my kids won't do it because there are so many distractions. And many people are working in office these days and neglecting their shrines. So that's the danger. If it is not taught in the class, the other side [meaning, learning by example] is no longer possible. It is vanishing. (Personal interview, Wangmo, conducted in Thimphu, October 2012)

The tradition known as *gomchen*, highly trained lay clergy who wear robes and are allowed to marry, also played a crucial role in the early education system. Gomchen taught villagers to read and write *Choeke*,[5] conducted rituals, and gave guidance, earning a great deal of respect from their communities.

These traditions are on the wane. In an article in the *Bhutan Observer* about the disappearance of gomchen, a villager from Rangshikhar stated:

> Young boys are not interested to stay behind and become gomchens. In future, there would be no gomchen in our village to conduct important religious rituals. The whole gewog[6] is feeling the dearth of gomchen.

In the absence of gomchen and learned family members, there is a widening gap in transference of Buddhist wisdom traditions. An emerging practice is to send favourite sons to boarding schools in India, not to the monasteries.

The Education Ministry does its part in promoting values education and linking to Buddhist wisdom traditions by including Buddhist texts in the Dzongkha language curriculum and requiring prayers in morning assemblies so that by graduation, every student will at least have encountered certain Buddhist texts. Lopon Lungten Gyatsho, the Director for the Institute for Linguistic and Cultural Studies in Semtokha which trains most of the country's Dzongkha teachers, stated:

> If one is to study spirituality, Dzongkha is a perfect language because of its rich spiritual terms that are mostly used in day to day conversation. Dzongkha largely talks about culture, values, spirituality, religion,

mind and mind related things. In fact Dzongkha language originally was used more for spiritual purpose than any other sciences. (E-mail interview, November 23, 2012)

But as many have confessed, Dzongkha class and the required prayers do not always translate into a true understanding of the Buddhist view of impermanence and emptiness or wisdom and compassion. "It's more of the ritualistic, rote, memorization, not necessarily understanding," said Tashi Lhamo, a graduate of a boarding school in Punakha (Personal interview, November 2012).

RELIGIOUS INFLUENCES

Buddhism was introduced to Bhutan in the 7th century AD by Tibetan King Songtsen Gyalpo. The Indian Buddhist saint Padmasambhava, also known as Guru Rinpoche, came to teach and practice in what are now holy sites across the region in the year 747. Today, it is estimated that between two-thirds and three-quarters of the Bhutanese population (estimated at 700,000) classify themselves as Vajrayana Buddhists (Center for Bhutan Studies, 2013). Those remaining are primarily ethnic Nepalis who practise Hinduism or Christianity. Christianity is on the rise, though it accounts for less than 1% of the population (Center for Bhutan Studies, 2013). The education minister of the past five years, Thakur Singh Powdel, was a practising Hindu.

Another non-Buddhist responsible for shaping the education system of Bhutan was Father William Mackey, a Canadian Jesuit who spent 32 years in Bhutan, from 1963 to 1995, by invitation of the third king. The country had resisted outside influence until the third king's reign; he opened the doors to tourism in 1964, the same year that he established the Ministry of Education. Mackey established Bhutan's first English-medium upper secondary school in an abandoned cowshed in Kanglung, Tashigang, with seven students, in 1973. He went on to become the beloved teacher of many of today's leaders of Bhutan, and the school has flourished, becoming the country's first accredited university, Sherubtse College. The number of schools grew from about 20 to around 100 during this era.

In 1999, the fourth king, Jigme Singye Wangchuck, made radical changes and lifted a ban on television and the Internet for the first time. Though it has been less than 15 years since the country opened its doors to modern media, youth have quickly been indoctrinated by powerful consumerist messages.

Television has rapidly changed social relationships in Bhutan, people spend a lot of time watching television, it's the centerpiece of many households. To be fair, it has had some positive effects, people watch educational programs, Discovery Channel, and some programs help open up once taboo topics for conversation. But certainly the consumerist and materialist messages present in advertising and programs produced in the West are having a strong influence. (Personal Interview with Mansoor Fassihi of the Bhutan Center for Media and Democracy [BCMD], March 2013)

Fassihi also said that television has created a cognitive dissonance surrounding Bhutan's mission to preserve its culture. "There is an anxiety about saying traditional things are boring, they have a difficulty squaring those traditions with what they are attracted to on television."

In many ways, the ancient cultural practices and Buddhist belief system of the Bhutanese people are contemporary and progressive, but in the face of modern 'development,' young Bhutanese are losing their connection to this wealth of tradition.

Currently, under the fifth king, His Majesty Jigme Khesar Namgyel Wangchuck, there are more than 550 schools. Bhutanese students are offered eleven years of basic education free of charge, with seven years of primary education beginning at age 6, followed by four years of secondary education. At the end of class X,[7] they sit for the National Board Examinations. Those who pass the exams can continue for two more years of higher secondary education, and the rest have the option to pay for private schooling, attend vocational training, or enter the labour market.

With high-stakes exams at the centre of the education system, the number of 'school leavers,' or drop-outs, is increasing and youth unemployment is exceptionally high in Bhutan. With unemployment at 7.3% (Ministry of Labour and Human Resources, 2012) gang activity and criminality have increased steeply. Gangs have sprung up in the capital with a style strongly influenced by popular Korean gangster movies. It is not the image of Bhutan as a Shangri-la as it is often portrayed in international media.

The fourth king is credited with introducing the concept of Gross National Happiness (GNH) *vis à vis* Gross Domestic Product, in 1974. GNH is now considered the backbone of policy making for Bhutan (Centre for Bhutan Studies, 2013). Culturally, Bhutanese are known to have a predisposition for certain gentle traits—for instance, few Bhutanese would kill a fly—however, it is difficult to expect that an entire population would value holistic happiness over economic development. In fact, it would be a dangerous assumption that the Bhutanese are naturally more spiritual and less materialistic than any other people. Buddhist pilgrims who come to Bhutan from the West are often surprised by the Buddhist practice they encounter, which, though prolific, is often ritualistic—almost deifying Buddha—and less about inner grappling with the essence-less ego. This was observed by Prakke (2005):

> I am frustrated to see (after I personally stumbled across Buddhism and was taken by surprise by its profundity) how most Bhutanese have no

clue about the jewel they hold in the palm of their hands. I can accept that people choose to disregard spirituality, setting other priorities in their lives. But I feel thwarted that a clumsy and shallow presentation of Buddhism puts off open-minded Bhutanese who are actually in search of the very inspiration, meaning and fulfilment that Buddhism can help you find. (p. 120)

THE LANGUAGE ISSUE

Since 1964, Bhutanese students have performed prayers as part of their morning assembly. They recite a homage to Manjushri—the sword-wielding god of wisdom—which includes a short refuge and Bodhicitta prayer and a dedication of merit.[8] Those in boarding schools often have more extended evening prayer sessions where they recite the *Sherab Nyingpo* and *Barche Namsel*. These prayers are recited in Dzongkha or Tibetan, neither of which is the primary language spoken in the country. "In Bhutan we say we chant mantra but hardly anyone knows what they are saying because it's all in complicated languages and the scripts and everything," said Pema Lhaden, a recent college graduate (Videotaped interview, January 10, 2012).

Students are expected to learn basic dharma principles in their Dzongkha language classes. Dzongkha is the official language of Bhutan but only a minority of students speak it as their native tongue. In fact, according to a survey by the Centre of Bhutan Studies,[9] it ranked fourth among the country's 24 other languages. The most popular, Tshangla (also known as Scharchopka from eastern Bhutan), is without a written script. Dzongkha uses *Choeke* script (classical Tibetan text).

Formal Dzongkha is a complex and somewhat stiff language that was traditionally used only by the elite in society; 'Dzong' means fortress and so it was the language of high officials who occupied positions of power. Dzongkha is not often a favourite subject of students; spelling and grammar are famously difficult. To make matters worse, the teachers of Dzongkha have a reputation for being very strict. One graduate of a school in Mongar recalled:

> I used to hate Dzongkha class. If you weren't correct you had to pull up your kira and recite again with your rear exposed getting beaten.

A Thimphu graduate said that poor spelling resulted in 50 whacks on the tips of her fingers. Corporal punishment is now prohibited in public schools, although debate about reversing this rule was hotly discussed as late as 2012.

Dzongkha teachers are meant to be scholars who have been rigorously trained in Buddhist traditions so the training of these teachers is essential to the transfer of these traditions.

There are basically two ways to become a Dzongkha instructor. One is through the monastic system and the other from the school system. Most of the Dzongkha experts come from the monastic background, although it focuses more on Choeke rather than Dzongkha. (E-mail interview with Lopon Lungten, Director for the Institute for Linguistic and Cultural Studies, Semtokha, November 13, 2012)

While many of these teachers are former monks, one Thimphu resident commented, "Those monks must have left for a reason. Teaching, then, became their only option." The rest of the teachers come from the college system where degrees in Dzongkha are offered.

Some say that the linkage of dharma to this rather tough course might serve to deter students from enjoying the actual subject matter. Phuntsho, a native Tshangla-lo speaker, asserted:

Dzongkha is just a language class, like English, it's not about spirituality. I became Buddhist despite Dzongkha class, not because of it. I really do think Dzongkha is important, it is our national language but it is not a way to teach spirituality. I think the curriculum is really wrong. (Personal interview, December 2012)

Phuntsho takes her 7-year-old son to weekend classes with Lama Shenphen Zangpo, a Welsh monk residing full time in Bhutan who conducts meditation courses in the capital city of Thimphu. He teaches the story of the Buddha and other saints, meditation, and compassionate action:

I can't help thinking, what if that was available in the schools! In our time if we had these opportunities I would have learned much more because they are enjoying. (Phuntsho, personal interview, December 2012)

Lama Shenphen is deeply engaged with disenfranchised youth, particularly drug addicts, and he finds most have many misconceptions about the Buddhist view. As he said:

The way dharma is presented in schools is moralistic, they (the students) are not looking at it as an inner practice. (Personal interview with Lama Shenphen at the Ambient Café in Thimphu, November 30, 2012)

Phuntsho also said that learning Dzongkha in school had nothing to do with her own spiritual growth.

Funny, in my case I think I learned more from when I was in touch with people from the outside [meaning foreigners] because they began questioning things we took for granted and that made me reflect and made me search for answers. So I looked at English language books from Thich Nat Han and Trungpa Rinpoche. (Personal interview, December 2012)

Some do benefit from Buddhism taught in Dzongkha class. Tshewang Wangchuk, Executive Director of the Bhutan Foundation, is a product of the 1964 system and an example of its success. In a personal communication to the author in November 2012 he said that he had been born a Buddhist and grew up in a household rich with Buddhist tradition but that in his Dzongkha classes his understanding increased and deepened. After completing his studies in Bhutan, he earned a BSc in Plant and Wildlife Management from the University of Maryland and an MSc from the University of Life Sciences, Norway. He is currently completing his doctoral degree at the University of Montana. He offered the following:

> There were a lot of good teachers in that time and they, in turn, were taught mostly by monks and lamas and learned scholars. When we went to school, we studied the Gyalse Laklen,[10] the 37 Practices of the Bodhisattva. A lot of the core tenets of Buddhism are there in that text. We would learn grammar in Choeke so our comprehension of the verses was a lot better from just rote learning. In fact when I listen to a lot of the teachings in the West, it's all covered in the texts we learned in high school in Bhutan—the teachers only enrich them with their unique life lessons and examples. We also studied epics like Khandro Drowa Zangmo, which is a biography of a great practitioner and Nagarjurna's *Letter to a Friend* in Dzongkha class.

But, he adds:

> The version of Gyalse Laklen they are teaching now is a very abridged dumbed down version. I think teachers are getting lazy. It's not like spiritual education does not exist in the Bhutanese education system. It's just that people don't pay attention to what we have. It is especially sad when Bhutanese have to learn Buddhism in English given that we have such a unbroken lineage of great masters. (Personal communication, November 26, 2012)

Lama Shenphen says that when he teaches from the 37 Practices, his students, who have memorized it in full, do not recognize the ideas and are surprised to find that they have spent so much time saying words without understanding the meaning. With proper instruction they suddenly understand how relevant these texts can be in day-to-day life.

Today, because of a shortage of Dzongkha teachers, not all are trained rigorously in Buddhism. "Just because I'm good at Dzongkha doesn't mean I can teach Dzongkha," said Nima Tshering, a lecturer at Paro College of Education. "Only at a primary level. But for the higher classes it's important that you have specific training, that you are a graduate of ILCS or a monk graduate of shedra."[11] (Personal interview, October, 2012).

WHAT'S BEING DONE?

The rate of economic growth and social change in Bhutan is bewildering, and there is an ever increasing stream of consultants and experts who come to "fix" the problems, drawn by the country's mystique. There are countless initiatives, sometimes parallel, sometimes contradictory, aimed at creating a 'truly Bhutanese' system of education. With so many eyes on Bhutan, the Bhutanese find themselves working fast to produce such a system. There have been numerous workshops, roundtable discussions, reports, and studies, where there seems to be a general consensus that a truly Bhutanese education must have a strong spiritual dimension. For instance, The Royal Education Council, a think tank for the Ministry of Education, recently published a new Education Framework which includes spirituality as one of 13 'capabilities' to be developed in learners (along with physical fitness, numeracy, teamwork, and technology, among others). It defines spirituality as "To be enquiring, compassionate, tolerant and self reliant citizens through right thought and action" (Royal Education Council, 2012, p. 75).

In January 2009, the then Prime Minister Lyonchoen Jigmi Y. Thinly said that bringing GNH fully into the education system was a top priority for Bhutan. Later that year, on December 7, he invited 25 education specialists from 18 countries to participate in a week-long conference on GNH Education. The aim was for His Majesty the Fifth King, the honorable Prime Minister, and Education Minister Powdel to seek advice for the creation of an educational system more in tune with their values of Gross National Happiness. Scholars in Contemplative Education were asked to speak about bringing contemplation and other holistic practices into schools. An additional 80 participants joined other invited experts including Bhutanese students, educators, and officials.

The primary outcome of the conference was the introduction of mandatory mindfulness practice during morning and afternoon assemblies in all Bhutanese schools. To that end, UNICEF sponsored a trip for 71 principals to study meditation with Professor Art Ong Jumsai Na Ayudhya, Chief Administrator of the Sathya School in Thailand, whose style is decidedly not part of the Vajrayana Buddhist path, but rather from the lineage of Sai Baba. This was an interesting choice for a Vajrayana Kingdom. Lama Sonam Phuntshok, a learned khenpo from eastern Bhutan who now teaches in India, reviewed the PowerPoint presentation and other materials provided to the teachers by Art Ong and said that while this meditation can be beneficial, it is important that everyone involved be aware of the traditions that are being promoted.

> We always begin teaching by identifying the sutra or source of text as it relates to Shakyamuni Buddha. I don't recognize where these practices are originating from. (Personal interview, October 2012).

Nevertheless, Bhutanese teachers participating in the Royal Education Council workshops said in their exit surveys and during group discussions that some meditation has been useful in calming students before and after classes.

Another initiative involves Lhomon Education which is a project of the Lhomon Society, a grassroots organization founded in 2010 by Bhutanese Lama Dzongsar Khyentse Rinpoche, with a mission to support and promote sustainable development in Bhutan through holistic education and training initiatives. Khyentse Rinpoche offered one of his *shedras*, the Chokyi Gyatso Institute in Dewathang, eastern Bhutan, as a laboratory where new ideas could be tested out. I was hired to oversee the project in 2009. Our primary recommendation is to eliminate high-stakes exams.

After a year of evaluating the existing initiatives in the country, we conducted a curriculum design workshop in July 2012. Teachers were given instruction on a number of strategies such as active learning, place-based learning, multiple intelligences, listening skills, integrated curriculum development, essential questions, and daily meditation. In the post-workshop evaluation questionnaires, the teachers resoundingly requested further instruction on meditation in the classroom. In response to this request, we have coordinated a one-week meditation practicum, the Mindfulness Camp for Bhutanese Teachers, in which more than 40 educators and college directors participated in January 2013. Many said that the intensive meditation they were guided through during the retreat helped them understand Buddhism for the first time and recommended that all teachers have an opportunity to explore and deepen their practice. We are also conducting a pilot project, introducing project-based learning with 18 students in eastern Bhutan.

At another level, the Ministry of Labour Department of Human Resources (MoLHR), which oversees all the technical training institutes in Bhutan, is actively seeking ways to infuse their curriculum with mindfulness practices, particularly at the two arts institutes. MoLHR has a keen interest in helping cultivate dignity of labour and job satisfaction at all of the institutes, and programme officers at the Training and Professional Service Division have expressed their belief that there is a direct correlation between achieving these goals and developing mindfulness/awareness practice. Additionally, more advanced philosophical study can contribute to the experience of students at the arts schools who are learning how to sculpt, paint, embroider, and carve traditional Buddhist crafts. Most of these crafts are based on Buddhist scripture, but the students do not receive any direct training on the concepts behind the images. In some cases, the instructors can impart knowledge ad hoc but the institutes are interested in formalizing the study by introducing mandatory courses in Buddhism.

Finally, the Royal University of Bhutan (RUB) has recently launched a four-year plan to completely overhaul the university system. Deborah Young of Naropa University in Boulder, Colorado, was brought in to oversee a participatory action research project on developing a GNH pedagogy and classroom practice that aligns with Gross National Happiness. Her first workshop in February 2012 at the Paro College of Education was designed "to identify the most deeply rooted values among the people of Bhutan, and to identify the gaps between those values and current educational practice" (E-mail correspondence to the author, October 8, 2012). Participants in the study are all lecturers at one of Bhutan's 11 colleges under the Royal University of Bhutan: Royal Institute of Health Science, National Institute of Traditional Medicine, Sherubtse (Liberal Arts), Gaeddu, Institute of Language and Culture Studies, Jigme Namgyal Polytechnic, Paro College of Education, Samtse College of Education, the College of Science and Technology, the College of Natural Resources, and Royal Thimphu College (an affiliate college).

The team came up with 22 themes by organizing and categorizing the 180 patterns that emerged from their initial study analysis.

> Mindfulness was one of the top five themes to be addressed, with little mindfulness practices in the college and in the classroom. One of the interventions recommended is that each of the four years represents one of the pillars where everyone in RUB undertakes a one week journey into the pillar. (E-mail correspondence from Young to the author, October 8, 2012)

The third year would be reserved for spirituality and mindfulness. Young recommended a one-week mandatory retreat for all college students in all the colleges and added in her e-mail:

> I believe many of the lecturers who were research team members were quite surprised by the overwhelming gap of GNH values and principles.

INNATE SPIRITUALITY

The Bhutanese have the Buddhadharma infused in every part of their lives—in the architecture, the patterns on their *kiras*, in their languages, their names, and in dance. Most Bhutanese practice nonviolence, even to the point of not killing mosquitos. Spirituality is not perceived as something separate from daily life, and there is a general willingness to respect the Buddha. It is uncommon to see Bhutanese emotions flaring; it is so deeply understood that negative emotions are poisonous. As Diederik Prakke (2005) said, he could never be as Buddhist as the Bhutanese who have suckled on the milk of Buddhism.

My own observations over the past several years suggest that even without formal study, certain beliefs appear to exist amongst Bhutanese, if not outwardly, then just under the surface. Like a child raised by multilingual parents who never formally studies or even speaks one of those languages, he or she is far more likely to quickly become fluent upon setting the intention to learn.

He or she will have the rhythm and sound of the spoken word deeply embedded in the psyche. Similarly, it seems Bhutanese understand the language and the values of Buddhism, even if these understandings are latent. At the very least, they are accustomed to sitting cross-legged for long periods of time!

So for the time being, Bhutan is still a fertile land for the dharma. But it would not take long for the unbroken lineage of Vajrayana Buddhism in Bhutan to become like that of Cambodia or Mongolia,[12] where the traditions nearly became extinct and are only now being reintroduced by outsiders. There are some Bhutanese who wonder if that will be the case for Bhutan. Or indeed, is it already the case? Certainly, the recent initiatives discussed here, I believe, are a move in the right direction.

NOTES

1. 'Zomdue' is a Bhutanese term for a village gathering. The Lhomon Society zomdus were designed as a platform for local educators to share ideas and discuss issues concerning their work.
2. There are three primary traditions of Buddhism: Theravada (a relatively conservative tradition as practised in Sri Lanka, Thailand, and Burma, for example); Mahayana (practised throughout China, Japan, and elsewhere, focussed on altruism); and Vajrayana (the 'swift path to enlightenment,' with a shamanic influence, also known as Tibetan or Tantric Buddhism).
3. 'Hindi-medium' means that they were taught in Hindi. Hindi was the medium of instruction.
4. Anecdotally, Bhutan has been mythologized as a Shangri La and many countries in the world are looking to it as a model for development. For instance, a UN team has requested the Prime Minister to establish a secretariat to develop a new economic paradigm document based on Bhutan's GNH philosophy. Many Buddhist Westerners who come to Bhutan on pilgrimage are surprised to find that not every Bhutanese citizen is a devout Buddhist and that they have the same material wishes as Westerners.
5. The Tibetan script in which most Buddhist texts are written.
6. Village or cluster of villages below the Dzongkhag district.
7. Roman numerals are used in Bhutan, coinciding with the Indian education system. Class X may be translated into grade 10 in Western countries.
8. Nearly all Buddhist practices begin with taking refuge in the Buddha, dharma, and sangha. This is followed by a Bodhichitta prayer, wishing that all beings may attain enlightenment. Then the main practice, mantra, or prayer is recited. At the end, all the merit accumulated from performing these acts is offered outward, so as not to increase the ego of the practitioner.
9. In the *GNH and GNH Index: A Short Guide to the Gross National Happiness Index* from the Centre for Bhutan Studies (Ura, Alkire, Zangmo & Wangdi, 2013), the authors offer results from the 2010 GNH Survey, the first official national survey on GNH in Bhutan. See http://www.ophi.org.uk/wp-content/uploads/Ura-et-al-Bhutan-Happiness-Chapter.pdf.
10. Wylie: rgyal sras lag len so bdun ma.
11. Traditional monastic college of higher Buddhist studies
12. Mongolia has an issue similar to the Dzongkha issues of Bhutan. Buddhist texts are in high Mongolian and are now being translated into the vernacular so that common people can benefit from the words.

REFERENCES

Centre for Bhutan Studies. (2013). *Gross National Happiness Survey Results.* Retrieved March 3, 2013, from http://www.grossnationalhappiness.com/survey-results.

Centre for Bhutan Studies (2013). *Gross National Happiness website.* Retrieved March 3, 2013, from http://www.grossnationalhappiness.com/.

Ministry of Labour and Human Resources. (2012). *Labour Force Survey.* Retrieved March 3, 2013, from http://www.molhr.gov.bt/molhr_site.

Prakke, D. (2005). The Buddhist truth of happiness, spirituality, and development—The case of governance in Bhutan. *Journal of Bhutan Studies*, 12, Winter 2005, pp. 119–165.

The Royal Education Council. (2012). *The national education framework: Shaping Bhutan's future.* Thimphu, Bhutan: Author.

Thinley, J. Y. (2013). What is Gross National Happiness?

13 Life Education in Contemporary Chinese Societies

Ngar-sze Elsa Lau

INTRODUCTION

In a classroom of a secondary school in Beijing, most students are deeply moved to tears while they are watching a video of childbirth, captured at hospital by another student. Having never imagined the difficulty and physical suffering of a mother, the students are amazed with joy when the small new life starts crying loudly on the vivid screen (Yuan Wang, 2004). After the lesson, these adolescents started making sense of their lives and understanding the meaning of respecting their parents and valuing the lives of others.

This is one example of 'life education' (LE) (*shengming jiaoyu*) teaching activities promoted in mainland China. LE has been gradually promoted and recognised in the last two decades as a formal or informal curriculum with the aims of preventing campus violence and suicide in Chinese societies among 'two shores, four places' (*liangan sidi*). 'Two shores' (*liangan*) refers to mainland China and Taiwan, while 'four places' (*sidi*) includes the 'two shores', Hong Kong and Macao. Mainland China, Taiwan, Hong Kong and Macao are geographically closely located but diverse given the historical, political, social and religious development in the last century. Nevertheless, similar social crises among children and adolescents caused by modernisation and globalisation have occurred in these Chinese societies. Common concerns about the challenges in education and society have provided opportunities for educators from the 'four places' to interact on the curriculum and pedagogy of LE.

Religious education has never been implemented as a statutory policy in these Chinese societies due to cultural, historical and political conditions. We may ask, then: How can LE relate to the spiritual needs of students? This chapter discusses the development of LE in the Chinese societies in 'two shores, four places' and how LE curriculum, particularly in Taiwan and mainland China, is related to spirituality in building resilience.

DEVELOPMENT OF 'LIFE EDUCATION' IN 'TWO SHORES, FOUR PLACES'

Taiwan

After taking over Taiwan[1] in 1949, the Nationalist Party of China (*Kuomingtang*) effectively implemented social policies with the political and financial support of the United States. The success of industrialisation beginning in the 1960s, especially in information technology, led to rapid economic growth in Taiwan, one of the four 'Asian Dragons'. Yet social problems created by alienation have emerged gradually, similar to those in most developed countries. Less government control of institutionalised religions has resulted in the gradual flourishing of Daoism, Buddhism and Christianity. Nevertheless, due to complex historical and political factors from early in the 20th century, since the Nationalist Party moved to Taiwan, religious education has never been launched in public schools. Religious education or religious rituals are permitted in private religious schools, but forcing students or teachers to join any religious rituals is forbidden by law (Shihangqing, 2002).

Since the mid-1990s there has been increasing number of students almost addicted to computer games and indulging in drugs, sex and violence. Negative incidents, such as the suicides of some top achieving female school students, aroused much attention in society, and in 1999, suicide was the third major cause of death among youth, following cancer and violence. In 1996 a Catholic girls school started implementing a life education program based on ethics.[2] In 1999, the 9.21 earthquake, in which over 2400 people died, greatly impacted society. In 2000 the government organised a Life Education Committee and issued a promotion plan in schools and universities with a TWD 200 million budget (Chen, 2004).

Since 2006, LE has been implemented as a credit-bearing elective curriculum for senior secondary and university students (Chen, 2004; Sun, 2004) and LE in Taiwan has developed rapidly with the publication of teaching materials and textbooks (see Ji, 2007; Lin et al., 2004; Wu, 2006). Forums and conferences on LE were organised for teachers by the Education Department and universities (see National Changhua University of Education, 2006). The Life Education Centre of the National Taiwan University (2008) was established, and the *Journal of Life Education* (n.d.) began publishing. Learning materials and lesson plans began to be shared on websites and forums (see Taiwan Life Education Association, 2004; Education Department Life Education Learning, 2012). Among Chinese societies, Taiwan, with great support from the government as well as the community, pioneered LE as part of the education system and thus became a model for others.

Mainland China

Mainland China, which is officially the People's Republic of China (PRC),[3] has been ruled by the Chinese Communist Party (CCP) since 1949, following the civil war. With a Marxist-Leninist policy criticising religious beliefs as the 'opiate of the masses', creating inequality, CCP members profess atheism. As a result of a rigorous political movement over the three decades since the 1950s, education systems, institutionalised religions and cultural heritage traditions were largely destroyed. However, control by authorities over religion and culture became more relaxed with the Open Policy in the early 1980s. In the 1982 PRC constitution, Article 36 states that citizens have the right to enjoy religious freedom and any 'normal religious activities' are protected by the state. However, religious education has been forbidden in schools since the founding of the PRC to ensure that "no one may make use of religion" to "interfere with the educational systems of the state" (People's Republic of China, 1982).

Under the Open Policy, industries, finance and the market economy have been established rapidly and successfully in China, resulting in the emergence of wealth disparity. Social problems have also arisen in both cities and villages, with mental health one of the most challenging issues.[4] For example, the suicide rate of adolescents in rural areas is higher than that in urban areas, and that of females is much higher than that of males[5] (Hawton, Saunders & O'Conner, 2012). It appears that the more mature the student, the higher the suicide ideation rate; hence suicide has become a major cause of death among college students[6] (Yu & Wang, 2004). Moreover, incidents involving family disasters and campus violence including child and adolescent homicide have occurred due to chaotic morality and twisted values about life and money. Recent youth crimes such as the case of Yao Jiaxin[7] have been rigorously discussed in public Internet forums.

One key issue in the education system is the dominating examination-oriented culture, resulting in unfair education opportunities involving great disparity between city and village. Most students, almost becoming 'examinations machines', aim for high marks and promotion in the competitive examinations. In light of the current birth control policy, parents put particularly high expectations on their only child. Moreover, many school teachers pay little respect to students, practising corporal punishment and identifying students with numbers instead of their names (Wu, 2010; Zheng, 2011). Indeed, problems and issues of psychological well-being and mental health have become concerns in schools and the wider society in the last decade.[8] This has led to a consensus in promoting LE, as in Taiwan, in cultivating students with right attitudes, teaching the knowledge and skills of psychological health and promoting values on life and safety.

Formal LE in mainland China started first in 2004 in Liaoning province, which issued a working plan of LE in schools (Ying Wang, 2004). The key aims offered guidance for students to experience the uniqueness and value of their lives, as well as understanding life and death, and their relationships with nature. Plans were made for centres of LE to be built in 100 counties for training teachers, medical professionals and volunteers in providing guidance, counseling service and support to students. Positive results of LE implementation were reported in the media, such as the gratefulness of students after visiting a hospice (Yuan Wang, 2004). In 2005 Shanghai and Hunan provinces also started promoting LE in their schools by issuing guiding outlines and policy documents (Shanghai Education Committee, 2005). Cultivating attitudes concerned with caring, valuing life, healthy lifestyle and respecting others was emphasised.

Following the 70,000 fatalities of the Sichuan earthquake, the Education Department of Yunnan Province (2008) was prompted to promote LE and publish a series of textbooks: *Life, Live and Living Education* (Lo, 2009a, 2009b, 2009c). Accordingly, LE became a compulsory subject in all kindergartens as well as primary and junior secondary schools. For senior secondary school, college and university students, there are 32 credit-bearing learning hours. Over 16 provinces and cities such as Shaanxi, Heilongjiang, Chongqing, Changchun, Suzhou and Shengzhen also implemented the policy and adapted the Yunnan curriculum (Zheng, 2011). The most recent government implementation plan in 2010 confirmed that LE had been accepted as a national agenda in the outline of the country's plan 2010–2020 (Central People's Government of the People's Republic of China, 2010).

Useful websites of teaching materials and seminars to train teachers and parents have been organised by NGOs and government agencies such as the National Life Work Committee of Education (2012) and *Sansheng Jiaoyuwang* (2009). The Beijing Normal University established the first Life Education Research Centre in the country in April 2010 with a resourceful website, China Life Education (2010). The centre also organised the First Summit Forum on Life Education for University Students in 2011. Further, there have been over 5,000 academic articles published in China (Liu, 2010).

Hong Kong

Hong Kong,[9] a British colony for 150 years before 1997, has been successful in industrialisation and modernisation since the 1960s as one of the four Asian Dragons. After the PRC resumed sovereignty, the Hong Kong Special Administrative Region (HKSAR) still maintains its position as an international financial centre with its laissez-faire capitalist system under the principle of 'one country, two systems'. Unlike other British colonial countries, the colonial government employed a non-intervening religious policy, though Christianity had replaced traditional Confucianism in playing a major role in society by dominating the political system, social establishment and education (Kwong, 2002). Nearly half of all schools are Christian based. Mono-religious education has been offered in religious schools but not in governmental or aided schools. Nevertheless, Hong Kong people have enjoyed religious freedom, and most major Chinese religions and rituals are still practised within the Chinese community.

The materialistic and competitive social environment has caused some adolescents in Hong Kong to suffer attention deficit disorders, Internet addiction, anxiety and depression,[10] and suicidal ideation (Research International, 2007). Indeed, suicide has become the leading cause of death for the 15 to 24 age group (Yip et al., 2004) which has aroused considerable concern in society (Sun, Hui & Watkins, 2006).

In 1996, a nonreligious secondary school first started LE[11] in Hong Kong (Chow & Yeung, 2002). The Hong Kong Anglican Church (Kwok, 2004) and the Evangelical Lutheran Church of Hong Kong (2006) later published textbooks on LE. The Centre of Buddhist Studies of the University of Hong Kong (2005) organised an LE seminar for teachers. The Catholic Diocese of Hong Kong and Methodist Church Hong Kong issued guidelines for promoting life and ethics education (Wong, 2010). Tertiary institutes such as the Centre for Religious and Spirituality Education (2006) and the Centre for Quality-Life Education (2010) have run yearly training programmes for teachers with the support of the Education Bureau. Nevertheless, LE is still not implemented in the formal school curriculum but is included as an aspect in Moral, Civic and National Education (Education Bureau, 2012; W. H. Ho, personal communication, August 30, 2012). Overall, LE has been recognised broadly by teachers for promoting positive values, strengthening resilience and preventing suicide and campus violence in schools (Yeung, 2005).

Macao

Macao,[12] which had been under Portuguese rule since the mid-16th century, was the last European colony in Asia before sovereignty was returned to the PRC on December 20, 1999. People in Macao have enjoyed religious freedom though Catholics, particularly, were privileged under the Portuguese regime. Religious education was offered in religious schools.

Macao's economy heavily relies on gambling so that corrupted colonial bureaucrats, organised crime and triad violence outside the casino have become the territory's image (Lo, 2008). Adolescents get jobs at casinos quite easily and this has raised concerns about the drop-out rate from secondary schools although 15-year free education is provided.[13] Violent behavior, smoking and psychological problems are common juvenile problems (Chen, 2003).

With the influence of Taiwan and Hong Kong, some schools in Macao started implementing LE as informal curriculum in 2000 (Su, 2005). While LE is not part of the formal curriculum implemented by the government, the official body has supported related events in the community. For example, the Macao Education and Youth Department (2002) promoted a

'Holistic cultivation scheme', supported by NGOs including Macao Caritas and Macao Anglican Social Services. The Drug Prevention Department established the Life Education Center in 2004 for preventing drug abuse, and the YMCA of Macao organised training workshops for teachers and social workers about life and death education.

Frequent Interchanges on LE in Liangansidi

Not only has there been great diversity in the historical, political, social and religious development of Taiwan, China, Hong Kong and Macao during the past century, their cultures have been quite distinct as well. Nonetheless, scholars and educators from the 'four places' have started sharing experiences in promoting LE by frequently organising *liangansidi* conferences or forums since 2000.[14]

There has been no state religion or RE policy in the four Chinese societies due to complex historical and cultural reasons but LE appears to have brought Chinese together from the different societies. This could be related to their recent histories. Almost all share similar hardships and there are many stories of previous generations undergoing arduous experiences during the Western invasions and bloody revolutions of the last two centuries, followed by the Japanese invasion and the civil war in the 1950s. Many Chinese died from wars or hunger. As Tu Wei-ming (1994) contends, the sufferings of the last generations including rootlessness, alienation and marginality have constituted 'the collective psyche of the modern Chinese' (p. v). Therefore, settling down with a satisfactory material life, sometimes by emigrating, has become a common dream. Most Chinese parents share similar aspirations for their children: a higher degree, a better job and a more stable life.[15]

Hence, most contemporary 'tiger parents' expect their children to perform well academically, following the model of those successful literati who were selected from the civil service examination system (*keju*) in imperial dynasties. The study goal of children is to get high marks in examinations. Science and technology, which offers better career paths, are favored subjects. Most parents in Hong Kong, Taiwan and also mainland China are willing to spend money for children to attend extra tuition classes to achieve good results. However, happiness, well-being, emotional needs and the mental health of children are easily neglected during the learning process. Approaching education with a utilitarian target is still a core notion and practice in education systems, though there have been recent reforms.[16] A complicating factor involves overprotected children from single-child families and young people who favor modern Western values, including individualism and materialism. Increasing rates of abuse (drug, sex, Internet and so on) among young people, along with mental health and self-harming problems of students, are symptoms of a distressed youth culture where morals and values have been influenced by capitalist global challenges resulting in a chaotic cultural clash between the East and the West

(Sun, 2004; Sun, Hui & Watkins, 2006; Zheng, 2011). Educators from the 'four places' have highlighted common concerns on these youth crises.

LE AND SPIRITUALITY IN BUILDING RESILIENCE

In this section, I review and discuss the curriculum and content of LE in Taiwan and mainland China and the relation between LE and spirituality in building resilience. Both societies have implemented LE as a policy, but with slightly different approaches.

Curriculum of LE in Taiwan

There have been briefly three stages in the development of LE in Taiwan (Chen, 2004). The first (1996–1999) promoted LE with four principles: 'understanding life, valuing life, appreciating life and respecting life'. There were three main parts and twelve units in the outline: 'Ultimate concerns' (i.e. dignity of life and death; religion and life), 'Ethics' (i.e. cultivating conscience) and 'Personality and relation development' (i.e. appreciating life; being myself is good). The third part, including understanding one's uniqueness and building up self-dignity, were related to 'awareness of self' in Hay and Nye's (1998) interpretation of children's spirituality. Yet the term 'spirituality' or 'spiritual growth' was not mentioned as a major theme.

In the second stage (1999–2002), discussion and debate focused on diverse interpretations of LE. Some argued that LE should not be restricted to suicide prevention and thanatology but should be extended to include cultivating values and investigating the meaning of life. Maintaining balance among different religious values in the curriculum was a concern. Some were critical about asking students to respect all people as it was seen as too idealistic and they argued that the discourse of LE, which affirms the values of life, may play down the notion that the "value of death is higher than life" (Chen, 2004).

In the third stage (2003–2004), a mature consensus was developed by a group of distinguished scholars who discussed and prepared a teaching resource scheme and refined a credit-bearing senior secondary curriculum with three main areas and eight units.[17] Three complementary areas inter-related to form a complete LE: 'Ultimate concern and practice', 'Ethical thinking and reflection' and 'Personality integration and spiritual development' (Chen, 2004; Taiwan Life Education Association, 2004).

The area of 'Ultimate concern and practice' aim at helping students to explore the meaning in human life, by way of building up ultimate concerns through enquiring about philosophical and religious issues. 'Ethical thinking and reflection' facilitates students to cultivate ethical thinking and reflection to reveal wisdom in life. This builds resilience in a globalised world which emphasises individuality and diverse values. 'Personality integration and spiritual development' highlight a principle of 'unity of knowledge and practice' (*zhixingheyi*) proposed by *Wang Yangming*, a famous educator and philosopher in the Ming dynasty. This principle understands that knowledge (*zhi*) is expressed in practice (*xing*); thus, there is no knowledge without practice. It may be likened to the understanding of 'authenticity' in the West to explain what you mean by authenticity. To work out this principle, it is necessary to firstly integrate one's knowledge and feelings, and also mind, body and spirit, and secondly, to develop spiritual aspects through spiritual practices, guiding students towards yearning for truth, beauty and transcendence. The curriculum (such as developed by the Life Education Resource Centre, n.d., or the National Yangmei Senior High School, n.d.) also introduces concepts about 'self' such as Freud's human psyche, Carl Roger's self-concept and Maslow's self-actualisation. Spiritual practices of the East and the West (e.g. Buddhism, Christianity) include stories of virtuous nuns and monks (e.g. Mother Teresa, Master Sheng Yen). In sum, the whole curriculum scheme emphasises an integrated approach towards understanding knowledge and practice about life through spiritual practice, with awareness of self and others.

Curriculum of Life, Live and Living Education (Sanshengjiaoyu) in Mainland China

Unlike Taiwan, there is no state LE curriculum in mainland China. Each province started promoting LE at different times depending on its own policy and resources. The Life, Live and Living Education (*Sansheng jiaoyu*) of Yunnan Province (Education Department of Yunnan Province, 2008; Lo, 2009a, 2009b, 2009c) will be discussed as it has been the model promoted in many cities. *Sansheng jiaoyu* consists of three main interrelated themes. *San* means three. *Sansheng* refers to *Shengming* (life), *shengcun* (live) and *shenghuo* (living).

The theme 'Life education' (*Shengming jiaoyu*) mainly helps students to understand the process of life and death, and respect for life. Students are guided to establish right views on the meaning of life through understanding the laws of development of natural species. The principle of developing harmonious relationships between self, others and nature are highlighted. For example, in the textbook, a case of saving others' lives in an earthquake disaster is discussed. Practical ways of showing gratitude to those who have helped are also introduced.

The theme 'Live education' (*Shengcun jiaoyu*) aims at enhancing the ability to exist and live in society. Key components include cultivating working and social skills, a sense of protection from danger or crime, building resilience to failures or challenges, collaborating with others, adapting to difficult environments and learning basic laws. For example, in the primary five textbook, the salience of obeying the laws in schools and society, and preventing abuse or duplicity is introduced by using specific cases. In the junior secondary textbook, campus violence and Internet traps are discussed with cases and solutions.

The theme 'Living education' (*Shenghuo jiaoyu*) aims at facilitating students to understand that the ultimate goal of life is yearning for the well-being of the individual, family, the country and the world. Cultivating good virtue and behavior/habits, social responsibility, love and gratitude is emphasised. Students learn how to make choices in their lifestyles to maintain balance between study and leisure, personal life and work, income and consumption. For example, in a unit of the junior secondary textbook, the pursuit of happiness does not rely only on money or materials. In the primary five textbook, how to make friends appropriately and keep healthy friendships is introduced. In sum, the curriculum emphasises cultivating right values of life, understanding the meaning of life and upgrading life quality by practising responsibility in daily life in the community.

Unlike the curriculum in Taiwan, the 'Life, Live and Living Education' curriculum in mainland China does not include religious aspects on life and death or spiritual practices. The terms 'religion', 'spiritual practice' and 'spirituality' are not mentioned in the curriculum. Instead, the aspect of harmonious community, awareness of others and relationship with others is more emphasised. For the differences, I argue that Taiwan is a more Westernised and modernised society with a greater level of religious freedom, while in China, religions are still under state restriction. Besides, there are various social challenges in China such as natural disasters and crimes. Some families in rural areas, due to poverty and hunger, are still unable to support their children to finish fundamental education. According to Maslow's hierarchy of needs, it would appear that many children are still striving to satisfy the basic physiological and safety needs. It may explain why 'live and living education' is so highlighted in China's curriculum. Nevertheless, it is possible that the spiritual aspects in the curriculum of China, as well as other societies, can be further enhanced by introducing more Confucian humanistic values,[18] which emphasise self-awareness, self-cultivation and harmonious relationships in daily life practice (Ching, 2003), especially given the recent craze involving the revival of the Chinese culture heritage (Tan, 2008). However, this is a topic for a further article.

CONCLUSION

In conclusion, this chapter reviews the development of LE in recent decades in four Chinese societies due to similar crises of children and youth. Formal curriculum has been implemented in Taiwan and China, whereas informal curriculum has been well recognised in Hong Kong and Macao. Emphasis on LE curriculum is slightly different among the four societies due to distinct social backgrounds and cultures; however, educators from the four places share similar directions in developing LE on ultimate concerns, values of life and death and spiritual practices in frequent interchanges for building resilience. Comparing the curricula of Taiwan and China, the former introduces religious and spiritual practice while the latter does not.

Nonetheless, there is a suggestion that Confucian humanistic spirituality, which focuses on daily life self-awareness, may be considered in developing LE to further strengthen resilience.

ACKNOWLEDGEMENTS

I warmly acknowledge the editors, particularly Marian de Souza and the two anonymous reviewers for their positive comments, and Bernard Hung-kay Luk for his encouraging advice on this work. I would also like to thank K. K. Yeung and W. H. Ho, who have been working on life education, provided me with useful information for this work in the early stage.

NOTES

1. Taiwan, an island located to the east of the People's Republic of China and to the northeast of Japan, has a population of 23 million people with an area of 36,009 square kilometers (Executive Yuan, Republic of China (Taiwan), 2012).
2. Stella Matutina Girls' High School (n.d.) first started life education in Taiwan. Then Chen Yinghao, former head of the Education Department, proposed an expanded concept and vision of life education in 1997.
3. With a population of over 1.3 billion people living in a total area of 9.6 million square kilometers, the PRC (Central People's Government of the People's Republic of China, 2011), which is located in East Asia and to the south of Russia, is one of the most populous countries in the world.
4. About 158 million people with diagnosable psychiatric disorders have never been treated and around 287,000 suicides have occurred every year from 1995 to 1999 (see Phillips et al., 2009; Phillips, Li & Zhang, 2002).
5. In 1999 the suicide rate of male and female adolescents was 8 and 12.9 per 100,000, respectively, in rural China, while it was 3 and 4.1 in urban China (Hawton, Saunders & O'Conner, 2012). A study reported that the rate of adolescent suicide attempts in Anhui, Beijing and Shanghai was 7.6%, 5% and 5.1%, respectively, in 2010 (see Wu, 2010)
6. For example, from 1989 to 1991, there were eight students from the same university who committed suicide over a period of 17 months (see Su & Wang, 1993). There are nearly five thousand published theses on school and university student suicide (China Knowledge Resource Integrated Database, n.d.).
7. On October 20, 2010, a male student, Yao Jiaxin, of Xi'an Conservatory of Music, accidentally hit a young woman, Zhang Miu, with his car. When he became aware that the young woman, who was still lying on the ground, was memorizing his license plate, he came out of his car and stabbed her to death. His case was finally processed in Xi'an Intermediate People's courts as murder, and his death penalty was executed on June 7, 2011 (BBC News, 2011).
8. For instance, 'psychological counseling' (*xinli zixun*) of a female student who experienced anxiety caused by examinations was discussed in detail on the website of the secondary school (see Changle No. 2 Middle School Shandong Province, 2008).
9. Hong Kong, located on the south coast of China enclosed by the Pearl River Delta and South China Sea, has a population of over 7 million with a total

area of 1100 square kilometers (Government of Hong Kong Special Administrative Region, 2012).

10. When I started as a teacher in a secondary school in Hong Kong, I knew a 16-year-old girl in one of my Form 4 classes. I still clearly remember that she showed me a few scars on her knees in one chat. She would cut herself when she was depressed and felt plagued. There were many other students as well who suffered from distress and emotional turmoil in schools.

11. SPHRC Kung Yick She Secondary School (n.d.) is the first school which has launched LE in Hong Kong.

12. Both 'Macao' and 'Macau' are commonly used to refer the same place. The present Special Administrative Region (SAR) government uses 'Macao', though others prefer 'Macau'. Located on the south coast of China on the western side of the Pearl River Delta and Hong Kong, Macao has a population of over 576,000 with a total area of 29.5 square kilometers (Government of Macao Special Administrative Region, 2012).

13. According to the 2011 statistics, among 1414 drop-out students, 41.6% were junior secondary students and 28.4% were senior secondary students. Reasons given by junior secondary students for dropping out included "To leave school" (25.5%) and "Violation of school regulations" (22.1%), while those of senior secondary students were "To study abroad" (24.6%) and "To leave school" (24.6%) (Government of Macao Special Administrative Region, 2012).

14. The China Soong Ching Ling Foundation (2008), a highly recognised NGO by the central government because Deng Xiaoping was the first honorary chairman, has organised yearly Chinese Youth Life Education Forums involving the 'four places' since 2005 and invites scholars to participate. Conferences have also been organised by universities in Taiwan (see, for example, WuFeng University, 2005), Hong Kong (see, for example, Chinese University of Hong Kong School Heads Alumni Association, 2011) and Macao.

15. Most Chinese children and adolescents before the 1980s did not have a chance to finish primary and secondary school education due to poverty and wars. Public education in Taiwan started in 1968; nine-year free education in Hong Kong began in 1979 and nine-year compulsory education in China started in 1985. Hence most expect the next generation to attain high education levels.

16. For example, enjoying learning was proposed in the education reform document in 2000 in Hong Kong (Education Commission, 2000).

17. The eight units are life philosophy and life philosophy education, life and death education, religion and religious education, basic ethics and ethical thinking education, gender and marriage ethics education, technology ethics and technology ethics education, personality integration and spiritual development, and education theory.

18. Confucianism spirituality is practised not only in a sacred place like temple, but also in family, in the public sphere and elsewhere in daily affairs. "The secular is the sacred; the transcendent is in the immanent" (Tu & Tucker, 2003, p. 1). The Confucian way is to become more fully human within the world, rather than outside the world.

REFERENCES

BBC News. (2011, June 7). China executes student for murder of hit-and-run victim. *BBC News*. Retrieved from http://www.bbc.co.uk/news/world-asia-pacific-13678179

Central People's Government of the People's Republic of China. (2010). 國家中長期教育改革和發展規劃綱要 (2010–2020年) [Outline of China's National Plan for Medium and Long-term Education Reform and Development (2010–2020)]. Retrieved March 30, 2013, from http://www.gov.cn.

Central People's Government of the People's Republic of China. (2011). 2010年第六次全國人口普查主要數據公報 [Major Figures of the 2010 National Population Census]. Retrieved March 30, 2013, from http://www.gov.cn.

Centre of Buddhist Studies of the University of Hong Kong. (2005). 佛學與生命教育交流會論文集 [Buddhism and life education forum proceedings]. Hong Kong: Centre of Buddhist Studies of the University of Hong Kong.

Centre for Quality-Life Education. (2010). 基督教生命教育文憑課程 [Diploma Programme in Christian Life Education]. Retrieved March 30, 2013, from http://www.cuhk.edu.hk/theology/cqle.

Centre for Religious and Spirituality Education. (2006). 協助小學規劃生命教育計劃 [Project for Supporting Planning of Life Education in Primary Schools commissioned by the Education Bureau of HKSAR Government]. Retrieved March 30, 2013, from http://www.ied.edu.hk/crse.

Changle No. 2 Middle School Shandong Province. (2008, Sept. 9). 一例高中生考試焦慮所致心理問題的諮詢案例報告 [A counseling case report of psychological problems of a senior secondary student who experienced anxiety]. Retrieved March 30, 2013, from http://www.sdclez.cn/neweb/Item/389.aspx.

Chen, L. Y. (2004). 生命教育在台灣的發展概況 [Development of Life education in Taiwan]. *Philosophy and Culture, 31*(9), 21–46.

Chen, X. X. (Ed.). (2003). 青少年偏差行為學術研討會論文集 [Conference proceedings of deviated behaviour of adolescents]. Macao: Macao Adolescents Crime Research Society.

China Knowledge Resource Integrated Database. (n.d.). Retrieved June 13, 2013, from http://www.cnki.net.

China Life Education. (2010). 中心概況 [About the Centre]. Retrieved March 30, 2013, from http://www.zgsmjy.com.

China Soong Ching Ling Foundation. (2008, Dec. 3). 第四屆中華青少年生命教育論壇在港舉行 [The Fourth Chinese Youth Life Education Forum organised in Hong Kong]. Retrieved March 30, 2013, from http://www.sclf.org/lajl/jldt/200812/t20081203_10982.htm.

Chinese University of Hong Kong School Heads Alumni Association. (2011). 兩岸四地生命教育論壇: 後現代及全球化下的生命教育 [Life education forum in two shores four places—postmodern life education under globalisation]. Hong Kong: Chinese University of Hong Kong School Heads Alumni Association.

Ching, J. (2003). What is Confucian spirituality? In W. M. Tu & M. E. Tucker (Eds.), *Confucian spirituality I* (pp. 81–95). New York: Crossroad.

Chow, W. Y., & Yeung, K. K. (2002). 香港的生命教育：文化背景, 教育改革與實踐方向 [Life education in Hong Kong: cultural background, education reform and direction of practice]. Hong Kong: Religious Education Resource Centre.

Education Bureau. (2012). Moral, Civic and National Education. Retrieved March 30, 2013, from http://www.edb.gov.hk.

Education Commission. (2000) *Reform Proposals for the Education Systems in Hong Kong.* Hong Kong: Hong Kong Special Administrative Region. Retrieved March 30, 2013, from http://www.e-c.edu.hk/eng/reform/index_e.html

Education Department Life Education Learning. (2012). 教材資源 [Teaching resources]. Retrieved March 30, 2013, from http://life.edu.tw/homepage/new_page_2.php.

Education Department of Yunnan Province. (2008, May 23). 雲南省教育廳關於實施"三生教育"決定 [The decision about implementation of "Sanshengjiaoyu"]. Retrieved March 30, 2013, from http://www.stats.yn.gov.cn/canton_model37/newsview.aspx?id=190325.

Evangelical Lutheran Church of Hong Kong. (2006). 生命之旅生命教育-中學篇 [Life education of life journey—secondary]. Hong Kong: Life Angel Education Centre of Evangelical Lutheran Church of Hong Kong.

Executive Yuan, Republic of China (Taiwan). (2012). 土地與人民 [Land and population]. Retrieved March 30, 2013, from http://www.ey.gov.tw/state/Content_List.aspx?n=9EC698333226EFEA.

Government of Hong Kong Special Administrative Region. (2012). Hong Kong Statistics—Population. Retrieved March 30, 2013, from http://www.censtatd.gov.hk/hkstat/sub/bbs.jsp.

Government of Macao Special Administrative Region. (2012). Statistics and Census Service. Retrieved March 30, 2013, from http://www.dsec.gov.mo/default.aspx?noredirect=true.

Hawton, K., Saunders, K. E. A., & O'Conner, R. C. (2012). Self-harm and suicide in adolescents. *Lancet, 379*, 2373–2382.

Hay, D., with Nye, R. (1998). *The spirit of the child*. London: Fount.

Ji, J. F. (2007). 生命教育課程教學資源與人力資源手冊 [Handbook of life education curriculum teaching resources and human resources]. Chiayi: WuFeng University.

Journal of Life Education. (n.d.). 本刊簡介 [Introduction of the Journal]. Retrieved March 30, 2013, from http://www.tlea.org.tw/jole.

Kwok, C. P. (2004). 成長列車: 小學生命成長課程 [Train of growth: Life Education curriculum in primary school]. Hong Kong: Wen Lin Publisher Ltd.

Kwong, C. (2002). *The public role of religion in post-colonial Hong Kong: An historical overview of Confucianism, Taoism, Buddhism and Christianity*. New York: Peter Lang.

Life Education Centre of the National Taiwan University. (2008). 認識中心 [About us]. Retrieved March 30, 2013, from http://www.lec.ntu.edu.tw/index.php.

Life Education Resource Centre. (n.d.). 人格統整與靈性發展 [Personality Integration and Spiritual Development]. Retrieved March 30, 2013, from http://life.ltsh.ilc.edu.tw.

Lin, Z. P., Pun, Z. D., Lin, J. W., Lu, Y. J., Jiang, R. G., Li, Q. Y., & Su, Y. R. (2004). 生命教育之理論與實踐 [Theory and practice of life education]. Taipei: Psychology Publisher.

Liu, H. (2010). 近十年我國生命教育的回顧與展望 [Review and prospect of our country's life education in recent decade]. *Sixiang lilunjiaoyu, 20*, 4–8.

Lo, C. M. (2009a). 生命生存生活—幼兒 [Life, live and living—Textbook for kindergarten level]. Yunnan: Renminchubanshe.

Lo, C. M. (2009b). 生命生存生活—小學 [Life, live and living—Textbook for primary level]. Yunnan: Renminchubanshe.

Lo, C. M. (2009c). 生命生存生活—中學 [Life, live and living—Textbook for secondary level]. Yunnan: Renminchubanshe.

Lo, S. S. H. (2008). *Political change in Macao*. New York: Routledge.

Macao Education and Youth Department. (2002). 教育暨青年局年刊 [Annual Report of Education and Youth Affairs Bureau]. Retrieved March 30, 2013, from http://portal.dsej.gov.mo/webdsejspace/internet/Inter_main_page.jsp.

National Changhua University of Education. (2006). 生命教育中心靈成長教育研討會: 論文資料暨研討會手冊 [Conference proceedings on spiritual growth in life education]. Changhua: National Changhua University of Education.

National Life Work Committee of Education. (2012). 生命教育論壇 [Life Education Forum]. Retrieved March 30, 2013, from http://www.pleedu.com/index.asp.

National Yangmei Senior High School. (n.d.). 人格統整與靈性發展 [Personality Integration and Spiritual Development]. Retrieved March 30, 2013, from http://www.ymhs.tyc.edu.tw.

People's Republic of China. (1982). *Constitution of the People's Republic of China*. Retrieved March 30, 2013, from http://english.people.com.cn/constitution/constitution.html.

Phillips, M. R., Li, X., & Zhang, Y. (2002). Suicides rates in China, 1995–99. *Lancet, 359*, 835–840.

Phillips, M. R., Zhang, J., Shi, Q., Song, Z., Ding, Z., Pang, S., & Wang, Z. (2009). Prevalence, treatment, and associated disability of mental disorders in four provinces in China during 2001–05: An epidemiological survey. *Lancet, 373*, 2041–2053.

Research International. (2007, Aug. 16). *The Wrigley Concentration Index—Understanding concentration amongst youth in Asia*. Press conference in Hong Kong.

Sansheng Jiaoyuwang. (2009). 資源中心 [Resources Centre]. Retrieved March 30, 2013, from http://www.ssjy.org/index.jsp.

Shanghai Education Committee. (2005, June 17). 上海市中小學生生命教育指導綱要 (試行) [Guiding outline of life education in secondary and primary schools in Shanghai (trial)]. Retrieved March 30, 2013, from http://wenku.baidu.com/view/1fa801d4360cba1aa811dade.html.

Shihangqing. (2002). 宗教教育辨義－兼論宗教研修機構體制化的問題 [The meaning of religious education—also discusses the problem of institutionalisation of a religious professional organisation]. *Special Issue on Religion Discourse, 4*, 249–292. Taipei: Ministry of the Interior. Retrieved March 30, 2013, from http://buddhism.lib.ntu.edu.tw/FULLTEXT/JR-AN/103828.htm.

SPHRC Kung Yick She Secondary School. (n.d.). 教育目標與方向 [Education objectives and directions]. Retrieved March 30, 2013, from http://www.sphrc.edu.hk/index.html.

Stella Matutina Girls' High School. (n.d.). 學校基本資料 [Basic information of school]. Retrieved March 30, 2013, from http://www.smgsh.tc.edu.tw.

Su, X. D., & Wang, G. Y. (1993). 福建師範大學8名學生自殺事件的調查分析 [Investigating analysis of the suicide of 8 students from Fujian Normal University—Abstract]. *China School Health, 6*. Abstract retrieved March 30, 2013, from http://www.cnki.com.cn/Article/CJFDTOTAL-XIWS199306017.htm.

Su, X. H. (Ed.) (2005). 生命教育: 推行現況, 課程及防治自殺 [Life education: current implementation, curriculum and suicide prevention]. Macao: Faculty of Education of University of Macau.

Sun, J. H. C. (2004). 當前台灣社會的重大生命課題與願景 [The grand education and vision about Life for the present society in Taiwan]. *Philosophy and Culture, 31*, 1–17.

Sun, R. C. F., Hui, E. K. P., & Watkins, D. (2006). Towards a model of suicidal ideation for Hong Kong Chinese adolescents. *Journal of Adolescents, 29*, 209–224.

Taiwan Life Education Association. (2004). 學校教育 [School Education]. Retrieved from http://www.tlea.org.tw/index.php.

Tan, S. H. (2008). Modernizing Confucianism and 'new Confucianism'. In L. Kam (Ed.), *The Cambridge companion to modern Chinese culture* (pp. 135–154). New York: Cambridge University Press.

Tu, W. M. (Ed.). (2004). *The living tree: the changing meaning of being Chinese today*. Stanford, California: Stanford University Press.

Tu, W. M., & Tucker, M. E. (Eds.). (2003). *Confucian spirituality I*. New York: Crossroad.

Wang, Ying. (2004, Dec. 24). 遼寧省昨日啟動中小學 "生命教育工程" [Liaoning province launched the 'Life education project' in secondary and primary schools yesterday]. *Xinhuanet*. Retrieved March 30, 2013, from http://edu.163.com/edu2004/editor_2004/school/041224/041224_171087.html.

Wang, Yuan. (2004, Dec. 23). 遼寧中小学開展生命教育 學生看分娩感悟生命 [Life education launched in Liaoning secondary and primary schools: students were touched after witnessing childbirth]. *Shenyangjinbao*. Retrieved March 30, 2013, from http://news.qq.com/a/20041223/000081.htm.

Wong, P. H. (2010, Nov. 28). 本地生命教育近期的發展 [Recent development of local life education]. *Kung Kao Po*.

Wu, X. B. (2006). 生命教育: 理論與教學方案 [Life education: theory and teaching scheme]. Taipei: Psychology Publisher.

Wu, Z. Q. (2010, May 10). 生命教育初探 [Preliminary exploration of life education]. Retrieved March 30, 2013, from http://wenku.baidu.com/view/9ff3a468a98271fe910ef9ff.html.

WuFeng University. (2005). 亞太地區生命教育教學研討會論文集 [Conference Proceedings of teaching life education in Asia Pacific]. Chiayi: WuFeng University.

Yeung, K. K. (2005). 香港生命教育的推動與發展概況 [Promotion and development of Hong Kong life education]. In X. H. Su (Ed.), 生命教育: 推行現況, 課程及防治自殺 [Life education: current implementation, curriculum and suicide prevention] (pp. 36–46). Macao: Faculty of Education of University of Macau.

Yip, S. F., Liu, K. Y., Lam, T. H., Stewart, S. M., Chen, E., & Fan, S. (2004). Suicidality among high school students in Hong Kong SAR. *Suicide and Life-Threatening Behaviour, 34*(3), 284–297.

YMCA of Macao. (n.d.). 專業培訓 [Professional training]. Retrieved March 30, 2013, from www.ymca.org.mo.

Yu, Q., & Wang, N. G. (2004). 大學生自殺問題研究進展 [Research progress of university student suicide problem]. *Medicine in Other Countries—Social Medicine, 21*(4), 159–165.

Zheng, X. Q. (2011, Sept. 21). 中小學生命教育的核心問題與解決方法 [Core problems and solutions of life education in secondary and primary schools]. Lecture presented at the Second Stage of Life and Safety Education Training in Jilin Province, China.

14 The Japanese Way of Spiritual Cultivation

Yoshiharu Nakagawa

ON THE EVOLUTION OF JAPANESE SPIRITUALITY AND EDUCATION

Japan, located in Far East Asia, is composed of four major islands and many smaller islands. About 70% of the land is mountainous. Having a high population density, most of Japan's people reside in towns and cities. In order to avoid conflicts and achieve 'harmony' (*wa*), people in Japan have created a society that praises conformity over individual uniqueness.

The land of Japan is endowed with a rich natural environment and a distinctive cycle of four seasons in a climate prone to monsoons. These factors of nature gave rise to animistic folk beliefs that evolved into Shinto, the indigenous religion of Japan. Shinto itself manifests a deep connection with nature that is at the heart of Japanese spirituality. The people of ancient times believed in spiritual forces behind visible phenomena. Such forces were called *kami* (deities) and this led to the rise of Shinto, which literally means *the way of kami*. Nature was believed to be the manifestation of *kami*. People conducted rituals to worship *kami* at special natural settings where people felt *kami* to reside, such as lofty mountains, great rocks, caves, forests, tall trees, and waterfalls. Shrines were built at those sacred places. Festivals (*matsuri*) of shrines are important Shinto rituals to worship *kami*. Purification (*misogi*) is also essential in Shinto practice—that is, a cleansing of negative energies (*kegare*) that disturb communion with *kami*. By describing a way of life, Shinto has been the dominant religious belief prevailing over Japanese society.

But also, during its long 2000 year history, Japan has been heavily influenced by Chinese culture. As the noted critic of Japanese culture Seigō Matsuoka (2006) remarks, the essential feature of Japanese culture lies in the skillful 'editorship' of associated multiple imported elements. Religions from outside Japan, such as Buddhism, Confucianism, and Taoism, became deeply embedded in Japanese culture, thereby adding depth and refinement to Japanese spirituality as it evolved. Buddhism with its theories and practices greatly contributed to the development of Japanese spirituality, whereas Confucianism provided moral, ethical, and political concepts. Taoism in particular offered a profound philosophy of the natural way and also spiritual practices including exercises for healing and wellness. Shinto was the native mythic religion but these imported religions variously affected the further formation of Shintoism. The best known is of course Buddhism, which fused with Shinto in a form of syncretism known as *shinbutsu-shūgo*.

It is said that this Chinese Buddhism was initially introduced by way of Korea in the 6th century. First adopted by Prince Shōtoku of the Yamato state, and eventually coming under the patronage of the government of the day, Buddhism long served as a state religion in order to give the state spiritual support and protection. Japanese Buddhism belongs to the Mahayana tradition. Two major sects, Tendai and Shingon, were founded by Saichō and Kūkai in the 9th century during the Heian period (794–1192). In the Kamakura period (1192–1333) when the warrior class took over power, new sects of Japanese Buddhism such as Zen (Rinzai and Sōtō), Jōdo (the Pure Land), Shin, and Nichiren emerged, through the efforts of Eisai, Dōgen, Hōnen, Shinran, and Nichiren, respectively. Most of them were gradually infused into the lives of the common people and have continued to be influential up to this day.

Zen Buddhism particularly impacted Japanese culture, contributing to the rise of such traditional arts as the *nō* play (theatre), the way of tea (*sadō, chadō*), the way of flower arrangement (*kadō*), the way of calligraphy (*shodō*), black and white ink-painting (*suibokuga*), poetry (*haiku*), landscape gardening, architecture, and the way of martial arts (*budō*) such as swordsmanship and archery (see Carter, 2008; Hisamatsu, 1971; Suzuki, 1959; Yanagi, 1972/1989). Many of these arts are called the 'way' (*dō*) of, expressing the involvement of spiritual cultivation (*shugyō*) as well as the mastering of artistry. The Japanese have indeed favored the concept of the 'way' and have frequently applied it to a variety of activities, provided that they involve the approach of spiritual cultivation. In a later discussion I will detail the way of the arts as a traditional form of spiritual education developed in Japan.

Prior to the adaptation of the modern educational system there had been a variety of educational institutions. Apprenticeship was the major way for people to learn practical and professional skills. Buddhist monasteries served as academic institutes and also provided children with basic literacy. During the Edo period (1603–1868), apart from monasteries, 'temple schools' (*terakoya*) were spread out over the country as the major educational institutions in communities where young children had training in reading and writing under the guidance of teachers. In the Edo period Neo-Confucianism became influential as the official ideology, adopted by the Tokugawa regime. Throughout this period, Confucianism laid a firm educational foundation, for children learned the classical Confucian texts as the common basis for their further study. Official schools (*hangaku*) in the feudal regions provided children of the ruling class with Confucian scholarship and swordsmanship. There were also private academies (*shijuku*) founded by scholars to offer an advanced study of Confucianism.

The modern educational system in Japan dates back to the Meiji period. The Meiji Restoration took place in 1868 when the feudal society in the Edo period came to an end. In order to establish a modern nation, the Meiji government imported the modern school system from Western countries in 1872, along with other important facets of modern society. Thus, modern schools became the central place for receiving a public education. In the formation of a modern nation, these schools also played a major role in building a national identity amongst the people, particularly through a moral education called *shūshin*, which transmitted Confucian social ethics and then later, the nationalistic ideology of State Shinto (*kokka shintō*). The Meiji government introduced State Shinto as a kind of national religion, under which traditional Shinto was assimilated.

With the end of World War II in 1945, the education system was completely changed, and the elements that had fostered nationalism and militarism were removed from schools. As part of this, any kind of religious education for any particular religion has been forbidden in the public schools, except for providing general knowledge about world religions. On the other hand, a new moral education (*doutoku*) was introduced in 1958, based on the values education approach. In addition to social values, without explicit reference to 'spirituality,' it has become more inclusive of 'spiritual' values such as compassion, caring for nature, reverence for life, and a sense of awe toward that which is considered sacred. But generally speaking, moral education has never been fully conducted in schools, and also the practice of moral education has been inclined to focus on the side of social values and the cognitive development of moral reasoning.

There also exist in Japan numerous private schools (about 80% of kindergarten, 30% of high schools, and 80% of universities, but only 1% of primary schools and 7% of junior high schools), many of them founded by Christian, Buddhist, or new religious organizations. Private schools affiliated with religious organizations address religious values in their educational policies and teach them in one way or another, which might include ways of ceremonies, prayer, and contemplation. However, in today's highly competitive circumstances, academic achievement seems to have been given far greater priority over religious and spiritual aspects.

As for the current situation of religion and spirituality in Japan, the traditional and organized religions have become less attractive to the majority of people in a society that has placed a higher value on economic and technological growth. Many people today think that they no longer have a specific religious belief. However, they still vaguely believe in *kami* and *buddhas* and visit shrines and temples to pray for wellbeing and happiness. Religious (mostly Buddhist) ceremonies for deceased family members also remain important. Even though people follow these 'religious' customs, they prefer to regard themselves as 'nonreligious' and tend to see religious matters as rather suspicious and even dangerous.

On the other hand, since the late 1970s there has been a growing phenomenon of those seeking spiritual growth without relying on a certain religion. Faced with a spiritual vacuum caused by a materialistic attitude in society, this new movement of spirituality has attracted a considerable number of people. Impacted by spiritual movements that have developed in Western countries during these decades, this movement has embraced diverse streams by accepting spiritual teachings and practices from the world wisdom traditions and other resources. It is gradually reaching a greater population who feel spiritual hunger in their lives.

Given the evolution of this new situation, discussions about spirituality in education have also begun to grow during the last ten years, although limited to a small number of holistic educators. However, it seems to me that the time has already come to invite some forms of spiritual education, including contemplative practices. The need for such initiatives can be reasoned from the fact that both students and teachers are suffering even more from a stressful and depressive environment. For example, according to governmental surveys, instances of bullying (*ijime*) reported in 2012 amount to over 144,000 cases (Monbukagaku-shō, 2012a). More than 60% of the teachers who are on leaves of absence from work are suffering from mental sickness (Monbukagaku-shō, 2012b). In dealing with these problems, spiritual education could provide opportunities in which students and teachers may recover the meaning and vitality of their existence.

To explore the possibility of a way of spiritual education in a Japanese context, it is important to recognize the essential aspects of traditional Japanese spirituality, which are embedded in Japanese culture but rarely considered in education. In what follows I will focus on this topic and then describe the way of spiritual cultivation that can be drawn from traditional Japanese culture.

THE NATURE OF TRADITIONAL JAPANESE SPIRITUALITY

Spirituality appears where the transcendental, infinite, and divine meets the visible, finite, and material. The manner of how these two dimensions relate has been differently manifested. In religions with a monotheistic tradition, these two dimensions are more clearly separated. The human world is distanced from the divine, and spirituality assumes forms of revelation, salvation, and grace. On the contrary, Japanese spirituality is marked as a seamless identity between these two dimensions. Ordinary reality is simultaneously seen as something sacred, infinite, and absolute. Hajime Nakamura (1964), an eminent scholar of Indian and Buddhist thought, highlighted this feature of Japanese thinking and remarked, "In the first place, we should notice that the Japanese are willing to accept the phenomenal world as Absolute because of their disposition to lay a greater emphasis upon intuitive sensible concrete events, rather than upon universals" (p. 350). According to Nakamura, this phenomenalist thinking is associated with "the Japanese traditional love of nature" (p. 355) and with an intrinsic tendency to cherish 'this-worldliness' and to affirm the natural dispositions of humans including desires, sentiments, and feelings.

The Japanese, in this sense, are fundamentally life-affirming. Because of this life-affirming thinking, they have explored a way of transforming the ordinary sensible reality into something absolute, made possible by incorporating the Buddhist concept of 'emptiness' (*sunyata*, *kū*) and 'nothingness' (*mu*). In the twofold way of negation and affirmation, that is, by way of negation, the ordinary world is first emptied to absolute nothingness, and in the way of affirmation, this nothingness manifests itself as the phenomenal world, in which the absolute and the phenomenal are unified. This twofold movement of negation and affirmation constitutes the core of Japanese spirituality.

A transformation of reality is to be conducted through transforming the self. Therefore, Japanese spirituality is concerned with cultivating the profound depths of consciousness. One's surface consciousness is composed of articulations of things that constitute the ordinary reality. By cultivating the depths of consciousness through contemplation, one dissociates from articulations and attains the deepest level of no articulation. In this unarticulated dimension, both the self and the world completely drop away and the self becomes 'selfless.' This is the ultimate dimension of absolute nothingness. The Eastern philosopher Toshihiko Izutsu (2008) calls this absolutely unarticulated dimension 'the zero-point' of consciousness and Being (pp. 147–149). It is from this zero-point that arises the 'selfless self.'

Scholars of Zen, mostly belonging to the Kyoto School of philosophy, have variously described the selfless self as 'the supra-individual Person' (Suzuki), 'contradictory self-identity' (Nishida), 'Formless Self' (Hisamatsu), and 'the selfless self' (Ueda). Because this concept embodies the fundamental structure of Japanese spirituality, I will briefly examine these various definitions below (for further discussion, see Nakagawa, 2000, pp. 62–68).

D. T. Suzuki (1944/1972) introduced the term 'the supra-individual Person' in his book *Japanese Spirituality*. He says, "Because the supra-individual Person transcends individuality, it is not within the realm of the individual self" (p. 76). But the supra-individual Person does not exist apart from the individual self. "The supra-individual Person is not without a relation to the individual self; there is a deep, in fact, inseparable, relation between them" (p. 76). The supra-individual Person is the individual self who has returned to his or her original nature of nothingness. Therefore, according to Suzuki, the key component of Japanese spirituality is the "realization that the supra-individual Person is none other than each individual" (p. 78).

Kitarō Nishida (1946/1987), the founder of the Kyoto School, referred to *kenshō*, the Zen experience of enlightenment, and remarked, "*Kenshō*, seeing one's nature, means to penetrate to the roots of one's own self. The self exists as the absolute's own self-negation. We exist as the many through the self-negation of the One" (p. 108). The absolute is not separate from the self. At the bottom of the self it negates and defines itself to appear as the self. In this sense, the self is none other than the absolute. Nishida continues, "Therefore the self has a radically self-contradictory existence. . . . Hence we always possess ourselves in something that transcends ourselves in our own bottomless depths" (p. 108). The self is selfless in its bottomless depths, opened up to the absolute, and arising as a finite being through the self-negation of the absolute. This is called 'contradictory self-identity.'

Shinichi Hisamatsu (1971) refers to 'the Formless Self.' The ordinary self, standing in opposition to the other, has distinction and, in this sense, has form, but the true fundamental self is totally formless. "Formlessness means the discarding of this ordinary self, of the self that still has form and still can be differentiated" (p. 48). *Satori* (enlightenment) is an awakening to the Formless Self. This Formless Self is 'the Fundamental Subject.' In the experience of Zen, an activity or a form emerges from this formless Fundamental Subject. The phenomenal activity of the Formless Self is called the 'wondrous being.' According to Hisamatsu, "This term signifies that, unlike ordinary being, this is at once being and nonbeing. Here, being never remains static, but is constantly one with Formlessness" (p. 51).

Finally, Shizuteru Ueda (1982) defines 'the selfless self' as "I am I because I am not I" (p. 13). In expounding on the *Ten Oxherding Pictures*, a textbook of Zen teachings that uses a series of ten pictures, Ueda says, "The ego-individual has to die for the sake of the true, selfless self" (p. 13). One must "leap once and for all into pure nothingness" (p. 13) and in this nothingness all forms drop away; "the self, free of form, discloses itself initially as formlessness pure and simple, as formlessness itself" (p. 23), which is described as an empty circle in the eighth picture. And, as the ninth and tenth pictures show, "the self resurrects from nothingness and into the selfless self" (p. 23). Japanese spirituality is concerned with realizing the wholeness of the selfless self. Therefore, it focuses not only on the side of 'selflessness' in the way of negation but also emphasis is laid on the 'selfhood' that arises from pure nothingness in the way of affirmation.

The selfless self is fundamentally empty and open, and thereby interrelational. When the self becomes selfless, the boundary of the self becomes fragile and easily open to others. And when the self is completely empty, the selfless self has no boundary with other beings. Selflessness means to be absolutely unarticulated and, because of this, unification takes place between the selfless self and the other. In this unity there is no outer existence, and everything is inseparably interrelated and arises as the manifestation of pure nothingness. Out of this unity, sensitivity to a unified field and caring for others evolves to the highest level. Attitudes toward another person take the form of compassion, for the existence of the other is sensed just as one's own. Nature is also experienced not as an objective reality but as an authentic manifestation of nothingness. Because the selfless self becomes one with any particular thing in nature, the relation to that thing assumes attentive caring and leads to aesthetic refinement without deformation of its original nature. This is typically realized in the Japanese arts.

On the other hand, in Japanese society the concept of selflessness has also been coupled with the Confucian emphasis on social relationships. Selflessness is required to some extent, in order for everyone to adapt to the social nexus. Although Western concepts of individualism have been introduced, in reality they have not been rooted deeply enough into Japanese society. On the contrary, an intrinsic tendency toward selflessness allows people to easily assimilate within social systems, such as family, school, community, organization, and nation. These larger systems often become the most important matrix in which one becomes a selfless collective self.

Selfless assimilation with the social nexus is so fundamental that many of the characteristics of the Japanese can be explained from this viewpoint. In this regard, there seems to be some negative consequences to selflessness. For example, social relationships tend to fall into exclusive sectarianism, in which the inner circle (*uchi*) is closed to others (*soto*). Within the circle, one feels forced to internalize the feelings and expectations of the other members as the basis for one's own behavior. What sometimes emerges is a strong bond within the circle and an indifference to outsiders. It is possibly this aspect that accounts for today's serious phenomenon of bullying in schools, often accompanied by violence and even the suicides of some victims.

Seen from a larger scale, manifestations of mass collectivism and nationalism may also take place, and Japan has experienced this with severity during wartime. Furthermore, selfless assimilation can make individuals become passive and dependent. It becomes difficult for them to develop the abilities of responsibility, critical thinking, and decision-making, all of which are based on the development of an independent self. The psychiatrist Takeo Doi (1973) explored the pathologies of dependence (*amae*) in Japanese who unconsciously long for union with others. In this respect, selfless assimilation within the social nexus is not an authentic form of selflessness, but rather a false objectification of the social nexus.

THE WAY OF SPIRITUAL CULTIVATION

Zen Master Dōgen's (1985) famous formulation on the practice of Zen in his masterpiece *Shōbōgenzō* may also define the way of spiritual education in Japan. He wrote:

> To study the buddha way is to study the self. To study the self is to forget the self. To forget the self is to be actualized by myriad things.

When actualized by myriad things, your body and mind as well as the bodies and minds of others drop away. No trace of realization remains, and this no-trace continues endlessly. (p. 70)

In forgetting the self, the self becomes selfless and formless. In this selflessness there remains no boundary, no differentiation, and the self is open to myriad things and becomes one with them. Here emerges an interpenetration of everything. In this sense, traditional spiritual education in Japan is a systematic training of forgetting the self. The primary aim of this education is to empty the self toward selflessness. Then, this selfless nothingness resurrects the self as a self-manifestation of nothingness. Hence, this spiritual education is the way of self-formation on the ground of selflessness.

In this regard, the way of the arts (*geidō*) in traditional Japanese culture provides an essential model of this spiritual education, for these arts have long held a central and formative place in the spiritual culture of Japan. The mastery of an art through practice (*keiko*) is inseparably associated with spiritual cultivation by its contemplative nature. Each traditional art developed its own educational system of transmitting artistry as well as spirit particularly through the relationship between master and disciple.

The story of Eugen Herrigel (1953) offers a remarkable example that illustrates the process of a spiritual cultivation. While residing in Japan from 1924 to 1929 as a German professor of philosophy, he learned the Japanese way of archery (*kyūdō*) under the master Kenzō Awa. Like other Zen-influenced arts, the way of archery essentially trains the student to become selfless. Herrigel initially struggled with letting go of his egocentric self, for he held the idea that *he* hit the target. At this stage he was a doer hitting the target and the target was an object. The master told him that he had "a much too willful will" (Herrigel, 1953, p. 31). The work of the master is to help the student release the doer and learn that "all right doing is accomplished only in a state of true selflessness, in which the doer cannot be present any longer as 'himself'" (p. 44).

In the practice of Japanese arts, 'patterns' (*kata*) play a decisive role as normative models. The teaching and learning process consists of the demonstration of patterns by the master and the imitation of them through the repeated practice of the student. Patterns are designed for the student to be unified with what is being learned. Concentrating on patterns, the student not only embodies them but also gives up his or her personal preferences and becomes selfless. In other words, in the learning process the student becomes the thing itself. As the religious scholar Keiji Nishitani (1961/1982) clarifies, "The Japanese word for 'learn' (*narau*) carries the sense of 'taking after' something, of making an effort to stand essentially in the same mode of being as the thing one wishes to learn about" (p. 128). Referring to the art of black and white ink-painting, for example, Toshihiko Izutsu

(1977/1982) remarks that "the painter should *become* the thing which he wants to paint. The painter who is going to paint a bamboo must, before taking up his brush, sit in contemplation until he feels himself completely identified with the bamboo" (p. 79).

In becoming the thing in a contemplative state, one's self is completely forgotten and "pure awareness" remains, which is unarticulated and unbounded—therefore, pure nothingness. What unfolds by means of aesthetic expression is this pure awareness. Izutsu (1977/1982) says, "By depicting a flower, tree, or bird, the poet or painter expresses the cosmic illumination of the pure Awareness" (p. 81). With similar meaning, Takuan (1986/2012), a Zen monk in the early Edo period, referred to 'No-Mind' (*mushin*) as pure awareness in his teachings on the way of swordsmanship. "It neither congeals nor fixes itself in one place. It is called No-Mind when the mind has neither discrimination nor thought but wanders about the entire body and extends throughout the entire self" (p. 22). The No-Mind is placed nowhere and it is present everywhere. When the mind stops at one place, this clinging obstructs spontaneity in movement.

One day, after Herrigel (1953) delivered a shot, the master Awa made a deep bow to the shot and cried, "Just then, 'It' shot!" (p. 52). The master said to Herrigel, "You remained this time absolutely self-oblivious and without purpose in the highest tension, so that the shot fell from you like a ripe fruit" (p. 53). Here is a conversation between Herrigel and his master in the final stage of his training:

> "I'm afraid I don't understand anything more at all," I answered, "even the simplest things have got in a muddle. Is it 'I' who draw the bow, or is it the bow that draws me into the state of highest tension? Do 'I' hit the goal, or does the goal hit me? . . . Bow, arrow, goal and ego, all melt into one another, so that I can no longer separate them. And even the need to separate has gone. For as soon as I take the bow and shoot, everything becomes so clear and straightforward and so ridiculously simple."
>
> "Now at last," the Master broke in, "the bowstring has cut right through you." (p. 61)

Bow, arrow, goal, and ego, all are no longer there, and nothingness comes to assume the form of a wondrous shot. As Herrigel remarks, "it is necessary for the archer to become, in spite of himself, an unmoved center. Then comes the supreme and ultimate miracle: art becomes 'artless,' shooting becomes not-shooting, a shooting without bow and arrow" (pp. 5–6). To describe such a state, art critic Sōetsu Yanagi (1972/1989) referred to it as "the realization of Non-dual Entirety" (*funi*), undifferentiated integrity, which is synonymous with enlightenment (p. 128). The aesthetic creation in this state is called *muge* or *jizai* (unobstructed freedom). In his *Zen and Japanese Culture*, D. T. Suzuki (1959) remarks:

> The artist's world is one of free creation, and this can come only from intuitions directly and immediately rising from the isness of things, unhampered by senses and intellect. He creates forms and sounds out of formlessness and soundlessness. (p. 17)

CONCLUDING REMARKS

As referred to earlier, Japanese society achieved rapid economic and technological development after the war and this has led to a situation where many people have moved away from traditional religious beliefs. In particular, young people have been affected by these changes and also by the wide exposure to today's materialism, including the emergence of many related health and social problems. In addition, Japanese education has been too focused on competition and the achievement of success, seriously disregarding spiritual needs of students and teachers. By briefly identifying these problematic elements and the need for spiritual education, this chapter has explored the essential aspects of traditional Japanese spirituality and the way of spiritual cultivation that may have a role in contemporary education.

Spiritual education in Japan has been about the cultivation of the selfless self, as embodied in the way of the traditional Japanese arts. In formal education, it is true that students get a taste of the traditional arts in regular lessons or club activities after school. The study of calligraphy, tea ceremony, flower arrangement, and martial arts are popular in school curricula. However, those cultural study programs are rarely seen in the light of a spiritual cultivation. Therefore, it is by casting a fresh light on these existing programs as prospective practices that it becomes possible to carry out a spiritual education rooted in Japanese culture.

Furthermore, it is also important to note that the way of cultivating the selfless self may become a unique contribution to spiritual education beyond a strictly Japanese context, for such a concept as the 'way' can be applied to any practice that involves the development of the selfless self.

REFERENCES

Carter, R. E. (2008). *The Japanese arts and self-cultivation.* Albany: State University of New York Press.

Dōgen. (1985). *Moon in a dewdrop: Writings of Zen Master Dōgen.* K. Tanahashi (Ed.). (R. Aitken et al., Trans.). New York: Farrar Straus and Giroux.

Doi, T. (1973). *The anatomy of dependence.* (J. Bester, Trans.). Tokyo: Kodansha International.

Herrigel, E. (1953). *Zen in the art of archery.* (R. F. C. Hull, Trans.). New York: Random House.
Hisamatsu, S. (1971). *Zen and the fine arts.* (G. Tokiwa, Trans.). Tokyo: Kodansha International.
Izutsu, T. (1977/1982). *Toward a philosophy of Zen Buddhism.* Boulder, CO: Prajna Press.
Izutsu, T. (2008). *The structure of oriental philosophy: Collected papers of the Eranos conference* (Vol. II). Tokyo: Keio University Press.
Matsuoka, S. (2006). *Nihon toiu houhō* [Japan as the method]. Tokyo: Nihon Hōsō Shuppan Kyōkai.
Monbukagaku-shō [Ministry of Education, Culture, Sports, Science and Technology in Japan]. (2012a). Ijime no mondai ni kansuru jidō-seito no jittai-haaku ni kakawaru kinkyū-chōsa ni tsuite [On an urgent survey on the situation of students regarding the problems of bullying]. Retrieved February 1, 2013, from http://www.mext.go.jp/b_menu/houdou/24/11/__icsFiles/afieldfile/2012/12/09/1328532_02_1.pdf.
Monbukagaku-shō [Ministry of Education, Culture, Sports, Science and Technology in Japan]. (2012b). Kyōin no mental health no genjyō [The current situation of teachers' mental health]. Retrieved February 1, 2013, from http://www.mext.go.jp/b_menu/shingi/chousa/shotou/088/shiryo/__icsFiles/afieldfile/2012/02/24/1316629_001.pdf.
Nakagawa, Y. (2000). *Education for awakening: An Eastern approach to holistic education.* Brandon, VT: Foundation for Educational Renewal.
Nakamura, H. (1964). *Ways of thinking of Eastern peoples: India, China, Tibet, Japan.* P. P. Wiener (Ed. & Rev.). Honolulu: University of Hawaii Press.
Nishida, K. (1946/1987). *Last writings: Nothingness and the religious worldview.* (D. Dilworth, Trans.). Honolulu: University of Hawaii Press.
Nishitani, K. (1961/1982). *Religion and nothingness.* (J. V. Bragt, Trans.). Berkeley: University of California Press.
Suzuki, D. T. (1959). *Zen and Japanese culture.* Princeton, NJ: Princeton University Press.
Suzuki, D. T. (1944/1972). *Japanese spirituality.* (N. Waddell, Trans.). Tokyo: Japan Society for the Promotion of Science.
Takuan, S. (1986/2012). *The unfettered mind: Writings from a Zen master to a master swordsman.* (W. S. Wilson, Trans.). Boston: Shambhala.
Ueda, S. (1982). Emptiness and fullness: Sunyata in Mahayana Buddhism. (J. W. Heisig & F. Greiner, Trans.). *The Eastern Buddhist, 15*(1), 9–37.
Yanagi, S. (1972/1989). *The unknown craftsman: A Japanese insight into beauty* (rev. ed.). Tokyo: Kodansha International.

15 Spiritual Education in Singapore and Hong Kong

Issues, Challenges and Prospects

Charlene Tan and Kaili C. Zhang

As Asian societies with a majority of ethnic Chinese people, Singapore and Hong Kong provide a useful comparative study of the governments' conceptions and implementation of spiritual education for their students. Both Singapore and Hong Kong emphasise the need for their students to understand various religious systems, preserve religious harmony and acquire moral values through religious studies. This chapter compares spiritual education in schools in Singapore and Hong Kong in terms of the issues, challenges and prospects. The chapter is divided into three sections. First, we discuss the nature of the spiritual education programmes in Singapore and Hong Kong. Secondly, we examine some key similarities and common challenges in Singapore and Hong Kong. The final section recommends some approaches and strategies to strengthen spiritual education in both societies.

At this point it may be useful to briefly explain the key terms used in this paper: 'religion', 'spirituality', 'morality', 'religious education', 'spiritual education' and 'moral education'. We define *religion* as an organised and shared system of beliefs and practices related to a transcendent entity such as God, a higher power or ultimate truth or reality, closely linked to a particular faith institution (Minney, 1991; Tan & Wong, 2012). It follows that *religious education* is the learning of one or more specific faith systems such as Christianity, Islam, Buddhism and so on. In contrast, *spirituality* is not necessarily associated with any named supernatural power, institutionalised doctrines or religious affiliations. Rather, it is essentially about things pertaining to one's spirit or soul. It propels the search for personal meaning, purpose and identity in life, connectedness with others (whether divine or human), and a commitment to contribute to others (Zhang & Tan, 2010).

Following Carr (1995), we define *spirituality* as "a function of appreciation or reflection upon ideals or goals which are both apt for positive moral evaluation and concerned with those aspects of human experience which attempt to reach beyond the mundane and the material towards what is transcendent and eternal" (p. 90). Examples of spiritual ideals are a sense of awe, feelings of transcendence, a search for meaning, peace and significance, self-awareness, self-knowledge, salvation and prayer (Tan & Wong, 2012). Spiritual ideals can be religiously 'tethered' or 'untethered' (Alexander & McLaughlin, 2003). A tethered ideal is linked to or housed within the tradition of a religious faith. It "takes its shape and structure from various aspects of religion with which it is associated and that make it possible for us to identify criteria for 'spiritual development'" (Alexander & McLaughlin, 2003, p. 359). Untethered ideals, on the other hand, are concerned with beliefs and practices that are disconnected from religion. This form of spirituality is not associated with any named supernatural power, institutionalised doctrines or religious affiliations. In terms of the search for meaning, personal cultivation, manifestations of spirituality in life, responses to aspects of the natural and human world, and the collective domain, religiously untethered spiritual ideals tend to be unstructured, less specific, more open-ended and diffused (Alexander & McLaughlin, 2003).

It follows that *spiritual education* focuses on enabling students to acquire insights into their personal existence which are of enduring worth, in order to attribute meaning to their life experiences and value a nonmaterial and transcendental dimension to life (Office for Standards in Education [Ofsted], 1994). It is apparent that there is a close relationship between spiritual education and religious education; the search for a wider framework of meaning for spirituality usually leads one to explore religious beliefs and practices (Tan & Wong, 2012). Spiritual education may include but is not confined to any set of religious beliefs, institutionalised belief system or any realm of worship.

Besides religious considerations, spiritual education also includes *morality*. Given that spirituality is about the search for personal meaning, purpose and identity in life, the exploratory process inevitably involves confronting, reflecting and clarifying beliefs and values about right and wrong, good and bad, justice and injustice, fairness and unfairness, and so on. This points to the close connection between spirituality education and *moral education*, the latter referring to a form of education that seeks to nurture in young people a set of normative beliefs and values so that students can become moral agents by applying these beliefs and values in their lives (Tan & Wong, 2010).

SPIRITUAL EDUCATION IN SINGAPORE

Singapore, a multicultural and multireligious country in Southeast Asia, has a predominantly Chinese population (74%) among its over 5 million inhabitants. A large majority (83%) of the population identify themselves as adherents of a particular religion, with the majority being Buddhists, followed by Christians, Muslims, Taoists, Hindus and other religions.

Currently, spiritual education does not exist as a formal subject in Singapore schools. But religious education was a compulsory subject in Singapore schools in the 1980s. Known as Religious Knowledge (henceforth RK), it was introduced to all upper secondary students (15–17 years old) in Singapore from 1984 to 1989. Students had a total of six options: Bible Knowledge (in English), Islamic Religious Knowledge (in English and Malay), Buddhist Studies (in Chinese and English), Confucian Ethics (in Chinese and English), Hindu Studies (in English) and Sikh Studies (in English).

Given the sensitive nature of religion, the government was acutely aware of the potential problems associated with the teaching of RK. The government stated categorically that there should be no attempt by RK teachers to preach, proselytise or engage in other religious activities. The phenomenological approach was chosen where the aim was for students to receive 'religious knowledge' and not 'religious instruction' (Curriculum Planning Division, 1988). The prescribed textbooks discussed the various religions in a historical, objective and detached manner (Tan, 2008a, 2008b). RK only lasted until 1989 when it was withdrawn and finally replaced by a common Civics and Moral Education (CME) course in 1992.

With the termination of RK, Singapore students learn about the basic facts of various religions and religious harmony primarily through CME and other learning programmes in schools (Tan, 2008b). Currently, CME is compulsory for all students but is not taken as an examination subject. Factual knowledge of the religions covered in RK is now incorporated into the secondary syllabus, although in a less detailed and potentially less divisive manner. There has been a shift from the careful study of one religion under RK to an overview of the major religions in Singapore under CME. The new policy aims to deemphasise religious differences, diffuse religious undercurrents and direct the students' attention to the importance of religious harmony and appreciation.

In other words, the purpose of CME is to inform students about various belief systems, and not to impart religious faith or induce religious experience in the students. This can be seen in the objective, neutral and crisp way in which the religious beliefs and practices are introduced. Information about seven belief systems (Buddhism, Christianity, Confucianism, Hinduism, Islam, Sikhism and Taoism) is provided in the Reference section of the textbook students use (Curriculum Planning and Development Division [CPDD], 2001, pp. 41–61). The treatment of the various religions is highly descriptive, and exclusive and controversial claims are omitted. For example, there is no mention of sensitive and potentially offensive words and issues like hell, condemnation and the fate of those who subscribe to other religions (CPDD, 2001, p. 53).

CME is not the only avenue whereby religious knowledge is taught in schools. The government explains that the promotion of greater understanding of different races and religions is achieved by infusing it into the formal curriculum through subjects such as Social Studies and History, as well as outside the classroom via co-curricular activities and enrichment programmes (Remaking Singapore Committee, 2004). This integrated approach to the teaching of religious knowledge with the purpose of citizenship training is part of National Education (henceforth NE) which was launched in 1997. One of the six messages of NE is the preservation of racial and religious harmony. For example, all schools celebrate Racial Harmony Day on 21 July every year where students learn about different religions through performances, exhibitions, funfairs and other activities.

Recently, the Ministry of Education announced the launch of Character and Citizenship Education (CCE). The CCE curriculum aims to bring together CME, NE and all other learning experiences that nurture students' character and cultivate them to be responsible citizens. CCE continues the stress on racial and religious harmony. One of CCE's learning outcomes is for students to "[d]emonstrate socio-cultural sensitivity and promote social cohesion and harmony in Singapore as a multi-cultural society" (Ministry of Education, n.d., p. 3).

Overall, it can be noted that the focus for religious education in Singapore schools tends to be on surface culture. According to Holtzman (2000), surface culture, represented by the aboveground part of the tree, is easily visible in the form of clothing, food, language, music and dance. This is reflected in the 'food and festival' or 'heroes and holidays' approach to multicultural education (Tan, 2009, 2011). On the other hand, deep culture, like the roots below the surface, "reflects less observable values, beliefs, and customs and includes child rearing practices, rules about courtship and marriage, treatment of elders, and proxemics" (Holtzman, 2000, p. 21). While surface culture covers areas that are often observable, shared and uncontroversial, deep culture engages with sensitive issues of cultural meanings and challenges cultural stereotypes (Bokhorst-Heng, 2007).

SPIRITUAL EDUCATION IN HONG KONG

As a special administrative region of China, Hong Kong is a city-state situated on China's south coast and enclosed by the Pearl River Delta and South China Sea. Like Singapore, Hong Kong has a predominantly Chinese population (95%) among its over 7 million residents. Approximately 43% of the population subscribe to some form of religion, with Buddhism and Taoism having the most adherents. Other religions include Christianity, Islam, Hinduism, Sikhism and Judaism.

In the past ten years or so, the term 'spiritual' has begun to gain more prominence in the educational discourse in Hong Kong (Ho, 2005). In 2000, in the overall review of the Hong Kong education system, the Education Commission indicated that "with the rapid development of information technology, the spiritual aspect of our life is being suppressed by materialistic influences. It is the society's expectation that education should enrich our moral, emotional, spiritual and cultural life so that we can rise above the material world and lead a healthy life" (Education Commission, 2000, p. 38).

Since then, all schools, whether religious or nonreligious, are expected to provide an environment in which students' spiritual development is supported. However, the term 'spiritual' is still seldom used by the nonreligious in Hong Kong schools (Cheung, 2003). Currently, most schools (including both primary and secondary schools) that claim to facilitate students' spirituality offer two main subjects: Religious Education and Ethics and Religious Studies (Cheung, 2003; Ho, 2005). In these schools, students learn about the role and rationale of religions through the ethics and religious education curricula.

As also indicated previously, part of the vision of the education reform put forward by the Education Commission is to acknowledge the importance of moral education:

> Moral education will be acknowledged as playing a very important role in the education system, and having an important social mission. Students will experience structured learning in moral, emotional and spiritual education to help them develop a healthy outlook to life. (Education Commission, 2000, p. 35)

Thus, although the government seemed to put a stronger emphasis on moral education, its implementation has been a matter for individual schools. In addition, since religious education and moral education are closely related, schools with religious backgrounds often implement moral education that draws its moral sources from faith (Cheng, 2004).

On the whole, according to Ho (2005), the attention given to moral education is hardly conducive to the professed balanced development of students. First of all, time allocated to moral education is often limited. Further, teaching methods for moral education are often on a large scale. In other words, in general, moral education is carried out through assemblies, talks, class teaching and whole-school interaction (Cheng, 2004). Little attention is given to individual students' specific needs when it comes to moral development.

Hill (2005) argued that "educators everywhere bear a moral imperative to provide opportunities for children to reclaim hope, reintegrate socially, learn well, reflect deeply, and act justly" (p. 155). Indeed, children need to be supported in their moral development in order to develop their full potential. Unfortunately, as we have seen, the provision of moral education is often neglected in practice in school situations.

In summary, as no formal subject on spiritual education is provided in schools, it seems that the meaning of 'spiritual education' is mainly from the religious and moral sense of spirituality only. Ho (2005) also questioned the extent to which the increased rhetorical emphasis on the spiritual in Hong

Kong is matched by the actual substance of education policy. His point is further supported when one considers the fact that 'spiritual education' is mentioned under the heading of moral education (Education Commission, 2000, p. 35).

Further, a closer look at different school curricula shows that the provision of ethical/religious and moral education lacks consistency across schools. Since in the Hong Kong education system academic excellence is mainly defined on the basis of performance in examinations, nonexamination courses such as Religious Education and Ethics and Religious Studies are often marginalised in the timetable compared with the importance attached to other academic subjects. Often, nonexamination subjects are reduced to occasional teaching. In some cases, these subjects are even exempted on the grounds of the demands of the examination subjects.

Secondly, while some religious schools do provide regular and frequent lessons in Religious Education and Ethics and Religious Studies for all classes, and these schools may have specialist teachers trained in these areas, many other schools, both religious and nonreligious alike, just assign teachers of other subjects to fulfil this task in order to make up their teaching load. As a result, the majority of teachers teaching these subjects in government or aided secondary schools, are non-subject-trained, meaning those who have not themselves studied the relevant subject in higher education (Education Department, 2002). Consequently, many of these teachers fail to go beyond a surface understanding of religions and are not equipped to recognise and respond to students' spiritual and moral needs.

KEY SIMILARITIES BETWEEN SINGAPORE AND HONG KONG

Singapore and Hong Kong share key similarities in their approaches to and content for spiritual education. First, due to the common influence of the British educational system, the governments in both societies keep religious conversion and instruction away from the formal education system, adopting instead a phenomenological approach in teaching *of* religion (not *teaching religion*). The phenomenological approach originated as a counter-response to the confessional approach (Tan, 2008c). The latter, traditionally used in both ancient and present-day churches, has been criticised as indoctrinating the learners with religious beliefs that are not scientifically justified. Rejecting this approach, the phenomenological approach abstains from leading students to embrace a religion and experience religious conviction. Characterised as informational, descriptive and neutral, this approach concentrates on the different social and cultural expressions of spirituality (Carr, 1996; Grimmitt, 2001). While the phenomenological approach usually involves the teaching of multiple religions, it can focus on the teaching of one religion as long as the aim is to teach religious phenomena in a factual, objective and detached manner.

As noted earlier, Singapore introduced Religious Knowledge from 1984 to 1989. The aim was for students to receive 'religious knowledge' and not 'religious instruction'. The prescribed textbooks discussed the various religions in a historical, objective and detached manner. The government in Singapore explained that religious knowledge aimed to inform the students "about the religion, its founder or its origins and the universal moral teachings and main beliefs of the religion" (as cited in Tan, 2000, p. 86).

The second local concern is the state's desire to use spirituality as a medium to transmit moral values in the school curriculum. In Singapore, religion is part of the cultural curriculum used to promote national unity and enhance political loyalty to the state (Tan, 2011). That was evident in both the Religious Knowledge and the current Civics and Moral Education courses, each with the aim to highlight the universal moral values shared by the major faiths in Singapore, such as love, good works and tolerance. Singapore's former Deputy Prime Minister Goh Keng Swee stated that religious knowledge would provide the "intellectual basis which will bind the various moral qualities we deem desirable into a consistent system of thought" (as cited in Ong & Moral Education Committee, 1979, p. iii).

The approach is also evident in Hong Kong. As indicated previously, the Religious Education and Ethics and Religious Studies courses or, for that matter, spiritual education that schools provide generally do not seem to adequately promote students' spiritual development (Ho, 2005). Students learn about the role and rationale of religions, ethics, and personal and social issues mainly from assemblies or talks, class teaching and counselling (Cheng, 2004). Furthermore, the overriding importance of public examinations in the Hong Kong education system inevitably lowers the status of religious and moral education in school. Subjects such as Religious Education and Ethics and Religious Studies are often considered to be of limited significance.

COMMON CHALLENGES FOR SINGAPORE AND HONG KONG

We highlight four broad challenges facing Singapore and Hong Kong for their spiritual education programmes. First, religious knowledge is imparted in a largely descriptive and superficial manner, with the result that the students generally lack an adequate empathetic awareness of religion. Just like many other countries in the world, the one-size-fits-all approach of religious studies in schools merely presents students with fragments from various traditions.

Secondly, since the teacher may adhere to a certain religion/belief or even be an atheist, trying to teach about *all* religions and/or spirituality to *all* students in common classes is likely to lead to distortion and indoctrination

(Baer & Carper, 1998/1999). The consequence is that "scraps and frag-ments of different religious traditions" are presented which are meaning-less, superficial and distortive of any real understanding of religion (Carr, 1996, p. 171). Hull (2001) noted that this approach tends not to grapple with the life-world of the student and often makes little or no explicit con-tribution to the students' search for moral and spiritual values. The phe-nomenological approach, with the ostensible aim to avoid indoctrination, has presented a truncated and superficial account of religion (Tan, 2008c). It is therefore not an option favoured by parents and educators who want their children and students to have an empathetic awareness of faith.

Thirdly, religious knowledge is often taught using didactic and uninter-esting ways or becomes marginalised in an exam-oriented school environ-ment. It should be acknowledged that in the case of Singapore, there is a strong attempt by the Ministry of Education and schools to make the learn-ing of religious knowledge fun and interesting. For example, the CME text-books include activities such as crossword puzzles and matching pictures to words (Tan, 2008a). Activities such as getting students to don religious attire during Racial Harmony Day and organising visits to temples and mosques also are interactive and novel for the students.

But the challenge for Singapore students and even teachers is the temp-tation to sideline the teaching of religious knowledge in favour of exam subjects, especially during the exam period. The limited success of the phe-nomenological approach in promoting religious harmony and appreciation in Singapore schools was confirmed by Chew (2005) in a study involving 2779 students aged between 12 and 18 in six educational institutions. Her research findings showed that the average adolescent in Singapore knows very little about faith in Singapore, despite learning about religions during the CME period. She also pointed out that the religious tolerance of many students is based primarily on ignorance and fear rather than an apprecia-tion of the different faiths in Singapore.

Similarly, in Hong Kong, the attention given to children's spiritual needs and spiritual development is inadequate, since the focus of education is generally on teaching basic skills and contributing to intellectual develop-ment. This neglect is a matter of grave concern, for the main problems chil-dren face in Hong Kong are criminal activity, suicide and the loss of moral values (Lau, 2001). In addition, among children in Hong Kong there is an increasing sense of insecurity, a growing resentment at the large influx of immigrants from Mainland China, and anger at the increasing socioeco-nomic burden brought by the immigrants (Zhang & Law, 2011).

Finally, spiritual education in both societies is limited to religious sys-tems and tends to neglect the broader concept of spirituality and the impor-tance of spiritual development for students. Gaining religious knowledge is not the same as acquiring spiritual education. We have already explained the difference between 'spirituality' and 'religion' at the start of the chap-ter. Spiritual education goes beyond religious education by encouraging students to acquire insights (that need not be religious in nature) into their personal existence which are of enduring worth.

PROSPECTS FOR SINGAPORE AND HONG KONG

In response to the above-mentioned challenges, we suggest that spiritual education be introduced and enhanced in both societies so as to help students to develop spiritually. The school should adopt a whole-school approach where its motto, vision, ethos and curriculum design converge on selected spiritual ideals such as the quest for knowing oneself and serving others (for details, please see Tan & Wong, 2012). These spiritual ideals can then be transmitted through subjects such as civics and moral education and activities such as community involvement and service learning. It is hoped that students will take the first step towards the construction and acquisition of spiritual values and beliefs that go beyond mere obedience to social and moral norms. With appropriate facilitation from their teachers, students can then be guided to reflect upon more universal and transcendental aspects of the human experience—essentially what spiritual education is about. Spiritual development could also take place in various school subjects across the curriculum, especially the arts—literature, poetry, drama, painting and music (Tan, 2010). Universal themes and values from both religious and nonreligious sources may be introduced to encourage students to reflect on, internalise and apply the moral values learnt. Situating our discussion in the Asian context, we also propose that spiritual education could be introduced to students by drawing upon Asian philosophies and different religions. For example, students could explore the concept of harmony or moral cultivation from Confucian, Muslim, Hindu and Christian sources.

Given that spiritual education (as described above) is currently not implemented in Singapore and Hong Kong, teachers in both societies are likely to be unfamiliar with it. Hence, we suggest that in order for spiritual education to be adequately addressed, the notion of a teacher training programme should be carefully revisited. For example, in order for student teachers to grow spiritually, our training programmes should include elements that encourage them to explore their inner lives, to foster positive values and to develop a deeper sense of self, understanding, and compassion for others.

Further, since research has found that practices such as student-centred pedagogy, service learning, meditation and contemplation enhance college students' spiritual development (Astin, Astin & Lindhom, 2011; Pascarella & Terenzini, 2005; Zhang, forthcoming; Zhang & Yu, 2012), we believe that encouraging and enabling pre-and in-service teachers to engage in such practices could substantially enhance the positive impact of the college experience and/or training programme on student teachers' lives, and ultimately the lives of their pupils.

CONCLUSION

This chapter offers a comparative study of spiritual education in two Asian societies. It has been pointed out that spiritual education curricula in Singapore and Hong Kong have underlined the importance of religious harmony by linking religion to morality. However, we have also argued that more can be done to promote spiritual development so that students in both societies can go beyond a surface understanding of religions to develop a deeper appreciation of human existence. We also submit that in order that spiritual education be adequately addressed, the notion of a teacher training programme should be carefully revisited.

REFERENCES

Alexander, H., & McLaughlin, T. H. (2003). Education in religion and spirituality. In N. Blake, P. Smeyers, R. Smith, & P. Standish (Eds.), *The Blackwell guide to the philosophy of education* (pp. 356–373). Malden, MA: Blackwell.

Astin, A. W., Astin, H. S., & Lindhom, J. A. (2011). *Cultivating the spirit: How college can enhance students' inner lives.* San Francisco: Jossey Bass.

Baer, R. A., & Carper, J. C. (1998, Dec./1999, Jan.). Spirituality and the public schools: An evangelical perspective. *Educational Leadership, 56*(4), 33–37.

Bokhorst-Heng, D. W. (2007). Multiculturalism's narratives in Singapore and Canada: Exploring a model for comparative multiculturalism and multicultural education. *Journal of Curriculum Studies, 39*(6), 629–658.

Carr, D. (1995). Towards a distinctive conception of spiritual education. *Oxford Review of Education, 21*(1), 83–98.

Carr, D. (1996). Rival conceptions of spiritual education. *Journal of Philosophy of Education, 30*, 159–178.

Carr, D. (1999). Spiritual language and the ethics of redemption: A reply to Jim Mackenzie. *Journal of Philosophy of Education, 33*, 451–461.

Cheng, R. H. M. (2004). Moral education in Hong Kong: Confucian-parental, Christian religious and liberal-civic influences. *Journal of Moral Education, 33*(4), 533, 551. DOI: 10.1080/0305724042000315626

Cheung, C. K. (2003). The use of popular culture in the teaching of ethics/religious education: A Hong Kong case. *Religious Education, 98*(2), 197–220.

Chew, P. (2005, Sept. 1–2). *Religious switching among adolescents in Singapore.* Paper presented at the IPS Workshop on Religious Diversity and Harmony in Singapore, Singapore.

Curriculum Planning and Development Division (CPDD). (2001). *Civics and moral education.* Pupil's Book, 3A. Singapore: Ministry of Education.

Curriculum Planning Division (CPD). (1988). *Guide book for principals on the implementation of religious knowledge subjects.* Singapore: Ministry of Education.

Education Commission. (2000). *Education blueprint for the 21st century: Learning for life, learning through life—Reform proposals for the education system in Hong Kong.* Hong Kong: Printing Department.

Education Department. (2002). *Teacher statistics 2001.* Hong Kong: Printing Department.

Grimmitt, M. (2001). Pedagogies of religious education for today and tomorrow: Identifying their principles, procedures and strategies. In T. Dodd (Ed.), *Developments in religious education* (pp. 1–23). Hull: The University of Hull.

Hill, C. M. (2005) Moral imperatives, professional interventions and resilience, and educational action in chaotic situations: The souls of children amid the horror of war. *International Journal of Children's Spirituality, 10*(2), 155–164.

Ho, W. (2005). The ambiguity of the term 'spiritual' in Hong Kong educational discourse: Rhetoric and substance. *International Journal of Children's Spirituality 10*(3), 243–261.

Holtzman, L. (2000). *Media messages.* Armonk, NY: M. E. Sharpe, Inc.

Hull, J. M. (2001, Nov.). *The contribution of religious education to religious freedom: A global perspective.* Paper presented at The International Consultative Conference on School Education in Relation with Freedom of Religion and Belief, Tolerance, and Non-Discrimination in Madrid, Spain. Retrieved March 30, 2013, from http://www.iarf.net/REBooklet/Hull.htm.

Lau, L. (2001). *Other initiatives in the Near East, Central and Eastern Asia.* Retrieved March 30, 2013, from http://www.freunde-waldorf.de/en/the-friends/publications/waldorf-education-worldwide/teil-3/near-east-and-asia.html.

Ministry of Education. (n.d.). *Character and citizenship education.: A toolkit for Singapore schools.* Singapore: Author.

Minney, R. (1991). What is spirituality in an educational context? *British Journal of Educational Studies, 39*(4), 386–397.

Office for Standards in Education. (1994). *Spiritual, moral, social and cultural development. An OFSTED Discussion Paper.* London: Office for Standards in Education.

Ong, T. C., & Moral Education Committee. (1979). *Report on moral education 1979.* Singapore: Author.

Pascarella, E. T., & Terenzini, P. T. (2005). *How college affects students: A third decade of research* (Vol. 2). San Francisco: Jossey-Bass.

Remaking Singapore Committee. (2004). *Changing mindsets, Deepening relationships.* Singapore: Author.

Tan, C. (2008a). The teaching of religious knowledge in a plural society: The case for Singapore. *International Review of Education, 54*(2), 175–191.

Tan, C. (2008b). From moral values to citizenship education: The teaching of religion in Singapore schools. In A. E. Lai (Ed.), *Religious diversity in Singapore* (pp. 321–341). Singapore: ISEAS & IPS.

Tan, C. (2008c). Religious education and indoctrination. In C. Tan (Ed.), *Philosophical reflections for educators* (pp. 183–192). Singapore: Cengage Learning Asia.

Tan, C. (2009). Maximising the overlapping area: Multiculturalism and the Muslim identity for madrasahs in Singapore. *Journal of Beliefs and Values, 30*(1), 41–48.

Tan, C. (2010). Dialogical education for inter-religious engagement in a plural society. In K. Engebretson, M. de Sousa, G. Durka, & L. Gearon (Eds.), *International handbook of inter-religious education* (pp. 361–376). Dordrecht: Springer.

Tan, C. (2011). Deep culture matters: Multiracialism in Singapore schools. *International Journal of Educational Reform, 21*(1), 24–38.

Tan, C., & Wong, Y. L. (2010). Moral education for young people in Singapore: Philosophy, policy and prospects. *Journal of Youth Studies, 13*(2), 89–102.

Tan, C., & Wong, Y. L. (2012). Promoting spiritual ideals through design thinking in public schools. *International Journal of Children's Spirituality, 1–13.* DOI: 10.1080/1364436X.2011.651714

Tan, J. (2000). The politics of religious knowledge in Singapore secondary schools. In C. Cornbleth (Ed.), *Curriculum politics policy, practice. Cases in comparative context* (pp. 77–102). Albany: State University of New York Press.

Zhang, K. C. (forthcoming). What I look like: College women, body image, and spirituality. *Journal of Religion and Health.* DOI: 10.1007/s10943–012–9566–0

Zhang, K. C., & Law, M. T. (2011). The education of new Chinese immigrant children in Hong Kong: Challenges and opportunities. *Support for Learning: British Journal for Learning Support, 26*(2), 49–55.

Zhang, K. C., & Tan. C. (2010). Exploring the spiritual needs of adolescent girls. *Religion and Education, 37*(2), 146–161.

Zhang, K. C., & Yu, E. D. (2012). Quest for a good life: Spiritual values, life goals and college students. *Asia-Pacific Psychiatry.* DOI:10.1111/j.1758–5872. 2012.00183.x

16 Buddha's Beacon and the Long Shadow of Thai Culture
Spirituality and Education in Thailand

Michael Ernest Jones

> *The contents of kitchens and closets may change, but the core mechanisms by which cultures maintain their identity and socialize their young remain untouched.*
>
> —Kenichi Ohmae (1995)

INTRODUCTION: REFORMS, THE THREE PILLARS, THE NATION

Until the mid to late 19th century, Thailand was known as the kingdom of Siam. During the reign of King Mongkut ('Rama IV,' reigned 1851–1868), colonial powers surrounded the region, and the king responded by annexing various smaller kingdoms in Northern, Northeastern, Southeastern, and South Thailand to form a consolidated kingdom. Mongkut then set a series of sweeping reforms in motion whereby the practice of Buddhism, along with regional customs, beliefs, and practices were altered considerably, while the foundations of a modern education system were put in place. The newly developed state took the profound step, during the reign of Vajiravudh (1910–1925), of creating the foundations that would lead to national legitimacy; namely, introducing a cultural platform of interlocking shared values of nation, religion, and monarchy which was proclaimed *The Three Pillars of Thai Nationalism* (Payulpitack, 1991, p. 41). This notion of the *Three Pillars* is modelled after the Buddhist *Triple Gems*, the central focus of devotion comprised of Buddha, the Dhamma, and the Sangha, but instead of professing refuge in the Gems, Thainess requires an allegiance to king, nation, and (Thai) Buddhism. The use of these *Pillars* provided the opportunity to unify a once multicultural region into a single nation by assigning similar cultural attributes, beliefs, and language to all in order to develop good, obedient citizens who were both educated and morally disciplined (Baker & Phongpaichit, 2005).

The 1932 political revolution that brought about a constitutional monarchy was led by the People's Party and steered by the right-wing military faction (Sattayanurak, 2002). After efforts to consolidate the region, sometimes forcibly, succeeded, the military quickly began capitalizing on the new education system. Consequently, Luang Wichit Wathakan, Minister of Foreign Affairs and the chief ideologue of the cultural campaigns, initiated an effective series of innovations in cultural indoctrination through the use of media, arts, theatre, radio, and the school curriculum. Inspired by the social fascism of Italy and the Japanese Meiji period, his efforts went towards locking in a mythic-based, exclusive cultural identity that would be invulnerable to outsiders and their influence. And, as Christopher Baker and Pasuk Phongpaichit point out, his "influence was broad, deep, and lasting" (2005, p. 29).

By the issue of seven 'cultural mandates' or 'state edicts' in 1939 (Baker & Phongpaichit, 2005, p. 132), what was once the amorphous Kingdom of Siam became the solidified nation-state of Thailand. The historical notion of education and spirituality in Thailand had been interwoven to creatively construct a cultural archetype that successfully consolidated an elaborate nation-state. This ingeniously managed design of a nation-state was initially driven, during the 20th century era of political modernization and industrialization, in order to keep colonial forces at arms' length and to establish a morally and intellectually capable population equipped with a distinct identity that set it apart from all others. These civil reforms relied heavily on the use of *reform utilities* (Jones, 2008), or state-determined notions of culture, Buddhism, and education, to manipulate social class restructuring with a view to creating in the population "a sense of national identity moulded into their blood permanently" (Wathakan, 1932, cited in Sattayanurak, 2002, p. 16).

THAI BUDDHIST EDUCATION—THEN AND NOW

In Thai language, 'spiritual' refers to Buddhist practices or the prevalent belief in ghosts and the magic that emanates from the spirit world where ghosts and spirits roam, haunt, bless, protect, or cause various mischiefs and beneficial actions. In talking about the Thai beliefs in spirits, one must recognize that they are a rich and complex heritage of ancient village folk traditions and animistic beliefs that have adapted to and entwined with the many spiritual traditions and interpretations that have passed through Thailand, e.g., Vedic tales, Brahmin practices, Hindu conceptualizations, both Theravada and Mahayana Buddhist traditions, and so on. Although these ghost and spirit world beliefs are not taught in public schools, they have been passed on through a wide variety of rituals and ceremonies by Buddhist monks, *maw do*, *maw pee*, *mae maw*, *paw tao*, and the many interpretative narratives of local contexts. To say Thai spirit beliefs and rituals are insignificant and superstitious is far from the truth as they are symbolic of how Thais interpret and express their Buddhist values and beliefs in everyday living (McDaniel, 2011).

For centuries, the Thai *wat* (or Buddhist temple) was the focus of public activity in every village and was the "the most important institution in Thai rural life" (Kusalasaya, 2006, p. 19). The *wat* fulfilled multiple village needs, "much like a combination of a school, social centre, hospital, town hall, playground, visitor inn, and community centre," while monks served a host of "regional Buddhist traditions (Khmer, Mon, Lao, etc.) and multiple cultural customs and languages" (Jones, 2008, p. 426). The responsibilities of a monk were far-ranging and required versatility and broad knowledge, since they were expected to perform as teachers and transcribers, healers of bones and minds, laborers and designers, veterinarians and agricultural extension agents, public leaders and arbitrators, prognosticators and fortune tellers, recreation coordinators and ritual organizers, and crucially, protectors against ghosts and evil spirits (Tiyavanich, 1997).

The 1902 *Sangha* Act decreed by King Chulalongkorn ('Rama V,' reigned 1868–1910), however, intended to reform the duties of monks, as well as alter monastic education through a standardized curriculum and administrative control from Bangkok over all monasteries in Northern and Northeastern Thailand. The intent was to shape Buddhism into a coherent and uniform state religion while mandating a more sedentary and administratively focused monk, splitting Buddhism from education to make them both more universally coherent and available to all citizens and placing villagers into a kind of cultural harness that would serve the purpose of developing a homogeneous nation. Even though the reforms destabilized local traditions and customs in North and Northeast Thailand for the sake of creating a homogeneous culture and nation-state, monastic schools changed little as "reforms were not actually implemented in any significant way" (McDaniel, 2008, p. 106).

Kusalasaya (2006) has surmised that even though Thailand had transformed from many tiny village kingdoms into one sovereign state, enduring many profound reforms and creating a large modern educational system, "one-half of the primary schools of the country are still situated in *wats*" (p. 17). The majority of *wats* and traditional *wat* schools are still found in Northern and Northeastern Thailand, the historical centres of Buddhist education in Southeast Asia. There are 31,071 *wats* in Thailand, 48% of which are in Northeast Thailand and 24% in Northern Thailand (McDaniel, 2008). Of these, 3554 (11%) have elementary schools, 2772 (78%) of which are in Northern and Northeastern Thailand. Elementary student numbers are also proportionally distributed in these two regions with the Northeast registering approximately 161,000 and the North registering approximately 21,600 students, while Central Thailand (including the densely populated and economically dominant Bangkok) has approximately 8000 elementary students. Though national figures vary, there are as many as 290,000 monks and approximately 150,000 novices throughout Thailand, presumably mostly in Northeast and North Thailand where, coincidently or otherwise, the incidence of poverty is greatest. In addition, 21,125 schools (67%) out of 31,424 have the word '*wat*' or temple in front of their school names, though they are not necessarily all run by monks or located on temple grounds (National Office of Buddhism, 2011).

According to the Buddha Dharma Education Association (2002), approximately 10,500 *wat* schools teach mainly Pali or Buddhism to nearly 260,000 students served by 34,000 teachers. Thailand also has two Buddhist universities and two Buddhist associations as well as affiliated provincial Buddhist associations. In general, the historic foundation of Buddhist education has been built upon studies in morality, meditation (mind), and wisdom (cognition).

In contemporary Thai public education, Buddhism, as well as Islam in the *pondok* schools of South Thailand, is a required subject. It is referred to in the Thai National Curriculum for grades 1–12 as "Religion, Morality, and Ethics" under the broad "Social Studies, Religion, and Culture" Learning Area (Office of the Basic Education Commission, 2008, p. 10). There are no teacher qualifications for teaching the subject of religion and teachers often teach their own beliefs and understanding of Buddhism or call in a monk from a local *wat*. But these efforts have not been completely satisfactory for many of the monks in the reformist vanguard, the voices of dissent. The amount and quality of Buddhist education in both public and *wat* schools has been at the centre of ongoing criticisms from Buddhist monk-scholars (Payutto, 1988; Visalo, 1999; Dhammasakiyo, 2004; Dhammasami, 2007) and they are in agreement that Buddhist education at all levels is remiss.

Making matters worse, Buddhist temple schools are not only deficient in their academic approaches, but they are unconnected to the Thai Ministry of Education, its curriculum, or its support as reported by Dhammasakiyo (2004). Until the last two decades, the majority of Thai *wat* schools refused to teach secular subjects, considering subjects such as mathematics and English to be 'animal sciences' (Dhammasami, 2007, pp. 17–18). Until recent years, few monks were taught secular subjects in large part because the Ministry of Education did not recognize *wat* schools or universities and the Thai *sangha* persists in refusing to teach secular subjects.

Reformist Buddhist monk-scholars such as Prayudh Payutto (1988) argued to the Thai government and to the *sangha* that monks were unable to assimilate into contemporary society and were unprepared to impart essential Buddhist values to a more secularized Thailand. Payutto also lamented the lack of capacity to produce quality monks or Buddhist scholars in Thailand even as non-Buddhist countries were producing both. While the government supports the overall idea of the secular within the Buddhist, the debate remains lively and contentious within the *sangha* since no one has clear ideas on just how this is to be done (Dhammasami, 2007), not least because the *wat* schools continue to hold a similar divisive and incoherent approach to the topic.

THAI EDUCATION—CHALLENGES TO BEING WHOLE

Thailand spends 28.3% of its entire budget on education (NationMaster. com, 2012), one of the world's highest percentages. However, it is apparent that Thai educational reform has not transformed education as intended. For example, after many years of exposing students to a large variety of English language programs, the English First *English Proficiency Index* was released and ranked Thailand 42nd out of 44 countries with a rating of 'very low proficiency' (2011). UNICEF, which has long been a supporter of Thailand's educational achievement, states on its website, "The quality of education that children receive in Thailand is also a major concern. Studies have shown that the learning level of Thai children in major subject areas has declined over the past 10 years" (2012). The litany of statistics UNICEF base these worrisome statements upon seems to tell an unhappy story for education in Thailand:

- Only 60% of Thai children attend early childhood development programs;
- Of 8276 Early Childhood Centres, only 34% meet the government's minimum standards;
- Roughly 600,000 primary school children (6–11 years old) are not attending schools or enrol late, with Thailand one of 15 countries in the world that together account for more than half of the world's out-of-school children of primary school age;
- Approximately 50% of the children who started grade 1 in 1998 did not finish grade 12;
- Among the 65 countries participating in the Program for International Student Assessment (PISA) in 2009, Thai students ranked 50th in reading, 50th in mathematics, and 49th in science;
- Of 30,010 schools nationwide, 65% fall below a 'satisfactory' level in terms of student education achievement, the quality of teachers, and overall school administration;
- In recent years, the average scores in the National Achievement Test for Grades 6 and 12 have fallen below 50% in English, mathematics, science, and social sciences (UNICEF, 2012).

UNESCO has also expressed concern regarding Thai education in its *World Data on Education* document, particularly in connection with students' abilities to become responsible contributors to the public good, to act ethically with mature moral development, to work together, and to think critically. "It has become imperative for the Thai people to be endowed with desirable moral values, intelligence, and sagacity. The direction of such human capacity development would focus on providing children and youths with a firm foundation for attaining morality and public-mindedness" (2011, p. 12). These are not alien to Thais; they are values that Thai

Buddhists cherish because they are attributes that result from following the *Noble Eightfold Path*, the means to purify one's discipline; however, they are not present in the Thai school curriculum.

Currently, the unification agenda promoted by the Association of South-Eastern Asian Nations (ASEAN) is a high priority for Thailand, and the organization has acknowledged the need to be more outward looking. Education is the preferred crosscutting method for achieving this goal (ASEAN, 2012), even if the path to integrating it into national curricula seems vague and without regard for the region's more pressing educational deficiencies. Nevertheless, ASEAN has released a curriculum calling for member nations to connect the global to the local. The curriculum is highly sophisticated and has embedded 'Pathways' (p. 9), four areas composed of *people, places, materials, and ideas* (religion and philosophies) that lead to perspective-taking in understanding multicultural issues. Understanding one's religion and the religion of others in the context of local and regional history and social proximity is an objective. However, as well designed as the curriculum is, it is not clear how many teachers in Thailand have the capacity to teach the curriculum in general, and in particular implement the *ideas* area of the curriculum given the fact that Thai monks are very displeased with current religious education in Thailand.

Thailand's own well-crafted reform document has failed to produce anticipated results and Thai students are not mentally or emotionally equipped to compete with other ASEAN countries. One must therefore ask why, after so much money and effort has been invested into Thai education, don't Thais learn more effectively. Is the Thai curriculum sufficiently integrated in a manner to take advantage of their refined spiritual heritage?

Perhaps it may be appropriate to ask if Thais have been traditionally conditioned to learn in a particularly patterned way. Robert St. Clair (2000) contrasts modes of learning in cultures that are print oriented with those that have arisen from oral traditions. Oral traditions employ visual patterns enriched with emotional content in unstructured and contextualized performances in order to lead learners to intuitively understand experientially, usually via apprenticeship or communal relationships. Printed word-oriented traditions, by contrast, cognitively process concepts and employ detached and sequential, analytic, and logical functions in seeking rational knowledge, generally in isolation. Meanwhile, the products of oral traditions often consist of cultural artifacts portraying spiritual representations in symbols, dance, song, art, and motifs, and visual metaphors for large caches of information (i.e., mandalas, traditional dance forms, objects representing the significance of place, etc.). For their part, print-mode traditions tend to generate products saturated with technologies that result from a deep fascination with mathematics and the sciences, the intellectually spiritual forms in Western countries.

In the case of Southeast Asia and Buddhism, both have relied on an oral tradition as a means of learning for many centuries. Until the 13th century,

Thai had no written form and even after the introduction of a written script, it was largely taught to the ruling elite only. Some monks learned various regional spoken languages and achieved varying degrees of proficiency in reading and writing Thai and Pali, the script used in most Buddhist texts. Monks had to commit to memory an enormous number of texts, tales, rituals, and prayers in order to conduct ceremonies and sermons, some lasting hours on end. However, they did not simply memorize everything by rote, but had a system for remembering things through the "use of word association, circular and interconnected glossing of terms within terms, and repetition" (McDaniel, 2008, p. 172). Moreover, the importance of meditation should also be mentioned as an essential learning device. To the Buddhist, reason is an insufficient way towards the insight required for altering the mind in order to know what is considered loftier forms of knowledge experienced in levels of *jhana* (*absorptions* leading to enhanced consciousness, deep insights, and profound concentration) during meditation.

For their part, the villagers also had a large repertoire of rites, rituals, prayers, ceremonies, festivals, and myths to retain in memory. Learning without the aid of texts implies the development of sophisticated memes, which must be repeated with associated visual and intuitive mental patterns, with the memorization itself embedded in the living, that is, representative series of actions. The tales, myths, understandings, and problems of the local thus became the spiritual capital the monks used in their teaching—a holistically integrated, feedback-based regional educational system (McDaniel, 2008).

However, *wat* schools did not operate in a vacuum as separate centres, but were networked and shared resources, teachers, and 'leaves' (the traditional material of Buddhist manuscripts). In brief, they formed a shared intercultural Buddhist community open to all. The *nissaya* (support) manuscripts became the medium of communication between teacher and students and formed the basis for what was taught. The Buddhist texts used in the Southeast Asian region were thus emergent, dynamic, and living heritages where past meets future in coherent philosophical and moral terms. From its inception, Buddhism was never a single set of doctrines conducive to study in the classroom, but an expansive set of sermons, scriptures, commentaries, discourses, interpretations, liturgical practices, codes, prayers, poetic verses, and established records of the interactions that have long been occurring in the life-learning process within Buddhist communities of practice, including the laity, royalty, and the monks themselves (McDaniel, 2008).

These traditional patterns of learning in multiple forms are faintly mimicked in contemporary school settings; however, students employ less effective rote memory skills, while a Westernized curriculum demands that teachers engage in less effective transmission of more personally detached information. Thai students are required to attend school to pass an endless series of examinations, all of which determine their social standing and economic fate. The emphasis on material success is overwhelming and students do not spend adequate time in spiritual aspects to learning such as reflection, meditation, extending concern for others, building community, or of the relationship to the environment. Inherent curiosity and love of learning is replaced by the overriding concern for entering the most elite schools, personal future job prospects, and social status.

BROAD SHADOWS: THE BOUNDARIES OF MULTICULTURALISM AND INTERCULTURAL COMMUNICATION

Multicultural policies in Thailand have been for the most part ignored or approached as a means of exploiting those not considered Thai. Hayami Yoko (2006) explains how the notion of 'Thai-ness' and homogeneity are "incessantly stressed in official and other discourse while repressing differences. . . . Those who do not fit into the narrowly defined 'Thai-ness' have therefore been deemed 'others' and outsiders, threats to the unity of the homogeneously conceived nation" (p. 283). A cultural feature adapted from Buddhism is the idea of nonconfrontation and disengagement from conflict. However, when confronted with difference and cognitive dissonance, they can be vulnerable to passive-aggression (a disconnect between expressed beliefs and contrary actions). A general tendency of societies is to assert nonchalance to difference but revert to primitive measures to deny—or make difficult—existence through acts of discouragement and the denial of the means to flourish (Bennett, 1998). The hilltribe peoples of Northern Thailand are an example of people considered outsiders and have never been granted citizenship even though their ancestral homeland is Thailand.

Milton Bennett (1998) details styles of intercultural communication within societies that can be characterized as preferring a monocultural communication style, that is, exhibiting a *similarity-based* pattern of relating "shared assumptions about the nature of reality" (p. 1). The style becomes corrupted when these assumptions of similarity encounter differences, and "difference represents the potential for misunderstanding and friction. Thus, social difference of all kinds is discouraged" (p. 1). Bennett referred to these as *"difference-based"* (p. 2) approaches to intercultural communication.

Thailand fits neatly within the description of a difference-based intercultural communication approach. In summarizing the work of Thongchai Winichakul, Chachavalpongpun (2010) considers that "Thai identity is illusive because of a lack of cultural coherence or uniqueness" (p. 2), relying instead on what is defined as *not* Thainess and adopting a sense of difference, as well as *wrongness* inherent in non-Thainess. Thus the sense of Thainess is contrived and manipulated by those wielding power and used as a means of retaining power and creating a sense of prestige. The construction of enemies is an aspect of differentiation, particularly of *farang* (people of European descent), the embodiment of this emblematic and archetypical non-Thainess. In effect, *farang* are often used as whipping posts in order to justify self-serving policies as a defense from the imagined intrusion of foreign concepts/social order, in an effort to further redefine Thainess (Chachavalpongpun, 2010). The treatment of non-Thais is thus a love-hate relationship that has been prevalent since the time of King Mongkut's initial reforms, which have been embedded in cultural mythology ever since, perhaps to the detriment of a nation aspiring to spiritual greatness with the ability to address the wider world.

Chai Podhisita (1998) believes Thailand's approach to outsiders is through "individualism and autonomy" (p. 51) but results in the negative effect of an inability to bond in social groups or teams, locally or globally. As Podhisita comments, "This perhaps partly accounts for the weakness of many social, economic, and political activities in Thailand which require strong grouping (group discipline, sense of belonging, etc.) to be successful" (p. 51). The evident lack of public goods, spaces, and projects can be linked directly to this inability to act as an organized group. Given the call from ASEAN for regional economical unification, the collective task of joining an even larger social community whose motto is 'One Vision, One Identity, One Community' (2011, title page) is daunting for Thai society.

In addition, ASEAN regional unification calls for educational institutions to meet international standards in order to instil learning beyond the technical know-how of industrial needs. Rather, it seeks intercultural competency, international and regional linguistic capacities, and ethical and moral decision-making. In the case of Thailand, these areas of required expertise are failing badly, particularly in those areas related to culture, including language, intercultural skills, and the responsibility for creating public good. Traditional Buddhism before the nation-state reforms was dependent on *wats* being interconnected institutions of public good across kingdoms and races of people. Intercultural competence was an essential feature of a *wat's* spiritual efficacy and the potency of its spiritual work. Essentially, intercultural competence has always been a spiritual element in Thai Buddhism. Contemporary Thai culture with its binary approach to multiculturalism and insular intercultural understanding has lost the spiritual significance in understanding other cultures and even its own fabricated identity. These conditions will not lead to what Bennett refers to as "intercultural competence" (1998, p. 2).

CONCLUSION: CULTURAL SHADOWS AND IDENTITY

Where once Buddhism and education worked in tandem to support and make live culture and community, education and Buddhism are now estranged; instead of the nation supporting them, they support the nation without their complementary functions. Monks' knowledge was once practical and worldly and met the needs of the people, and the *wats* functioned as networked centres of public good. And although the interface between education and Buddhism was dissolved in the series of reforms beginning 150 years ago, both continue to play significant roles in the implementation of important educational reforms, as conceived in the 1999 National Education Act (Office of the National Education Commission, 2002) and the call for regional integration by ASEAN. The challenge for Thailand has been to make the historical spiritual significance of Buddhism and the education of an intelligent nation coherent and relevant to themselves and to the world, as intended 150 years ago at the onset of the reforms.

Thai educational reform has not shown to be potent nor has it addressed the learning needs of students. The pedagogical heritage modelled from the West is not understood deeply by Thais, nor is it adapted with the aim of preserving indigenous learning traditions (still used in learning Buddhist prayers). The necessary understanding of Western pedagogy with its print-based learning approach appears ill suited to the once appropriate student-centred approaches that were discarded as 'uncivilized' and replaced with borrowed Western concepts that do not fit the sociocultural context of Thailand. It is as if those making educational decisions in Thailand do not understand their own cultural tendencies and believe that the same cultural forces that moulded Thai identity so successfully can also bend the global culture into its own mythology. A more appropriate course would be for Thai education to utilize the Buddhist practices of reflection, contemplation, and experiential learning, while eliminating the emphasis on testing to measure materialistic success.

Thai Buddhism has also wavered in its educational efforts, although remaining a compelling spiritual heritage for the majority of Thais. The common plot that has attempted to bridge the schism between education and Buddhism has been the engineered cultural narrative stitched together by Central Thailand elitists who were fascinated by right-wing fascist means of consolidating a nation-state. This cultural narrative was contrived with the idea of replacing established identities with a more celebrated one that represented exceptionalism, separate from and in defiance of all other nations and cultures. It is this cultural foundation that has led to the weakest aspect of both Thai education and Buddhism—the inability to create a truly diverse multicultural state comprising citizens able to interact with intercultural competence.

Nevertheless, there are tendencies within nation-building that try to recapture the past and enshrine it in a graveyard of dreamy abstract ideas and unfertile spaces. Examples of this abstract feature of cultural mythology abound in all nations, e.g., American exceptionalism, and it is this abstract feature that distorts national characteristics and identity, affecting sociopolitical ideology that make intercultural relations arduous. Fathoming these issues of identity and their relationship to education and Buddhism is crucial if Thai people are to understand the challenges of combining identity with an engaged relationship with the world. While the benefits of having the state define identity and what is culturally appropriate are apparent, this assurance becomes a culture that is complacent, closed to other perspectives, and unable to collaborate or ask critical questions. This cultural certainty contains vulnerabilities, particularly at a time of significant global interaction, and this is an area that threatens Thailand in a most significant manner and perhaps even holds back the nation from further development—spiritually, educationally, and culturally.

REFERENCES

Association of South-Eastern Asian Nations (ASEAN). (2011). *ASEAN community in figures (ACIF) 2011.* Retrieved March 30, 2013, from http://www.aseansec.org/22073.htm.

Association of South-Eastern Asian Nations (ASEAN). (2012). *Curriculum source book: A teaching resource for primary and secondary schools to foster an outward-looking, stable, peaceful, and prosperous ASEAN community.* Retrieved March 30, 2013, from http://www.seameo.org/images/stories/Publications/Centres_publications/2012ASEAN_Curriculum_Sourcebook/ASEAN_Curriculum_Sourcebook.pdf.

Baker, C., & Phongpaichit, P. (2005). *A history of Thailand.* New York: Cambridge University Press.

Bennett, M. J. (1998). Intercultural communication: A current perspective. In M. J. Bennett (Ed.), *Basic concepts of intercultural communication: Selected readings.* Yarmouth, ME: Intercultural Press.

Buddha Dharma Education Association. (2002). *Buddhism in Thailand.* Bangkok: World Buddhist University. Retrieved March 30, 2013, from http://www.buddhanet.net/pdf_file/bud-thailand.pdf.

Chachavalpongpun, P. (2010). *A plastic nation: The curse of Thainess in Thai-Burmese relations.* Pasir Panjang, Singapore: Institute of Southeast Asian Studies.

Dhammasakiyo, A. (2004, Aug.). *A modern trend of study of Buddhism in Thailand.* Paper presented at the Exploring Theravada Studies: Intellectual Trends and the Future of a Field of Study Conference, National University of Singapore.

Dhammasami, K. (2007). Idealism and Pragmatism: A dilemma in the current monastic education systems of Burma and Thailand. In I. Harris (Ed.), *Buddhism, power and political power* (pp. 10–25). Abingdon, UK: Routledge.

English First. (2011). *English Proficiency Index.* Retrieved March 30, 2013, from www.ef.com/epi.

Jones, M. (2008). Thailand and globalization: The use of reform utilities—Culture, education, engaged spirituality, and social movements. In R. Hopson, K. Yeakey, C. Camp, & F. Boakari (Eds.), *Power, voice, and the public good: Schooling and education in global societies* (pp. 419–453). Oxford: Elsevier.

Kusalasaya, K. (2006). *Buddhism in Thailand: Its past and its present* (rev. ed.). *Wheel* Publication No. 85. Kandy: Buddhist Publication Society.

McDaniel, J. T. (2008). *Gathering leaves and lifting words: Histories of Buddhist monastic education in Laos and Thailand.* Seattle: University of Washington Press.

McDaniel, J. (2011). *The lovelorn ghost and the magical monk: Practicing Buddhism in modern Thailand.* New York: Columbia University Press.

National Office of Buddhism. (2011). *Basic information of Buddhism.* Retrieved March 30, 2013, from http://www.onab.go.th/attachments/912_2554.pdf.

NationMaster.com. (2012). *Education of Thailand—Statistics.* Retrieved March 30, 2013, from http://www.nationmaster.com/country/th-thailand/edu-education.

Office of the Basic Education Commission. (2008). *The basic education core curriculum B.E. 2551 (A.D. 2008)*. Retrieved March 30, 2013, from http://academic.obec.go.th/web/doc/d/147.

Office of the National Education Commission. (2002). *National Education Reform Act B.E. 2542 (1999 AD) and Amendments: Second National Education Act B.E. 2545 (2002 AD)*. Bangkok: Author.

Ohmae, K. (1995). *The end of the nation-state: The rise of regional economies*. New York: Simon and Schuster.

Payulpitack, S. (1991). Buddhadasa's movement: An analysis of its origins, development, and social impact. (Doctoral dissertation). Universitat Bielfeld, Germany. Retrieved March 30, 2013, from http://bieson.ub.uni-bielefeld.de/volltexte/2003/124.

Payutto, P. (1988) *Thit thang karn suksa khong khana song* (Directions of the Education of the *sangha*). Bangkok: Mahachulalongkorn University Press.

Podhisita, C. (1998). Buddhism and Thai world view. In A. Pongsapich (Ed.), *Traditional and changing Thai world view* (pp. 23–53). Bangkok: Chulalongkorn University Press.

Sattayanurak, S. (2002). The establishment of mainstream thought on 'Thai nation' and 'Thainess' by Luang Wichit Wathakan. *Tai Culture—International review on Tai studies. Nation and Culture*, 7(2), 7–34.

St. Clair, R. (2000). Visual metaphor, cultural knowledge, and the new rhetoric. In J. Reyhner, J. Martin, L. Lockard, & W. Gilbert (Eds.), *Learn in beauty: Indigenous education for a new century* (pp. 85–101). Flagstaff: Northern Arizona University.

Tiyavanich, K. (1997). *Forest recollections—Wandering monks in twentieth century Thailand*. Honolulu: University of Hawai'i Press.

UNESCO. (2011). *World data on education VII Ed. 2010/11*. Retrieved March 30, 2013, from http://www.ibe.unesco.org/fileadmin/user_upload/Publications/WDE/2010/pdf-versions/Thailand.pdf.

UNICEF. (2012). *Thailand—Quality of education*. Retrieved March 30, 2013, from www.unicef.org/thailand/education.html.

Visalo, P. (1999). Buddhism for the next century: Toward renewing a moral Thai society. In B. Payutto, *Socially engaged Buddhism for the new millennium*. Bangkok: Sathirakoses-Nagapradipa Foundation & Foundation for Children. Pp. 235–252.

Yoko, H. (2006). Redefining "otherness" from Northern Thailand—Introduction: Notes towards debating multiculturalism in Thailand and beyond. *Southeast Asian Studies*, 44(3), 283–294.

Part III
Spirituality and Education in the Americas

Part III
Introduction

Ann Trousdale

This section brings together voices from North and South America to provide perspectives on spirituality and education which share common themes, influences and concerns but which also reveal quite different tensions and challenges to those interested in supporting children's spiritual lives in public education.

In Chapter 17, Michael Dallaire provides an overview of spirituality in Canada, a nation that has developed from bilingual, bicultural roots in the Judeo-Christian tradition to become a multicultural, multifaith secular democracy. Within Canada's diverse population, Dallaire describes characteristics of what he sees as a common Canadian soul and argues for a pedagogy of engaged spirituality as a way to educate for civic spirituality.

Four chapters in this section come from the United States. In the first of these, "Pluralism and Polarity," I describe the historic, religious, political and cultural context in which the other contributors write. In one of the most religious of the 'developed' nations, public schooling has moved from a dominant Protestant Christian influence to become a secular endeavor in which little attention is given to the spiritual nature of children. While the increasing diversity of the US offers rich opportunity for cross-religious and -spiritual education, various influences, including increasingly polarized religious and political views, stand as impediments.

In Chapter 19, Tobin Hart outlines the ways in which the practice of contemplation may effect a shift in epistemic norms in education, away from a focus on *what* to know to a focus on *how* we know. Promoting no religious views, contemplation awakens the learner to three dimensions central to both education and spirituality: presence, resonance and transcendence. Such a shift, Hart proposes, can have a sustainable influence in returning the many dimensions of our humanity, including the spiritual, to the center of education.

Robert London, in Chapter 20, explores the experiences of students enrolled in his graduate courses in Holistic and Integrative Education at California State University, San Bernardino. London focuses on three aspects of the program's pedagogy: the students' process of transformation and nourishing their inner life, stages that students went through in completing the program, including obstacles, and effects of the process on their teaching. The students' responses reflect a heightened sense of their own spiritual natures as they seek ways to bring a holistic approach to education into nonholistic school settings.

Also working with graduate students in education, Elizabeth Tisdell, in Chapter 21, discusses her research exploring intersections of spirituality and culture in the lives of a diverse group of female educators as well as the effects of the research process on herself as the researcher. In this longitudinal study, Tisdell traces the participants' deepening spirituality and expanded sense of identity as she notes new understandings within herself of the nature of wisdom and the wisdom in nature.

In the final chapter from the Americas, Dora Incontri describes the complex scenario affecting spirituality and education in Brazil. She outlines the efforts of educators promoting secular and interreligious educational programs in this heavily Roman Catholic nation, mentioning a specifically Brazilian project, Spiritist Pedagogy, as well.

17 Spirituality in Canadian Education

Michael Dallaire

There is a gentle wind summoning Canadian educators to deepen their practice of spiritual education. It is a wind sourced in the history of our country and aided by contemporary developments in educational theory. It is a wind that flows today over our corner of the global village. Carried within this wind lies a hope for educational renewal that meets the challenges of our age. To appreciate the significance of this wind we need to understand the socio-political-historical context for Canadian spiritual education.

THE CANADIAN CONTEXT

For several thousand years indigenous peoples inhabited the large landmass of Canada. However, our indigenous peoples were almost totally eradicated when, during the 15th century, Europeans, particularly the French and English, fought for control of the resources and land found in this new place. The adversarial relationship between the French and English, along with their attempt to eradicate aboriginal peoples, became imbedded within the soul of our nation. Canada was formally established as a colonial nation in 1867 by virtue of the British North America Act passed in the British House of Commons. Over a hundred years later Canada achieved full nationhood with the repatriation of its constitution in 1982. Now part of the British Commonwealth of Nations, rather than the former British Empire, she belongs to the bioregion of North America populating the northern portion of the continent. Between then and now the population has grown from a few hundred thousand people of European ancestry and First Nations people to approximately 35 million people from all over the globe.

Culturally and linguistically Canada has historically been a bilingual nation of French and English, a reality that found expression in our Constitution and subsequent legislation. From the beginning the predominant religious horizon of meaning for Canada was Judeo-Christian. Due to colonization practices the more communal, earth-centered spiritualities of indigenous peoples were rejected as paganism although these were never completely eradicated. Today, due to immigration, Canada is growing beyond its original foundational identity of a bicultural (French/English) Judeo-Christian nation into a more multicultural, multifaith nation under the umbrella of secular democracy.

The primacy of God was always presumed as a given and is embedded within our Constitution. A case could be made that this constitutional presumption has protected religious and spiritual voices as Canada has slowly moved towards a clearly secular democracy. Our contemporary secular and multicultural society found support in the Canadian Charter of Rights and Freedoms (Department of Justice, Canada, 1982), which provided protection for both individual and religious rights. The Canadian Constitution today continues to maintain an appeal to God but recognizes that Canada is a secular and pluralist democracy that encompasses religious diversity.

Politically, Canada has a federal system of government including a central federal government, ten provincial governments and three territorial governments. For our purposes here we note that education is the responsibility of the provinces and territories. There is no federal government responsibility for education. This constitutional exclusion of the federal level from education has undermined Canada's ability to educate for a cohesive civic identity, let alone a civic spirituality, that would serve Canadians as members of the new global village brought about by technology and migration.

However, where our political structures have been handicapped in terms of fostering an education for a common civic identity economics has succeeded. That is, in the era of globalization it is the economy that has had the largest impact upon shaping educational policy at the provincial levels. The trend towards standardized testing, which has swept across our country in response to the business sector call to be competitive, has resulted in a substantial shift in the raison d'être of education from citizen preparation to job preparation (Jacobs, 2005). Of course, education retains some faint residuals of the classical approach to education as formation in citizenship, but predominantly education today has become preparation for employment. Due to the lack of federal political oversight of education, we have seen the rise of a monolithic approach to education driven by economics and the inability of the state to resist the reduction of education to job preparation in the face of the post–Cold War rise of capitalism.

Canada is the second largest country in the world in terms of landmass. Within this huge landmass lie various regions each with their own climates and geographical challenges. Canadians living in the Atlantic region are influenced by their close proximity to the American northeast states, the maritime climate and European countries, while Asia and our American neighbors to the south influence those residing in the Pacific province of British Columbia. While all of Canada is impacted by winter, northern Canadians are especially shaped by the cold of arctic winters, a sparse population and a closeness to the land. Central Canada is marked by the rolling hills of the Canadian Shield and the Great Lakes and is populated predominantly by Canadians of European ancestry. Canadians living in the west, with its prairies and mountains, rely upon agriculture and natural resources while embracing the variables of cold winters and hot summers.

Contained within each region is a struggle between urban and rural sensibilities. While it is true that the majority of Canadians live within cities, many reside in rural settings. There are differing concerns depending upon whether you live in a rural context or in an urban one. Life in a coastal fishing village, on a prairie ranch, an arctic hamlet or one of many small towns that dot the country is very different from the cosmopolitanism that characterizes Vancouver, Calgary, Winnipeg, Toronto, Montreal, Quebec City or Halifax. These differences have not only to do with economics and the often large discrepancies in terms of public expenditures to support infrastructure and social services, education and health care, but also with the vastly different ways of adapting to change, particularly when it comes to change in social values. Underlying all these struggles there has historically been in Canada a constant political tension between social democratic and free enterprise capitalist political philosophies.

Such is the context within which Canadian teachers teach. If educators, more than being trainers of workers for the state, are co-responsible with parents for the formation of citizens capable of embracing the challenges of our time, then attention must be paid to the civic identity of students. An essential ingredient in such identity making is spirituality. There is today a nascent movement within Canadian education that recognizes spirituality is an essential ingredient in this formation. This movement recognizes that today's Canadian educators need to promote a civic spirituality that would respect Canada's multicultural, multifaith and secular horizons of meaning.

CIVIC SPIRITUALITY AS UNIFYING NARRATIVE

Seeking to give voice to this civic spirituality requires a unifying narrative to support identity formation. However, Canadians abide in a country where postmodernism and its suspicion of grand narratives permeates our social discourse and our educational practice. Seen positively in Canada, this trend has enabled the revival of aboriginal spirituality, our openness to diversity and our legitimization of individualism. However, the postmodern mistrust of grand narratives, particularly religious ones, has undermined the appeal of any common unifying story, which is necessary for a healthy civic life.

Postmodernism, however, has a reconstructive trend as well. In this trend hermeneutics and critical theory are integrated to provide for pedagogies of hope beyond suspicion and doubt. The hermeneutical tools used incorporate the root metaphors of the grand narratives, but with substantive changes and modifications arising from critical discourses. Some Canadian spiritual educators align themselves with this reconstructive postmodernism. I find myself in sympathy with this trend and uphold that the narrative of a national soul can provide a unifying myth, one that allows diversity to flourish within a common horizon of meaning.

From the beginning Canadians recognized that education had as one of its goals an appreciation for the soul. Indeed, the philosophy of education that permeated the early years of Canadian education was one that was essentially humanistic and which saw education as preparing citizens to serve the common good. Part of this education involved the classical Platonic approach of turning the soul of the student to the world. Education was seen as crucial to civic life and a sense of duty to the polis was an integral part of education (Emberly & Waller, 1994, pp. 148–157). Obviously, there was not necessarily a clear sense of a Canadian national soul during the founding of our nation but there was an intuitive understanding that education by its nature was spiritual, although not necessarily religiously confessional, in its process and goals. The openness to the spiritual dimension of the student as a constitutive dimension of Canadian education was considered essential during the earlier days of Canadian history, then was overlooked during the second half of the 20th century, but is now beginning to re-emerge in our time.

CANADIAN SOUL

While there may not have been a clear articulation of a Canadian soul at the beginning of our national project there has emerged over time a pattern of deeply held values that we as Canadians keep and which give expression to our soul. Our Canadian soul is rooted in our indigenous peoples, in our history as a nation and in our contemporary experience. It finds expression in our artists, writers, poets and songwriters as well as our laws and our symbols. Our Canadian soul is found within our diverse citizenry, across our regional challenges and throughout our national discourse. It is found within our enduring national values, values that have given shape to our national identity.

A deeply held value of the Canadian soul is our appreciation of the natural world. Our connection to nature is rooted in the histories of our indigenous peoples who, despite their threatened extinction with the arrival of the Europeans, provided a foundation to our Canadian identity. Our indigenous peoples live within and from a sense of communion with nature. Many of the settlers and pioneers who came to this land learned over time to share this appreciation for nature. An attitude of working in communion with nature rather than against nature became an essential part our Canadian soul.

On top of our respect for the natural world is the fact of our being a nation within a northern climate. No matter where you live across this vast land, the reality of winter and snow is a constant reminder that we are a people of the northern hemisphere. Our soul is shaped by this northern exposure. In addition to our northern climate, the vastness of our land shapes us. Unlike some European countries that you can drive an auto- mobile across in a matter of hours, it takes a full week to drive across this country. The vast and often beautiful textures of our landscape reach deep within the Canadian soul (Leddy, 1987).

Another core Canadian value is inclusion. Canadians are generally hos- pitable people and are open to the new, whether it is in the field of ideas or in our relationships. We generally welcome strangers, turning them into honored guests. Is it not our openness that leads us to entertain new ideas, sifting them through our collective lens and incorporating them into our social matrix, making Canada a truly progressive country? Indeed, our inclusiveness of the *other*, whether the *other* is a newcomer or a new idea, is part of our collective soul.

When we look at our history, we can see our capacity for openness in our immigrant roots and in our preference for cultural and religious inte- gration rather than assimilation. Regrettably our preference for integra- tion was not extended to our First Nations who for generations endured the attempt to assimilate them and to wipe out their distinct cultures. The legacy of our Residential Schools, where many experienced years of abuse and were subjected to forced assimilation, has come back to haunt us as a nation and will require many years of deliberate attention in order to heal and to reconcile.

Assimilation is very different from integration. When a people are assim- ilated, their identity is subsumed within the predominant culture and is lost. Apart from our treatment of First Nations, our Canadian practice has been to favor integration rather than assimilation. With integration, a culture can belong to a larger collective culture without losing its particu- lar cultural identity. Integration means to "come into equal membership of society, without regard for race or religion" (*The Concise Oxford*, 1976). Distinct cultures and races are able to achieve equal membership in the larger Canadian society. This equal membership is achieved by focusing on what different cultures hold in common, eliminating any barriers to equal- ity between cultures, and valuing differences in such a way that the unify- ing bond is enriched rather than diminished. The result is one of a cultural tapestry rather than a melting pot. The Canadian soul's propensity towards inclusion has given rise to a nation where integration and multiculturalism are considered key features of Canadian identity.

Another notable value of the Canadian soul is our pursuit of a just soci- ety. Our appreciation of justice is a core value that has served us well during our experience with nation building. The Canadian ideal of justice is deeply rooted in the religious communitarian philosophies that have influenced the formation of Canada from the beginning. The core insight of communitarian philosophy is that a human being becomes a person *vis-à-vis* the community. Thus community provides the context for the flourishing of the person. There are limits to this communitarian philosophy, one of which is the tendency to suppress creativity in individuals. Nonetheless, the Canadian notion of justice finds one of its roots within the religious, communitarian notion of justice. The communitarian notion of justice helped to give birth to our lauded social programs, from public pensions to universal health care and social welfare. Deep within our communitarian philosophy of justice is a sense of duty to care for others and it is this motivation to care for others that animates the movements for social justice.

Still, as Canada moved into the secular age, the communitarian understanding of justice has been increasingly challenged within Canada by the libertarian view of justice based on the principle of contract and individual rights. In this view, justice is achieved by balancing the rights of rational beings who agree to exchange goods and services for mutual benefit. There is a fine balance in society then to promote and maintain this mutuality of benefit (Rawls, 1971). This principle of justice is invoked whenever there is a violation of this mutuality and equality, whenever someone is harmed.

There have at times been significant tensions between the communitarian and libertarian interpretations of justice, for example during our recent political struggle over the state's recognition of same-sex marriages. However, thus far our Canadian practice has been to seek to balance these two different approaches so that the core value of justice is upheld for Canadian society.

Compassion is another strong Canadian value. The notion of being compassionate towards one's neighbors is deeply connected to our sense of attachment to land and our climate. From neighbors helping neighbors in order to survive till the next harvest, to the sharing of food during the Great Depression, to the food banks today and to the multitude of community fundraising initiatives that exist across the land, we see the efforts of ordinary citizens to help out their neighbors in need. Our compassion, when wedded to the current of justice, led to the creation of our social safety net. It is rooted in our Judeo-Christian heritage in which the care of others was sustained through various church organizations and programs. These continue today within the growing diversity of religious organizations that exist in our land.

Our compassionate impulse was also carried forth into our foreign policies, which have been strongly marked by a humanitarian thrust. Our involvement in NATO grew out of our sense of sharing in the international responsibility for peace and the rebuilding of Europe during and after the Second World War. Similarly, a former prime minister, Lester B. Pearson, won the Nobel Peace Prize for his contribution to the resolution of the Suez Canal Crisis and his idea for the creation of a United Nations peacekeeping force. Finally, we see further evidence of our compassion in the proliferation of Canadian nongovernment organizations serving humanitarian goals worldwide, in the growth of our volunteer sector and in the number of nonprofit organizations addressing multiple communities' needs.

Compassion then is a salient value of the Canadian soul, one rooted in our history and in our present realities. Moreover, partly due to the growing influence of Buddhism in Canada (Harding, Victor & Alexander, 2010) and aboriginal spirituality, we see today our compassion being extended to include all sentient beings and the natural world. Compassion, rooted in our hearts' ability to walk with the other in their time of need, is part of the Canadian soul.

Finally, Canadians value the place of compromise in order to sustain the common good. Perhaps due to the vastness of our land and our living in a challenging climate, we recognize that in order to survive we need to seek the middle path whenever possible. This is a testimony to the health of our democracy, for democracy is the practice of the middle way in politics. Our ability to compromise sustains our practice of democracy, which, as the exercise of public reasoning (Sen, 2009), provides the political framework for the progressive pursuit of justice and the common good.

This ability to compromise is closely aligned with one of the main characteristics of spiritual growth, the ability to live with ambiguity. The spiritual path is never a straight path of clear answers, but rather a meandering path through the various exigencies that face us as we journey. To be able to live with ambiguity then points to a largesse in our soul and to a capacity to hold the seemingly incommensurable factors of life together for the common good. There is plenty of evidence throughout our history that we as a people are able to live with ambiguity and that we express this through our willingness to compromise when necessary to uphold the common good within a secular society like Canada.

In sum then, Canadians appreciate that living attuned to the natural world, being inclusive, valuing justice, being compassionate and accepting compromise are enduring values of our national soul. These values are present in greater and lesser degrees throughout different points of our history and across the various regions of our vast land. Taken together, they point to the ways in which the soul of our country is alive and how our soul can be discerned. They operate in the background of the public discourse about our country and through the parts of our identity that we continue to express through our national project.

CANADIAN EDUCATIONAL PRACTICE

Our national soul provides the energy for our education systems to thrive. Within these systems there are many ways in which educators today are seeking to promote a spirituality that affirms this national soul. Such ways can be gathered under a category called education for civic spirituality. There are a number of examples of how Canadian educators today are seeking to educate for such a civic spirituality. Let us now turn to a few of these initiatives.

Like many Western countries Canada has a network of faith-based schools. These exist with varying degrees of public support, from full public financial support for Catholic schools in the provinces of Ontario and Alberta to partial financial support for all faith-based schools in some provinces like British Columbia. However, faith-based schools in Canada are a continually changing reality (Sweet, 1997) subject to demographics, politics and economics. In fact during the last few decades we have witnessed the ending of publicly mandated funding for faith-based schools systems in the provinces of Quebec, Manitoba and Newfoundland/Labrador where their provincial governments revoked the constitutional requirement to fund denominational schools. Despite the economic and political pressures which faith-based schools often experience, they demonstrate a particular resilience and continue to thrive, particularly in regions where new immigrants gravitate. The existence of provincial associations of independent schools, many of which are faith based, provides support and structures for such schools. These faith-based schools are vital locations for teachers to turn the souls of students to the requirements of citizenship and civil engagement.

In the province of Quebec where the previously confessional school systems have recently been reconfigured along linguistic lines, French and English, we are witnessing a flagship initiative in the area of spiritual education with the establishment of an institutional animator of spiritual care and community service whose role is "to help students explore the world of the inner life and community involvement" (Ministry of Education, Quebec, n.d.). This outgrowth of the previous role of faith animator or chaplain in faith-based schools is now a nondenominational effort. The focus is on spirituality as an inner journey and service to others as an outer journey. This new role has had mixed support from the religious authorities of that province, but has been strongly supported by the political and educational establishment which seems intent upon promoting a sense of spirituality within a very secular society.

On the West Coast of the country, we see in the Vancouver public school board, the largest in the province of British Columbia, a program to promote mindfulness. Buddhist-inspired mindfulness practices are being incorporated within the K–8 curriculum and schooling under a program called Mindup (The Hawn Foundation, n.d.). A new initiative that requires time to determine its efficacy, it is a good example of how schools within the secular public education system in Canada are seeking ways to promote spirituality.

In addition to faith-based schools and public school spiritual initiatives we have numerous alternative schools like Montessori and Waldorf, which incorporate spirituality as part of their practice. Moreover, there are many First Nations schools across our nation that use aboriginal spiritualities as a way of educating students about the life of the community. These schools often use experiential learning activities in nature, storytelling, hunting and rituals to teach aboriginal spiritualities to First Nations' youth.

Also noteworthy is the fact that across this land, in various schools, colleges and universities, there exist quiet rooms, chapels, meditation rooms and outdoor gardens where teachers and students are permitted, and encouraged, to practice yoga, meditation, chanting and religious rites. For examples there is an Interfaith Chapel on the grounds of the University of Victoria and there are seven interfaith quiet spaces or chapels integrated within the University of Toronto. At the secondary level most Catholic high schools in Ontario have a chapel or dedicated sacred space of some sort. These spaces are sometimes contested places, particularly when the questions of capital and maintenance costs arise. Sometimes funding for such space has to be provided from sources external to the educational institution when curricular or philosophical arguments in support of spiritual education fail to convince decision-makers as to the importance of including such spaces within the learning establishment.

Finally, I myself for years have used the traditional method of contemplation and action to introduce high school students to the practice of integrating spirituality and social justice. The method of engaged spirituality (a spiral hermeneutic of presence, discernment, action and reflection) is one that is easy to incorporate across subject specialties and within a school context. It particularly lends itself to what I call 'engaged spiritual retreats'. These are structured learning experiences during which students are exposed to concrete social issues and given opportunities to serve and learn. These retreats include input sessions from learned people and times for meditation, solitude and prayer. This method of engaged spirituality is one that finds support in many world religions (Dallaire, 2011).

THE POLITICS OF CANADIAN EDUCATION

While it is possible to recognize that Canadians from the beginning have understood that education for a soulful life is integral to Canadian citizenship and to naming the core values of the Canadian soul, it has to be acknowledged, even while recognizing the growing use of spiritual pedagogies, that we do not have a clear national approach to educating for civic spirituality. Beyond the hesitation from some religions within Canada regarding spirituality due to the fear of undermining dogma and the hesitations of some secularists to including spirituality within education due to a fear of religious indoctrination, there are three major impediments to a national approach to educating for spirituality. The first, and possibly the most important, is a weak public awareness of a civic spirituality grounded upon the notion of a national soul. The second is the lack of federal government oversight of education itself, and the third is the lack of professional preparation of teachers for spirituality.

While I have sketched briefly the values of the Canadian soul it needs to be acknowledged that the awareness of a civic soul is fragile. It is not that our national soul is weak or fragile, but the awareness of it is. This is due to the fact that the voices of this national soul are too often muted and silenced within the secular mainstream and the fact that many Canadians hesitate to move beyond a privatized understanding of the spiritual life towards the societal dimensions of spirituality. Moreover, while there is a national soul, one that needs to be given room within our society and therefore within our educational practice, there is a fear amongst many teachers that attempts to promote any spirituality will be met with censure by the public or by education managers. Such fear stifles the voicing of a civic spirituality and works against the promotion of our national soul. As a result, many people, parents, teachers and students withdraw into the personal realm and give up seeking the spiritual in the outer realm of civil society. This is unfortunate especially given the fact that our country is shifting towards a more multifaith and diverse population. The inability to promote a unifying national identity, part of which includes a civic spiritual identity, risks undermining the long-term efficacy of multiculturalism and religious diversity. A stronger recognition of our national soul will be required if spiritual education is to grow in Canada.

Another impediment to a national approach to spiritual education lies in the fact that education from the beginning of Canada has been the responsibility of the provinces rather than the central, federal government. Without an overarching national policy it was simply never possible to promote a national educational strategy for spiritual education. Each province moved in its own way to address the issues of religious education and civic education, but none was obligated or challenged to promote a national approach that supplemented their own provincial concerns. Indeed, we have seen in recent decades a fundamental shift in provincial education policies away from citizen preparation to one of job skill training. While the federal government has overall responsibility for immigration and for the economy, it has little direct hand in education, which is nonetheless impacted upon by changes in immigration and the economy. The engines driving educational policy today are more economic than religious or spiritual. But if the human person is a spiritual as well as physical, emotional, intellectual, communal and economic being, then it is imperative that schools embrace education for spirituality. However, without a coordinating federal body to oversee the development of spiritual education and the drafting of policies and curriculum aids that serve the Canadian soul, then the nascent movement for including spirituality within education runs the risk of never fully flourishing. This is a stumbling block that must be addressed if education for spirituality is to grow across Canada.

Finally, turning to the levels of professional training there are a few lone individuals who are providing some direction in teachers' spiritual formation. Examples include Professor Jack Miller at the University of Toronto, Professor Heesoon Bai at Simon Fraser University and Professor Daniel Vokey at the University of British Columbia, working in the Faculty of Education at their respective institutions, either by offering courses on spirituality or including spiritual practices within their curriculum. However, overall in Canada there is a lack of teacher preparation in spirituality and this threatens the nascent movement for spiritual education in Canada. There is a need to train teachers to be capable of teaching spirituality in nonsectarian and interdisciplinary ways. There is a need to channel resources to the writing of textbooks, to promote spiritual pedagogies and to create teaching aids to assist in the integration of spirituality as a common thread throughout the full range of teacher training. There is a need to legitimize the creation of spiritual spaces on campuses where student teachers can practice meditation, mindfulness, reflection and prayer. There is a need for more valuing of engaged learning experiences, service learning, exchange programs and volunteerism as constitutive of a healthy civic spiritual life. Finally, there is a need to create retreat experiences that provide the context for the deepening of the appreciation of the soul of Canada and how this can be recognized across our land.

CONCLUSION

Despite a weak appreciation of our national soul and the professional and political obstacles to spiritual education in Canada there remains much hope for those educators who seek to promote a civic spirituality that serves the soul of Canada. The histories of faith-based schools, the emergence of a vibrant multifaith citizenry within a secular state and the existence of a myriad of school-based programs and strategies designed to turn the soul of the student to the soul of the world all point to a renaissance of the spiritual within the life of Canadians. There are many Canadian thinkers, writers, artists and community leaders who are advocating a spiritual way of life today. Canadian educators have much to celebrate and much to offer as the global village now gathers in the classrooms of our nation. There is, in all this, then a new wind that gently flows across our nation today. Where will it lead? Only the spirit knows. We know, though, that we are being summoned further and deeper.

REFERENCES

The concise Oxford dictionary of current English. (1976). Oxford: Oxford University Press.

Dallaire, M. (2011). *Teaching with the wind: Spirituality in Canadian education.* Lanham, MD: University Press of America.

Department of Justice, Canada. (1982). *Canadian charter of rights and freedoms. Part 1 of the Constitution Act, 1982.* Retrieved March 30, 2013, from http://laws-lois.justice.gc.ca/eng/charter.

Emberly, P. C, & Waller, R. N. (1994). *Bankrupt education: The decline of liberal education in Canada.* Toronto: University of Toronto Press.

Harding, J. S., Victor S. H., & Alexander S. (Eds.). (2010). *Wild geese: Buddhism in Canada.* Montreal: McGill-Queen's University Press.

The Hawn Foundation. (n.d.). *MindUP.* Retrieved March 30, 2013, from http://www.thehawnfoundation.org/mindup.

Jacobs, J. (2005). *Dark age ahead.* Toronto: Vintage Canada.

Leddy, M. J. (1987). Theology in the Canadian context. In M. J. Leddy & M. A. Hinsdale (Eds.), *Faith that transforms: Essays in honor of Gregory Baum* (pp.127–134). New York: Paulist Press.

Ministry of Education, Quebec. (n.d.) *Developing the inner life and changing the world: The spiritual care and guidance and community involvement service.* Ministerial framework. Retrieved March 30, 2013, from http://www.mels.gouv.qc.ca/dgfj/csc/asec/pdf/26–0001-A.pdf.

Rawls, J. (1971). *A theory of justice.* Cambridge, MA: Harvard University Press.

Sen, A. (2009). *The idea of justice.* Cambridge, MA: The Belknap Press of Harvard University Press.

Sweet, L. (1997). *God in the classroom: The controversial issue of religion in Canada's schools.* Toronto: McClelland and Stewart, Inc.

18 Pluralism and Polarity
Spirituality and Education in the United States

Ann Trousdale

Spiritual education in the United States today traces its roots through a complex interplay of historic, religious, political and cultural influences. An examination of those influences can help explain the fact that, while the United States is one of the most religious of 'developed' nations (Putnam & Campbell, 2010), its public school system is one of the most secular, despite notable efforts contrariwise. The beginnings of the religious-secular controversy began with the emergence of the nation from its colonial beginnings.

A NEW NATION FORGED FROM BRITISH COLONIES

The 13 British colonies in the New World won their independence from England in 1783, and delegates from the various colonies immediately set about writing a constitution that was to govern the new nation. Ratified in 1788, the United States Constitution was a radical document for its time. The Bill of Rights, comprising ten amendments to the Constitution clarifying the principles set forth in that document, was adopted three years later. The first issue addressed in the Bill of Rights was the relation between state and religion. The First Amendment states, "Congress shall make no law regarding an establishment of religion or prohibiting the free exercise thereof; or abridging the freedom of speech, or of the press; or the right of the people peaceably to assemble, and to petition the Government for a redress of grievances."

Guarantee of such freedoms on a national scale was uncharted territory at the time; indeed, interpretation of the First Amendment remains controversial to this day. And while spirituality is not to be conflated with religion, the interplay of law and religion in the U.S. has had a pronounced effect on spiritual education in this country.

Revolutionary though the First Amendment was, it is perhaps not so remarkable if one considers several factors. The generation who framed it were, for the most part, either immigrants from England or descendants of English subjects who had suffered vicissitudes and violence deriving from imposed state religion for generations. The Roman Catholic Church had been the established church in England and on the European continent from the Dark Ages until well into the 16th century, when the authority of the Church was challenged on three geographical fronts. In 1517 Martin Luther's posting of his 95 theses protesting abuses in the Roman Catholic Church led to the Protestant Reformation in Germany, which subsequently extended to other nations. In 1534 John Calvin, a French Catholic lay person, left the Roman Catholic Church and emigrated to Switzerland where he set up a model of a church-state that became the foundation of the Presbyterian Church, which soon spread to Scotland. Ties with the Roman Catholic Church were severed in England in 1534 when Henry VIII established the Anglican Church as the state church of England with himself as its head.

At the time in England a group of devout Christians had begun a movement to purify both church and state according to biblical teachings. Their hopes were not realized during Henry's reign, and were further dashed when the Catholic Mary Tudor ascended to the throne. "Bloody Mary" began a massive persecution of Protestants, many of whom were martyred while others fled to Protestant strongholds on the European continent.

The ascension of Henry VIII's daughter Elizabeth I brought many of the Protestants back to England. Exposure to Lutheranism and Calvinism had intensified their hopes of purifying the English church and state along biblical lines, but Elizabeth was more interested in returning order and political stability to England than in religious extremism. By the late 16th century, two parties had developed within the Anglican Church, those who favored a rationalistic approach to the role of church and state and those who agitated for the purification of church and state according to the teachings of the Bible. It was during this time that the first group coined the derisive term 'Puritan' for the second group.

James I's ascension to the throne in 1603 increased the Puritans' discomfort and discontent. James supported high church forms of elaborate worship in the Church of England, requiring all citizens not only financially to support the lavish ceremonies but to attend them regularly. A group of Puritans separated themselves from the English Church and emigrated to Leyden, Holland; others remained in England but suffered persecution if they absented themselves from Anglican worship or violated laws forbidding unauthorized religious meetings.

During James I's reign, British interest in colonization in the New World was revived, an early attempt during Elizabeth's reign having failed. Exploration of the New World continued to bring back reports of the natural richness of the land, promoting an interest in financial gain. In 1606 James I issued a charter providing for British colonization of America, in Virginia and Massachusetts. These two locales were to prove significantly different in spiritual tenor.

The first group of settlers in Virginia landed on the banks of the James River in 1607 to found the Jamestown colony. While the settlement was officially under the authority of the Bishop of London, religious practice was not its primary purpose. Two groups of settlers in Massachusetts—the Pilgrims and the Puritans—emigrated for explicitly religious reasons. Arriving in 1620 and 1630, respectively, they sought to live together in accordance with their religious convictions, granting Scripture final authority on all aspects of life: political, civil, personal, religious.

A challenge to the identity of church and state in the Puritans' Massachusetts Bay Colony arose a year after its founding, with the arrival of Roger Williams, who questioned the close tie between state and religion as well as British claims on the Native people's land. In 1635 Williams was banished from the Massachusetts Bay Colony and settled in what is now Rhode Island.

Both Massachusetts colonies set up schools to teach children, both boys and girls, to read, again for religious reasons: it was only through reading the Bible that one could escape the wiles of the Devil and understand the way one was to live in order to be saved. Early reading material featured biblical texts and references.

While the Massachusetts colonies strove to maintain the purity of their theocracies, the Mid-Atlantic and Southern colonies began to attract people representing noteworthy religious diversity. In 1624, Dutch colonists arrived in what is now New York, bringing the Dutch Reformed tradition to the colonies and welcoming Belgian and French Huguenots as well. Maryland was established as a colony in 1632, as a speculation in real estate and as a refuge for Roman Catholics who were victims of religious persecution in England. In 1658, the first Jewish synagogue in the colonies was established in Rhode Island, which also attracted Quakers who had come to Massachusetts only to be persecuted there for their beliefs. In 1681, William Penn was granted a charter for a colony to be called Pennsylvania, founded specifically on Quaker beliefs, which differed from those of the Massachusetts settlers in several ways. Quaker beliefs included emphasis on the individual's direct relationship with God; a conviction that the individual's conscience, not the Bible, was the ultimate authority on morals; equal rights for women; and just and respectful treatment of the Native peoples. Further religious diversity was introduced by Presbyterians arriving from Scotland and Ulster, Ireland, and by German immigrants including Lutherans, German Reformed and Mennonites.

By the early18th century, there was remarkable national and religious diversity in the British colonies in America. By the time of the drafting of the Constitution, there was sufficient religious diversity in itself to rule out the likelihood of the establishing of a state religion. The memory of the power exercised by established churches in Europe and England to coerce orthodoxy of belief and practice was not forgotten, including, for the British, the persecution of Protestants under Roman Catholic Queen Mary, the persecution of Roman Catholics under Church of England rulers and the persecution of the Puritans under James I and his successor Charles I.

Yet religious feeling—or an assumption of a Divine presence—clearly persisted. The Declaration of Independence, drafted in 1776, refers to "nature's God" and the belief that all people are "endowed by their Creator with certain inalienable rights," and a final appeal to the "Supreme Judge of the World for the rectitude of our intentions." When the U.S. Constitution was ratified in 1788 there was no mention of religion other than that "no Religious test shall ever be required as a qualification to any Office or public Trust under the United States." It was three years later that the First Amendment attempted to make clear the separation of state and religion in the new nation: "Congress shall make no law regarding an establishment of religion or prohibiting the free exercise thereof. . . . " In the late 20th and early 21st centuries the interpretation of these words was to prove hotly controversial.

THE 19TH CENTURY

We shall paint the vast changes in the new nation that occurred during the 19th century with very broad brush strokes, focusing on those developments that were to have an ultimate effect on spiritual education in the United States. A strand running through these developments was increasing ethnic, racial, cultural and religious diversity.

Westward Expansion

The 19th century opened with the doubling of the size of the new nation. The Louisiana Purchase in 1803 incorporated the vast lands stretching from the Mississippi River to the Rocky Mountains, formerly explored and claimed by Spain and France. In these territories mission churches and early schools had been established by Roman Catholic religious orders.

The new westward expansion involved appropriation of the Natives peoples' land through war, genocide, forced migration and relocation of Native Americans to 'reservations,' leaving the frontier open for white settlers. The movement west also included the establishing of residential schools for Native American children. In many cases taken forcibly from their homes and families, the children were forbidden to speak their native languages or to observe their native customs and spiritual practices; they were also forced to convert to Christianity.

Eventually the westward expansion of U.S. boundaries led to the coastline of the Pacific Ocean. Into these lands Latino and Asian immigrants were soon to flow.

Slavery and Its Aftermath

Perhaps the central irony of the American Revolution was that it was founded on the belief that "all men are created equal," yet many signers of the Declaration of Independence and supporters of the Constitution were people who held other people in slavery.

From colonial times, African men, women and children had been brought to America to be sold as slaves. Slave-holding was particularly economically advantageous in the agrarian Southern states. Protestant Christianity was preached to the slaves, but it represented a highly selective version, primarily those passages that admonished slaves to be obedient to their masters as to God (Eph. 6:5, Col. 3:22). Despite these efforts, a powerful Christian tradition valuing freedom and self-respect grew among the enslaved people (Genovese, 1976; Lester, 1968; Osofsky, 1969; Trousdale, 1990). In the mid-19th century the issue of slavery came to a crisis. The American Civil War, fought from 1861 to 1865, freed the slaves but issued in a 'Jim Crow' period characterized by legalized social, political, educational and economic inequality for African-American citizens.

Dominance of Protestant Christianity

Despite the increasingly multicultural nature of the population, Protestant Christianity remained the dominant social, cultural, political and religious force. Common practice in public schools was the reading of a portion of the Bible at the beginning of the school day, followed by the Lord's Prayer and the Pledge of Allegiance. Christian holidays such as Thanksgiving, Christmas and Easter were celebrated, often marked with school plays or pageants in which all students were expected to participate. The Bible that was used was the King James Version, a translation not acceptable to the Roman Catholic Church. Protests over the use of the Protestant Bible in public schools led to street rioting in Philadelphia in 1844. A subsequent appeal by Roman Catholics to the New York Board of Education to request a change in the practice was rebuffed. Soon afterward the Roman Catholic Church began a movement to organize and fund its own schools. Meanwhile, the Protestant King James version of the Bible continued to be read and recited in public schools.

THE 20TH CENTURY

The 20th century began with what seemed gradual changes in American society, including a slight flagging of interest in religious feeling and expression. In 1936, John Dewey's *Art as Experience,* a landmark in philosophical pragmatism, was published. Not religious in intent or perspective, Dewey encouraged individuals to develop their philosophy from their experience of the world as an immediate and nondualistic event. Dewey's sense of the meaningful wholeness in experience has remained influential in educational and philosophical circles, and is certainly consonant with how many educationalists envision spirituality today, but it was not able to stem a torrent of events that flowed in very different directions in the United States in the following decades.

In the second half of the century the nation was to experience events that Putnam and Campbell characterize as a series of "seismic shocks and after-shocks" in social, political, cultural, religious and educational life (2010, p. 80). An ultimate effect was increasing plurality and polarity in American society. First was a resurgence of religious feeling and expression following the anxieties of World War II. Postwar affluence, with returning veterans and their wives starting families and the looming Cold War with Russia and its nuclear threat, combined to produce a renewed appreciation for traditional values including patriotism and religion (Putnam & Campbell, 2010). In 1952, 75% of Americans said that religion was "very important" in their lives; 81% said that religion was "relevant to today's world" (Gallup & Lindsay, 1999, pp. 7, 19). The importance of religion prevailed across denominational, racial and cultural boundaries; later events were to affect the philosophical and political nature of these religious feelings.

A second factor in the rise of religious and nationalistic sentiment was the Soviet Union's emergence as a global power following World War II. As the Soviet Union invaded and annexed nation after nation in Europe and Asia and set its avowed sights on the West, many Americans joined together under the banner of fighting 'godless Communism,' claiming a national identity as a religious people. In 1954 Congress voted to insert the words 'under God' into the Pledge of Allegiance. Two years later, as war grew colder, Congress declared the national motto to be "In God We Trust"; the words were to be printed on national currency. During this period, as Sydney Ahlstrom put it, "Religion and Americanism were brought together to an unusual degree" (cited in Putnam & Campbell, 2010, p. 88).

As much as the Cold War of the 1950s united people in a mission to combat a common enemy, it also was precursor to the beginnings of polarity along political lines. On the one hand, anti-Communist fervor gained an obsessive intensity, paving the way for U.S. Senator Joseph McCarthy of Wisconsin to work through the Congressional House Un-American Activities Committee to conduct a series of witch hunts for individuals suspected of having Communist ties or leanings. People accused of being Communists were blacklisted from the workforce; reputations were ruined and livelihoods lost as friends and associates turned against one another in fear for their own well-being. A fissure developed between those having the self-proclaimed 'American' religious, traditional, conservative beliefs and more philosophically liberal individuals whom the first party branded as 'Communist' and 'atheistic.'

While many Americans were clutching at traditional values and a solid white Protestant nationalistic identity, the continuing influx of immigrants from many parts of the world was producing an increasingly pluralistic society. As sociologists of religion have pointed out, inevitably the presence of multiple views of the world threaten the assumed dominant religious perspective of a country, undermining its authority, depriving it of its tak-en-for-granted status, leading to the secularizing of a society (McGuire, 2002). In many cases a decline in religious belief is an accompanying effect. In the United States, while there were indeed movements to agnosticism or atheism, for the majority of the population, religious belief persisted but gradually began to play a different, more private role both in individual lives and in society (Putnam & Campbell, 2010). More seismic shocks and aftershocks were to follow.

Since the American Civil War in the mid-19th century, public schooling in the United States had largely been segregated, with white students going to 'white' schools and black children going to 'black' schools. In 1954 the Supreme Court ruled that all public schools must admit black students. Violent resistance followed in many parts of the country, but the law of the land ultimately prevailed. Formerly all-white public school systems became more open in admission policies, but in many parts of the country, and par-ticularly in the Deep South, white parents began to send their children to parochial schools or to found private 'segregation academies,' abandoning their support of public school systems. Thus, while plurality was the goal in United States schooling, economic and racial polarization was a result.

The 1960s and 1970s are commonly described as the 'Civil Rights Era,' a period of struggle for people of African descent to gain voting rights, rights of access to public places and amenities, and legal recourse for vio-lence committed against them. These rights were won at the cost of many lives, but gradually white perpetrators of such violence, formerly immune to legal repercussions, began to be brought to justice.

The dominance of the white male Protestant citizenry was challenged on another front by the 'women's movement.' In 1920 the Nineteenth Amend-ment to the Constitution had granted women the right to vote; now women began to agitate for greater equality in the workforce, in public life and in family life. In the spiritual and religious realm, recognizing women's equal-ity was to come more slowly. Such mainstream Christian denominations as the Presbyterian, Episcopal, United Methodist and United Church of Christ gradually extended ordination to women, as did the Unitarian Universalists and Reformed Jewish congregations, yet today the two largest Christian denominations in the U.S., the Roman Catholic and the Southern Baptist, still deny women ordination, as do Orthodox Jewish congregations.

Efforts for women's equality were given greater practical effectiveness with the development of the birth control pill in the latter part of the century, freeing women from the fear of unwanted pregnancy. It also produced a seismic shock on a broader cultural level; America's young people began to experiment with premarital sex with a heretofore un-thought-of sense of freedom. In the religious world, such loosening of sexual mores provoked strong reaction from more conservative quarters. The Roman Catholic Church issued a papal encyclical in1968 forbidding contraception by any means. While some Catholics chose simply to ignore the decree, Putnam and Campbell (2010) claim that the ban on contraception accounts for much of the decline in church attendance during the latter part of the century

A second movement on the sexual front was the 'gay rights' movement, beginning in the 1970s, seeking to affirm the value and equality before the law of homosexual individuals. This movement has had a long-term, still unresolved polarizing effect within the religious world; three large mainstream Christian denominations, the Southern Baptist, Roman Catholic and United Methodist, refuse to perform marriages between or to ordain homosexual individuals. Entrenched homophobia was also to have a remarkable effect in the tenor of public schooling in the 21st century.

The 1960s began to see greater and greater experimentation with religious and spiritual practice as alternatives to mainstream religious practice beckoned. Early efforts to welcome Eastern spiritual traditions to the United States had included Swami Vivekananda's participation in the World Parliament of Religions in Chicago in 1893; in 1920 the International Congress of Religious Liberals brought the Hindu leader Paramahansa Yogananda to speak at its conference in Boston. Returning to the States in 1935 and drawing many disciples, Yogananda was to be a forerunner of later, more widespread Eastern spiritual influences, including Transcendental Meditation, Zen Buddhism, Scientology and the New Age Movement. Increasingly, young and older adults found that they could be 'spiritual' without being 'religious.' A tenor of greater religious tolerance in the nation—or at least an overcoming of a former religious prejudice—was evidenced by the election in 1960 of the first Roman Catholic president, John F. Kennedy. Further spiritual and religious diversity included increased immigration of people of the Muslim faith. Attendance at mainstream church services declined and continues to decline to the present day (Glenn, 2013).

A major shock to a century and a half of Protestant religious practice in the public schools occurred in 1963 with a pair of rulings handed down by the Supreme Court. Both suits had to do with state requirements that each school day begin with mandatory Bible reading and recitation of the Lord's Prayer. In this landmark dual decision the Court pointed out that the state was financing a daily religious exercise that only some of the people wanted and that violated the sensibilities of others. It ruled that publicly funded schools cannot enforce a practice of prayer, Bible reading or religious ceremony (*School District of Abington Township v. Schempp* and *Murray v. Curtlett*, 374 U.S. 203). The written opinion of the Court did not preclude "teaching about the Holy Scriptures or about the differences between religious sects in classes in literature or history," noting that "whether or not the Bible is involved, it would be impossible to teach meaningfully many subjects in the social science or humanities without some mention of religion." Nevertheless, this ruling has been widely misconstrued by educators and the general public to mean that neither religion nor holy scriptures may be so much as mentioned in public classrooms.

The 1964 decision broke the dam on what seemed to have been an underground stream of resentment at the overtly religious tone set in U.S. public schools. Other lawsuits were to follow, argued from local courts to district courts to the U.S. Supreme Court. The state cannot provide salary supplements to teachers in parochial schools (*Lemon et al. v. Kurtzman*, 403 U.S. 602, 1971); the First Amendment protects students' individual rights to freedom of speech and expression, including private prayer and expression of religious views, so long as they do not impinge on the rights of others (*Tinker v. Des Moines School District*, 393 U.S. 503, 1969); public nonsectarian prayer offered at football games or commencement exercises by either faculty or students is unconstitutional (*Lee v. Weisman*, 505 U.S. 577, 1992; *Santa Fe School District v. Doe*, 145 Ed. Law Rep. 21, 1999); efforts to remove the teaching of evolution from the science curriculum and replace it with Creationism is a violation of the First Amendment, as is the requirement that evolution can only be taught if it is accompanied by Creationism (*Edwards v. Aguillard*, 482 U.S. 578, 1987).

With each cultural 'shock,' the seismic fissure between religious and secular views grew, and with it a backlash from ultraconservative Christian groups who equated Americanism with Christianity. The threat of such social changes as equality for women, sexual liberation and gay rights found many conservative Christians gathering under the banner of 'Family Values.' As ultraconservatives began to claim Christianity as justification for their stance, a fissure developed within the religious world between those of conservative and those of more liberal and inclusive understandings.

The last decades of the 20th century saw growing recognition and respect for minority cultures, as the former desire to assimilate to the dominant culture was replaced by a conscious reclaiming of linguistic and cultural heritages. Observers of the U.S. Census Bureau statistics began to predict that the majority white population would, in the 21st century, become a minority.

21ST CENTURY

Whites still held majority status at the close of the first decade of the 21st century, but a significant landmark was reached in 2011 when, for the first time, more than half (50.4%) the children born in the U.S. were racial and ethnic minorities (Yen, 2012).

As demographics changed, the interplay of plurality and polarity on political, religious and educational levels in the United States became more pronounced—and more complex. In 2008, the United States elected its first African-American president, the Democratic candidate Barack Obama, who defeated the conservative white Republican candidate, John McCain; both candidates claimed Protestant Christian affiliation. The 2012 election was to see more evidence of plurality, now along religious lines: Obama's opponent was white Republican candidate Mitt Romney, whose supporters overlooked his minority-religious status (as a Mormon, a member of the Church of Jesus Christ of Latter Day Saints) in favor of his conservative political views. While the 2012 election might suggest increasing tolerance of racial and religious diversity, the kind of backlash against plurality predicted by sociologists of religion also became more evident.

The number of violent 'hate groups' in the nation among the radical right wing topped 1000 in 2011, a growth of 7.5% over the previous year. The growth was fueled by several factors, according to the Southern Poverty Law Center: resentment over immigration and changing racial demographics, the spreading of conspiracy theories aimed at minorities and the national government, frustration over the lagging economy and the election of the first black president (Southern Poverty Law Center, 2011).

In this increasingly polarized atmosphere, it is not surprising that efforts to bring spiritual or religious perspectives into the public school classroom are played out on either end of a rather polarized scale. On the conservative religious right, and despite the Supreme Court's 1987 *Edwards v. Aguillard* decision in Louisiana regarding the teaching of Creationism in public schools, proponents of Creationism continue to barrage state legislatures and textbook adoption committees to include a biblical version of the creation of the world along with the teaching of evolution—or replacing evolution altogether. These efforts have been successful in some states or school districts, but the controversy has spawned numerous lawsuits across the country (Putnam & Campbell, 2010; Stutz, 2011).

At the other end of the spectrum are movements to introduce Eastern spiritual practices into the public schools. Such programs have been successfully implemented in some locales, as described in other chapters in this section, yet they are fraught with fear of arousing resistance from parents or objections from the religious right. A case in point is the 2008 effort to bring meditation into public schools in the Charlotte Mecklenburg school district in North Carolina, whose schools are predominantly African-American of conservative—but not necessarily fundamentalist—religious backgrounds. Program director for the school district, Missy Crews, and Dr. Russ Greenfield, M.D., director of Carolinas Integrative Health, approached the school system with a program to offer techniques in yoga and meditation to middle school students. School administrators and the assistant superintendent for the county system saw potential in the program for benefiting the students, but felt that bringing the practice of yoga into the school would be seen by parents as religious in nature. The effort was abandoned; Crews continued to use stillness practices as a means of centering in her own classes, but did not call it meditation (Crews, personal communication, November 21, 2013).

In other generally conservative communities the language in which such programs are couched seems to have made a difference. In Louisiana, therapists Joan Stewart and Janice McDermott developed a program based on mindfulness describing it in terms that would be acceptable to their local East and West Feliciana Parish school systems. The goals of the program, called *Grand Ideas from Within*, were expressed as raising students' awareness, reducing stress, maintain self-control and envisioning success. The program was so successful on both academic and behavioral levels that the local public television station broadcast a special documentary about it.

Implementation of such programs tends to be dependent upon their promotion as nonreligious in nature as well as upon the general tenor of the local community (Johnson & Neagley, 2011), but even such carefully framed efforts do not always have an easy path. In 2012 the Encinitas Union School District in California accepted a grant to introduce yoga into its kindergarten through grade 6 classes in a wellness program that includes twice-weekly sessions of stretching, breathing and relaxing; learning about healthy dietary habits; and cultivating small gardens. One might have expected few bumps in the road: Encinitas, as the home of the Self-Realization Center founded by Paramahansa Yogananda in 1935, is perhaps the earliest and longest-continuing site of the practice of yoga in the United States. Encinitas has been described as 'the yoga center of America,' hosting numerous yoga centers; yoga is even taught at the Young Men's Christian Association (Calvert, 2013).

In bringing yoga into the school system, the use of Sanskrit was omitted along with the traditional Namaste greeting. Poses were renamed in 'child-friendly' terms. Teachers reported that after yoga, students appeared calmer and more focused, and a decrease in playground problems and fewer suspensions for unruly behavior were also noted. Nevertheless, four dozen parents protested to the school board, claiming that teaching yoga is tantamount to religious indoctrination into Eastern religion and threatening a lawsuit (Perry, 2012). As of this writing, the school board has held firm and the wellness program continues.

Regardless of the content of the academic or physical education curriculum, ensuring that schools are places where children have a sense of safety and well-being might seem a commonly shared concern for people across the political and religious spectrum. In the U.S., however, for some citizens that concern does not extend to students who do not display overt signs of heterosexual sexual orientation.

Particularly in the 21st century educators have become aware of bullying in the schools, the use of some students' sense of power to intimidate, harass or physically harm other students for perceived weakness or lack of acceptability. According to Henkin (2005), bullying has for years taken place 'under the radar' of teachers' and administrators' awareness. The growing problem has recently prompted anti-bullying bills to be brought before local and state governmental bodies, specifying causes for bullying, including race, ethnicity, physical appearance, language, gender and sexual orientation. Efforts in many states to outlaw bullying for the above specific reasons have been stymied by religiously conservative groups such as the Family Research Council, the American Family Association and local expressions of such groups, voicing objection to outlawing bullying because of a student's sexual orientation, claiming that homosexuality is unbiblical and that forbidding students verbally to harass such children is a violation of their First Amendment right to freedom of speech. In several locales it has only been when language specifying sexual orientation has been removed from anti-bullying bills that they have been enacted into law (Southern Poverty Law Center, 2010; *Bullying in Louisiana*, 2012).

For the first decade of the 21st century, the U.S. Department of Education's No Child Left Behind Act with its reductionist approach to curriculum and its emphasis on high-stakes testing, influenced educational policies on state and local levels. The recent national initiative, Common Core State Standards, reveals a more holistic approach to education though no explicit reference is made to children's spirituality.

CONCLUSIONS

Children in the U.S. are growing up in an increasingly diverse society, bringing a variety of different spiritual backgrounds to their classrooms. These classrooms could be sites for nurturing the spirits of children while they learn about spiritual diversity in the United States and around the world; yet except in isolated cases, there is little acknowledgment of children's spirituality in U.S. public classrooms. There are a host of reasons that these opportunities are not taken advantage of: in addition to polarization along the political and religious spectrum, there is a conflating of spirituality with religion, a lack of education about children's spirituality, overinterpretation of the First Amendment and case law surrounding it, fear of litigation, as well as simple public relations concerns for parental and local community response.

A perception of spiritual education as an area separate from religious education or indoctrination has not gained widespread understanding in the United States, yet there are efforts in that direction. In addition to the initiatives mentioned in other chapters in this section, there are educators in the field of literacy who are attuned to the need and who see the possibility of using literature to support children's spiritual lives in the public school classroom (Trousdale & DeMoor, 2005; Trousdale, 2008, 2009, 2011; Trousdale, Bach & Willis, 2010; Wilhelm & Novak, 2011). The National Council of Teachers of English supports a special interest group that promotes attention to children's spiritual lives, the Assembly for Expanded Perspectives on Learning; the American Educational Research Association hosts an active special interest group, Spirituality and Education. These and the prophetic voices speaking through this book remain on the margins of mainstream education in the United States as they seek ways to nurture children's spirituality in the public classroom, a challenge indeed in a nation characterized by such rich diversity and increasingly entrenched polarity.

REFERENCES

Bullying in Louisiana. (2012). Retrieved March 1, 2013, from http://www.lpb.org/publicsquare/topic/08_12_bullying_in_louisana.

Calvert, K. (2013). *Promoting Hinduism? Parents demand removal of school yoga class.* Retrieved March 1, 2013, from www.npr.org/2013/01/09/168613416.

Gallup, G., & Lindsay, D. M. (1999). *Surveying the religious landscape: Trends in U.S. beliefs.* Harrisburg, PA: Morehouse.

Genovese, E. E. (1976). *Roll, Jordan, roll: The world the slaves made.* New York: Vintage.

Glenn, H. (2013). Losing our religion: The growth of the nones. Retrieved April 5, 2013, from http://www.npr/org/blogs/the two-way/2013/01/14/169164840/losing-our-religion.

Henkin, R. (2005). *Confronting bullying: Literacy as a tool for character education.* Portsmouth, NH: Heinemann.

Johnson, A., & Neagley, M. W. (Eds.). (2011). *Educating from the heart: Theoretical and practical approaches to transforming education.* Lanham, MD: Rowman & Littlefield Education.

Lester, J. (1968). *To be a slave.* New York: Dell.

McGuire, M. B. (2002). *Religion: The social context* (5th ed.). Belmont, CA: Wadsworth.

Osofsky, G. (Ed.). (1969). *Puttin' on ole massa.* New York: Harper & Row.

Perry, T. (2012, Nov. 11). Parents view yoga in school as religious indoctrination. *The Advocate, 19A.*

Putnam, R. D., & Campbell, D. E. (2010). *American grace: How religion divides and unites us.* New York: Simon & Schuster.

Southern Poverty Law Center. (2010). SPLC national campaign counters anti-gay bullying. *SPLC Report, 40*(4), 1–3.

Southern Poverty Law Center. (2011). U.S. hate groups top 1,000. *SPLC Report, 41*(1), 1–3.

Stutz, T. (2011, Jul. 20). Texas Board of Education set to dive back into science, evolution debate. *The Dallas Morning News.*

Trousdale, A. M. (1990). A submission theology for Black Americans: Religion and social action in prize-winning children's books about the Black experience in America. *Research in the Teaching of English, 24*(2), 117–140.

Trousdale, A.M. (2008). An endangered relationship, *Journal of Children's Literature, 34*:1, 37–44.

Trousdale, A. M. (2009). Peak experiences explored through literature. In M. deSouza, L. Francis, J. O'Higgins Norman, & D. Scott (Eds.), *International handbook of education for spirituality, care and wellbeing* (pp. 491–506). Dordrecht: Springer Academic Publishers.

Trousdale, A. M. (2011). Nurturing the spirit through literature. In A. Johnson & M. Webb Neagley (Eds.), *Educating from the heart: Theoretical and practical approaches to transforming education* (pp. 37–47). Lanham, MD: Rowman & Littlefield Education.

Trousdale, A., Bach, J., & Willis, E. (Eds.). (2010). Freedom, physicality, friendship and feeling: Aspects of children's spirituality expressed through the choral reading of poetry. *International Journal of Children's Spirituality, 25*(4), 317–329.

Trousdale, A. M., & DeMoor, E. A. (2005). Literature that helps children connect with the Earth. *Encounter: Education for Meaning and Social Justice, 18*(3), Autumn, 44–49.

Wilhelm, J. D., & Novak, B. (2011). *Teaching literacy for love and wisdom.* New York: Teachers College Press.

Yen, H. (2012). Minority birth rate: Racial and ethnic minorities surpass whites in U.S. births for first time, Census reports. Retrieved March, 2, 2013, from www.huffingtonpost.com/2012/05/17/census-minority-birth-rate_n_1523150.html.

19 Presence, Resonance, Transcendence
Education, Spirituality and the Contemplative Mind

Tobin Hart

Within a secular education system in a society deluged with technology, is there a place for spirituality? The constitutional firewall in the United States between religion and state has almost universally been interpreted to mean there can be no explicit religious content in the public classroom. The exceptions might be a course examining world religions, although this is rare, or time for silence during the school day. At the same time there has been a recognized need for the development of that which we might label 'spiritual'—that is, capacities or understanding that balance our concerns for preparing students for the marketplace with attention to growing their humanity. Recent initiatives in North America toward this larger end have taken the form of character and values education, social and emotional learning, service learning, anti-bullying campaigns, ecological awareness, self-reflection and creativity.

But it is unclear how successful these have been. However noble and well-conceived these programs may be, it is difficult to sustain them in a climate fixated on test scores. The history of North American education is strewn with excellent initiatives that have had a shelf life of an assistant principal. When the economic, political or personnel winds change, long-term teachers recognize that the next good idea will be coming along, eclipsing the previous 'new' idea. For change to be sustained on a large scale it must somehow be fundamentally integrated into teaching and learning.

Perhaps a more foundational approach to spirituality, and one that has been gaining recent momentum in North American education, has to do with *how* we know rather than *what* to know. Contemplation in education serves to alter our epistemic norms complementing the traditional forms of rational-empiricism and emphasis on information downloading that characterize conventional schooling. What the contemplative offers education is not a different set of knowledge so much as an expanded approach to knowing without any necessary imposition of religious doctrine whatsoever or even a fundamental change in curriculum. Essentially this approach recalibrates the relationship between knower, knowing and knowledge. We might say that the Mind—knower and knowing—becomes both the goal and the means, the object and the instrument of inquiry.

Today the emerging orientation called Contemplative Teaching and Learning or Contemplative Education emphasizes knower and knowing, helping to foster an inner technology of mind designed to quiet and shift habitual internal chatter in order to cultivate a capacity for deepened awareness, concentration and insight. While various practices may evoke different kinds of awareness, such as creative breakthrough or compassion, they share in common a typically nonlinear process that invites an opening of the mind. This opening *within us* in turn enables a corresponding opening toward the world *before us*.

Expanding education's epistemic status quo today might include deep reflection, empathic understanding, imaginative inquiry, enhancing sensory sensitivity, radical questioning, journaling, the use of silence and stillness, absorption in nature, beholding beauty, mindful service, meditation and so forth. A contemplative approach does not take away from literacy and numeracy; it deepens our ability to engage and thus understand information.

The contemplative has the potential to impact spirituality through education by engendering

- an *epistemology of presence* that helps us stay awake in the here and now, just what we hope for in the classroom, but also what we see as central in many spiritual traditions.
- a *pedagogy of resonance* that shapes our graciousness and spaciousness toward meeting and receiving the world nondefensively, developing a more intimate and integral empiricism. This more empathic, connected knowing provides an experiential base for ethics, complementing the objectivist, reductionist style of knowing that has dominated the modernist episteme.
- the *capacity for transcendence* through overcoming habitual patterns of mind and behavior in order to see new possibility, catalyze creativity and expand identifications, freeing us from a more limited view.

PRESENCE

Perhaps the most fundamental injunction for learning is to pay attention. Yet we rarely help children to do this; we just insist that they do.

At the most basic level, a skill set (e.g., learning to read) or knowledge set (e.g., vocabulary)—the predominant emphasis in schooling—is dependent largely on the *mindset* that one brings to the task. The simple but subtle ability to intentionally deploy and sustain attention is both an outcome of contemplative inquiry and the most fundamental mind skill needed for learning. Especially when young people are bombarded with flashy information and threatened from within by high levels of anxiety, developing the capacity for sustained attention—central to a contemplative approach—is essential for learning.

A wide range of practices—experiments with knowing—help to develop the muscle of attention and can be introduced safely in most classrooms (Hart, 2004). For example, at the beginning of a class or at a transition time we might turn the lights off and ask students to

> Take a few deep, slow clearing breaths. Let your body release and relax; let any parts of you that need to wiggle or stretch do so. Now feel the gentle pull of gravity and allow the chair you're sitting on, and the floor beneath you to gently support you as you as you sit upright without effort. Know that you are safe and welcome here. You are invited to relax and allow yourself to be silent and *not do* for a few minutes. Close your eyes if you are able to do so comfortably. You may want to focus only on your breathing, allowing it to flow in and out without effort. For some it can be helpful to count: perhaps 1, 2, 3, 4 beats on the in-breath, and 1 to 8 as you exhale, but find a rhythm that works for you. If you find yourself thinking, distracted, working on a problem, or whatever don't fight it, don't get stuck in it. Just notice it, allow it to be for a moment and then see if you can redirect your awareness back to your breath, and to *not doing*.

We might add a ring of a bell, perhaps three rings to begin and one to end, in order to add to the power of ceremony that helps students to recognize this as a different and important activity.

We are also discovering that such simple contemplative practices, so important for developing the muscle of attention, engender a host of significant *states* such as mental clarity and calmness as well as *traits* like emotional resilience, flexibility and compassion (Hart, 2007).

An epistemology of presence allows us to stay awake in the here and now, just what we hope for in the classroom, and also what we see as central in many spiritual traditions. We might stretch this a bit and call this a kind of spirituality of immanence. Most wisdom traditions emphasize either transcendence or immanence and sometimes both. The metaphysical concept of immanence implies that the world is infused with the spiritual. The challenge for the spiritually inclined has something to do with realizing or recognizing this dimension in the world around us. But how is this world revealed?

Presence opens knowing. The great texts of the wisdom traditions are often depicted as *living words*: They are in some mysterious way described as alive on the page. But the words, while right in front of us, are not always so easy to comprehend. As *living words* the implication is that their meaning is somehow encrypted and compressed. This is why in all of the traditions there is invitation to return to the words again and again in order to see what light might be revealed this time around. To gain access to the mysteries and reveal the meaning, we have to break the code.

The process of deep learning in a secular text or in knowing our neighbor may actually not be so different. The biology text, the notes on the board, the 'text' that is the person or situation in front of us, and the world as a whole are living words—awaiting expansion in order to be more fully understood. Their richness, beauty and dimensionality already exist here and now but must be decompressed to be realized. So how do we break the code?

The secret lies in *knowledge by presence*, which involves looking not only at the outer words or data but also opening into our selves. The code is broken, the words come alive, and the world is opened only through a corresponding opening of consciousness within us.

The instructions to return to the words is an invitation to enter into relationship with the symbols and signs and allow ourselves to both open *to* them and be further opened *by* them. This is like a two-headed key opening a series of locks that lead simultaneously into ourselves and into the data, the other. In this sense the symbol and the surface, whether a holy book or a textbook, will disclose itself only to the degree that we can open to it. This highlights that *what* we know is bound to *how* we know. And this *how* has a lot to do with presence.

RESONANCE

The common way we are trained to know through contemporary education tends to invite categorical identification rather than intimate meeting of the subject. This is largely because of the domination of the assumptions of contemporary science, which is based on objectification (Schrodinger, 1945). The notion of objective knowing has led to a new level of control over the natural world, and its presuppositions have dominated educational practice. Cartesian subject-object division provides the cornerstone. However, the maintenance of this separation between observer and observed is artificial, justified in the name of objectivity and reinforced by a cognitive repression of the awareness of interconnection. I am not speaking of the valuable arm's-length perspective that the intellect can provide; instead, I refer to the inflation, distortion and institutionalization of this approach into objectivism, which reduces the world to a collection of objects.

With the distance between knower and known maintained and without recognition of their interplay, we remain separate from (above or outside) the world we are perceiving. The modernist objectification of the other, including the natural world (environment and body), contributes to difficulties in relationships and limits the experience from which to make ethical choices. At the beginning of the 20th century, William James (1909/1977) recognized that "materialism and objectivism" tend to lead human beings to see their world as alien. And "the difference between living against a background of foreignness [i.e., treating the world as alien] and one of intimacy means the difference between a general habit of wariness and one of trust" (p. 19). The result of habitual wariness and distance is anxiety, depersonalization, alienation and narcissism. Objectivism is an insufficient ground on which to fashion character or human values. Such objectivist knowing tends to invite self-separateness and a lived solipsism in which we never experience the other or the other's subjectivity (Schroeder, 1984).

The opposite of objectification is understanding. Objectivity creates distance from the other whereas understanding invites dialogue and participation. The word 'understanding' literally means to stand under or among, implying a more participative knowing. This way of knowing is as useful in science as it is in human relationships. For example, Nobel Laureate Barbara McClintock made remarkable discoveries in genetics. When asked about her scientific process she said, "You have to have a feeling for the organism. . . . You have to have an openness to let it come to you" (Keller, 1983, p. 198). The organisms with which she worked were not monkeys or mice that you could imagine some kind of responsive relationship with; instead she worked with simple corn plants who were hard to get a smile or a squeak out of. The key to her astounding and extremely advanced understanding of genetics was, as she described, "feeling for" and "openness to let it come to you."

The shift in knowing is very simple but subtle; it takes place when we lead with curiosity instead of judgment, when we make contact instead of categories, accommodate rather than just assimilate, when we appreciate rather than defend against. Rather than objective, this may be considered a more empathic way of knowing. The spiritual traditions have something to say about this.

In Zen Buddhism, this attitude or way of seeing is called 'Beginner's Mind.' It means being open to the world, appreciating and meeting it with fresh eyes—just watching it (and ourselves) without preset expectations or categories. In the same vein, the Bible tells us that one enters the kingdom of heaven only by becoming like a child: "And calling to him a child, he put him in the midst of them and said, 'Truly, I say to you, unless you turn and become like children, you will never enter the kingdom of heaven'" (Matthew 18:3). This has something to do with openness and purity of heart. The same principle is captured in Taoism, whose alleged founder's name, Lao-tzu, means 'old child' (Lao-Tzu, 2000). This does not mean 'childish,' but 'childlike'—full of wonder and openness, allowing one to see as if for the first time.

This more empathic-contemplative knowing allows us to begin to see from multiple points of view. To get to know the other, *feel into* the other, take up their position or see through their eyes—whether a person or a plant—engages the empathic heart as a legitimate and complementary source of knowledge. While the intellect tends to *hold*, categorize, cut and re-form the world, contemplative knowing tends toward *beholding* it. In so doing the gap between us and it shrinks. With this knowing we begin to see the world, in the words of Thomas Berry (2000), as a communion of subjects rather than merely a collection of objects.

TRANSCENDENCE

Transcendence is a principle of virtually all spiritual traditions. Not only in the metaphysical sense of the existence of another realm—the spirit world in whatever form: heaven, God, the absolute—but also in terms of a *process* or *capacity* characteristic of human nature. At our best we can transcend our greed, ignorance, selfishness, primitive drives, and strive for something greater as we seek what is good and true and beautiful. We can transcend our circumstance through creativity and a bit of grace perhaps. We may even help transcend oppression and ignorance on a larger scale (think Gandhi, Martin Luther King, Jr., and others).

A rise in the belief in human transcendent agency began to take hold in the Renaissance. Following the rediscovery of ancient Greek texts and after the Bubonic plague wiped out a quarter of the population of all of Europe, the value of human life became significantly reappraised. For example, Pico Della Mirandola's *Oration on the Dignity of Man* celebrates the wonder of humanity, especially of human potential. The capacity that makes us most worthy of admiration, he contends, is precisely our ability to create what we are to be, to sow our own seeds from the gifts we have been given. Essentially, this shift gave new confidence in the human capability for agency and self-transcendence, both internal and external, material and spiritual, geographic and economic. From Dante to da Vinci the Renaissance mind took flight. Importantly, this elevation of the person was not anti-spiritual but instead provided an expanded way of considering it; the 'humanist' mind celebrated spirituality through much of the art, literature and philosophy of the day. We might say that the spiritual could now come through us, not just exist beyond us.

In the West most of the attention on personal agency has been about transcending external circumstances. We move westward, make our fortunes, create our dreams, dam the river, smash the atom. However, the primary starting point for the contemplative is to pay attention not to the outside but instead to our inside circumstances, noticing the quality and kind of our thoughts, feelings and sensations. For the contemplative the *capacity for transcendence* can involve overcoming habitual patterns of mind and behavior in order to see new possibility, catalyze creativity, open to insight, and even enter mystical union, freeing us from a more limited view. We might say that the contemplative seeks to change nothing but the way we look at things, opening the aperture of consciousness.

The capacity for *witnessing* the contents of consciousness rather than merely reacting is a key. This permits us to transcend our own habits of thought and inquire not only into the question at hand but also toward the asker of the question. We can become the object of inquiry as well as the instrument, as we inquire into self and subject. Action may follow but the idea is that it may come from a more aware and awake perspective.

With just a little turn we direct our gaze inward, witnessing the content (sensations, thoughts, feelings) and the process of one's own consciousness. This invites an embodied (somatic) and reflective awareness. For example, if we pause and ask internally, "Where am I now?" and allow impressions to arise on their own, in a few moments we may become aware of our body in some way, perhaps hunger, tightness somewhere, tiredness, or whatever sensations may arise. Likewise, thoughts or images may come to mind. We may notice that we are thinking about the list of things we need to do today, a previous unresolved conversation that seems to linger, or the fantasy of something we would rather be doing. We may notice that our awareness seems out in front of us, or overhead, or perhaps stuck in some nook in our body such as when pain grabs our attention. We might have a more existential response thinking about where we are in the course of our life, ready for a change, happy with our lot or whatever. Other possibilities exist as well but the point is that a moment of contemplative focusing, in this case through the use of a simple question, can help us notice how and by what our attention is held. When applied repeatedly over time, we can metacognize, noticing the patterns of our thought process. For example, are we always thinking about the next thing or often feel like we are racing ahead rather than attending to the moment at hand. Or even something so practical for learning as "Do I understand what I just read?" A simple moment of awareness gives us an option to transcend the habits of thought as we notice our internal reaction to that math problem, the history lesson, to our neighbor or our life. (Hart, 2009).

Young people are growing into a world of unthinkable violence. In the United States, for example, stress is implicated in the top six causes of death; the third leading cause of death for 10–14-year-olds is suicide and the second and third leading causes of death for 15–24-years-olds are homicide and suicide, respectively (National Center for Injury Prevention and Control, 2004). Meanwhile, millions of children are on antidepressants, and constant electronic stimulation gives access not only to dizzying amounts of information but also to sex, violence and sophisticated advertising.

The greater the complexity and demands—the external stressors—the greater is the need for internal balance and resilience. In a state of chronic stimulation or low-grade anxiety it is difficult to concentrate, comprehend and create. In other words, our emotional state is significant not only for our well-being but also for our capacity to learn.

Perhaps the most grounded way to talk about the ability to rise beyond limits is as a kind of biology of transcendence. During stress what has come to be referred to as the HPA axis (hypothalmus, pituitary, adrenal cortex) coordinates autonomic nervous system response that gets us ready for fight or flight in part by increasing levels of cortisol. But in an age of constant stimulation designed to grab our attention, shock or arouse us, not to mention the accelerated pace of the day, we may not return to an optimal baseline state, instead living in a constant state of frazzle. The hyper-arousal of the HPA axis and elevated levels of cortisol have been related to obesity, memory deficit (Raber, 1998), even the neurobiology of suicide (Lopez, Vazquez, Chalmers & Watson, 1997). In general, we know that anxiety, depression and significant levels of stress can impair mental processing and thus learning. The good news is that contemplative practice has been shown to reduce the level of cortisol during nonstressful events, increase response during stress and quicken the return to baseline levels (Maclean et al., 1997).

In addition to the activity of the HPA axis, general brain activity shifts under stress, inhibiting our higher capabilities of mind. If we are agitated in some way the more primitive limbic system tends to dominate brain activity; essentially this means our emotional and instinctual survival responses are in high gear. When this happens, the cerebral cortex, including the prefrontal cortex, recedes in influence. The activity of the prefrontal cortex, the most recently evolved part of the most complex thing we know of, the human brain, helps coordinate sophisticated integration of thought, emotion, planning, meaning, empathy, compassion, executive function and more, just those capacities that we could consider part of spirituality. (While the prefrontal cortex does not come into full integrative operation until emerging adulthood and beyond, the capacities with which it is associated are part of our repertoire prior to its full bloom.) Contemplative practice invites a state shift, calming limbic firing and allowing the cortex to come back on line, giving us fuller human functioning and thus potential for mental, spiritual, moral and creative capacities. We regain our capacity to think more clearly, weigh information carefully, consider long-range consequences and moral imperatives and much more. In addition to a shift in state, contemplative practice may also have an effect on long-term traits, such as compassion and equanimity, allowing easier and more stable access to our most important human capabilities. Both state and trait shifts engendered by contemplation imply a capacity for transcending circumstances and habits of mind.

NORTH AMERICAN TRENDS

Currently in North America there is initiative to develop contemplative teaching and learning as a field or to consider it as a movement. A number of programs have sprung up with an emphasis on K–12 education and/or higher education. The Center for Contemplative Mind in Society has spearheaded an effort to bring contemplative approaches to higher education pedagogy across a surprisingly wide range of disciplines from contemplative architecture to music to law. The Garrison Institute has instituted a field development initiative across North America especially targeting K–12 education. This involves research, program development, training and networking. Groups like the Mindfulness in Education Network provide resources and host conferences for educators. Naropa Institute in Boulder, Colorado, was perhaps the first explicit teacher training program in Contemplative Education. Other programs such as the University of Toronto's Holistic Education program (Ontario

Institute for Studies in Education) and numerous initiatives for educators throughout North America such as San Bernardino State's (California) master's program in Holistic and Integrative Education and the University of Michigan's undergraduate major in Jazz and Contemplative Studies incorporate the contemplative as do many courses at every level in the Department of Psychology at the University of West Georgia. There are well-established programs emphasizing the inner life of the teacher, especially The Courage to Teach work founded by Parker Palmer as well as The Center for Education, Imagination and the Natural World in North Carolina inspired by the work of Thomas Berry. Learning to BREATHE, CARE for Teachers (Cultivating Awareness and Resilience in Education), Inner Kids, HeartMath's Test Edge and The Impact Foundation's SMART in Education are among active programs that are training teachers and students explicitly in contemplative practice with stated goals of personal resilience and school success. Organizations such as Montessori and Waldorf education, CASEL (Collaborative for Academic, Social and Emotional Learning), and the Passageways Institute integrate contemplation within a larger pedagogical framework. The majority of initiatives involve both an emphasis on developing one's own contemplative knowing as an educator, whether through formal meditation practice, journal work, wilderness experience or other means and then integrating age-appropriate approaches into the classroom.

These are just a sampling of initiatives large and small, local and national, that have sprung up around this topic. Some are part of well-established networks, while others are fairly independent. The diversity and sheer number of these programs reflect some real momentum for this approach in North America. A reasonable question at this point can ask, Are they making a difference? We do see a meaningful spread of this general approach, ranging from a local initiative for the small Warren County High School in Vermont to thousands of teachers in the New York City public schools through The Inner Resilience Program. Both small and large school districts, individuals and groups of teachers are being exposed to contemplative practice for the classroom and for nourishing the inner life. The qualitative reports of the impact on individual teachers and students are compelling. There are also various outcome studies in progress. These may be useful in understanding relative effectiveness and making an argument for inclusion in contemporary schooling. However, the nature of both contemplation and spirituality are such that it will be important not to reduce either to a simple quantitative outcome measure toward a truncated end—tests scores, for example. The risk is that contemplation gets used as an improved means to an unimproved end.

In sum, it appears that a *bona fide* field is emerging with new research, training, frequent gatherings and scholarship. At the same time, education in the United States remains rigidly fixated on standardized test scores. Despite more than ten years of the national plan labeled 'No Child Left Behind' which places major emphasis on standardized assessment, meaningful improvement in test scores has *not* occurred and there is considerable evidence that this initiative, having cost billions of dollars and person hours, has not improved society or engendered better students, teachers, attrition rates or schools. Yet both major political parties for the past several national elections have offered essentially the same recipe for education: higher test scores. Whether contemplative teaching and learning makes a sustained and substantial impact in North American education is uncertain but I think it will depend largely on whether a bigger view of education can be advanced, a view that has as much to do with developing our humanity as it does with training workers for the marketplace.

Essentially this will require recognizing that *how* we know affects *what* we know. The general approach called contemplative teaching and learning provides an epistemic recalibration to contemporary schooling. This places an emphasis not only on *knowledge* but especially on *knower* and *knowing*—the inner life and processes that make us go and know. Without imposition of religious doctrine or significant curricular revision, contemplative teaching and learning develops the inner art and inner technology that affect human capacities for presence, resonance and transcendence. Essentially, this returns the cultivation of our humanity to the center of education.

REFERENCES

Berry, T. (2000). *The great work: Our way into the future*. New York: Random House.

Hart, T. (2004). Opening the contemplative mind in the classroom. *Journal of Transformative Education, 2*(1), 28–46.

Hart, T. (2007). Interiority and education: The neurophenomenology of contemplation and its potential role in learning. *Journal of Transformative Education, 6*(4), 235–250.

Hart, T. (2009). *From information to transformation: Education for the evolution of Consciousness* (rev. ed.). New York: Peter Lang.

James, W. (1909/1977). *A pluralistic universe*. Cambridge, MA: Harvard University Press.

Keller, E. F. (1983). *A feeling for the organism: The life and work of Barbara McClintock*. New York: Freeman.

Lao Tzu. (2000). *Tao te ching*. (S. Mitchell, Trans.). New York: Harper Perennial.

Lopez, J. F., Vazquez, D. M., Chalmers, D. T., & Watson, S. J. (1997). Regulation of 5-HT receptors and the hypothalamic-pituitary-adrenal axis. Implications for the neurobiology of suicide. *Academy of Science, 29*(836), 106–134.

MacLean, C., Walton, K., Wenneberg, S., Levitsky, D., Mandarino, J., Waziri, R., . . . , & Schneider, R. H. (1997). Effects of the Transcendental Meditation program on adaptive mechanisms: Changes in hormone levels and responses to stress after 4 months of practice. *Psychoneuroendocrinology, 22*(4), 277–295.

National Center for Injury Prevention and Control. (2004). *10 Leading Causes of Death, United States.* Retrieved January 16, 2007, from http://webappa.cdc. gov/cgi-bin/broker.exe.

Raber, J. (1998). Detrimental effects of chronic hypothalamic-pituitary-adrenal axis activation. From obesity to memory deficits. *Molecular Neurobiology, 18*(1), 1–22.

Schrodinger, E. (1945). *What is life? Mind and matter.* London: Cambridge University Press.

Schroeder, W. R. (1984). *Sartre and his predecessors: The self and the other.* Boston: Routledge & Kegan Paul.

20 Transformative Approaches to Teacher Education

Robert London

This chapter explores the experience of students that were enrolled in the MA program in Holistic and Integrative Education at California State University, San Bernardino (CSUSB), an approach that has worked with 11 cohorts over a period of more than 15 years, recognized by its students and the professional community as an exemplar program in transformative education (e.g., identified as one of three exemplar transformative programs in higher education in Duerr, Zajonc & Dana, 2003). Students take six courses over a two-year period as a cohort, which typically consists of a diverse group of 15 to 25 students of varying professional backgrounds, ages and experience. This chapter discusses the distinctive features of our geographical, political, and professional context, and then our pedagogy, including a discussion of our framework and the transformative components of the program, especially our focuses on the students' vision of education, nourishing their inner lives, and building a supportive learning community. The discussion of pedagogy will be clarified with quotes from students from three sources: final documentation papers by the students in the tenth cohort, comments from the eleventh cohort's summative evaluation, and a group documentation of the transformative components of the eighth cohort's experience. The following topics are integrated into the discussion: (1) our focus on the students' process of transformation and nourishing their inner life, (2) stages that students went through in completing the program, (3) obstacles in the process, and (4) effects of the process on their teaching.

CONTEXT

CSUSB is one campus in the state-supported CSU system and is a federally recognized Hispanic-serving institution with approximately 40% Hispanic students, 28% Caucasian students, and 11% African-American students. Approximately 64% of the students are female, and approximately 62% of the freshman class are first-generation college students. Many of our MA students experience stress connected with their work environment, financial situation, and/or family responsibilities. Many of our students work in public schools which perform poorly on standardized high-stakes testing and which have adopted methods inconsistent with a holistic philosophy. To clarify, one student in the tenth cohort describes her situation entering the program:

> I started [my first year teaching] as a second grade teacher and got very personally involved with my students' stories and worked very hard to connect their learning environment with their own life experiences. This took a lot out of me but I figured this was the way it needed to be. . . . My students' needs came before my own needs. . . . That first year I drove an hour to work, worked between 10 and 12 hours a day, drove another hour home and then worked some more. . . . That was a hard year personally! I still loved teaching though. As I gave my students top priority in my life, the balance of my marriage, children, friends, extended family and self suffered. I saw a future of burn out. . . . Professionally, there was a lot of pressure to perform. Achievement on the standardized tests was the focus of my district. Administrators were constantly in my room and meeting with me to make sure that I was identifying students' weaknesses and determining ways to enhance their mastery of the standards. I put a lot of pressure on myself as I worked to make sure every student . . . worked to meet my ideals. . . . The team of teachers I worked with, for the most part, were burnt out. . . . I considered that I might be headed towards that direction myself.

It seems appropriate to briefly describe the transformation of this student two years later:

> [Attending to my needs] used to make me feel guilty but now I can separate from the guilt and allow my own needs to become a priority when it is essential. By allowing myself to be connected to my own needs, I can see how I am more aware of my students' needs and can help them to find ways to get their needs met. . . . What I discovered is that inside of me lies who I am and not inside of the orders that are given to me. Discovering and accepting my true self as a teacher and human being has been one of the most powerful lessons . . . throughout this journey.

She then quotes Emerson: "To be yourself in a world that is constantly trying to make you something else is the greatest accomplishment."

To further clarify, I will describe one student's response to an assignment to experiment with methods that might nourish her inner life. She had practiced yoga in the past and thought this would be nourishing for her. This student had no time for this assignment with her perceived responsibilities. She already woke up at 6 am and was unwilling to get up earlier. Finally, she realized that she arrived at work an hour before the students arrived, and decided that she would spend about five minutes practicing yoga at home each morning before leaving, resulting in her arriving at school a little later. This little adjustment made a significant difference in her day.

Finally, a different student's account of her professional setting follows:

> Imagine my shock . . . to find that most of the theories of educational leaders were de-emphasized in favor of political agendas . . . and teaching to the test in order to get school dollars. Proven curriculum and pedagogies were discarded in favor of drilling, pre-scripted curriculum, and anthology readings from the class text. . . . *I was a holistic teacher in an unholistic environment* [emphasis added].

While these quotes give a good sense of our context, it is certainly not a description of all our students and the schools in which they work. Some enter the program with significantly fewer demands on their personal life and time compared to others, and some work in supportive professional settings; however, the descriptions give a sense of the specific characteristics of our setting that are an appropriate focus for this chapter.

PEDAGOGY

In this section I discuss the conceptual framework for our pedagogy, followed by an exploration of the relevant components of our program. First, it is necessary to clarify that the pedagogy of the program has been deeply influenced by my colleagues and input from our students, especially Dr. Sam Crowell, who has co-taught and planned with me for over 15 years, and David Reid-Marr, who during the past few cohorts has taught our third program course which experientially examines the metaphor of teacher as artist. Some of the principles in this section represent my revision of material Sam Crowell and I co-wrote for professional presentations; therefore, I use the pronoun 'we' in this section. Although this section may not accurately represent Sam's views, it seems more appropriate than using 'I.'

Framework

A principle that we believe essential is the need for the teacher to be open to, and cooperate with, what is needed. As stated by Doll (1993), "ends emerge from within process itself; they are not external to it. This means that prior to the process' development the ends can be delineated only in general, even 'fuzzy,' terms" (p. 31). For things to work we had to be open to the needs of our students and to what is expressed in a variety of ways in different spiritual traditions; for example, 'cooperating with the Tao,' 'being sensitive to the reconciling force,' or 'listening to higher intuition.' We saw the primary method associated with this principle to be 'not doing,' approximately meaning that we were careful not to let our habitual patterns of teaching prevent us from seeing what was needed. This meant a disciplined strategy of planning learning opportunities that we considered consistent with our vision, yet allowing ourselves to be open to what was needed and perhaps not considered in our initial planning.

In addition, we have tried to implement a constructive postmodern pedagogy, particularly as implied by Doll (1993) and Oliver (1989), as well as allowing ourselves to be influenced by our work in identifying the implications of a spiritual perspective in education and studying transformative approaches to learning (e.g., London et al., 2004; O'Sullivan, Morrell & O'Connor, 2002). We believe that postmodernist science reveals the inadequacy of modernism to explain a significant portion of our experience and that our interpretation of a spiritual perspective clarifies what a postmodern pedagogy might mean in our context. Specifically, we see our pedagogy consistent with a spiritual perspective that acknowledges the role that sacred experience plays. Our interest is not in defining explicitly what a spiritual perspective is; rather, we affirm its place and role in life. We introduce the question of the spiritual as it applies to our work as educators. We invite theory to emerge from experiences, relationships, and questions. Doll (1993) states, "These [postmodern] relations will exemplify less the knowing teacher informing unknown students, and more a group of individuals interacting together in the mutual exploration of relevant issues" (pp. 3–4).

Interdependent Components

Three interdependent components were integrated into all six program courses and are consistent with the above framework: (1) development of a transformative vision of education by each student, (2) exploration of how to nourish their inner life and the inner life of their students, and (3) development of a supportive learning environment.

Vision of Education

The major focus of our program is helping each student develop a transformative vision of education and clarifying how to implement that vision in their professional context. We expected their vision of education to be transformed, in the sense of "a transformation in your overall view of teaching, resulting in a significant change in the way you view teaching." I will mention that 92 to 100% of our students in the last four cohorts have identified the program as transformative in this sense in their summative evaluations.

In exploring one's vision of education we identified three key questions to address:

1. What is my vision of education? This question is primarily a matter of connecting with one's purpose in life particularly in the context

of one's profession. Clarity for this question allows one to 'see' or 'notice' opportunities to move one's teaching toward practice more consistent with one's vision.

2. What practices and methods are consistent with my vision? Clarity for this issue allows one to have a variety of tools to use to teach in a way consistent with one's vision.

3. What is needed in my situation? Receptivity to what is needed allows one to 'see' what is needed to reconcile one's vision and methods with the actual classroom situation. This process requires the teacher to maintain a strong connection to a vision of education in the midst of the limiting nature of the actual classroom situation. The terminology 'Seeing what is needed' is meant to be consistent with a spiritual perspective. It does not refer primarily to what we would rationally plan, referring more to an intuitive grasp of what is necessary.

The students described the transformation of their vision of education in a variety of ways. I will illustrate four major (interdependent) patterns in their descriptions. The first pattern was an increased feeling of empowerment and confidence in their teaching. One student wrote:

> I've learned to be more confident in my understanding and abilities. This has transformed my attitude towards the educational process. I used to think that perhaps some of these tenured teachers in the school system were educational experts with their "drill & kill", "practice 'til it's perfect", and other mechanical methods. . . . I've learned that my understanding and methods are just as good.

A second student writes:

> I feel lucky to have found a program that spoke to my soul as well as to my professional context. I find a consistency between who I am on the inside and in my personal life and who I am as a successful professional. . . . [W]hile I may sometimes feel alone on my campus . . . I am more confident taking risks in my classroom. . . . I am a more confident person and teacher and feel empowered to grow professionally.

The second pattern involved a shift from an emphasis on the 'end product' to an understanding that transformation is an ongoing process that will continue beyond the temporal end of the program. One student wrote, "The revival [of my teaching] is ongoing even as I attempt to describe my journey . . . and will continue beyond this program." Another student writes, "The changes were transformative. . . . I see them [my goals] differently now. My goals are part of an ongoing process."

The nature of this shift is caught in the following quote: "my vision has changed dramatically since I started this program. Although I started off as a holistic teacher years ago, I quickly fell into the trap of teaching to the test and producing test scores. This program has brought me back to the [holistic] frame of mind." This quote captures a typical pattern for educators in our region who teach in schools overemphasizing testing results.

The third pattern involved a movement from lack of clarity to a clear vision of education and how to implement that vision in their professional setting. One student wrote, "My vision of education was made clear during the program and I find myself constantly finding random things that I can incorporate into my lessons that maybe other educators would never consider." Another student writes, "The program was very effective in helping me to develop a vision of education that fit with my actual professional context, rather than having just an abstract idea of what an 'ideal' vision might be without knowing how to implement it in my classroom." I will mention that both teachers were in teaching situations not supportive of holistic approaches to education—their clarity concerning their vision of education allowed them to determine how to integrate their vision in an 'unholistic' institution.

One student indicates the significance of requiring them to experiment in their professional context: "I felt extremely supported . . . throughout this process. I greatly appreciated that we were able to tailor every single activity to our own individual situation/context."

The fourth pattern involved movement from feeling isolated in their professional context to understanding the 'bigger picture.' The two examples relate to earlier remarks concerning our emphasis on a postmodern paradigm, describing movement toward a postmodern pedagogy in institutions 'stuck in a modernist paradigm,' unfortunately not an uncommon occurrence in our context. One student writes:

> Today's schooling is so crippling to students and teachers alike. It is based on standardized testing and superficial curriculum. I felt guilty whenever I strayed from the modernist lesson plans and created lessons that taught life skills. This program did not relieve me of my guilt, but helped me to be aware of the feeling and to control my responses. If I am guilty of giving my students experiences that are meaningful, I do not retreat back to the terrible ways of the current education system; I continue to teach the whole child and nothing less.

A second student notes that

> how I perceive my students . . . has gone from attending to what they produce to how they are going about it [i.e., process]. . . . My perception of curriculum has changed as well. . . . My focus was on standards and how best to ensure each student met those requirements. . . . Now my perception of curriculum is transforming into one that views the environment and its inhabitants, the students, as the curriculum.

To give a more complete sense of their journey of transformation I partially quote one student's description of the six phases she went through in the program.

> [Phase 1: Becoming Aware of Dissonance] began prior to the program. Initially, I expected the dissonance to "clear up" in subsequent classes but . . . this dissonance did not subside. But neither did it intensify. Rather, my awareness of it became sharper empowering me to move on to Phase 2 [Becoming Re-enchanted With Education]. The empowerment came in the realization that transformation would come from within. . . . The dissonance in Phase 1 necessitated this second phase . . . that would lead to a transformation within me and enable me to formulate my vision of education.
>
> In [Phase 2], [Phase 3: Learning to Nourish Myself] was beginning to reveal itself. Becoming re-enchanted meant a new kind of involvement in my role as educator. The demands of a successful transformation into an educator whose pedagogy is holistic and integrative necessitate a caring of the self, physically and spiritually and so, I began to learn, or re-learn, how to nourish myself. . . . I was able to be more receptive of the world outside myself and thus, able to choose more effectively behaviors that would enable me to emerge as the educator I desire to be.
>
> [Phase 4: Constructing a Curriculum Reflective of My Pedagogy] The culmination of the course Education 617 came in the form of a paper in which I described a curriculum with a holistic and integrative pedagogy. . . . The transformation in me as an educator was moving from my role as an integrator of content areas to the role of incorporating discovery learning. . . . Phase 4 was the materialization of my pedagogy and called upon me to be aware of integrating holistic practices into my daily teaching.
>
> In [Phase 5: Creating a Vision of Education] I reflected on Phase 4 . . . which led to an articulation of my vision of education. . . .
>
> [Phase 6: Believing My Actions Are Connected to a Bigger Picture]: By this sixth phase, my senses were sharpened enhancing a transformation in my practices. Because of this heightened awareness, I am able to convey to my students the importance of interconnectedness. Previous to this, my teaching was more linear. . . . Now my teaching is more of a spiral; I connect what I teach to my students' lives, spiraling out from the classroom and to the world beyond.

Students noted that a focus on developing their ability to be present in the moment as an educator, including an emphasis on observation, facilitated transformation of their vision of education. We emphasized observation in the sense of 'seeing' our actions in the present moment and then reflecting on the significance and implications of those observations. For example, I assign 'No Time Assignments' which bring attention and awareness to ordinary moments in which being present and aware can provide insights into our behavior (London, 2007). In one assignment, participants observed how they listened to others; many were surprised to observe how seldom they actually listened attentively (e.g., "In this argumentative conversation I was thinking of what I was going to say next rather than attentively listening," or "I really wasn't *just* listening. I was constantly thinking about my behavior"). These observations led to experiments in which they deepened their ability to listen well to their students.

One participant summarized the significance of the No Time assignments: "The no time assignments allowed for growth in ways that otherwise I would have never truly taken the time to focus on in my life. They were key in developing my sensitivity."

Nourishing the Inner Life

A second major component of the program is a two-year curriculum on developing the students' ability to nourish their inner lives and the inner lives of their students. The fact that many of our students work in professional contexts that 'create' obstacles to nourishing one's inner life is a reality we addressed directly in our processing of relevant activities. One student describes her lack of nourishing her inner life on entering the program:

> Previously, . . . I thought that the more I did, the better I would feel. I was spiraling downward. I was giving more than I was receiving, a very unhealthy way to live. . . . I was struggling to be there for my students physically, emotionally, and spiritually, but things were not working out. I was constantly getting sick and interrupting the precious moments with my students. The students were draining me of my emotions; they can be so needy because of the lack of love in their lives. Lastly, my spirituality had gone out like a fire that nobody attends to.

Later she writes about her experimentation that

> to nourish myself, I had to find a practice that I was comfortable with. . . . At first I tried going on mini-nature walks with my dog, but the routine became another item on my agenda and lost its power to nourish. . . . Then I tried driving in my car to and from work without listening to music and that worked for quite some time, but eventually it lost its luster. Lastly, I have discovered a practice that had not occurred to me before. Whenever I felt stressed . . . I did something kind for someone else. . . . I actually felt nourished because my path

was crossing with someone else's and we were connected. . . . These small acts of kindness became an ongoing practice.

An art teacher in the program illustrated and described the phases she went through in her process of nourishing her inner life in part of a booklet she created: (1) Label: Before I came to this program I thought 'nourishing me' meant—Picture: A beach with a palm tree on a remote island; (2) Label: Daily thing? Yet another thing I had to get done. Picture: A To Do list of five items, third one, 'nourish myself'; (3) Label: Then I went through a phase where I was reveling in the permission to be selfish. Picture: A door with the sign "Go Away . . . Nourishing"; (4) Label: Finally, through time and the practices: a way of life and a way of intention, consistently and with a level of relative ease. Picture: The teacher walking up the school steps to the office, carrying material with the label 'work,' thinking "I'm nourishing myself right now!"; and (5) Label: Life more peaceful and enjoyable; not living weekend to weekend. Picture: The teacher sitting in the full lotus position, peacefully meditating, with images of typical school distractions in the background, not disrupting her internal peace.

Many students, in describing both their development of a transformative vision and a process to nourish their inner lives, mention feeling they were granted permission by the program both to experiment with their pedagogy and to nourish their inner lives. For example, one student wrote concerning nourishing her inner life:

> Early in the program we were given an assignment to go find a place in nature and spend a minimum of twenty minutes or so a few times a week there. When this came up I was all giddy inside. Again wondering why I had never given myself *permission* [italics added] to just be outside doing nothing but being there . . . now if I am driving and am called by some place off of the road I know that it's O.K. to get out of the car and just be there for a while. I always feel better for having done it.

In the program courses we invited students to experiment with a variety of techniques as part of developing their own process for nourishing their inner lives, as well as reflecting on the implications for their teaching. For example, we invited them to experiment with secular meditative practices (based on Miller, 2010), body work, centering activities, walking meditation, being in Nature, the process of starting the day, and journaling. Without defining terms or pointing to any specific spiritual or religious traditions, we encourage our students to nourish their inner lives, however they interpret what that means. I have noticed three common patterns in this process: (1) Each student develops a unique process that works for him or her, many times including activities that were not introduced in class. (2) Most students report a qualitative difference in their process of nourishing their inner lives, including, for many, a change from a view that time spent nourishing their inner lives 'interferes' with their need to spend time planning, to a view that time nourishing their inner lives, in fact, improves the quality of their teaching. (3) Students realize that nourishing their inner lives is a continuing process, needing regular adjustment and requiring discipline. One student explains how she applied these concepts to her job as a substitute teacher, a stressful job in her geographical location.

> I like to begin a day of subbing by entering the classroom, finding some-where to sit, and spending a few minutes meditating in the new and unfamiliar classroom. Since beginning this practice . . . I have found that my day as a substitute teacher goes a lot smoother. I feel calmer, and more connected to what I am doing. I no longer leave the schools exhausted and emotionally drained.

Students consistently noted the positive effect on their teaching.

> What I realized when I started this program was how much I had been neglecting my inner life. What I also realized after continuous assign-ments regarding the subject was, how much more in tune I was with myself and that made me more relaxed and in tune with others. The walls came down and there was an openness that I think is critical for teaching and education.

A Supportive Learning Environment

A third major component of the program is creating a supportive learn-ing environment. Two student quotes capture the positive effect of this focus. First,

> The strength I received through this community of [holistic educators] is something I could not have achieved on my own. This cohort pro-vided a place where my voice could be heard and where I could hear others' voices as well. The exchange of feelings, ideas, insecurities, and wisdoms was the vehicle through which I gained confidence and inspi-ration to develop and redevelop my vision of education.

Second,

> The community we formed was a home for our souls.

Although many of our activities addressed this focus on community, three approaches were consistently identified by students as significant: (1) Quar-terly retreats at the James Reserve at a lodge in a wilderness area, (2) the

Mesa activity, and (3) activities involving art that were part of our third program course.

Each program course includes a weekend retreat. One student addressed the significance of the retreats:

> I was reluctant to go to the James Reserve the first time. . . . I had many reservations: a group of strangers spending the weekend together, why is this necessary, couldn't we accomplish what we need to do in a regular classroom, I went anyway. I still remember the feeling I had at the end of the first weekend driving home from the Reserve. . . . It was a feeling of power, of contentment, relaxation, a bonding with my friends and with nature.

The Mesa activity was usually part of our first quarter retreat and, briefly, required students (and faculty) to bring artifacts that reflected who we were to place on a created 'mesa' (i.e., a specially prepared table) at James Reserve. This seemingly simple activity, combined with our initial establishment of community, elicited much deeper responses than we expected. One student tried to capture the significance of her feelings at the end of the Mesa activity:

> It was at this moment that I truly saw each person and they saw me. It was more than a physical presence that permeated the circle, but a spiritual essence that guided us through an emotional experience that would forever bond us together.

Finally, the activities of our third program course focusing on the educator as artist were consistently identified by students as being transformative. One student wrote of the importance of process: "in art, the process is more important than the finished product. In a meaningful educational process this is also true."

The following statement concerns one of the activities and captures some of the initial hesitation of some students to engage in these experiential activities:

> Our cohort created a mandala. It was an unexpected experience of unification and connection. Initially I felt stilted and disingenuous. I embarked on this task because it was part of the day's agenda though I did not feel connected—yet. As I worked with my cohort, I discovered our actions revealed the ability of a group of people to come together and create something—individually and as one—in a peaceful and caring manner. The effect of this activity and my reflection was transformative, causing me to be more aware of providing opportunities for my own students to discover their connectedness to others.

CONCLUSION

This chapter explored the process of transformation for our students, focusing on some of the distinctive characteristics of our context, especially the fact that a good portion of our students work in 'unholistic' institutions, and experience additional stress connected with time management, their financial situation, and/or family responsibilities. The students were able to implement a holistic pedagogy in an 'unholistic' environment and manage their stress in a way that had a positive effect on their teaching and students.

REFERENCES

Doll, W. (1993). *A post-modern perspective on curriculum*. New York: Teachers College Press.

Duerr, M., Zajonc, A., & Dana, D. (2003). Survey of transformative and spiritual dimensions of higher education. *Journal of Transformative Education, 1*(3), 177–211.

London, R. (2007, October). *No Time assignments: A spiritual perspective in teacher education*. Paper presented at the Holistic Education Conference, University of Toronto.

London, R., Arguelles, L., Brown, R., Crowell, S., Donnelley, J., & Johnson, A. (2004). What does it mean to teach in a way consistent with a spiritual perspective? *Encounter: Education for Meaning and Social Justice, 17*(2), 28–37.

Miller, John P. (2010). *Whole child education*. Toronto: University of Toronto Press.

Oliver, D. (1989). *Education, modernity, and fractured meaning: Toward a process theory of teaching and learning*. Albany: State University of New York Press.

O'Sullivan, E., Morrell, A., & O'Connor, M. (Eds.). (2002). *Expanding the boundaries of transformative learning*. New York: Palgrave.

21 Research as Transformative Learning

A Longitudinal Study of Spirituality, Cultural Identity, and Unfolding Wisdom in the Lives of US Educators

Elizabeth J. Tisdell

Research can be transformative, especially when one is researching one's passion. For more than 12 years I have had the honor of listening to research participants narrate stories of deep spiritual experiences related to cultural identity. Many of the spiritual journeys shared by these adult educators of varied backgrounds involved transformative learning experiences related to their cultural and religious history. The sharing of such stories has the effect of helping both the teller and the listener unfold their own inner wisdom; as the teller relates and shares powerful memory of spiritual experiences it evokes memory in the listener and potentially leads to greater wisdom for each. As I've discussed elsewhere (Tisdell, 2003, 2013), for the teller, this process of significant spiritual experience is not simply a recalling process: tellers usually re-member such formative spiritual experiences in light of their cultural background and identity in new ways. As Frederick Buechner notes in speaking of this re-membering: "Memory is more than a looking back to a time that is no longer; it is a looking out into another kind of time altogether where everything that ever was continues not just to be, but to grow and change with the life that is in it still" (cited by Wuthnow, 1999, p. 141). These kinds of memories do indeed change in the re-telling, with the "life that is in them still." The process of narrating experience leads to the further development of identity, for the narrator and can transform listener/researcher (Clark & Rossiter, 2008). The purpose of this chapter is to discuss the transformative process of conducting the research itself as well as the findings related to spirituality, cultural identity, and unfolding wisdom of educators in a US context.

PASSIONATE RESEARCH: FOLLOWING THE INVISIBLE THREAD

Researching one's passion, particularly if it's about spirituality, can be analogous to a form of pilgrimage. In discussing the stages of pilgrimage, Cousineau (1998) likens it to walking a labyrinth, and "following an invisible thread" that connects to the Source or the sacred (p. 150)." This research on the connection of spirituality and culture emerged to some extent out of my personal background and passionate interests, where I have been unconsciously following my own invisible thread. My 1998 study of how spirituality informs the educational work of a multicultural group of 31 adult educators in the US grew out of my own teaching. I had been teaching classes dealing with diversity issues related to race, gender, class, and sexual orientation, and had developed a passion for doing so. I saw teaching for equity as rooted in my own spiritual commitments which, both then (1998) and now, are partly informed by my own cultural background growing up in a white Irish-American-Catholic family.

Such commitments are also informed by my theological training as part of a master's degree in religion and my earlier work as a campus minister for the Catholic Church strongly informed by feminist theology and the liberation theology movement of Latin America. Feminist theology focuses in part on women's experience of the Divine, as well as women's often overlooked contribution to theology and academic discussions of religious experience; liberation theology focuses more specifically on Jesus's injunction to care for the poor and the oppressed and to set the captives free. Both feminist theology and liberation theology are concerned with equity and social justice and have strongly informed my educational background and understanding of spirituality as connected to social justice. When I began teaching graduate-level diversity classes in 1994, I saw such work as an extension of my spiritual commitment that also required that I do some of my own internal work. A participant in one of my studies described spirituality as "a journey toward wholeness" (Tisdell, 2003, p. 80). Understanding my own whiteness as a system of privilege and unpacking how other social systems based on race, gender, and culture inform my identity are part of this journey toward wholeness. My desire to understand the intersection of spirituality and culture and its connection to wisdom through a research project began in 1998, but it is an interest that continues to this day, as I follow the invisible thread.

THREADING THE NEEDLE: PURPOSES AND DATA COLLECTION

The purpose of the initial study was to examine the spiritual development of North American adult educators of different cultural groups in the US who were teaching for social justice and were motivated to do so because of their spiritual commitments. A total of 31 narrative interviews were conducted from December 1998 through October 2001, initially with 22 women, then later with 9 men. There were 17 people of color (6 African-American, 4 Latino, 4 Asian-American, 2 Native American, 1 of East Indian descent) and 14 Euro-Americans. The results of various aspects of that study have been published elsewhere (Tisdell, 2003, 2007).

Given the limited longitudinal studies of spiritual development, the second follow-up study (still in process), involves narrative interviews with these same participants ten years later. I provided participants with a transcript of their original interviews from ten years ago and asked them to share their reflections on the original interview, to describe significant spiritual experiences they have had since then, and to note how these relate to their understanding of the world. Thus far 18 participants have been reinterviewed. This research on spirituality and culture increased my knowledge of the participants' spirituality and cultural identity as well as my own.

The data were collected in each one of these studies through a one-and-a-half- to three-hour taped narrative interview that focused on their spiritual journeys, significant spiritual experiences, how their spirituality relates to their cultural identity, and how spirituality relates to their teaching. Given that I am a Euro-American white woman, and I was trying to do culturally sensitive research across borders of race, culture, and gender, each narrative interview was approached as a shared conversation (Fine, 1998). Data were analyzed via a thematic analysis and/or a narrative analysis (in some instances).

WEAVING THEORETICAL THREADS

The weaving together of multiple theoretical influences formed the framework of this longitudinal study. It was initially rooted in the faith development literature (Fowler, 1981; Loder, 1998). Fowler has discussed the significance of unconscious and symbolic knowledge construction processes as part of spirituality, but he doesn't discuss their connection to culture; yet symbol is always cultural. Thus, those who consider the connection of spirituality and culture in a US context (Abalos, 1998; hooks, 2000) also informed these studies, as did the notion that spirituality is different from religion, but related to spiritual development for those who were religiously and culturally socialized in a religious tradition, even though many no longer define their spirituality in those terms (Wuthnow, 1999). To some extent the transformative learning literature that is grounded more in cultural-spiritual perspectives, as opposed to that grounded in the individualist-rationalist perspective of Mezirow (as summarized by Taylor, 2008), informs this work. This particular paper is also informed by the literature on wisdom (Goldberg, 2005; Hall, 2010; Sternberg & Jordan, 2005), and how it develops over time and connects to spiritual development and cultural identity.

As I've discussed elsewhere (see Tisdell, 2011), in the literature on wisdom, many authors refer to the Proverbs 24 reference from the Hebrew Bible, where Wisdom is building *her* house. Wisdom has also been the subject of philosophy; indeed, the very root of the word 'philosophy' means love of wisdom. Many authors also recount the story of Socrates, seen by his contemporaries as having knowledge and wisdom but who is rumored to have denied being knowledgeable or wise. Hence, humility is deemed a characteristic of wisdom, as the recognition that all knowledge is partial. This tension of wisdom as having knowledge but recognizing that at the same time, one does not have knowledge, connects wisdom to the notion of paradox, a connection made by numerous authors (Hall, 2010; Goldberg, 2005).

THE TAPESTRY OF FINDINGS

The findings of the initial study are described in detail elsewhere (Tisdell, 2003, 2007), though a brief summary is helpful here, and will pave the way for an analysis of some of the longitudinal findings.

Initial Study: Multiple Threads

The findings in the first study indicated that participants focused on the role of spirituality in (1) dealing with internalized oppression and re-claiming aspects of their own cultural identity; (2) mediating among multiple identities (race, gender, class, sexuality); (3) crossing culture to facilitate development toward a more authentic identity; and (4) unconscious knowledge-construction processes that are connected to image, symbol, ritual, and metaphor that are often cultural. While nearly all were socialized in a religious tradition, only 6 of the 31 regularly practiced in the tradition of their childhood; all of them saw themselves as spiritual and most defined themselves as 'spiritual but not religious.' Nevertheless, most of them continually *spiraled back* to re-claim images, symbols, and music that still had important meaning for them from their childhood religious traditions. Two brief examples are provided here.

Julia

In her 1999 interview, Julia, who is Chicana and an educational consultant who grew up Catholic, described the journey of re-claiming a positive cultural identity as a spiritual experience and emphasized the significance of the cultural symbol of *La Virgen de Guadalupe* in that process. This is an example both of dealing with internalized oppression and the role of unconscious knowledge production processes. In 1999, Julia had long since moved away from the Mexican-Catholicism of her youth, but in reflecting back, she noted:

> I think part of my journey is going back to my heritage, my Aztec and indigenous roots. . . . Ana Castillo . . . gives a different picture of what *La Virgen* could represent in terms of powerful women. . . . But there's another side to it. . . . I don't always just go with 'this is the way that it is' because I do question 'was that a way for the Spaniards to . . . convert the Aztecs into Catholicism?' Or is it really an Aztec goddess? . . . But I do believe it's a spirit—a spirit that kind of watches over me.

Further she discusses some of the affective significance she holds for this image of *La Virgen de Guadalupe* in her family and cultural history:

> We have this ritual in my family—every time I go home, and when I'm getting ready to leave, I ask for my parents' blessing, and so they'll take me into their room, and each one of them will bless me. . . . And I don't feel complete if I don't do that. . . . So my father will bless me, 'te encomiendo a Dios Padre, y a *La Virgen de Guadalupe*' and ask my grandmother and *La Virgen* to watch over me, and so I feel like my Grandmother's watching over me!

For Julia the importance of the cultural symbol in her 1999 interview is in its significance to her ancestral connection, to her cultural roots, and the affective dimension associated with the family ritual of blessing.

Anna

At the time of our interview in 1999, Anna was 53, and an African American education professor. She shared the deeply significant experiences, which resulted from her spiritual searching as a child that extended into her adulthood. She explained that while her parents were Presbyterian, she attended a Methodist church as a child and then a Black Baptist church before becoming a Catholic in high school, but then stopped attending church sometime in her college years, moving away from religion as many young adults do. She became an atheist and a Marxist until into her 30s, and then spiraled back and re-claimed the sense of spirituality that she initially knew about as a child, but from an adult perspective. While she does not affiliate with any organized religion, she had developed her own individualized spirituality that is very much connected to her cultural background. In her 1999 interview she referred to the African-American singer Aretha Franklin as an important figure who helps her tap into her spiritual self, providing connections to her cultural identity and spirituality:

> I grew up in a Black community doing and understanding and experiencing things of Black culture, so when I say Aretha takes me back, she takes me back to my childhood and the things that I understood then—things like music and dance, and the way of walking, the way of talking, the way of knowing, the interactions, the jive talk, the improvisations, you know all those things that I learned coming up—the music of the church, the choir that I sang in, all of that. And because I was raised in that community with that knowledge her music takes me back even farther than I know, because I don't know where all of those things come from. As I've gotten older, the more I am able to let go of the material plane and accept things on

a spiritual plane that I am in touch with spiritually, but I'm not in touch with necessarily materially.

This seeming tension of the positions that Anna had embraced in her life—of a Marxist perspective, with its emphasis on human agency, and a spiritual perspective that acknowledges the divine spark both within and beyond us, and its connection to her African-American ancestors—had been integrated into Anna's spirituality by 1999. Loder (1998) discusses at length the ability of those mid-life adults who are generative to integrate the tension of opposites. Perhaps the moving forward and spiraling back process that is the shape of spiritual development is part of the integration process at work as well as the development of wisdom. This paves the way for a consideration of the follow-up study.

New Weavings: The Follow Up

The follow-up interviews conducted ten years later with 13 of the women revisited some of the same issues, but also have yielded some themes related to the longitudinal development of spirituality. Here I summarize some of these themes with particular attention to the narratives of Anna and Julia throughout.

A Deepening Spirituality and Expanded Sense of Identity

For the most part, these new narrative interviews were characterized by spiraling back, settling into their lives now, and going deeper into their spirituality. In general, their spirituality didn't change profoundly over the years, as most of them had a fairly developed spiritual view of the world ten years earlier; rather they embraced their spirituality, pondering some things more deeply as they began to make new meaning. Not surprisingly given their ages, almost all of them had experienced either a life-threatening illness themselves and/or the death of a loved one. Three of them had had breast cancer, including Julia; two had experienced the death of their partners, and several had walked the journey of death with a parent. While these experiences had touched them deeply, they didn't fundamentally change their spirituality, which was already established ten years earlier; rather such experiences deepened and affirmed their spirituality.

Julia, 58 at the time of my second interview with her in 2010, had just completed chemotherapy for breast cancer. She reflected on both her cultural identity and her more expanded sense of identity in light of her spirituality:

In terms of my culture, my culture has embraced many different ways of being, or different cultures, and being Latino or being a person of color is just some of being a woman. There are just some aspects of it. It's all part of who I am and, in that way, it feeds into my spirituality.

She has also now joined another cultural group that is also informing her identity: the culture of survivors of breast cancer, which also relates to her spirituality:

My spirituality has grown because of having cancer. . . . I feel like I'm more in touch with the sacred or not taking things for granted. . . . I really had to slow down a lot and I think the lesson in that was that you can't take life for granted, that you have to appreciate everything: people and just everything out of blessing. And so I would go for walks, especially when I had the chemo in me. I had just gone through a bunch of chemo and I would go for walks and I would feel like I was walking slow motion but I was really focusing on each flower and people's gardens and the sky and the birds. It was really an experience, and that was like a spiritual experience, just going for a walk!

She also talked about aspects of her Catholic background that are important in spite of her ambivalence to many things about the Church, such as praying the Rosary in Spanish partly because of its connection to her grandmother. In essence, Julia, like many of the women in this study, have continued to build on the power of memory to root themselves in a spiritual sense, but also to develop a more expanded sense of identity.

Anna, who was 63 at the time of our 2009 interview, spoke to this point and said about pondering spiritual questions:

I guess as I'm more conscious of my mortality, they loom a little bit bigger than they used to, but not so much as I'm going to become something that I've never ever thought about. It was interesting reading myself again and visiting those ideas. . . . I really don't think I've changed that much, but there have been a couple things that have really kind of stirred up my spiritual self and made me think more about it.

In spite of the fact that their worldview hadn't changed significantly in the past ten years, overall they appeared to value a spiritual perspective even more. This is not to say that they necessarily always consciously sought out a spiritual way of being; the busyness of life pulled them away from it at times. Nevertheless, they always came back to a center point that had a sense of spirituality to it.

Making New Memory/Spiraling into a Deepened Sense of Self

Memory is powerful, and memory related to spirituality is even more powerful, because it seems to help people develop a stronger and more integrated sense of self. Throughout our lives we tend to revisit significant past events, particularly events that touch the core of our being as related to our life process, serving as moments of transformative learning. Theologian and spiritual writer Frederick Buechner, as previously noted, hints at how this process works when he notes significant memory is more than simply looking back on a past event, that significant memory is "a looking out into another kind of time altogether" where everything changes "with the life that is in it still" (cited in Wuthnow, 1999, p. 151). Many of these women talked about earlier memories that they had, but spoke specifically about how they've made new meaning of these memories that have "life in them still."

Shirley, an African-American woman and community college professor, had talked about the significance of her grandmother and other women in organizing for civil rights in the 1950s and 1960s in her interview in 1999. In her interview in late 2009, she said that one of the things that struck her from re-reading that initial interview transcript was the significance of these many women mentors: "They were great black women teachers who were into 'lifting as we climb,' and one white woman who was also on a similar mission. These women were important role models," and she went on to discuss the significance of her grandmother in particular. She had become a doula (birth coach) since her last interview, and, recalling her presence at her grandmother's death about five years before, noted the intense similarities of birth and death, as she made further meaning of the births and deaths that she had been present for and the fact that many people are afraid of these things and miss the powerful spiritual lessons that can be learned from them. "Lots of people are terrified of these things and are afraid of things like ghosts, and blood, and the whole issues of death, that often we can't be open to them [spiritual experiences]."

She discussed the fact that in the ten years since I interviewed her she had gone on various trips and as part of them explored "aspects of these traditional religions of the African Diaspora and Indigenous spiritualities as part of the journey" and talked about the significance of women in these spiritual traditions, with her experiences in Bahia, Brazil, with women in the Candomble tradition being particularly important. She said that some of these women reminded her of her grandmother and the women that raised her; memories of them have life in them still. While she embraces her African-American cultural heritage, she also emphasized that her spirituality, culture, and identity are much bigger than can be "boxed," and noted "I came to black consciousness in my 20s because of what was going on, but my sense of spirituality is bigger than that and is extremely vast. This vastness of the divine is huge."

Moving Toward Wisdom

Many of the participants discussed wisdom and what it means to them as they age, as I asked specifically about it. They reported ways they have grown in their spirituality in finding a rhythmic balance between inner reflection and outer action as a key component of aging well. Two themes discussed here in relation to wisdom are listening to the 'inner voice' and love and interconnectedness.

Listening to the "Inner Voice"

Many of the participants indicated that wisdom was the result not only of life experience, but also of listening with a more integrated sense of self and one's whole being. In general they saw themselves as better at being able to access an internal sense of wisdom, by meditating, journaling, or cultivating some sense of spirit. Maureen, for example, age 63 at the time of the second interview, explains: "I do have a kind of channeling process that happens to me in my journal writing when I contemplate something that is particularly troubling me; I will sometimes get a kind of a different inner voice that is very strong and it comes through with a lot of wisdom. The voice will say: 'No, that is not what is happening; this is what is happening and this is what you need to do next.' Which in Siddha Yoga [her tradition] we would call that the 'inner guru.'" Others described a meditation process aiding them in their decisions that would be seen as more wise.

Love and Interconnectedness

Many of these women also talked about the importance of love and the recognition of the interconnectedness of everything as being part of wisdom. Returning again to Anna, in her 2009 interview she talked about the interconnection of love, spirituality, and wisdom:

> Wisdom is a spiritual knowing. My spirituality is based on the notion that there are no separations in the universe. We are all interconnected across time and space and whatever other dimensions and matter that exists, existed. I am because we are, because everything is everything. Love is a central factor. I love my sons enough to let them find their path with me as a supporting person because I know that they have that moral center and the trials they suffer will strengthen them in the long run. In some ways it's a gift to them to let them learn so they can add to the family [social] narrative. It is empowering to know that you are a part of the human journey, can shape it, add to it. Besides, I know I cannot control the world anyway, I am but a speck of the cosmos on a wonderful adventure for this material pulse of time, who am I to deny them the thrill of their pulse. It is so fleeting, this moment, held together and passed by the dreams and wonder of those before us. I am at peace with that.

She seemed to indicate that wisdom is also contextual; one is not 'wise' in all aspects of life. She ended by saying in a somewhat humorous way: "On another note, wisdom is not all pervasive. There are some things I am not wise about. Never been really wise about men! Still something I have to learn!"

SPIRALING AROUND AGAIN:
TRANSFORMING THE RESEARCHER

I learned a lot from the process of conducting these studies, both from an academic and a personal perspective. The most important academic insights can be summarized in considering the main findings of the studies, with the core theme being *we always spiral back* to make further meaning of memory of events *"with life in them still."* This theme relates to other significant findings in regard to the connection between cultural identity and spirituality, namely that such memories are connected to (1) unconscious knowledge production processes relating to image, symbol, music that are also cultural; (2) that people draw on their spirituality to deal with their own internalized oppression around race, gender, and other sociocultural factors as well as individual dimensions to re-claim their cultural identity and mediate among multiple identities; (3) that, while not discussed so much here, they often cross cultural and religious traditions to draw on aspects of spirituality to facilitate their own spiritual development and claim a more authentic identity. They draw on the wisdom of their own cultural traditions as well as the wisdom traditions of other cultures in doing so. Some discuss particular *moments* of transformative learning; others focus on the journey as transformative learning.

But from a personal perspective, the experience of examining the connection of spirituality and cultural identity of study participants in the US also made me explore my own cultural and religious roots more deeply, in relation to my Irish-American Roman Catholic culture of origin. This has been like 'following the invisible thread' that has been a continually unfolding process, gleaned from reflecting on the actual interviews as well as what they prompted me to think about and to do. For example, Shirley's discussion of traveling to other countries to better understand her own cultural roots and connection to the African Diaspora prompted me to consider my own connection to the Irish Diaspora and to recognize the different systems of power and privilege inherent in our respective cultural histories. Shirley's ancestors were forced to come on slave ships to what would eventually be 'the United States'; while my ancestors were poor, they came from Ireland on their own accord in search of a better life. Both her ancestors and mine also relied on their own culturally grounded sense of faith. The differences and similarities in our stories made me ponder how systems of power and privilege in the US also affect how people forge their cultural identities in light of their spiritual commitments.

As noted above, a number of the participants also discussed the notion of spiritual pilgrimage in the sense of travel for a spiritual purpose. From a personal perspective, their stories to some extent influenced my own undertaking of two significant pilgrimage experiences: climbing the sacred mountain of Croagh Patrick in the West of Ireland in 2009 and very recently walking the more than 1000-year-old pilgrimage route of the Camino de Santiago stretching from Southern France across Northern Spain in the summer of 2012. These walking pilgrimage experiences have been personally transformative in many ways. I learned that we do indeed 'make the road by walking' (literally and metaphorically), as adult educators Myles Horton and Paulo Freire (1990) suggest. I also learned something about a sense of a spirituality related to the land and to nature that is so often lost in our computerized lives, and which relates to my more recent academic examination of wisdom (Tisdell, 2011). I learned that while we can learn a lot from the literature about *the nature of wisdom*, we often ignore *the wisdom of nature*. We can do an academic study of wisdom, but real wisdom comes only from walking the journey of life and attending mindfully to the rhythms of nature, oneself, and others.

Over the past 12 years, the various influences on my spirituality have broadened and increased, but I've learned that a *spiritual practice* can be embodied in every step, in every breath; I've also learned that the role of *beloved community* in that process is crucial to my own pursuit of wisdom. While I've always valued a regular spiritual practice *in theory*, in reality I have often found it difficult to maintain a regular practice without the support of community; the demands of academic life have made it too easy to discard the meditation time in favor of my never-ending 'to-do' list. And because I also do academic research (like this!) related to spirituality and culture, in the past it was easy for my spiritual commitment to erode to another academic exercise. I am finding more balance in the *being and doing* than I did 12 years ago, through the support of a church community that focuses more on *doing* and social justice, and a meditation group that focuses more on *being* and spiritual practices. Although the living out of spiritual practice will always be a struggle, I'm inspired by the figure of Lady Wisdom in the Old Testament Book of Proverbs 9: "Wisdom has built her house; she has carved out her seven pillars." The silence of my own attempts at regular meditation practice, my pilgrimage experiences, and my morning walks are among the ways I try to build the house of my life in the hopes that the divine spark of feminine Wisdom might dwell within me as I follow the invisible thread. I continue to be inspired by the insights from those in beloved community (including the beloved community of my research participants), and other academics who share their moments of wisdom grounded in their cultural identities and transformative learning experiences with me. Hopefully our collective insights result in culturally responsive transformative educational experiences for our students that lead to greater wisdom for all of us.

REFERENCES

Abalos, D. (1998). *La Communidad Latina in the United States*. Westport, CT: Praeger.

Clark, M. C., & Rossiter, M. (2008). Narrative learning in adulthood. In S. Merriam (Ed.), *The third update on adult learning theory* (pp. 61–71). San Francisco: Jossey-Bass.

Cousineau, P. (1998). *The art of pilgrimage*. Berkeley, CA: Conari Press.

Fine, M. (1998). Working the hyphens. In N. Denzin & Y. Lincoln (Eds.), *The landscape of qualitative research* (pp. 130–155). Newbury Park, CA: Sage.

Fowler, J. (1981). *Stages of faith.* San Francisco: Harper and Row.

Goldberg, E. (2005). *The wisdom paradox.* New York: Gotham Books.

Hall, S. (2010). *Wisdom: From philosophy to neuroscience.* New York: Knopf.

hooks, b. (2000). *All about love.* New York: Harper Collins.

Horton, M., & Freire, P. (1990). *We make the road by walking.* Philadelphia: Temple University Press.

Loder, J. (1998). *The logic of the spirit.* San Francisco: Jossey-Bass

Sternberg, R., & Jordan, J. (Eds.). (2005). *A handbook of wisdom.* New York: Cambridge University Press.

Taylor, E. (2008). Transformative learning theory. In S. Merriam (Ed.), *The third update on adult learning theory* (pp. 5–15). San Francisco: Jossey-Bass.

Tisdell, E. (2003). *Exploring spirituality and culture in adult and higher education.* San Francisco: Jossey-Bass.

Tisdell, E. (2007). In the new millennium: The role of spirituality and the cultural imagination in dealing with diversity and equity in the higher education classroom. *Teachers College Record, 109,* 531–560.

Tisdell, E. (2011). The wisdom of webs a-weaving: Adult education and the paradoxes of complexity in changing times. In E. Tisdell & A. Swartz (Eds.), *Adult education and the pursuit of wisdom* (pp. 5–13). New Directions for Adult and Continuing Education No. 131. San Francisco: Jossey-Bass.

Tisdell, E. (2013). Re-searching spirituality and cultural identity. In J. Hocheimer & J Fernandez-Godborough, *Spirituality in the 21st century: Conversations* (pp. 3–18). Oxfordshire, England: Inter-disciplinary Press.

Wuthnow, R. (1999). *Growing up religious: Christians and Jews and their journeys of faith.* Boston: Beacon Press.

22 Spiritual Education in Brazil
Debates, Trends, Proposals, and Experiments

Dora Incontri

INTRODUCTION

Brazilian history has roots in Catholic tradition: during the first 200 years from the arrival of Portuguese conquerors, in 1500 C.E., education was fully in the hands of the Jesuits, and after their deportation, was both in the hands of the state and other religious orders. The 20th century has seen a strong effort to make public education fully secular (85% of elementary Brazilian students go to public school). This effort is prompted by the continued presence of confessional teaching in state schools. The still powerful Catholic Church, and more recently the several Protestant Pentecostal churches, act against this secular trend. For some scholars and advocates of secularism, public school is no place for religion. Roseli Fischmann (2012), of the University of São Paulo, states that religion in public school always brings proselytism pushed by majority religions, and this is a constraint for minorities. For Sergio Junqueira (2009), from the Catholic University (Paraná), Director of GPER (Research Group Education and Religion), and the members of Fonaper (Forum Nacional Permanente de Ensino Religioso—Permanent National Forum of Religious Education), pluralism should be guaranteed in religious education, but spirituality must be inserted both in private and public school. However, recent research provides evidence that proselytism and constraints, both illegal under Brazilian law, are widely practiced in various public schools all over Brazil (Fischmann, 2012).

In 2009, a document signed by President Luiz Inácio Lula da Silva provoked a strong reaction from non-Catholics (both secularists and followers of other religions): *The Concordat between Brazil and Vatican* (*Concordata Brasil-Vaticano*). In this bilateral agreement, many privileges are granted to the Catholic Church. In Article 11, particularly controversial, religious teaching becomes compulsory in public schools and it is mentioned as a teaching of Catholicism "and other religions". An Action of unconstitutionality (n. 4439) has been proposed against this document (Fischmann, 2012, p. 7).

On the other hand, programs proposed by Fonaper (2008), textbooks like *Todos os Jeitos de Crer* (*All Ways of Believing*) (Incontri & Bigheto,

2004), along with other practical experiments, tend towards pluralism, interdisciplinary projects, interreligious dialogue, and tolerance with respect to minorities. Such programs are based on the understanding that religion is a knowledge field that must interact with other areas for a better understanding of the human being, using terms like 'spirituality' or 'religiousness' instead of religion.

This chapter examines this complex and sensitive scenario, offering a review of developments, contradictions, and trends in spiritual and religious education in Brazil. Note that this discussion does not apply to the Brazilian Indian population, which was almost extinguished by a chronic genocide and today numbers 896,900 with 305 ethnic groups speaking 274 languages (IBGE, Instituto Brasileiro de Geografia e Estatística, 2010). These different cultures are quite isolated and have no influence in Brazilian education, although a few anthropologists try to recover their traditions.

LEGISLATION AND REALITY

The Brazilian Constitution ensures freedom of worship, and Brazilian educational law (Lei de Diretrizes e Bases da Educação, n. 9.394, 1996) proposes an interfaith teaching in elementary school. Article 33 says that the law shall guarantee respect for religious diversity in Brazil, rejecting all forms of proselytism, and states that religion has to figure as an elective discipline. However, enforcement depends on local legislation in each state, where legislators face opponent groups striving for the prevalence of their positions: Catholics and Protestants willing to have their priests and teachers inside the school, secularists desiring to leave religion outside public education, teachers and scholars of other groups like Fonaper making claims for interreligious teaching which is not led by clergy.

For instance, the State of São Paulo restrains the presence of religious representatives in the classroom and assigns religious education to history, sociology, and philosophy teachers or to generalist primary school teachers. The State Board of Education of São Paulo, in the law resolution of July 27, 2001, says:

> Religious education in schools should be, first of all, founded on the principles of citizenship and the understanding of each other. Religious knowledge should not be a cluster of content aimed at evangelizing or seeking followers of doctrines; it should not be associated with the imposition of dogmas, rituals or prayers, but instead it should be a way to learn more about human societies and about human beings themselves. (Conselho Estadual de Educação, 2001, p. 2)

Otherwise, in Rio de Janeiro, local legislation, strongly influenced by Catholic and Protestant churches, requests religious institutions to certify representatives to teach their confessional doctrines to children in public schools with the consent of parents.

The local legislation (n. 3459, September 14, 2000) says that the religion teacher has to be accredited by the competent religious authority. Advocates of secularism and religious minorities, like Afro-Brazilians, Spiritists, indigenous movements, and others, are critical of such an arrangement, because only powerful and strongly organized religions are able to access these teaching places.

A large study carried out in ten cities in six Brazilian states, funded by the National Council of Technological and Scientific Development (CNPq), revealed that many public schools are far away from a secular institutional model where religions would be equally respected (Fischmann, 2012; Cunha, 2012; Medeiros, 2012; Grassi, 2012; Molina, 2012; Seffner & Santos, 2012; Pereira & Nishimoto, 2012). The researchers also found irregular procedures in more than 90% of the surveyed schools, such as the following:

- Religious symbols like crucifixes and Bibles in classrooms, board-rooms, and playgrounds;
- Students required to repeat Christian prayers;
- Students and parents misinformed about the nonmandatory character of religious teaching;
- Lack of alternative activities for students during religion classes;
- Classes with specific indoctrination of Christian dogmas;
- The silencing of minority expression.

For researchers in that study, the causes of this situation are most likely due to factors such as the following:

1. a historical problematic fusion in Brazil between public and private, state and religion; and
2. a lack of training of the teachers involved with religious education.

The regular pedagogy faculties never touch this subject; religious teaching is nowhere mentioned in the current curricular guidelines for a bachelor's degree in pedagogy (Conselho Nacional de Educação, 2006).

According to Seffner and Santos (2012), "the need for specific training of teachers for religious education is identified as a problem for several of the actors involved, as pedagogical advisers of municipal departments of education, school principals and the teachers themselves. Some respondents claimed a lot of insecurity to start in the discipline" (p. 76). Instead of an understanding of religious teaching as a field of knowledge, which has to consider plural points of view, teachers tend to bring to the school their own religion as the universal truth, to be preached to all students. As Seffner and Santos (2012) report, "there are teachers who make a strict program, based on their own beliefs, setting aside important aspects of respect to the religious diversity. They grant an avowed privilege to Christian religions, emphasizing the Roman Catholic denomination" (p. 73).

Searching evidence for the hypothesis that this situation is related to the teachers' training, we can mention Amaral and Junqueira (2010). They examined 23 specialization courses of religious teaching in five Brazilian states and verified that all except two are offered by confessional colleges. Out of the teacher training courses analyzed in the research, only 10% are offered and fully funded by some institution. The tuition of 90% of them must be undertaken by the students—mostly public school teachers, who are poorly paid in the country.

Another reason for proselytism may be the agreements between public schools and religious organizations. States and counties do not allocate sufficient funds to assure public education for all children, so they offer places in private confessional schools. As well, religious entities lend buildings and infrastructure to public schools. Many times, as shown by Molina (2012), Cunha (2012), and Medeiros (2012), this fusion results in interference or even in evident control practiced by the religious organizations.

In 2008, after the X Seminário Nacional de Formação de Professores para o Ensino Religioso (X National Seminar on Teacher Training for Religious Education), Fonaper drafted a document proposing some curriculum guidelines for a Graduation Course of Religious Teaching. This document reveals the concept of Religious Education as a field of knowledge and not as a confessional crusade to indoctrinate students. Articles 1 and 2 are very specific:

1. The teaching of Religious Education is understood as an educational activity built and focused on the valuation and recognition of religious diversity present in Brazilian society, through the exercise of dialogue, research, study, construction, reconstruction and socialization of knowledge, developing the relationship between scientific and cultural, ethical and aesthetic values. . . .
2. The pedagogical and didactic exercise in teaching of Religious Education considers the prior knowledge of learners and the socio-historical context in which they are circumscribed, . . . developing a process of recognition, respect and appreciation of differences and different individuals. (Fonaper, 2008, p. 2)

Although this document was delivered to the National Council of Education, no action has been so far undertaken to improve teaching training in this area.

INTERRELIGIOUS AND INTERDISCIPLINARY WAYS

Public education—the scenario of the debates mentioned above—accounts for 85% of 31 million Brazilian children. Private education, which accounts for the other 15% of Brazilian children, is offered by numerous Catholic and Protestant schools and a few Jewish, Spiritist, and nonreligious institutions.

In this context, approximately 75,000 students (data provided by publisher Editora Ática, referring to the years 2008–2011), mostly in Catholic schools, follow an interreligious program, with the books *Todos os Jeitos de Crer* (*All Ways of Believing*) and *Jeitos do Crer* (*Ways of Believing*), altogether nine volumes of interreligious education, by Incontri and Bigheto (2004, 2009). This program introduces Brazilian and world religions in a plural and interdisciplinary view, so students can develop an empathy with different cultures and beliefs while deepening their own faith. Materialism and atheism are also discussed, so that the students may take notice of the diversity of viewpoints in society. All perspectives are treated respectfully, so that children can learn tolerance to others' worldviews. These textbooks could avoid proselytism in public school, but although Brazilian educational law proposes religious teaching, the government does not allocate a budget to cover the costs of teaching materials in this area. Paradoxically, many Catholic schools, which could proselytize, adopt an interreligious program.

These textbooks are not only concerned with the solution of the conflict between secular schools and religious schools by providing interreligious education but, similarly to Junqueira (2009), Incontri and Bigheto (2010) assert that traditional schools (public or private) must be totally reformed to become places where children and young people can research, debate, think freely, and make contact with different philosophical, scientific, political, and religious points of view. Quoting the great Brazilian educator Paulo Freire (2011), who called the traditional school a 'banking model' of education, Junqueira declares that this model still exists:

> The student receives knowledge passively, becoming a "depository" of the educator. Education is to archive what is deposited. But the curious thing is that the archive is the human being, who thus loses his power to create, becoming less human, like a part of a machine. Instead, man's destiny should be to create and transform the world, being the subject of his action. (Junqueira, 2009, p. 247)

A plural and active school is one where students are stimulated to develop critical capacity, personal judgment, and independence of mind (Incontri & Bigheto, 2010). One must, however, take care to ensure that pluralism does not turn into skepticism or relativism, in the sense of equating all speeches as mere narratives, as the postmodern philosophers defend, emptying them of the possibility of truth or inducing a thought from which no ethical parameter can be proposed as universal.

Another urgent change in school is to break up this system of tight disciplines that are swallowed into short periods of classes and where no discipline connects with another. Spirituality stimulated by interreligious education should not be the subject of a discipline, with a time schedule, but it should pervade projects, research, attitudes, debates, and actions. We should not expect the awakening of spirituality in a simple lesson, isolated and unconnected with the experience of the learner. Of course, even in traditional teaching, even in the shortest time, even under adverse conditions, an educator can always leave a mark on his or her students. But structural change in schools to allow them to become places of research, projects, experiences, and interactions would open a new horizon in education and a healthy spirituality could result in involvement with the whole community.

These pedagogical views were not only embodied in the *Todos os Jeitos de Crer* textbooks, but have been experienced also in public schools, in a project (2002–2004) funded by Fundação de Amparo à Pesquisa do Estado de São Paulo (Fapesp, Foundation for Research Support of São Paulo State), with research under the title 'Ethic, Philosophy, Religions and Arts—An interdisciplinary project in public school'. This involved 300 children from 8 to 10 years years old (Incontri & Bigheto, 2003).

SPIRITIST PEDAGOGY AND INTERRELIGIOUS EDUCATION

Within this scenario, a new pedagogical trend is emerging. It has a strong focus on the spiritual dimension of the child. It is important to be mentioned because of its originality and because it is based on an idea that is widely accepted in Brazil: reincarnation. This pedagogical proposal is a project which is specifically Brazilian (Incontri, 2006).

In spite of the strong Catholic roots in Brazilian culture and the increasing acceptance of Pentecostal Protestantism among popular classes, 37% of Brazilians believe in reincarnation and 18% consider that it is possible (Data Folha, 2007). This idea is widely spread in Brazil, influenced by the concepts foundational to Spiritism, a French doctrine founded by Allan Kardec (1804–1869). Spiritism was introduced into Brazilian culture in the second half of the 19th century and became very popular in the 20th century. Although only 3% of Brazilians declare themselves as Spiritists, it has a strong influence in society, with mediums like Francisco Cândido Xavier (1910–2002) and with a large number of 'Spiritist centers' (in the city of São Paulo, for instance, using data supplied by the Union of Spiritist Societies from São Paulo, there are around 240 centers) and recently from many films and soap operas focusing on life after death, reincarnation, and mediumship (communication with spirits).

Based on the social relevance of this influence, Brazilian psychologists, among them Julio Peres (2012), propose that psychotherapy should consider patients' beliefs like reincarnation. Likewise, a groundbreaking pedagogical stream also takes into consideration this hypothesis and suggests that education would change if children were seen as reincarnated beings (Peres & Incontri, 2010). Since Spiritism belongs to a Greek and Western tradition with a strong Enlightenment heritage and a pronounced rationalistic accent, reincarnation acquires a specific nuance, emphasizing the concept of the individual identity of the human being. This is different from Eastern concepts of reincarnation, like Buddhist and Hindu doctrines, where the ego has to be dissolved to avoid the wheel of karma. Spiritist philosophy defends the permanence of the spirit—that is, retaining an individual identity through the various lives, through time. The spirit maintains its personality, animating successive human bodies (never animals) whilst evolving towards perfection. (Distinct concepts of reincarnation are discussed in Obeyesekere, 2002, and Donnet, 1986.)

Spiritist Pedagogy was born in Brazil with the innovative praxis of Eurípedes Barsanulfo in the Allan Kardec School in 1907, and with the theoretical formulation of the philosopher J. Herculano Pires in the 1950s (Pires, 1985). It is an educational proposal, which sees the child as a reincarnated being, bringing spirituality into the education experience as interreligious teaching practice (Incontri, 2006). This proposition intends to be built theoretically and practically using what Spiritists consider empirical evidence that has become available in the last few decades concerning the hypothesis of reincarnation (see Stevenson, 1977, 1997a, 1997b, 2000, 2001; Haraldsson, 1991, 2000, 2003; Tucker, 2005, 2008).

In collaboration with other researchers, Ian Stevenson, from the Division of Personality Studies at the University of Virginia, analyzed more than 2000 cases of children who had supposed memories of previous lives. The study targeted Asian, European, and American children who spontaneously told detailed stories about personalities already deceased. The methodology consisted of 1) verifying whether the information came to children otherwise than from a personal past memory; 2) verifying whether such personalities really existed by checking their certificates of death, autopsy reports, former relatives, and other evidences; 3) comparing data of these suggested spontaneous memories through behavioral analysis. Researchers then presented the following psychological characteristics (Stevenson 1997b):

- Nonacceptance of present existence by the child (rejection of his or her present family, culture, gender, social status);
- Present psychological traits belonging to previous life regarding gender, including homosexual behavior;
- Innate feelings towards relatives and others in the present life (love, hate, and so on);
- Nostalgia for previous life places and for previous life affective bonds;
- Innate phobias;
- Knowledge of specific games showing abilities or interests that were not learned or stimulated in the present life;
- Uncommon behaviors not belonging to present environment status such as racism, preference for types of food typical from where the previous life occurred, alcoholic tendencies, and so on;
- Birthmarks (not genetically explained) that correspond to the means of death of previous personality.

Spiritist Pedagogy takes these studies into account in order to consider children in a deeper way and to deal with this psychological heritage coming from previous lives. From this point of view, learning can be understood as the awakening of past skills.

In spite of the concept of reincarnation, Spiritist Pedagogy has principles and proposals that may be common to several other pedagogical theories because it comes from the same tradition which many contemporary pedagogies fit into, one that dates back to Comenius, Rousseau, and Pestalozzi. The founder of Spiritism, Hippolyte Léon Denizard Rivail (known as Allan Kardec), was himself an educator, a disciple of Johann Heinrich Pestalozzi. Principles such as education with an affective bond, education for autonomy, valuing the uniqueness of each human being—and therefore of each child, active education, and interdisciplinary learning proposals are examples of these connections with other pedagogies of the last 200 years.

Simultaneously, this pedagogical stream aims to strengthen this very tradition that considers human beings in an integral manner because the spiritual dimension of humankind has been lost in the 20th century. Piaget, for example, defined himself as an heir of Comenius, but discards any aspect of spirituality presented by the Czech educator, considering it to have a medieval resonance (Comenius, 1957). The psychoanalytic and Marxist visions of human beings disqualify spirituality. Freud thought any form of faith was a pathological illusion (Freud, 2010) and Marx considered religion a manner of alienation. Behaviorism considers all human development as social conditioning, with no autonomy and no spiritual awareness. All these theories have greatly influenced education in the 20th century.

The findings of Rousseau (1712–1778), defining the child as a developing being who needs respect for his or her child status to blossom healthily, were confirmed in the 20th century by psychologists of child development. But these researchers did not take into consideration Rousseau's idea that development would be intertwined with a divine essence, which manifests itself in human consciousness—as Rousseau proposes in his *Emile* (1967).

Pestalozzi (1746–1827), in turn, can be considered one of the pioneers of the pedagogy based in experimental observation of the child's nature (see Incontri, 1996), something that all his successors, among them Claparède, Piaget, and Vygotsky, have practiced in the 20th century. But after Pestalozzi, in the work of most of these authors, the articulation of these observations is divorced from any aspects of human transcendence. This concept was banished from education with the influence of Marxism, psychoanalysis, behaviorism, and more recently, by postmodern philosophy.

Spiritist Pedagogy wants to bring back recognition of the child's spiritual nature in an evidence-based practice and therefore proposes to resume a path in which the achievements of psychological and pedagogical research of past centuries could be open to the spiritual dimension of children and human beings. This openness should be made by moving the spiritual dimension from the assumption level to a consistent scientific ground. This proposition comes from Spiritism itself, as Kardec conceived it, in the 19th century. He thought of a possible integration of spirituality and empirical research, gathering science and philosophical articulation of knowledge with an ethical approach.

In line with other scholars in Brazil, who argue for a nonconfessional religious education in school, Spiritist Pedagogy works with interdisciplinary methods, critical thinking, the use of arts, and universal moral values, as well as the virtue models of great spiritual world leaders like Buddha, Jesus, Gandhi, Saint Francis of Assisi, Teresa of Calcutta, the Dalai Lama, and others. However, different from other points of views, and as a specific trait of Spiritist Pedagogy, students are seen as reincarnated beings whose spirituality can only be awakened and retrieved by spiritual education but which should nevertheless be seen as something rooted in human nature.

Since Spiritist Pedagogy is a new proposition, made from a new epistemology, it is under constant construction. It can present at this time some practical experiences accumulated in the last hundred years, such as the first school founded in 1907 by Eurípedes Barsanulfo in Minas Gerais (Bigheto, 2004); the more than 100 kindergarten schools spread throughout São Paulo from 1901 to 1919 (some of them still working) by Anália Franco (Christo & Lodi, 2012); the children's town built by Ney Lobo in the 1970s in Paraná (Incontri, 2006); the Pestalozzi Foundation in Franca (State of São Paulo), led by Tomás Novelino (Incontri, 2006), among others. More recently, beginning in 2005, the Brazilian Association of Spiritist Pedagogy (ABPE) in partnership with the University Santa Cecília (Universidade Santa Cecília—Santos, São Paulo) has offered postgraduate studies in Spiritist Pedagogy. Since 2011, ABPE has worked in partnership with Capemisa Social, a social organization which supports more than 200 educational NGOs in Brazil. The Brazilian Association of Spiritist Pedagogy is providing pedagogical guidance and didactic material for these NGOs. The impact of that action is still unknown.

Spiritist Pedagogy continues to present guiding principles for its practice and to search for a systematization of theories that takes into account the contemporary scientific discourse and the educational tradition in which it operates.

CONCLUSION

In a country where 97% of the citizens claim to believe in God (Data Folha, 2007) and where religion has strong historical roots, it seems difficult or almost impossible to have secular schools, where religion is never mentioned. Not to study or to discuss religion and spirituality in Brazilian schools would mean excluding a vital dimension of being human and an important source of moral values and cultural perspectives. Therefore, spiritual education plays an essential role in human development and in bringing justice, fraternity, and peace to society.

This is true, however, only if religion does not turn into a cause of fanaticism and violence and if spirituality is inspired by great leaders of all times, who teach love to all human beings and to all forms of life. When law, government, educational policies, teachers training courses, textbooks, and projects ensure that proselytism, intolerance, or discrimination do not take over, all ways of believing or not-believing may be respected and expressed in school and in society.

REFERENCES

Amaral, V.L. & Junqueira, S.R.A. (2010) Cursos de pós-graduação Lato sensu de ensino religioso no cenário brasileiro. [Graduate courses Lato sensu religious education in the Brazilian context]. *Caminhos,* Goiânia, v. 8, n. 2, p. 133–146.

Bigheto, A. C. (2004). *Eurípedes Barsanulfo, um educador de vanguarda na Primeira República*. [Eurípedes Barsanulfo, an avant-garde educator from the first republic]. Bragança Paulista: Editora Comenius.

Christo, E., & Lodi, S. (2012). *Anália Franco, a educadora e seu tempo*. [Anália Franco, the educator and her time]. Bragança Paulista: Editora Comenius.

Comenius, J. A. (1957). *Selections*. (Introduction by Jean Piaget). Paris/Lausanne: UNESCO.

Conselho Estadual de Educação. (2001). *Resolução de 27/7/2001 que regulamenta o Artigo 33 da Lei 9394/96*. [Resolution of 27.07.2001 which regulates Article 33 of Law 9394/96]. São Paulo: Author.

Conselho Nacional De Educação. (2006). *Diretrizes Curriculares Nacionais para o Curso de Graduação em Pedagogia, licenciatura*. [Curricular guidelines for bachelor's degree in Pedagogy]. RESOLUÇÃO CNE/CP No. 1, de 15 de maio de 2006.

Cunha, L. A. (2012). O estado do Rio de Janeiro e o ensino religioso na educação pública: a experiência dos municípios de Duque de Caxias e Petrópolis. [The state of Rio de Janeiro and religious teaching in public education: the experience of the counties Duque de Caxias and Petrópolis]. *Notandum, 28*, 17–21. Retrieved March 22, 2013, from http://www.hottopos.com/notand28.

Data Folha. (2007). País altera mapa da fé. [Brazil changes the map of faith]. Retrieved June 20, 2012, from http://datafolha.folha.uol.com.br/po/ver_po.php?session=446.

Donnet, D. (1986). La Réincarnation et la problématique de l'égo. *Revue Philosophique de Louvain, 84*(2), 229–241.

Fischmann, R. (2012). Inconstitucional: o ensino religioso em escolas públicas em questão. [Unconstitutional: teaching religion in public schools in question]. *Notandum, 28*, 5–16. Retrieved June 20, 2012, from http://www.hottopos.com/notand28.

Fonaper (2008). *Propostas de diretrizes curriculares nacionais para o curso de graduação em ciências da religião—Licenciatura em ensino religioso*. [Proposals for national curriculum guidelines for undergraduate degree in religious studies—BA in religious education]. Retrieved June 20, 2012, from http://www.fonaper.com.br.

Freire, P. (2011). *Pedagogia do oprimido*. [Pedagogy of the oppressed]. São Paulo: Paz e Terra.

Freud, S. (2010). *The future of an illusion*. New York/London: Norton.

Grassi, L. G. I. (2012). O ensino religioso nas escolas municipais de ensino fundamental no município de São José dos Campos. [The religion teaching in public elementary schools of São José dos Campos]. *Notandum, 28,* 45–52. Retrieved June 20, 2012, from http://www.hottopos.com/notand28.

Haraldsson, E. (1991). Children claiming past-life memories: Four cases in Sri Lanka. *Journal of Scientific Exploration, 5,* 233–261

Haraldsson, E. (2000). Birthmarks and claims of previous-life memories. *Journal of the Society for Psychical Research, 64,* 16–25.

Haraldsson, E. (2003). Children who speak of past-life experiences: Is there a psychological explanation? *Psychology and Psychotherapy: Theory Research and Practice, 76,* 55–67.

IBGE. Instituto Brasileiro de Geografia e Estatística. [Brazilian Institute of Geography and Statistics] (2010). *Censo 2010: população indígena é de 896,9 mil, tem 305 etnias e fala 274 idiomas.* [Census 2010: Indian population is 896,900, and has 305 ethnic groups speaking 274 languages]. Retrieved June 20, 2012, from http://www.ibge.gov.br.

Incontri, D. (1996). *Pestalozzi, educação e etica.* [Pestalozzi, education and ethic]. São Paulo: Scipione.

Incontri, D. (2006). *Pedagogia Espírita: um projeto brasileiro e suas raízes.* [Spiritist Pedagogy—A Brazilian project and its roots]. Bragança Paulista: Comenius.

Incontri, D., & Bigheto, A. C. (2003). O ensino inter-religioso, como fazer? [Inter-religious teaching, how to do it?] *Revista Mirandum, 15.* Retrieved June 20, 2012, from www.hottopos.com/mirand15/dora.htm.

Incontri, D., & Bigheto, A. C. (2004). *Todos os jeitos de crer* (Vols. 1–4). [All ways of believing]. São Paulo: Ed. Ática.

Incontri, D., & Bigheto, A. C. (2009). *Jeitos de crer* (Ensino Fundamental 1o. a 5o. Ano). [Ways of believing—Primary School 1–5 years]. São Paulo: Ática.

Incontri, D., & Bigheto, A. C. (2010). Educação e espiritualidade, quando, como e por quê? [Education and spirituality, when, how and why?] In D. Incontri (Ed.), *Educação e espiritualidade: interface e perspectivas* [Education and spirituality: interfaces and perspectives], pp. 414–422. Bragança Paulista: Comenius.

Junqueira, S. R. A. (2009). Ensino religioso na perspectiva da escola: uma identidade pedagógica. [Religious education in the perspective of the school: an educational identity]. *Interações—Cultura e Comunidade, 4,* 245–256. Retrieved June 20, 2012, from http://www.gper.com.br.

Medeiros, L. B. (2012). O ensino religioso na escola pública: o sistema municipal de ensino de Petrópolis. [The religion teaching in public school: the educational system of the county of Petrópolis]. *Notandum, 28,* 33–44. Retrieved June 20, 2012, from http://www.hottopos.com/notand28.

Molina, T. S. (2012). Ensino Religioso em Escolas Públicas de Salvador-BA: da catequese oficiosa ao catolicentrismo. [Religion Teaching in public schools of Salvador, Bahia: from unofficial catechesis to Catholic-centric proselitysm]. *Notandum, 28,* 53–66. Retrieved June 20, 2012, from http://www.hottopos.com/notand28.

Obeyesekere, G. (2002) *Imagining karma: Ethical transformation in Amerindian, Buddhist, and Greek rebirth.* Berkeley: University of California Press.

Pereira, J. H. V., & Nishimoto, M. M. (2012). Homogeneização religiosa, proselitismo e ameaças ao estado laico: ensino religioso em escolas públicas municipais de Mato Grosso do Sul. [Religious homogenization, proselytism and threats to the secular state: Religion teaching in public schools of Mato Grosso do Sul]. *Notandum, 28,* 81–90. Retrieved June 20, 2012, from http://www.hottopos.com/notand28.

Peres, J. F. P. (2012). Should psychotherapy consider reincarnation? *The Journal of Nervous and Mental Disease, 200,* 174–179.

Peres, J. F. P., & Incontri, D. (2010). Implicações terapêuticas e pedagógicas da reencarnação. [Therapeutic and pedagogical implications of reincarnation]. In D. Incontri (Ed.), *Educação e Espiritualidade: interface e perspectivas* (Education and spirituality: Interfaces and perspectives), pp. 374–408. Bragança Paulista: Comenius.

Pires, J. H. (1985). *Pedagogia Espírita*. [Spiritist Pedagogy]. São Paulo: Paideia.

Rousseau, Jean-Jacques. (1967). *Œuvres complètes* (4 vols.). Bibliothèque la Pléiade. Paris: Éditions Gallimard.

Seffner, F., & Santos, R. B. (2012). Ensino Religioso no interior do Estado Laico: análise e reflexões a partir do estudo de caso em três municípios gauchos. [Religion teaching in a secular state: Analysis and reflections from the case study of three counties of Rio Grande do Sul]. *Notandum, 28,* 67–80. Retrieved June 20, 2012, from http://www.hottopos.com/notand28.

Stevenson, I. (1977). The explanatory value of the idea of reincarnation. *Journal of Nervous and Mental Disorders, 164,* 305–326.

Stevenson, I. (1997a). *Reincarnation and biology: A contribution to the etiology of birthmarks and birth defects* (2 vols.). Westport, Connecticut, Praeger Scientific Publishers.

Stevenson, I. (1997b). *Where reincarnation and biology intersect*. Westport, Connecticut, Praeger Scientific Publishers.

Stevenson, I. (2000). The phenomenon of claimed memories of previous lives: Possible interpretations and evidence. *Medical Hypotheses, 54,* 652–659.

Stevenson I. (2001). *Children who remember previous lives, a question of reincarnation*. Jefferson, NC: McFarland.

Tucker, J. B. (2005). *Life before life: A scientific investigation of children's memories of previous lives*. New York: St. Martin's Press.

Tucker, J. B. (2008). Children's reports of past-life memories: A review. *Explore (NY), 4,* 244–248.

23 Global Perspectives and Contexts for Spirituality in Education

Jacqueline Watson, Marian de Souza and Ann Trousdale

INTRODUCTION

The various contributors to this book have provided insights into historic, political, religious and cultural influences that have shaped the relationship between spirituality and education in their countries. In this final chapter we have made an analysis of their contributions to provide some general statements about the place of spirituality in education globally today.

The chapter reflects the structure of the book as a whole and has three parts; we found this to be the most suitable way to address the complexity of the narrative from different parts of the world. Finally, some conclusions are offered as a result of our analysis. We hope these conclusions, and the book as a whole, will extend the conversation about spirituality and education and be helpful both to researchers in this field and to educationalists generally.

EUROPE AND ISRAEL

In many countries in Europe, although not all, religious education (RE) is an accepted part of the public school system, and this is also true of Israel. All the authors who contributed to this section of the book discussed spirituality largely in the context of state (secular and/or religious) school systems where religious education is compulsory. It is not surprising then that most, though not all, of these authors make a strong correlation between spirituality and the school subject of religious education. As can be seen in these chapters, religious education is often influenced by a particular denomination of Christianity, but pupils are given options to study other faiths or secular beliefs, or, as in the UK, are presented with a form of religious education introducing them to a number of religions or worldviews—including Humanism in England and Wales.

Each author has concern for the spirituality of children and young people. The authors from Flanders (Belgium), Malta, Finland and Israel give close attention to religious education because this is a *central* way in which spirituality is addressed in education in these countries. In the UK and the Republic of Ireland, however, recent law and educational policy have required schools to develop the spirituality of children and young people within the curriculum as a whole and not just in religious education.

Spirituality across the Whole Curriculum

In the UK and Ireland, the law requires that spirituality is addressed across the whole curriculum of all schools (secular and religious). Best, in his detailed examination of the place of spirituality in education in the UK, shows how, especially in England and Wales, Scotland and, to a lesser extent, Northern Ireland, spirituality is not equated solely with religious education. He makes clear that 'spiritual education' is not 'religious education', but he also points out that, nonetheless, this is a "tacit assumption for many people, and for most schools [in the UK] until at least the 1980s" when an explicitly cross-curricular approach to spirituality was introduced by the 1988 Education Act. O'Higgins Norman and Renehan explain that, in Ireland, the 1998 Education Act introduced for the first time the notion that spirituality was not exclusively about "the acquisition of religious knowledge" and, importantly, gave "official recognition by the state that spiritual development and Religious Education are separate concepts and activities in schooling."

Defining 'Spirituality'

Best, along with Adams, discusses the challenges of disengaging spirituality from religion, and he devotes some space to discussing the debate this has generated, especially in the UK, about defining spirituality for a cross-curricular approach to spiritual development. Best refers to Terence McLaughlin's (2003) distinction between religiously 'tethered' and 'un-tethered' spirituality, and explores how a broadening of what is meant by spirituality in the context of education has driven much discussion and debate, in the UK but also globally. Adams continues with this theme by focusing on the unusual, or special situation in England, where secular state schools are advantaged by being legally obliged to give attention to children's spirituality, but where there is an attendant lack of confidence about what this means in the two-thirds of schools "which have no religious affiliation." O'Higgins Norman and Renehan celebrate the recognition of spirituality as a whole school matter because of the new possibilities this opens up for children and young people to "understand and learn how to live life with concern for others, to solve issues related to global perspectives, to contribute to society and experience a sense of belonging to that society." While there may be variation in what individual educationalists mean by 'spirituality', Best concludes that, nonetheless, they share fundamental values.

While there is great variety in the kinds of experiences which are labelled 'spiritual' by different groups, there are some (such as those which often happen between adults and children) which seem to me to epitomise what it is to be fully human, fully alive, and wholly at-one with another. It is what it is to love and be loved. To facilitate the development of a capacity for such experiences should surely be a fundamental purpose of education.

Spirituality and Religious Education

While educational policy in the UK and Ireland recognises spirituality as a whole school issue, a significant focus of all the contributions to this section is the school subject of religious education. The contributions from Malta, Belgium, Finland and Israel in particular present spirituality as a means to transforming religious education for the 21st century.

The authors from Malta, Belgium, Finland and Israel share a view that a 'weak confessional' approach to religious education may best encourage spiritual sensitivity. In Israel, Katz has used instruments to measure and compare children and young people's spirituality in the three different types of Jewish schools in Israel and was able to use statistical data to suggest that "education for the enhancement of spirituality among students seems to be better served by an integrative approach to religious education that promotes a combination of faith-based (religious values) and knowledge-based (humanistic values) religious education." Current policy suggests this would not be acceptable in the context of publicly funded schools in the UK, although recent government policies are strengthening and increasing publicly funded faith-based schools in parts of the UK, which raises new issues as discussed by Ron Best.

Spiritually Reconceptualising Religious Education and Education Generally

Whatever the specific curriculum focus of the authors in this section, all would, to some degree, characterise spirituality as both a spiritual transformation of religious education *and* of education in general. Their discussions of the potential and actual spiritual transformation of religious education, and education more broadly, is contextualised in and driven by the same social changes brought about by immigration and diversity, secularism, individualism and a move toward post-secularism, and issues around children's rights.

Religious Diversity

Authors agree that a strong driver of change to a more spiritual form of religious education is the recognition that we must now develop an openness to difference, partly because we all need to be more understanding in a diverse global context. In response to diversity, Dillen describes how, in Flanders, a small number of Catholic parents and leaders want to strengthen the Catholic identity of their schools through reconfessionalisation. However, she says, the larger proportion of parents "would prefer a form of 'recontextualization', a renewed thinking about what Catholicism can mean when it is accompanied by an openness toward individuals' beliefs and toward plurality in society in general," and is "focused on an open dialogue with other religions."

Secularisation, Individualism and Post-Secularism

At the same time, while Belgium, Ireland and Malta are historically strong Catholic countries, and Finland strongly Lutheran, authors describe how, in each country, there has been a gradual move away from the Church in recent decades. They describe a lack of confidence in the Church's ability to address people's concerns, and a lack of confidence in parents to bring up their children within the religion. Children and young people are therefore increasingly brought up within a more secular and individualistic culture. Adams, like Tirri and Ubani, also points out that contemporary spirituality—or religiosity—is changing because of a growing interest in a range of novel and individualised, sometimes eclectic or hybrid worldviews, including New Age spiritualities.

It has been argued that, in recent decades, Western societies have been transformed from secular to post-secular societies, with a new interest in inviting religiosity back into the public sphere (see especially Habermas, 2010; Habermas, Brieskorn, Reder, Ricken & Schmidt, 2011; see also Watson, 2012). The interest in spirituality appears to be part of that post-secular landscape in many countries. "[P]ost-secularity represents a discursive mode of religiosity," where increasing numbers of people are calling themselves spiritual rather than religious because of a reluctance to commit, or submit, to authorities, including traditional religions. As a result, there is a need to place greater emphasis on spirituality in education and to move away from traditional doctrinal religious education.

Children's and Young People's Rights and Voices

Adams and Gellel also point to educational change being driven by the United Nations Convention on the Rights of the Child (United Nations, 2001) and by the UNESCO Delors Report (Delors, 1996) which established that education should address spiritual development. If adults are to fully understand children's spirituality, it is essential that children's voices are heard in the debate and, Adams says, "incumbent upon us all to give children the opportunity to develop resilience against those who seek to ridicule or dismiss what is at the very heart of being human—so that they may flourish themselves". In Ireland, O'Higgins Norman and Renehan refer to several reports into child abuse which have raised issues around children's rights and generated special concern for children's healing, wholeness and wellbeing. For Dillen, a spiritual religious education is one which recognises the competencies of children because "children are often much more competent than we believe." And Tirri and Ubani recognise the novelty and positivity of young people's spiritual responsiveness to today's social concerns.

> This new generation also wants to act in ways that promote peace and human rights. Understanding spirituality as an expression of post-secular religiosity gives more room for young adults to participate in communicative actions concerning religion. This promotes discursive religiousness in the spirit of Habermas, in which a plurality of religious beliefs and practices are acknowledged and a dialogical and interreligious approach advocated.

Spirituality, Pedagogy and Teachers

Globally, recent instrumental approaches to education have given less attention to spiritual values and placed an emphasis on competition, individualism and consumerism. Authors in this section—and in the book more generally—point to numerous problems associated with this approach which often conflict with spiritual values and spiritual education. Gellel argues that "the fragmentation of knowledge and a labour market–oriented education have led to utilitarian curricula that leave little or no space for spiritual education"; O'Higgins Norman and Renehan argue this generates an educational environment where teachers are "reducing the time and space available to develop and model personal and empathetic relationships with their pupils." For many of the authors in this section, a spiritual approach to religious education and education more broadly embraces many of the principles and values of progressive education. However, and as several authors in this section acknowledge, this dialogical, hermeneutic and democratic approach to education—whether in religious education or the wider curriculum—is challenging for educators. Several contributors point to a need for changes to teacher education, and Adams places particular attention on this issue in relation to higher education.

A spiritual education, understood in this way, acknowledges the competencies of children or young people, their ability and wish to contribute their voices to discussion, and the need, therefore, for both knowledge and for the teacher to be responsive to young people's individual perspectives. Knowledge must be presented with a more hermeneutic or interpretative focus, and teachers must recognise they no longer have complete control and power over children, and need to be willing to listen. Dillen refers to "a dialogical approach, where it is not the teacher/catechist who knows everything, but where the interpretation of children and exchanges in the group are stimulated." For Gellel, a spiritual religious education is "a less doctrinally based approach to RE . . . [and] is not understood as religious learning but as a contribution towards meaning-making." Gellel and Dillen are keen to emphasise, however, that spiritual religious education continues to require religious content, because "communication can only be stimulated when it is centred on something—which may however be interpreted in various ways."

Gellel points out that education is very dependent on the approach the teacher takes, and O'Higgins Norman and Renehan refer to the need for a new approach to teacher training that develops empathy for healing, integration and wholeness. They argue for a "democratic process of education" and also suggest it is "essential that those who 'teach' spiritual development have experienced spiritual growth themselves."

AUSTRALASIA

The authors from the Australasian section of this book have revealed a variety of concepts and issues linked to the role of spirituality in both culture and education. They have identified the links between religion and spirituality, and in some instances they have shown how, from some perspectives, the two remain almost inseparable. This is particularly obvious in countries with a colonial history (for instance, Australia, Hong Kong and Singapore). Nevertheless, Aotearoa New Zealand, which also shares a colonial history, offers another point of view. Arguably, this may relate to the fact that Maori culture has a distinct place in New Zealand society. In other words, the dominant colonial culture, Christianity, and its particular interpretation of spirituality within a colonial setting has been blended with an indigenous culture from which new understandings and applications have emerged.

The countries in this section include China, Bhutan, Thailand, Singapore, Japan, Australia and Aotearoa New Zealand, and the authors provide insights from different levels of education—early childhood, primary and secondary. Despite the vast differences between these regions and their cultures and histories, many shared elements emerge in the discussions. In this overview, the following aspects are examined:

- the concept of spirituality and how it may be interpreted within a religious, cultural and educational framework;
- pedagogical approaches that recognise spirituality in education;
- the role of politics in determining whether spirituality is addressed in education.

These three facets provide a framework for understanding how different perspectives have shaped the way spirituality and education have operated in the Australasian region.

The Concept of Spirituality

Over the past 50 years for many in the West, discussions of spirituality were, more or less, restricted to Christian theological frameworks (Principe, 1983). Carrette and King noted that Principe's attempts to define spirituality derived from Christian thinking and did not explore influential Eastern teachings and traditions, an important consideration for this section of the book. Given the large movements of people over the past few decades, Eastern and Western religious and cultural philosophies, traditions and practices have, for the first time, found themselves in close encounter with one another in many countries. This has spawned a series of initiatives that encompass interreligious, interfaith and interspiritual movements[1] and this has become a feature in contemporary education. The chapters in this section, then, demonstrate the desire of many to encourage their students to seek understanding, empathy and wisdom from belief systems other than their own which may encourage them to be accepting and understanding of people who are different.

Traditionally, there has been recognition in most cultures that religion has a place in society, whether that place is seen as something foundational to the society as a whole (for instance, in some Middle Eastern and Eastern countries) or whether it is one where religion is restricted to the private sphere of individuals' lives (for instance in many secular societies, like Australia and New Zealand). Spirituality, on the other hand, has remained a fairly ambiguous concept, often used interchangeably with religion. In the past two decades, as the distinction between spirituality and religion has been identified, examined and acknowledged (for instance, de Souza, 2003; Hay with Nye, 1998/2006; Tacey, 2003) there has been ongoing confusion about what the concept may mean and this may be linked directly to the multiple interpretations arrived at.

For instance, it is interesting to note the different perceptions about spirituality, religion and education in relation to countries with a colonial heritage in comparison to Bhutan, Thailand and Japan, which were independent kingdoms. The influence of colonialism led to religion and religious education being perceived and treated as belonging to the private realm in society. Accordingly, education in a particular faith tradition has been excluded from state school curricula but sometimes, as discussed in Tan and Zhang's chapter on Singapore, a phenomenological approach to studying different religions may be offered where all religions are given equal emphasis. Buddhist education, on the other hand, is seen as something foundational to Thai and Bhutanese societies. Noa Jones and Michael Jones have both shown how in Bhutan and Thailand, respectively, Buddhist teachings have played a significant role in education. As Michael Jones points out, "Thais interpret and express their Buddhist values and beliefs in everyday living." Similarly, Noa Jones asserts that Buddhist values are implicit in Bhutanese culture. It would seem, then, that in such contexts, when spirituality in education is linked to Buddhist teachings and practices, such teachings and practices are a way of life for Thai and Bhutanese people. In other words, such education is not confined to a particular aspect of life, the religious aspect, but it incorporates learning that applies to all areas of life, for and in the everyday.

This holistic view of spirituality is also apparent in Nakagawa's discussion of traditional Japanese spirituality. Recalling the religious history of Japan, Nakagawa investigates the influence of Shintoism, Buddhism, Confucianism and Taoism on education. He claims that Buddhist philosophy and practice was the most influential since it was the state religion at one time and was instrumental in developing Japanese spirituality. As well, Confucianism provided a moral, ethical and political foundation with Taoist philosophy offering spiritual practices for healing and wellness. Once again we see a close link between religion and spirituality which provide the essence for everyday living.

The holistic nature of spirituality is also identified in Fraser's chapter on Maori spirituality in Aotearoa New Zealand and this is affirmed by Bone. Both authors identify that spirituality is about a strong sense of connectedness to the land which generates an inbuilt sense of belonging and responsibility. According to Fraser, spirituality permeates the daily lives of Maori people and it is important for their sense of wellbeing. Bone calls this an 'everyday spirituality' and claims that it is an "orientation to life [which] . . . heralds the mind, body, and spirit connections and connectedness of society, culture and nature in the ways we come to know ourselves and our worlds."

Fraser observes that the New Zealand government used to acknowledge the importance of Maori culture so that in a secular public school system, spirituality had been part of the curriculum since it was named in the education policy statement in 1937. Despite this long history of spirituality and education, in particular at the level of early childhood education where spirituality was articulated and addressed in policy documents in the mid-1990s, the most recent education document from 2007 has failed to mention the word. Fraser suggests that this may result in Maori students being disenfranchised since there is much evidence internationally to show that indigenous people fare badly in colonised countries.

It is also significant to note that in Thailand and Bhutan, education moved away from spirituality once their countries were influenced by a Western education system which emphasised cognitive learning and assessment or by a Western media that promoted a lifestyle driven by consumerism. Michael Jones makes an interesting observation that the modes of learning in cultures that are print oriented lead to dominance on cognitive learning as compared to those methods that have arisen from oral traditions where a contemplative approach to education ensures that affective and spiritual learning are given attention. The print-oriented mode of learning would certainly apply to most Western education systems and may explain the long-standing concentration on the attainment of knowledge and skills.

For many contemporary Japanese, a modern system of education was introduced after World War II and religion was promptly excluded from the curriculum. In response to a powerful media, materialistic values have overtaken the place that religion once held. Nonetheless, many people may still resort to Buddhist practices in their search for spirituality although moral learning in the form of values education is offered in schools and compassion, caring for nature, reverence for life and a sense of awe toward the sacred is facilitated.

Influences of a Colonial Culture on Concepts of Spirituality, Religion and Education

Three authors, Rossiter from Australia and Tan and Zhang from Singapore, discuss spiritual education mostly in the context of religious education and this may, in part, be related to the influences of a colonial history. Both chapters begin by discussing religious and values education in Australia (Rossiter) and Singapore and Hong Kong (Tan and Zhang), respectively. Speaking specifically from the field of Catholic education, Rossiter claims that, historically, attention to the spiritual and moral dimension of the curriculum has resided in religious education but, more recently in both religious and secular schools, there are programs that address personal and values education. Rossiter asserts that these are examples of a nonreligious spirituality in education. The life-encompassing spirituality which is reflected in Eastern thinking is not obvious in Rossiter's discussion.

Speaking out of a different context, Tan and Zhang take care to describe the perceived differences between religious and spiritual education at the beginning of their chapter. They present a comparative study of spirituality and religious education in Singapore and Hong Kong and make the point that the colonial influences both countries shared resulted in the intention to keep religious conversion and instruction out of the education system. However, given the multicultural nature of Singaporean society today, Character and Citizenship Education is offered where the aim is to build students' character and to cultivate them to be responsible citizens. It also focuses on the promotion of racial and religious harmony which will lead to social cohesion and accord. Implicit in these aims are tolerance, acceptance, inclusion, empathy and compassion, all spiritual traits, and there is also an underlying aim to unite religiously diverse students by highlighting universal moral values which are shared by the major faith traditions that exist in Singapore.

Tan and Zhang's discussion of the situation in Hong Kong shows a different process where over the past decade, spirituality has entered the educational discourse at the level of government and the level of classroom practitioners. Here we find spirituality linked to health and wellbeing as well as moral learning although there is little consistency in the development of moral education programs since they are often linked to the teachings of different religious traditions. The authors conclude that any spiritualising of education in both countries tends to be derived from religious and moral education and they argue that more needs to be done in spiritualising education rather than limiting it to an understanding of religious traditions and teachings. Clearly, the situations in Singapore and Hong Kong reflect a point made by Rossiter that there is a gap between theory and practice in spirituality and education.

Pedagogical Approaches to Address the Spiritual Dimension of Learning across the Curriculum

Some of the authors have offered discussions on pedagogical theory and practice in spirituality and education. Hyde notes that recent policy documents in Australia include the words 'spiritual' and 'spirituality' alongside the physical, social, emotional, spiritual, creative, cognitive and linguistic aspects of learning—thereby indicating that spirituality is being recognised as one element among many that compose the human person. Drawing on his research, he offers a particular pedagogical strategy—the recognition and application of learning dispositions—which is a way of identifying and addressing spiritual characteristics.

Another approach from the four Chinese societies or political regions where there is an attempt to address spirituality in education is presented by Ngar-sze Lau–a program called Life Education. However, the differences apparent between the histories, the religions and the cultures of these four Chinese societies have meant that there is little consistency in their curriculum offerings. Thus, Life Education is part of the formal curriculum in Taiwan and Mainland China but remains part of the informal curriculum in Hong Kong and Macau. With their respective colonial histories, both Hong Kong and Macau have religious schools which attend to spirituality as part of their religious and moral education programs. This could be why Life Education is not yet part of the formal curriculum.

Life Education is about understanding life, valuing life, appreciating life and respecting life. Subthemes are Ultimate Concerns, Ethics, and Personality and Relationships. The aim of the program is to enhance the ability of students to live well in society and therefore may be perceived as one form of spirituality in education.

Finally, Rossiter describes a pedagogy to study spirituality which lends itself to a "critical, inquiring, research-oriented, student-centred pedagogy in which the students themselves investigate contemporary spiritual and moral issues." This approach in itself is indicative of the perspective of the author where religious and spiritual education are used interchangeably. It is clearly a cognitive-driven approach to the study of spirituality where spirituality has become the object of study. Thus Rossiter's approach does not focus on a recognition that spirituality is an innate characteristic of all sentient beings which requires that environments, resources and activities should be developed to address and nurture the spirituality of the learner.

Undoubtedly, if the goal of education is to educate the whole child, that is, where all the elements that compose the child are identified and provided for, it must necessarily attend to the spiritual dimension—that is, the relational character of the child, the connectedness the child experiences to everything outside itself along with the thoughts, emotions, behaviours, attitudes and actions that are generated by this experience of connectedness. To achieve this, education needs to be extended past a concern that restricts learning to the cognitive domain and incorporate strategies that address and enhance affective and spiritual learning.

Politics, Spirituality and Education

Throughout the chapters in this section, the intervention by governing bodies as to whether spirituality will have a role in education becomes quite evident. All the authors have explored the historical antecedents of the education offered in their respective countries in terms of the role of religious education and spirituality. From having spirituality as a vital part of education (Aotearoa New Zealand, Bhutan, Japan, Thailand), to having religious education offered in faith-based schools (Australia and Hong Kong), to having a study of religion program offered in state schools (Singapore and Australia) to having no religious education (Mainland China and Taiwan), we have witnessed through their discussions, a move backwards and forwards, where religion and/or spirituality has or has not played a role in state education systems.

The most recent movement in the past decade has been toward the recognition of spirituality as a framework distinct from but linked to religion that needs to be identified and addressed. In most cases, this has come about in response to the problems and crises that appear to be growing amongst the children and young people in many countries where materialistic and consumerist values and a highly competitive culture have been dominating factors in the lives of children and young people, causing them much stress and anxiety. Different authors have referred to statistics showing the rise of health and addiction problems as well as other predicaments which young people face. Alongside these issues exists the declining influence of religious teachings and, given the compartmentalisation of religion, spirituality and education, the acute lack of understanding about moral and spiritual values amongst the young. These things have been noted and each author across the different countries and regions has called for a response that comprehends the role of spirituality in education.

To sum up, these authors clearly show that indigenous and traditional Eastern spirituality has encompassed daily lives with corresponding thinking, behaviour and actions. They have observed that the influences of Western concepts of compartmentalisation, materialism and consumerism have impacted on the spirituality of young people, arguing persuasively that a return to spirituality in education which is generated by religious and secular philosophy and practices will be beneficial for their students and for the future of their societies. They have also noted that significant problems have emerged amongst the young people in each of their countries, problems relating to health, drug abuse, overcompetitiveness in education and in careers, and the breakdown of traditional values. They each believe that the most valuable response to these problems will be to rediscover spirituality in education. In particular, they mention the importance of learning from wisdom traditions, developing compassion and understanding multicultural issues which, they argue, are important for the flourishing of both the individual and the community/society in today's pluralistic world.

Moving from countries where indigenous and certain religious teachings and practices have been influential to those countries where the curriculum is cognitively driven and assessment focused, these authors offer ideas and research findings that will inform and enhance efforts to combine spirituality and education as a potent force which will combat the challenges confronting the contemporary world in respect to the problems and crises threatening their young people. Equally important is the notion that spirituality in education promotes a position that affirms pluralism which is a significant benefit in societies that have become religiously and culturally diverse.

THE AMERICAS

Perspectives on spirituality and education from the Americas reflect historic, political, religious and cultural realities very different from those in other parts of the world. In neither Canada nor the United States is there a national policy mandating religious or spiritual education; indeed, in the United States any attempt to acknowledge or introduce spirituality into the classroom puts a teacher or school system at risk of costly legal reprisal. While the Brazilian constitution makes a provision for religious tolerance in public schools, it is largely ignored by the individual states. The contributors to the Americas section of the book do not write from mainstream—or even publicly accepted—policy or practice, but from the margins, as pioneers in the field of spirituality and education in their respective countries, working against strong contrary currents in an effort to bring about what change they can, given the challenges they face.

As varied as the historic, political, religious and cultural contexts of the three American nations are, there emerge common challenges and impediments to effecting a sustainable approach to spirituality in education. First, of course, is the lack of any overarching national policy to support spiritual education. Although there do exist individual or local initiatives aimed at enhancing teachers' awareness of and sensitivity to their own and their students' spiritual lives, contributors from all three nations note a need for informed, intentional professional preparation in the field. In the public classrooms, nonholistic, reductive approaches to teaching that emphasise standardised testing as evidence of learning are cited as further impediments to nurturing children's and young people's spiritual lives. These issues are made more difficult in the United States and Brazil by the reluctance of historically dominant religious groups to relinquish control of public schooling.

These factors play into themes common to other nations, including the historic or lingering effects of colonisation, transitions from a religious to a secular perspective in education, the influence of an increasingly diverse population and challenges in addressing public school policy and practice.

Effects of Colonisation

The three American nations represented in this book share a history of European colonisation dating from the late 15th century C.E. In many parts of the world 500 years is recent history, but in terms of accessible written records, it comprises the known history of the Americas. That half-millennium has been one of extraordinary growth and change politically, culturally, racially, ethnically, religiously and spiritually, affecting educational practices in varied and profound ways, but the effects of European colonisation linger. One of those effects was the colonisers' Christian beliefs systems which marginalised other religious and spiritual traditions and ultimately influenced public education.

Canada, the northernmost of the American nations, was colonised by both England and France. While some provinces give greater evidence of French cultural roots and others of British, Canada has evolved from a bicultural, bilingual nation founded on Judeo-Christian beliefs to a land of considerable cultural diversity, brought about by immigration from Asia and from other European countries as well as by a revival of respect for aboriginal cultures.

The colonial history of the United States has had a complex effect on the political and religious nature of the nation and its schools. Religious persecution in England and in the original colonies themselves contributed to a firm separation of the powers of state and religion in the U.S. Constitution, but the effects of the predominantly Protestant Christian beliefs of the British colonisers was not challenged in public schools until the mid-20th century.

Effects of colonisation linger in Brazil, particularly in regard to the spiritual and religious dimensions of public schooling. Brazil attracted early Portuguese colonists who brought with them a Roman Catholic belief system, the influence of which has remained strong for 500 years.

Emerging from Religious to Secular: A Political Struggle

The effects of religious education and its relationship with spiritual education differ among the American nations represented here. In various ways each nation is struggling to emerge from its history as a predominantly Christian nation to becoming a secular society with secular school systems. Canada is the least religious of the three nations (Putnam & Campbell, 2010), and the formerly dominant Judeo-Christian perspective has given way to a secular approach in the schools, although in some provinces there is a revival of interest in First Nations' spirituality. In the United States, the dominance of Protestant Christianity in public schools has, since the mid-20th century, been ruled unconstitutional by the Supreme Court. While the Constitution does not prohibit teaching *about* religion, many teachers and school systems think the topic of religion must be avoided altogether. At the same time there remain efforts from rather polarised perspectives to bring some attention to religion and to spirituality into the public school classroom. From the religious right come efforts to teach a literal interpretation of the biblical version of Creation alongside—or replacing—evolution in the science curriculum; from the progressive end of the spectrum come efforts to introduce Eastern spiritual practices devoid of professed religious beliefs into the schools. Such efforts remain local in nature and always run the risk of being challenged in courts of law.

Brazil is the most religious of the three nations in this section (Putnam & Campbell, 2010), with 73.6% of its population claiming Catholic beliefs (Brazil Demographic Profile, 2013). Despite the Brazilian Constitution's calling for a pluralistic and nonproselytising approach to religion in the public schools, the influence both of Catholic and, more recently, Protestant Pentecostal voices persist. In many Brazilian public schools, confessional Christian religious education is the sole contribution to spiritual education. In short, because of differing circumstances, spiritual education as distinct from religious education has yet to gain recognition and support on national levels in Canada, the U.S. and Brazil.

The very different political systems of the three American nations offer quite different dynamics between federal and local authority over public schools and, consequently, over practices regarding spirituality and education. In Canada, responsibility for educational policy rests with the provinces and territorial governments rather than with a central governing authority. In the United States, local school policies are set by local and state governments but are influenced by a national Department of Education and are subject to U.S. Supreme Court decisions. In Brazil, enforcement of provisions for spiritual and religious tolerance stated in the Brazilian Constitution rests with each state legislature and thus depends upon local legislation and enforcement. The one commonality among the three nations is the fact that neither state nor national governmental bodies have adopted an educational policy regarding spirituality.

Effects of Diversity

Issues of diversity have affected North and South American schooling in significant but different ways. The effects of its vast and varied terrain contribute to the diversity that is found in Canadian educational systems. The second-largest national landmass on the globe, Canada extends from the Atlantic to the Pacific Ocean, from Arctic regions to the northern boundaries of the United States. This huge nation is divided into ten provinces and three territories, each characterised by different population demographics, different economic concerns, and each with its own public school system. In some, but not all provinces, there are concerted efforts to recover the spiritual traditions of displaced indigenous peoples.

Despite the diversity of the Canadian population, Dallaire notes commonly held values which characterise what he describes as a Canadian civic soul: appreciation for the natural world, inclusion, openness, justice, compassion and the ability to compromise. Dallaire makes a case for educating for civic spirituality based upon this Canadian soul, an education which would include a unifying myth that would respect the multifaith and secular horizons of meaning among today's Canadians.

The cultural and ethnic diversity of the U.S. is particularly reflected in the chapters by Trousdale, London and Tisdell. London's chapter emphasises the growing Latino population and its emergence into the field of education, but his focus is not on the students' cultural and ethnic backgrounds but rather on their spiritual formation as they progress through his program in Holistic and Integrative Education. Notably, many of his students are the first generation in their families to attend college.

Tisdell's chapter goes more deeply into the interplay of culture, gender, religion and sexuality in the spiritual lives of female educators. She focuses on the interrelatedness of the participants' spiritual journeys toward wisdom, their significant spiritual experiences, how their spirituality relates to their cultural identities and how spirituality relates to their teaching. In the follow-up phase of a study ten years later, Tisdell found that the participants' narratives "were characterized by spiraling back, settling into their lives now, and going deeper into their spirituality . . . as they began to make new meaning." The core theme Tisdell found was that "*we always spiral back* to make further meaning of memory of events '*with life in them still*'." She notes that her participants often drew on the wisdom of their own cultural traditions as well as the wisdom traditions of other cultures, ending her chapter with the hope that the collective insights we gain will result in "culturally responsive transformative educational experiences for our students that lead to greater wisdom for all of us."

Diversity in Brazil bears a rather different face from either Canada or the U.S. While there is a slight majority of European ancestry among the Brazilian population (53.7%), more than a third (38.5 %) are of mixed ethnicity (Brazil Demographic Profile, 2013). With almost three-quarters of its population claiming the Roman Catholic faith, public schools are still largely influenced by Roman Catholic beliefs despite the Brazilian Constitution's call for interreligious teaching. In this nation, the aboriginal peoples, including 305 Indian ethnic groups speaking 274 languages, remain quite isolated from the mainstream population.

Critique of Modernism

A critique of modernist approaches to education emerges from all three nations, although postmodernist philosophy alone is not seen as the panacea. Dallaire, London, Hart and Incontri point to the limitations of rationalist, empirical approaches to education in which the child is seen as a passive recipient of a preordained set of knowledge, but they offer a variety of approaches that they consider more salutary in regards to the spirit of the child. Dallaire acknowledges the contributions postmodernism has made to education in Canada but points to its limitations as well, particularly in its distrust of grand narratives, which could give expression to a unifying myth.

London's approach to teaching in his masters-level program in the United States is informed by constructivist postmodern pedagogy combined with a transformative approach to learning and by identifying a spiritual perspective in education. He charts carefully the transformations his students experience as they pursue such a course of study.

Drawing from various fields, Hart calls for an epistemic recalibration of the relationship between knower, knowing and knowledge, a shift away from the objectification of knowledge and a fixation on standardised assessment to a contemplative approach. A contemplative approach ties together three dimensions central to both education and spirituality: knowledge by presence, empathic knowing or resonance, and the capacity for transcendence both internal and external, material and spiritual, geographic and economic. Such an approach complements "traditional forms of rational-empiricism and emphasis on information downloading that characterize conventional schooling. . . . . A contemplative approach does not take away from literacy and numeracy," he writes; "it deepens our ability to engage and thus understand information." Hart sees that it is through such a transformation of the central epistemological question that the cultivation of our humanity to its greatest potential will return to the centre of education.

From a Brazilian perspective, Incontri adds Paulo Freire's philosophical insights in arguing for a transformation of the view of schools as places where children are seen as passive recipients of knowledge to places where children can think freely, debate, make contact with and discuss different philosophical, political and religious points of view. Like Dallaire, she cautions against a postmodernist trend to equate "all speeches as mere narratives . . . emptying them of the possibility of truth . . . from which no ethical parameter can be proposed as universal."

To sum up, in none of the three American nations is there an overarching national policy regarding spirituality in the public school. Educationalists— teachers and researchers—who seek to promote attention to spirituality outside a religious frame do not work in social, political, religious or educational climates that support their work. The forces that impact spirituality in education are intense and often complex, presenting distinct challenges for those who have chosen to work in this field. Yet various contributors to this section offer visions of promise in this regard.

Dallaire sees hope for spirituality in Canadian education through the work of several university professors who offer courses on spirituality or include spiritual practices in their curricula. The recognition of a common Canadian soul can, Dallaire believes, lead to the development of a unifying myth, a 'grand narrative' with a particularly Canadian stamp.

In the U.S., Trousdale and Hart mention practices that have found traction on local levels in public school classrooms. Hart points out that many local initiatives are short-lived, offering instead a shift in the epistemological question that frames educational practice. London and Tisdell focus their attention on the spiritual lives of teachers in their graduate programs, with an aim toward affecting teachers' classroom practice thereby. Incontri describes a program implemented in some Brazilian schools that is interreligious in nature, aiming to develop in children a critical capacity, personal judgment and independence of mind while avoiding scepticism or relativism. She adds a potential component, Spiritist Pedagogy, which is unique to these pages.

FINAL CONCLUSIONS

The contributions to this book represent multiple perspectives on the relationship between spirituality and education around the world. The contributions do not represent all parts of the world, but there are sufficient perspectives to give a sense of the diverse ways in which policy and practice in relation to spirituality and education have been shaped by historical, political, religious and cultural contexts. While writers have demonstrated substantive differences in the way in which the relationship between spirituality and education has been developed in their different countries, there are commonalities in considering ways forward.

Many contributors refer to the changing nature of societies where diversity has become a prominent feature. This has led to the need for a different relationship between education and religiosity, and a focus on spirituality in education is seen as a way of recognising that the religious or worldview landscape is changing and complex. In some regions a movement away from religious content or practice has resulted in secularised school systems which make no provision for nurturing students' spirituality. In some countries, a continued correlation of spirituality with religion has made it difficult and challenging for a spiritual approach in education to flourish. In other countries, spirituality has been introduced to schools through new nonreligious subjects, such as life skills education. In regions where religion is included in public schools, spirituality has often had the greatest impact on the curriculum subject of religious education. In some countries, pre-existing religious education has been reconceptualised to include discussion of a wider range of worldviews, including in some cases nonreligious views. Some contributors suggest that a spiritual transformation of religious education extends beyond mere multifaith education, to recognise that a spiritual religious education enables children and young people to voice new and diverse spiritualities, through dialogue and hermeneutics.

In some regions, the spiritual dimensions of religions encompass everyday living to the extent that there is no clear boundary separating one from the other, spilling over into educational curriculum and practice. This is true in Buddhist nations and is also a feature where indigenous belief systems have been influential, as in New Zealand and Japan. In such situations there is a prevalent worldview that is holistic so that it becomes difficult to disentangle the various intertwining strands of culture, religion, spirituality and education. There appears, instead, to be a certain unity in consciousness that permeates all human activity in such regions.

Despite writing from diverse cultural, political and geographical regions, many of the writers identify the problems and challenges that their countries' children and young people face in highly competitive, performance-orientated, consumerist cultures. Their discussion of spirituality often forms a critique of performativity and consumer-driven society. Educationalists struggle with the logistics and pragmatics of trying to put the principles of spiritual education into practice within these cultures, but are driven by a concern for children's healing and wellbeing, and for enduring human values. As part of this critique, some authors take a special interest in indigenous spirituality's emphasis on connectedness to others and to the environment. There appears to be a consensus that addressing spirituality in education may be one way forward in promoting belonging and self-esteem, as well as tolerance and acceptance of diversity, which should lead to community wellbeing and social cohesion, and to human flourishing.

The contributors refer to research identifying particular pedagogical practices found useful in addressing the spiritual dimension of learning. There is a call across regions, cultures and societies for renewal in pedagogical approaches that incorporate a spiritual dimension, and these often embrace values associated with progressive education, such as learning through experience, engaging in dialogue with children and young people, and with notions of the whole child, holistic education and education for human flourishing. Incorporating spirituality represents a new approach to education, necessitating new and novel research and fundamental changes to teacher education. As Tirri and Ubani assert:

> We need new research instruments that are relevant for the new generation and which acknowledge the current ways of expressing religiosity. These new ways include taking quiet moments in the midst of everyday life, mystical and aesthetic experiences to complement rational thinking and the search for meaning and values in life.

NOTES

1. One classic example of this is the renewal of a global event—The Parliament of World Religions, which was first held in Chicago in 1893. The second Parliament was held exactly 100 years later, also in Chicago in 1993 and since then there have been other Parliaments held across the world, the last one in Melbourne, Australia, in 2009. For more information see http://www. parliamentofreligions.org. However, interreligious/interfaith and interspiritual movements are found at the local level in many countries. A Google search of 'interfaith' + 'Melbourne' alone report 429,000 websites.

REFERENCES

Brazil Demographic Profile. (2013). Retrieved June 13, 2013, from Index Mundi website, http://www.indexmundi.com/brazil/demographics_profile.html.

Delors, J. (1996). *Learning: The treasure within*. Report to UNESCO of The International Commission on Education for the Twenty-First Century. Paris: UNESCO Publishing.

de Souza, M. (2003). Contemporary influences on the spirituality of young people: Implications for education. *International Journal of Children's Spirituality, 18*(3), 269–279.

Habermas, J. (2010). *Between naturalism and religion*. Cambridge: Polity Press.

Habermas, J., Brieskorn, N., Reder, M., Ricken, F. & J. Schmidt (2011). *An awareness of what is missing: Faith and reason in a post-secular age*. Cambridge: Polity Press.

Hay, D., with Nye, R. (1998/2006). *The spirit of the child* (rev. ed.). London: Jessica Kingsley.

McLaughlin. T. H. (2003). Education, spirituality and the common school. In D. Carr & J. Haldane (Eds.), *Spirituality, philosophy and education* (pp. 185–199). London: RoutledgeFalmer.

Principe, W. (1983). Towards defining spirituality. *Sciences Religieuses/Studies in Religion, 12*, 127–141.

Putnam, R. D., & Campbell, D. E. (2010). *American grace: How religion divides and unites us*. New York: Simon and Schuster.

Tacey, D. (2003). *The spirituality revolution: The emergence of contemporary spirituality*. Sydney: HarperCollins.

United Nations. (2001). *Convention on the rights of the child. Appendix general comment 1 (2001): The aims of education.* Retrieved May 10, 2012, from http://www.unhchr.ch/tbs/doc.nsf/(symbol)/CRC.GC.2001.1.En?OpenDocument.

Watson, J. (2012). Religion, spirituality and state-funded schooling: Revisiting a fractured relationship with guidance from Habermas. *Journal for the Study of Spirituality, 2*(2), 186–202.

Contributors

DR KATE ADAMS

Reader in Education at Bishop Grosseteste University, Lincoln, UK

Kate Adam's research interests focus upon understanding childhood from children's perspectives, especially the spiritual dimension of their lives. She is interested in how children's spiritual voices often go unheard, particularly in the education system. Kate's most recent book is *Unseen Worlds: Looking through the Lens of Childhood*, published by Jessica Kingsley.

DR RON BEST

Emeritus Professor of Education, University of Roehampton, UK

Ron Best's interest in spiritual education dates from the early 1990s when spiritual, moral, social and cultural development (SMSC) became an issue for curriculum policy. He is interested in the connection between spirituality and the emotions, and the implications of faith schools for children's autonomy. He has researched, lectured and written about aspects of pastoral care and personal-social education for almost 40 years, most recently focusing on support for students who deliberately self-harm. He is a volunteer counsellor and a trustee of the Caspari Foundation which provides educational psychotherapy for children with learning difficulties based in the emotions.

JANE BONE, PHD

Monash University, Melbourne, Australia

Dr Jane Bone is involved in research in the area of early childhood education in Australia (and formerly in New Zealand). Her expertise is in holistic approaches to pedagogy, including research involving Steiner, Montessori and Reggio Emilia–based preschools. Her main research area explores spirituality and is internationally recognised. This research involves sensitive areas of research about values and beliefs. Jane has also published work about ethical approaches to research with young children. Her research contributes to wider understandings about the significance of early childhood education in terms of wellbeing and social justice.

MICHAEL DALLAIRE, EDD

Educator and Writer

Michael Dallaire is a Canadian educator and writer. In addition to undergraduate degrees in the humanities, theology and education, he holds a Masters of Arts in Theology from St. Paul University in Ottawa and a Doctorate in the Philosophy of Education from the University of Toronto. He served for 25 years as a chaplain in various locations, mostly within Ontario's Catholic education system. Michael currently lives in Vancouver, BC, and devotes his energy to educating for engaged spirituality, a spirituality that seeks to integrate the inner life with the building of just and sustainable civic communities. A member of the Canadian Academy of Independent Scholars, he is researching and writing on spirituality and hope. His most recent book, *Teaching with the Wind: Spirituality in Canadian Education*, was published in 2011.

DR MARIAN DE SOUZA

Australian Catholic University, Australia

Dr Marian de Souza is a Senior Lecturer at Australian Catholic University. Marian has published extensively about her research into the spirituality of young people and the implications for education in a globalised, pluralistic world and was the Coordinating Editor of the *International Handbook of the Religious, Moral and Spiritual Dimensions of Education* and the *International Handbook of Education for Spirituality, Care and Wellbeing*, published by Springer.

DR ANNEMIE DILLEN

Associate Professor in Practical Theology, Faculty of Theology and Religious Studies, KU Leuven, Belgium

The main themes in the research of **Annemie Dillen** are families in relation to Christian theology and ethics, children and spirituality, pastoral care and power issues. She is the Chair of the Academic Center for Practical Theology at the Catholic University Leuven, Belgium.

ASSOCIATE PROFESSOR DEBORAH FRASER

University of Waikato, New Zealand

Deborah is an Associate Professor who has taught in a range of inclusive and multicultural settings in New Zealand and the UK. Her research interests include curriculum integration, creativity and spirituality in state education. She is on the board of four journals and editor of two national texts. She has won a range of external grants including two Teaching-Learning Research Initiatives that highlight university-school partnerships in research.

DR ADRIAN-MARIO GELLEL

University of Malta

Adrian-Mario Gellel is a Senior Lecturer in Catechetic and Religious Education in the Department of Arts and Languages, and in the Department of Pastoral Theology, Liturgy and Canon Law at the University of Malta. His main areas of interest are Child and Adolescent Spirituality, Religious Education and Youth Ministry. Adrian is also actively involved in Ministry within the Maltese Archdiocese. Between 2006 and 2010 he was appointed as the National Coordinator for Religious Education in Schools for the Catholic Church and coordinated and led the publication of *Religious Education in Malta: Reflections by the Catholic Community*, the syllabus, and the Form 1 Religious Education scholastic textbook, *My Adventure*. He is currently a Board member of the Pastoral Formation Institute and was formerly a member of the Secretariat for Catechesis.

TOBIN HART, PHD

University of West Georgia, USA

Tobin Hart's research, writing and teaching live at the nexus of spirituality, psychology and education. He is especially interested in how we know, especially the knowing that integrates the analytic and intuitive, information and awe, quantity and quality. His recent books include *From Information to Transformation: Education for the Evolution of Consciousness* and *The Secret Spiritual World of Children*.

DR BRENDAN HYDE

Australian Catholic University, Melbourne, Australia

Brendan Hyde is a Senior Lecturer in Religious Education on the Melbourne campus of the Australian Catholic University, and the author of the book *Children and Spirituality: Searching for Meaning and Connectedness*

(Jessica Kingsley Publishers, London and Philadelphia). He has research interests in children's spirituality and in how a dispositional framework might nurture children's spirituality in educational contexts. He is a fellow of the Centre for the Theology of Childhood in Denver, Colorado, as well as a member of the Godly Play Australia Advisory Board. Presently, Brendan is a co-editor of the *International Journal of Children's Spirituality.*

DORA INCONTRI, PHD

Universidade Santa Cecilia, Santos SP, Brazil

Dora Incontri is Coordinator of Post-Graduation Courses at Universidade Santa Cecilia in Brazil. Her research focuses on spiritual education in Brazil, interreligious teaching, Spiritist Pedagogy, reincarnation and education. Her postdoctoral work was entitled *Ethic, Philosophy, Religions and Arts: An Interdisciplinary Project in Public School.*

DR MICHAEL ERNEST JONES

Michael Ernest Jones received his PhD from Indiana University-Bloomington majoring in Comparative International Education Policy with a minor in Intercultural Communications from the Intercultural Communication Institute, Oregon. Additionally, he was awarded a one-year Fulbright-Hays overseas grant to study spirituality in Thai alternative education. He has worked for more than 25 years in six countries in the fields of education, dispute resolution and human development. Most recently, he served as Chair of the PhD program at the Contemplative Education Center at Mahidol University, Thailand, where he created an international interdisciplinary PhD program designed to highlight the interdependency of the human condition and the fostering of transformational capacities.

NOA JONES

Lhomon Society, Bhutan

Noa Jones is a journalist and education coordinator. She often writes for *The New York Times, The Los Angeles Times, Body + Soul, Buddhadharma, Shambhala Sun*, and is currently a columnist for *Tricycle Magazine: The Buddhist Quarterly.* She has written several books including *Nature, Creativity, and Our Collective Future* (Palace Press, 2007) and *A Story in Bhutan,* about the film *Travellers and Magicians* (Prayer Flag Pictures, 2005). She edited *What Makes You Not a Buddhist* (Shambhala, 2006), for Dzongsar Khyentse Rinpoche. Since 2009, she has been volunteering for the Lhomon Society, coordinating teacher training and developing classroom materials and alternative curricula for Bhutanese educators.

PROFESSOR YAACOV J. KATZ

Senior Faculty Member at the School of Education, Bar-Ilan University, Israel

Yaacov Katz specializes in research in the fields of religious education and values, affective education and spirituality, and social attitudes in education especially with regard to attitudes toward the use of digital technology in learning and instruction. In his administrative capacities, Yaacov has served as Head of the School of Education at Bar-Ilan University and has also served as Chief Pedagogic Officer of the Israel Ministry of Education where he was responsible for all subject matter taught in the Israeli national school system.

NGAR-SZE ELSA LAU

Ngar-sze Lau has served as a Teaching Fellow at the Centre for Religious and Spirituality Education in the Hong Kong Institute of Education after having been a secondary school teacher of religious education for six years. She is interested in mindfulness education, spirituality, contemplative education, life education, values education and mental health. Apart from doing research on mindfulness and adolescents in Hong Kong as a pioneer, she has offered many mindfulness workshops for university students, in-service teachers and educators, as well as the general community. She is now a postgraduate student in Oxford.

ROBERT LONDON, EDD

Professor, California State University, San Bernardino, USA

Robert London is a Professor at California State University, San Bernardino and Program Coordinator for the MA in Holistic and Integrative Education, recognized internationally as an exemplar of transformative approaches to higher education. Bob also directs the Spirituality and Education Network and chairs the AERA Spirituality and Education Special Interest Group. His professional interests include integrating a spiritual perspective in education, our connection to nature from a spiritual perspective and research methodology consistent with a spiritual perspective.

PROFESSOR YOSHIHARU NAKAGAWA

Doshisha University in Kyoto, Japan

Professor Yoshiharu Nakagawa earned his PhD from the Ontario Institute for Studies in Education at the University of Toronto. His current interests include holistic education, Eastern philosophy and contemplative education. He is the author of the book *Education for Awakening: An*

Eastern Approach to Holistic Education (2000) and co-editor of the book *Nurturing Our Wholeness: Perspectives on Spirituality in Education* (2002). His contributions have appeared in *Nurturing Child and Adolescent Spirituality* (2006), *Cross-Cultural Studies in Curriculum* (2008), *International Handbook of Education for Spirituality, Care and Wellbeing* (2009), and *International Handbook of Inter-Religious Education* (2010).

DR JAMES O'HIGGINS NORMAN

Senior Lecturer and Chair of Graduate Teacher Education, School of Education Studies, Dublin City University, Ireland

James O'Higgins Norman's research is rooted in a sociological view of education and is concerned with the overall wellbeing of young people within the school system. He is co-editor of the *International Handbook on Education for Spirituality, Care and Wellbeing* (Springer, 2010) and is a member of the Centre for Spiritual Capital at All Hallows College in Dublin City University.

DR CAROLINE RENEHAN

Senior Lecturer and Head of Religious Studies and Religious Education, St Patrick's College, Dublin City University, Ireland

Caroline Renehan's long-term research interests include the interdisciplinary relationship between spirituality and theology and between spirituality and religious education in the context of primary and post-primary teacher education. Her other research interests include the spirituality of Marian Theology and its mediatory potential for women in the Judeo-Christian tradition.

PROFESSOR GRAHAM ROSSITER

Professor of Moral and Religious Education, Australian Catholic University, Sydney

Professor Graham Rossiter's research interests include the changing landscape of contemporary spiritualities with implications for education in the secular curriculum as well as in religious education; he is also interested in interpreting and evaluating the shaping influence of cultural meanings on personal meaning, identity and spirituality. His publications include *Reasons for Living: Education and Young People's Search for Meaning, Identity and Spirituality. A Handbook* (Australian Council for Educational Research, 2006).

ASSOCIATE PROFESSOR CHARLENE TAN

National Institute of Education, Nanyang Technological University, Singapore

Associate Professor Charlene Tan, a philosopher by training, has published articles on spirituality and spiritual education with a focus on Singapore and other Asian societies. Her most recent publications include *Islamic Education and Indoctrination: The Case in Indonesia* (Routledge, 2011) and *Confucius* (Bloomsbury, forthcoming). Among her current research interests is an exploration of Confucian, Islamic and Western traditions against a backdrop of Huntington's 'clash of civilisations' thesis.

PROFESSOR KIRSI TIRRI

University of Helsinki, Finland

Dr Kirsi Tirri is a Professor of Education and Research Director at the Department of Teacher Education at the University of Helsinki, Finland. She is also a visiting scholar with the Stanford Center on Adolescence, USA. Her research interests include moral and religious education, gifted education, teacher education and cross-cultural studies.

PROFESSOR ELIZABETH J. TISDELL

Penn State University-Harrisburg

Dr Tisdell is Professor of Adult Education at Penn State University-Harrisburg. She holds the EdD in Adult Education from the University of Georgia and the MA in Religion and Religious Education from Fordham University. Dr. Tisdell's research interests are in spirituality and its intersection with culture and wisdom, and its role in adult teaching and learning. She is the author of *Exploring Spirituality and Culture and Higher Education* and is co-editor with Ann Schwartz of the source book *Adult-Education and the Pursuit of Wisdom*.

DR ANN TROUSDALE

Louisiana State University, USA

Ann Trousdale is Associate Professor at Louisiana State University where she teaches courses in children's literature and children's spirituality. She is also an ordained Deacon in the United Methodist Church, having completed her seminary work at Perkins School of Theology. Her research interests include critical analysis of theological and social issues in children's literature, reader response to literature, children's embodied spirituality and using literature to support children's spiritual lives and religious understanding.

DR MARTIN UBANI

University of Helsinki, Finland

Martin Ubani, PhD, MTh, is a Senior Lecturer in Religious Education at the Department of Teacher Education, University of Helsinki, Finland. His research focuses on religion and spirituality in education and teacher education.

DR JACQUELINE WATSON

University of East Anglia, UK

Jacqueline Watson is Lecturer in Educational Research in the School of Education and Lifelong Learning at the University of East Anglia, UK. Jacqueline's long-term research interests are spiritual and religious education, including the response of religious education to Humanism. She also has interests in citizenship education, art education, and issues around children and young people's participation and voice. Jacqueline is currently Director of the Centre for Spirituality and Religion in Education at the University of East Anglia.

DR KAILI C. ZHANG

Senior Advisor, Andrew and Grace Education Consultancy and Community Services, Singapore

Kaili Zhang has a background in educational research, learning and development, and educational policy and planning. Her special interests are values/character development, emotional intelligence, and children and youth's spiritual and worldview formation.

Index

#0068 - 310517 - C0 - 229/152/18 [20] - CB - 9780415636193